PURSUING JUSTICE
FOR THE CHILD

Contributors
Egon Bittner
Robert A. Burt
Fred Cohen
Tove Stang Dahl
Geoffrey C. Hazard, Jr.
Charles E. Lister
Jerome Miller
Paul Nejelski
Lloyd E. Ohlin
Michael J. Power
Margaret K. Rosenheim
J. Lawrence Schultz (Deceased)
Charles H. Shireman
Michael H. Tonry
Michael S. Wald
Patricia M. Wald
Marguerite Q. Warren

PURSUING JUSTICE FOR THE CHILD

Edited by
Margaret K. Rosenheim

With a Foreword by
Robert Maynard Hutchins

THE UNIVERSITY OF CHICAGO PRESS
Chicago and London

KF
9709
A2
P87

The University of Chicago Press, Chicago 60637
The University of Chicago Press, Ltd., London
© 1976 by The University of Chicago
All rights reserved. Published 1976
Printed in the United States of America
80 79 78 77 76   9 8 7 6 5 4 3 2 1

LIBRARY OF CONGRESS CATALOGING IN PUBLICATION DATA

Main entry under title:

Pursuing justice for the child.

(Studies in crime and justice)
Includes index.
1. Juvenile courts—United States—Addresses,
essays, lectures.   2. Juvenile justice, Administration of—United States—Addresses, essays, lectures.
3. Juvenile corrections—United States—Addresses,
essays, lectures.   I. Rosenheim, Margaret Keeney.
II. Title.
KF9709.A2P87   345'.73'08   75-43238
ISBN 0-226-72789-0

3 3001 00672 8512

CONTENTS

Foreword

When I graduated from law school some fifty years ago, the aspiring liberals among us thought we knew what was the trouble with the law. It was too narrow and too formalistic: from Pleading, Evidence, and Criminal Law to the new subjects like Administrative Law and Trade Regulation, we hailed those developments which emphasized the differences in "fact situations," which required the interposition of the social sciences, and which sought to temper the wind to the shorn lamb by the exercise of discretion.

In those far-off days the word *bureaucracy* was never heard; perhaps it had not been invented. The liberal hope was in the agents and agencies of government.

The juvenile court, then only twenty-five years old, reflected the responsibility of the state as *parens patriae,* which could rescue children from the law, and from those agents of government whom we did not trust, like policemen, prosecutors, judges in criminal courts, and wardens of jails and penitentiaries. It could even rescue children from their parents. To us the juvenile court, with which few of us had any experience, looked like the fulfillment of our dreams. It had come into existence through the efforts of persons whose ideals we shared. It was packed with discretion from stem to stern. It relied on social workers. It aimed at "saving the child," not punishing him. If it had not existed, we would have tried to invent it.

This calm, judicious, comprehensive book shows how wrong we were. At the same time it is free of the panic that has overcome many aspiring liberals of late. They are so impressed by the danger of discretion that they seem on the verge of attacking every vestige of it, from the indeterminate sentence through probation, parole, to the idea of rehabilitation. What they want is punishment, on the ground that the system of criminal justice can supply little else. Their usual view is that punishment should be severe, though they offer no evidence that increasing severity of punishment lowers the crime rate.

Of course they cannot be friendly to the juvenile court. Yet as Professor Francis A. Allen reiterated up to the last of the old *Encyclopaedia Britannica,* "The juvenile court remains one of the most important social inventions of the modern period." He was aware of the difficulties; but he thought we had to overcome them. After seventy-seven years of experience, we know how onerous the task is. We also know it has to be performed. We have to pursue justice for the child. This book shows how to do it.

ROBERT M. HUTCHINS

Acknowledgments

Clearly the greatest debt I owe, in the long list of obligations accumulated throughout the history of this book, is to the contributors. They have been creative, cooperative, and tolerant of their editor. This book is theirs, and I hope they are pleased with the results.

In addition, I want to thank all those who, along with me, spontaneously and independently had the thought sometime in 1972 that it would be timely to initiate a review of the developments affecting the juvenile court. This group had a decisive influence upon the fashioning of questions which ultimately took form in chapters. Many of them are represented within these pages, but I am profoundly grateful to them all: to Bernard Fisher, Geoffrey Hazard, Norval Morris, Paul Nejelski, the late Lawrence Schultz, Charles Shireman, and Michael Tonry. For help and useful criticism later on, my warm thanks also to Ben Meeker and Franklin Zimring.

The informal discussion of a book led to two conferences in 1973 to plan and review such papers as were submitted in advance. These conferences were sponsored by the same organizations which have supported the entire editorial enterprise: the Juvenile Justice Standards Project of the American Bar Association and the Institute of Judicial Administration; and, at the University of Chicago, the Center for Studies in Criminal Justice and the Center for the Study of Welfare Policy. To their continuing interest this enterprise owes its life.

On behalf of all who have contributed to the book, I want to thank the following for their support: Grateful acknowledgment is made to the National Institute of Law Enforcement and Criminal Justice, the American Bar Endowment, the Andrew W. Mellon Foundation, the Vincent Astor Foundation, and the Herman Goldman Foundation for support to the Juvenile Justice Standards Project. For the Center for Studies in Criminal Justice, thanks are offered to the Ford Foundation. For the Center for the Study of Welfare Policy, University of Chicago, thanks are expressed for a Ford Foundation grant in Urban Studies made to the University of Chicago. The views expressed herein, however, are those of the authors and do not necessarily represent positions of the Juvenile Justice Standards Commission, or of the sponsoring organizations and funding sources.

Over the years many have provided help and good cheer to the editor; I want to single out Lynn Carter, Barbara Flicker, Helen Flint, Lee Gudel, Paul Harder, Yvette Hennings, Jan Lawrence, Anne Moses, Wayne Mucci, Lynn Vogel, and Donna Levine Walker. For their encouragement and patience, my special thanks to Norval Morris and Harold Richman. My appreciation also goes to Lucretia Davis, who knows how much she has helped. And to Ned Rosenheim and Dan, Tina, Jim, and Andy, love.

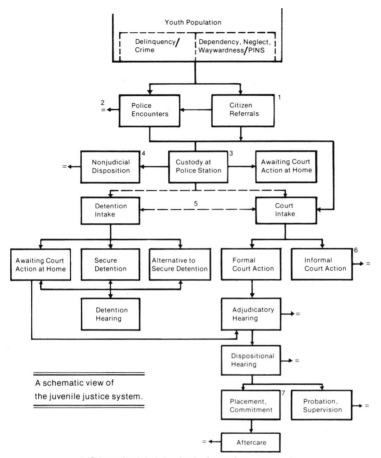

Youth Population

Delinquency/ Crime | Dependency, Neglect, Waywardness/PINS

2 = Police Encounters ← Citizen Referrals 1

Nonjudicial Disposition 4 = ← Custody at Police Station 3 → Awaiting Court Action at Home

Detention Intake ← 5 → Court Intake

Awaiting Court Action at Home | Secure Detention | Alternative to Secure Detention | Formal Court Action | Informal Court Action 6 =

Detention Hearing | Adjudicatory Hearing =

Dispositional Hearing =

A schematic view of the juvenile justice system.

Placement, Commitment 7 | Probation, Supervision =

= ← Aftercare

1. Citizen referrals include referrals of cases from parents, schools, welfare agencies—even occasionally children themselves.
2. This symbol (=) indicates a point at which the juvenile leaves the system as depicted here. Youth may avail themselves of services, counseling, or other arrangements on the recommendation of individuals in the system. However, formal control over the youth has ceased.
3. This point includes the options of station adjustment, referral to community services, or return home. Police screening decisions are made by the police juvenile unit in communities whose police departments have established such units. Police juvenile policies typically delineate cases appropriate for station adjustment or court referral. Presumably, serious or repeated offenders are routed directly to the juvenile court.
4. Youth Services Bureaus exist in an increasing number of communities but are still the exception rather than the rule. Where they or other appropriate resources are unavailable, a greater proportion of juvenile cases are probably routed directly to the juvenile court by the police (or other community agencies) for intake screening and decision as to further action.
5. Detention and court intake processes are related. One concerns the pre-judicial arrangement for custody and care of the child, whereas the other concerns the judicial process surrounding the child's case.
6. Informal court action can include the youth's and parents' consent to (informal) supervision or the use of community services and must be agreed to by parents and child.
7. Placement or commitment can cover a wide range of dispositions, from training schools and other correctional facilities to psychiatric institutions, foster family homes, hostels, relatives' homes, and so on.

Introduction

Pursuing Justice for the Child is concerned with the future of the juvenile court. Collectively, its chapters both sum up a period of great activity in the field and propose new standards and sources of legal analogies to guide the improvement of juvenile justice.

Geoffrey Hazard, in the opening chapter of this book, asserts that: "The aims of the juvenile court are now in perhaps more serious doubt than ever before ... [I]n rethinking the purposes of the juvenile court it is no longer sufficient simply to differentiate juvenile law from the criminal law or to borrow from family law. The law of the juvenile court needs a coherent theory of its own." Hazard then describes "The Jurisprudence of Juvenile Deviance" in seeking to define a proper set of goals for juvenile justice. His vision of these goals is far less ambitious than that of the court's founders.

In this restraint he speaks for all the contributors to this volume. Though individual authors differ in general philosophy and optimism about prospects for the future, they are all cautious in their estimate of how much the juvenile justice system can contribute to the prevention or control of juvenile delinquency—or, for that matter, how much it can contribute to the protection or correction of nondelinquents, whether they are truant, neglected, or generally incorrigible.

In holding minimal expectations for juvenile justice, the authors are certainly members of the majority at present. A central theme in the field, as in this volume, is that the goals of juvenile justice should be modest and selective. Authoritative statements endorsing a limited role for the juvenile justice system appear in sources ranging from the reports of national commissions (the 1967 President's Commission on Law Enforcement and Administration of Justice and the 1973 National Advisory Commission on Criminal Justice and Standards and Goals) to the work of courts and legislatures and the contributions of authors like Francis Allen, Joel Handler, Anthony Platt, and Edwin Schur. It appears that by at least a decade ago, many critics and analysts had reached agreement upon a much more limited agenda for the system of juvenile justice and were insisting on due process protections at critical junctures of coercive intervention. Yet, on reflection, the agreement was mostly about what was wrong with contemporary theory and practice. There was no accord on prescriptions for change.

It has been suggested that exploring procedural questions will bring real issues of substance to light. Exploration to date has not identified all such issues, but it does seem that we are much further along than we were in the sixties (compare, for example, the 1962 *Justice for the Child,* which I edited). For one thing, we are better prepared to consider what should be the role of the future juvenile court. For another, we are better able to debate intelligently what should be the role of other youth-serving institutions.

The themes running throughout the present book demonstrate this increasing concern for matters of function rather than form. What is the purpose of the juvenile justice system? What are the basic aspects of "minority" that should guide the jurisprudence of the court? What are principles upon which nonjudicial alternatives might be developed? Also addressed is the problem of where the juvenile court should go. What efforts are more properly undertaken under different auspices, and whose auspices should be used?

Pursuing Justice for the Child is arranged so that the chapters are closely related. The organization assumes that a reader without a working knowledge of juvenile justice will read from beginning to end. The chapters fall into four major sections. The three chapters in part I pose the central questions and themes that underlie all the remaining chapters. Part II deals with a range of developments affecting juvenile delinquents. The number and diversity of topics dealt with here give evidence that the bulk of statutory, judicial, and administrative effort to date has been directed at the delinquent population. Part III is composed of two chapters on the nondelinquent child. Part IV contains comparative and historical discussion of the aims of juvenile justice.

The dominant theme of this book is the proper function of the juvenile court. It is clear, and understandable, that the court plays only a minor role in preventing or controlling juvenile delinquency. Other institutions and informal arrangements, notably the family, are far more important in directing juveniles away from the law violations in which nearly all apparently engage at one time or another and toward law-abiding social behavior. Nevertheless, limited as they may be, the duties of the juvenile court and allied agencies are inescapable. And the way in which they are discharged is important, if not decisive. A civilized society has the right to demand fair, firm response to deviant behavior. Serious misconduct by youth should not and cannot be ignored, nor can threat of serious harm to children.

Agencies of law enforcement and justice are the usual instruments to implement social condemnation of intolerable conduct. That they perform their duties faithfully is eminently desirable; that they perform them with scrupulous attention to fairness and procedural regularity is vital to the health of a democratic country. The commitment to due process is as important in juvenile justice as it is when adults are held to account for antisocial conduct. The state, in seeking to promote the "best interests of the child," is not licensed thereby to proceed in irregular ways.

The pressing questions of the moment concern the degree to which principles and rules applicable to adults, as in the criminal law, should be modified for children and upon what rationale. J. Lawrence Schultz and Fred Cohen address these questions, analyzing *Gault* for guidance and suggesting analogues from both criminal law and other sources. In part III similar questions arise.

Here, in the context of the proper function of state authority over the nondelinquent child, Robert Burt and Michael Wald likewise consider the rationale for intervention when the child's conduct or situation is admittedly unharmful to others; each author proposes principles to guide and limit the exercise of state power.

"A coherent theory of juvenile court," to use Hazard's phrase, would supply the necessary foundation for a reformed juvenile justice system. Yet the system does not stand in isolation. The juvenile court gets its business from the community; the court's actions alter the responsiblities of other organizations and affect general public attitudes toward young people. What is said about the court could be said with equal force about other components of juvenile justice. Police, probation officers, detention personnel—they all interact with the public and with organizations like the schools, recreational agencies, churches, and the rest of the array of youth-serving instrumentalities.

Reform of juvenile justice therefore must involve change of other institutional arrangements. In my chapter I ask, under what principles shall this effort proceed? The question is useful not only because more attention should be paid to the development of nonjudicial responses to juvenile misconduct (and to juvenile mistreatment) but also because it forces us to consider what positive ends we contemplate when arguing for juvenile justice reform. Apart from the important aims of reducing the risks of stigma and harmful intervention, what gain in social provision for children can reasonably be sought? I describe a modest set of expectations and suggest principles of helping as guides to the translation of goals into resources for youth.

A diversity of views on the prospects and limits of reform is presented in part II, "Justice for the Delinquent Child." If there is one lesson to be learned from the experience of the past decade, it is that changing the juvenile justice system is much more difficult than it appeared in the first flush of excitement over *Gault*. During this time, we have come to appreciate aspects of juvenile justice little noticed previously. The critical role of certain agencies is now well accepted. The police are the most notable example, as Egon Bittner demonstrates. The persisting prominence of the detention facility is yet another example, discussed by Patricia Wald. In the main, reform efforts so far have centered on the court—on the formal hearing stages of adjudication and disposition—and they have been achieved through legislation. Now it is recognized that decisions at other stages are significant. Long-standing debates about the nature and justification of correctional dispositions acquire fresh importance. Marguerite Warren describes a pioneer effort to assess juvenile corrections. We need to find out what kinds of "sentences" or interventions work, and for whom, and to apply the knowledge we have. This will alter professional practice and organizational routine and highlight the fact that there is a major job to be done in developing additional resources for handling juvenile problems.

In part, the stress on interconnectedness comes from a modern tendency to view juvenile justice agencies as a system. To call present arrangements a "system," however, would be an over-simplification. Perhaps the agencies established to handle juveniles—on their way into court and out, and as they eventually return to the community—feel like a system to the young people who move through them all, but they would be the only ones to have such an overall perspective. For those working in them, or planning or criticizing, or paying the bills, each element in the "system" is an independent unit with its own priorities, constraints, constituencies, and methodologies. The term "juvenile system" is thus a loose shorthand phrase covering a collection of separate entities.

Just the same, to talk of "system" prepares us to seek out interrelationships. It is in this area that efforts to conduct fine-grained analysis in a more inclusive context have been most productive. The diverse array of papers in part II includes the recognition that, for example, court expectations bear on the work of the probation officer; Charles Shireman analyzes the probation task in this context. Correctional reform, as Jerome Miller and Lloyd Ohlin point out, has implications for the detention practices of local courts. The "spillover" from correctional change flows in two directions. It affects detention; it also affects diversion practices. As Paul Nejelski shows, diversion is at once the product of many agencies' attitudes and routines and the source of new conceptions of juvenile justice. Repeatedly, the chapters show new connections among component agencies. The discussion of possible solutions to existing shortcomings demonstrates how change in one place sets off reverberations in others.

Some aspects of juvenile justice can be fully understood only by taking a horizontal view. Recordkeeping practices, for instance, are seen in quite a different light if regarded solely in the context of the police, or the court. Charles Lister explores the opportunities for damage to juveniles and the acute difficulties of record control that are apparent when one looks at practices among several large-scale information keeping and disseminating agencies.

Paralleling the themes of limitation and restraint in juvenile court expectations is a strong preference for nonjudicial models of dealing with juvenile misconduct and mistreatment. Several authors endorse the use of crisis intervention theory in formal agencies of juvenile justice and in any alternatives that may come into being. The chapters stress the merit of noncoercive, speedily delivered services, while recognizing that coercive intervention is inevitable in some situations. Different authors propose different ways of dealing with the threat of coercion, but all of them emphasize varied and flexible community-based services, and none wish to return to wholesale reliance on the judicial model. It should be noticed, however, that methods of monitoring the nonjudicial alternatives to juvenile justice may result in placing larger responsibilities upon the courts than they presently carry. The juvenile court could be formally removed from certain areas of juvenile justice only to become a brooding omnipresence over youth-serving activities in general!

Such speculations lead back to basic questions concerning the aims of the juvenile court. What should we expect of it? What jurisprudential analogues are helpful in considering its mission and the procedures appropriate to it? How do the aims of the court fit into our vision of the role of youth in contemporary society? These questions, directly addressed in a few chapters and illuminated by all, are certainly not answered fully in this book, but part IV does attempt to offer a measure of perspective by placing them in historical and cross-national contexts. Michael Tonry describes the major American proposals for reform from the thirties to the seventies. Michael Power and Tove Stang Dahl review foreign approaches which have often been recommended as possible models for America. Power evaluates recent changes in Britain and Dahl considers to what extent apparently dissimilar models of juvenile justice are actually different in purpose and impact.

Many other questions concerning juvenile justice might have been considered in the book. Some issues concerning broad social aspects of youth policy are entirely ignored. *Pursuing Justice for the Child* is not intended as a catalog of current issues or as a general inquiry into the future of youth in America. It takes as its focus the institution of the juvenile court and seeks to move from that to examine what is happening throughout the system and what crucial problems should be tackled next. If, in the process, readers are inspired to identify essential questions that are here unasked, and to ponder the future of American children and the contribution of juvenile justice to it, the authors will feel well satisfied that they have done their job.

I   JUSTICE FOR THE CHILD

1

The Jurisprudence
of Juvenile Deviance

Geoffrey C. Hazard, Jr.

The juvenile court is an instrument for administering the law's expression of concepts of justice. It is constituted by law through the political process and is staffed with government officials whose responsibilities and procedures are specified, in greater or lesser detail, by law. Its specific function is to consider and decide cases tendered to it by other agencies of government (usually the police), and occasionally by private citizens, in which legally defined norms of conduct are said to have been violated.

It ordinarily has the further function of deciding, within legally prescribed limits, whether a sanction or remedy should be ordered and, if so, of what kind. Like other courts, it is subject to certain limitations upon its equity and effectiveness. Among them are: the gap between the community's sense of wrong and harm and the legal definitions of wrongs and harms; the dependence of legal tribunals on objective proof; the remoteness of courts from the origins of the events that they must judge; and the element of chance involved in whether judicial authority will be invoked in any particular case that falls within its formal purview. The juvenile court, that is to say, is only a court and no magic words can make it anything else.

3

The juvenile court is nevertheless distinguishable from other courts in many vital respects. It has different connections with the social and legal institutions that route cases to it, such as the police, the welfare department, and the school system. It is influenced by different sources of information that feed into its decision-making process—such as the probation department, youth service agencies, interested intercessors, and the school system—and affected by the responses to its dispositional alternatives. It is perceived differently by the various constituencies to which it must answer. The composition and organization of its judicial and auxiliary staff are different from those of other courts. Most important, the juvenile court is distinct from other courts in its jurisprudence—the norms it is supposed to enforce and the social purposes and expectations that it is supposed to serve. Unless the operating assumptions and goals of the juvenile court make sense, the quality and utility of its institutional connections will be ultimately unintelligible.

The aims of the juvenile court are now in perhaps more serious doubt than ever before. The doubts, expressed most forcefully by Francis Allen (1964, chap. 3), have been provoked primarily by the failure of the juvenile court to be demonstrably successful in achieving its professed rehabilitative goals. But the doubts would remain even if the court were to acknowledge or adopt other goals, for example, ones akin to those of the criminal courts handling adults or the domestic relations courts handling problems of the family. Neither criminal law nor family law these days can claim much success in accomplishing its professed goals, either. Hence, in rethinking the purposes of the juvenile court it is no longer sufficient simply to differentiate juvenile law from criminal law or to borrow from family law. The law of the juvenile court needs a coherent theory of its own. Such a theory must finally relate to concepts of legally significant deviance, that is, legally expressed definitions of the kind of behavior by or affecting young people that the state should try to do something about. That is the reason for the title of this paper.

The norms enforced in the juvenile court fall into three general categories. The first category consists of matters of the criminal law—prohibitions against murder, assault, smoking marijuana, driving without a license, and the like. The second category contains a group of more or less ill-defined types of conduct that are regarded as seriously improper or protocriminal—transgressions such as truancy from school, gross insubordination at home, and hanging around in a public place under suspicious circumstances. The third category is concerned with persons responsible for the child's welfare—principally parents—who are enjoined to exercise their responsibility properly and continuously, with specific remedies to be applied to them when they do not.

The first two categories have traditionally been given the heading of "delinquency," while the third is generally known as "dependency." The statutory definitions of the events or circumstances conferring jurisdiction on the juvenile court characteristically blur the pertinent distinctions. The older statutory language often defined the behavior involved by naming its legal significance—using terms like "delinquency" and "neglect." Newer statutes often define the behavior by the remedies the juvenile court ought to invoke—such as "persons in need of supervision" (PINS), and the like. When the labels and euphemistic wrappings are peeled away, however, the conduct referred to is either misbehavior by the child (delinquency) or misbehavior toward the child (dependency), or both. The focus of this paper is the norms of law enforced in the juvenile court's delinquency jurisdiction.

JUVENILE DELINQUENCY AND ADULT CRIME

In considering the norms enforced in juvenile court, it is useful for a number of reasons to begin by comparing them with those enforced against adults in criminal court. As a matter of historical development, the criminal court preceded the juvenile court in dealing with misconduct by juveniles that violated criminal law. As a matter of contemporary jurisdictional arrangement, the criminal court is the place of referral for cases involving criminal law violations that are remanded out of juvenile court. It is also the tribunal to which such cases are consigned when the jurisdictional age of the juvenile court is lowered, as it has been in a number of states. The procedure of the criminal court is the standard of comparison in assessing the fairness and constitutionality of juvenile court procedure. Finally, as a matter of substantive jurisdiction, violations of the criminal law are the entire jurisdiction of the criminal courts and a large component of the business of juvenile courts as well.

The "delinquency" jurisdiction of the juvenile court differs from that of the criminal court in three notable respects. Two of these have already been mentioned: the procedure in juvenile court is somewhat less elaborate, and the kinds of misconduct cognizable in juvenile court include behavior that is not criminal and usually not subject to sanction when engaged in by adults. The third difference is that the supposition and social purpose of enforcing the criminal law through the juvenile court are not the same as those served through the criminal court. The procedural characteristics of the juvenile court are significant in this discussion for what they imply about the substantive juvenile law they implement, but they will be touched on only incidentally. The focus here is on the substantive law—that is, conventional criminal norms and special protocriminal norms applied to young persons—articulated in the juvenile court.

In turning first to the juvenile court's jurisdiction over proto-criminal conduct (such as truancy and domestic insubordination), it is difficult to add much to the extended discourses in the literature, particularly those concerned with civil liberties. It has been pointed out many times that the definitions sanctioning this aspect of the juvenile court's jurisdiction are vague and suscep-tible of wide variations in interpretation and application. It is also recognized that they are often invoked in cases where the prosecuting authority suspects but cannot prove a criminal violation, or are used to reduce the charge and moderate the consequences in cases where a criminal violation can be proved. In this respect, protocriminal charges serve a purpose similar to that of the pervasive undercharging in adult criminal law and occasion similar abuse and criticism. Yet the dubieties inherent in the protocriminal aspects of juvenile law are perhaps even more serious when they are appraised by the standards ordinarily applied to other bodies of substantive law—such as criminal law, domestic relations law, and the law of torts.

One source of difficulty is that many of the protocriminal norms of the juvenile law deal with inchoate crimes, forms of behavior comparable to attempts and conspiracies in the adult criminal law. Inchoate crimes in adult criminal law are elusive enough in such respects as intent, acts "in furtherance," scope, complicity, and proof. In their more attenuated form in juvenile law, inchoate protocrimes become nearly ineffable except in the minds of the apprehensive. What distinguishes being in a gang from belonging to a group, loitering from hanging around with nothing to do, acquiescing from participating, knowing from misprisioning—particularly in the fluid social relationships typical of young people? If these distinctions cannot be formulated in ways susceptible of objective proof and disproof, how can the juvenile court's enforcement of protocriminal norms avoid being exercises in suspicion, ascription, and projection? If conspiracy is the "darling of the prosecutor's nursery," and the law of attempts of nearly equal attraction, their attenuated versions are no less than beauty's unrealized image in the judicial nursery. On fairly elementary legal grounds, these concepts of liability are sustainable only on the almost certainly wrong assumption that the behavior of young persons is easier to comprehend and predict than that of adults. And if the administration of the juvenile law is regarded as being somehow educational for its clients, its method is very strange: what lesson is taught by official action that is inevitably based on conjecture?

Another source of problems is that the protocriminal norms of juvenile law incorporate rules of behavior laid down by other authorities. Truancy is a violation of school attendance laws, trespassing is a violation of regulations asserted by custodians of private and public property, domestic undiscipline is the violation of parental rules, disrespect for a police officer is a violation of whatever may be his rules of deference. Except for isolated instances of specification such as the school attendance laws, these regulations are neither regularly formulated and published nor subject to any process of prior review in which the young person in any sense participates. In the case of parental rules, the reasonableness of the rules is subject only to the most hesitant review, which itself reflects only the juvenile court judge's own ideal of family structure. In the case of school law, little or no consideration is permitted of the value to the particular child of the school attendance that is being enforced.

This aspect of the law of the juvenile court may thus be thought of as a branch of the law of associations. Other branches of that kind of law have a fully developed jurisprudence—for example, corporation law and church law. The juvenile court administers what amounts to the same thing—corporation law, so to speak, of the family unit, the school community, and the neighborhood.

Yet in doing so, the juvenile court has not gone very far in appropriating the concepts of reasonableness, notice, specification, reciprocity, and fiduciary duty that are the basic stuff of association law. If the school requires the child to attend, does it not have a duty to provide real tutelage? (Of all applications of the "right to treatment" concept, surely school attendance is potentially the most salient.) If young persons may not dally in tenement corridors, where can they dally? If they must obey their parents, what are they entitled to get in return? Again, on fairly elementary legal grounds, this branch of juvenile law is sustainable on the assumption that the persons subject to it can be regarded as having substantive legal responsibilities but no substantive legal rights. That, indeed, has been the assumption in the past, and even today the concept and content of substantive legal rights for children is barely in the formative stage.

Underlying these difficulties with the protocriminal norms of the juvenile law is the more fundamental problem that law is a grossly inadequate device for achieving positive socialization. Its proper role is that of backing up anterior processes in the family and the community. That role can be effectively performed only if there exist coherent and substantially consistent concepts of young peoples' place in society and of society's responsibilities to them. Although the juvenile law purports to have a "philosophy," there is no social philosophy on which it can draw, except perhaps for the question-begging precept that it serve the "best interests of the child." It often seems that the juvenile law is operating on an unarticulated wish that young people would behave as though they were members of an integrated and static society living in untroubled times. Such a wish, though understandable, is no substitute for policy.

JUVENILE LAW "PHILOSOPHY" REGARDING CRIME

If the protocriminal aspect of juvenile law is legally and educationally problematic, so is that aspect that applies the criminal law to young people. If the jurisdiction of the juvenile court over protocriminal conduct were swept away, there would remain formidable questions of a theoretical and practical character concerning delinquency jurisdiction. These are cases that involve murder, manslaughter, rape, assault, burglary, larceny, extortion, malicious destruction of property, gross disorder in public places and school buildings, unauthorized use of another's vehicle (joy-riding), driving without a license, driving with suspended license, drunk driving, use or possession of alcohol by a person under age, use or possession or marijuana, and use or possession of addictive drugs. Even if some of the victimless crimes among those last listed were eliminated, the inventory would remain heavy. The basic task of the delinquency jurisdiction of the juvenile court is to deal with it somehow.

From this perspective, two much mooted issues concerning the juvenile court seem less important. The first is the charge that the jurisdiction of the juvenile court expresses white middle-class values and thereby involves judging lower-class or ethnic minority children by some alien standard. This assertion is one of those observations that combines fact and nonsense in a way that is difficult to refute. There are, without doubt, many unjust judgments when the juvenile court exercises authority over lower-class or ethnic minority "dependency" cases and cases involving protocriminal conduct. It is probably true also that patterns of deviance are different among lower-class or ethnic minority children from those which the middle class has come to expect and more or less tolerate among its own children. This may be especially true of some types of drug use and some types of nonlethal group or gang fighting. It is true as well that the sanctioning system is staffed largely by personnel who are white and almost entirely middle class. Hence, the values implicit in the penal code are expressed to offenders by people from whom they feel different or alienated. This feeling may be transferred to the values themselves and result in the offenders' trying to reject values that they actually share even though they violated them on the occasion in question. But surely murder, rape, robbery, arson, and burglary are behaviors that people of lower income or different ethnic identity from the white middle class would also proscribe if they ran the government.

The other mooted issue, a related one, is the matter of "labeling" and the consequent processes of stigmatization, trans-formation of the accused's self-image, and the redefinition of the accused by those with whom they later come in contact. The matter of stigmatization is of course very important. To the extent that the juvenile law can, without hypocrisy, avoid labeling, it may facilitate young offenders' redefinition of themselves as worthwhile persons. At the same time, it must be recognized that the stigma attached to serious criminal conduct is not merely an official conjuration. Crimes are real happenings that involve or threaten injury, sometimes fatal injury, to valuable personal interests that society is bound to try to protect. The participants in them—victim, perpetrator, onlookers, acquaintances of the immediate parties, as well as officials—give the events names in remembering and recounting them. The names, whatever the words, are not pleasant or positive because the events are not pleasant or positive. There is no way to avoid labels unless memory of the events is somehow to be suppressed. Indeed, the history of euphemism in the juvenile court suggests that the attempt to avoid labeling is not only fruitless but fatuous and conducive to hypocrisy. The real problem with labeling appears to be not labeling as such but the risk that events may be made more portentous than the facts warrant and that responses will be inflated as a result. Thus labeling in regard to real criminal offenses by juveniles is only an aspect of the much more complicated problem of interpreting and responding to criminal behavior in an appropriate way.

The problems of substantive values and labeling are not serious in themselves, but they become serious in practice when the cases of middle-class juvenile offenders are resolved differently from those involving their lower-class counterparts. The difference is that middle-class children have access to means of mediation through private resources that are not available to lower-class children through public resources. These means include intervention by parents, teachers, clergy, lawyers, and others skilled in interpreting offenders' behavior in a way that elicts a more lenient response from legal authority and in formulating alternatives to the sanctions of juvenile law—dispositions such as psychological treatment or special educational plans, for example. In essence, middle-class children can to a considerable extent escape the hand of the juvenile law because there are private hands in which to put them, whereas such resources are in short supply for the poor. The only way to avoid this discrimination would be to foreclose such diversions to the middle class or to make equivalent resources available to the lower class. Neither alternative is a realistic possibility, and those administering the juvenile law cannot be held responsible for that fact. They can be held responsible, however, for recognizing that the law they administer is the official part of a two-part regime whose unofficial counterpart works more tenderly.

This brings us to theories concerning the nature of criminal deviance and what, through law, should be done about it. The questions here are the same as those to which the law and procedure of the adult criminal courts are a response. The answers in juvenile law differ, however, because certain assumptions embraced by the criminal law have been modified in relation to offenders who are young. The character of these modifications at the same time expresses the special theory of deviance implicit in juvenile law and reveals the theory of deviance in the criminal law at large.

Assumptions about Offenders

The departures in juvenile law from the assumptions in criminal law begin with an uncertainty about whether young persons should be held fully responsible for their conduct when they violate the criminal law. The particular underlying notions are rarely articulated: Is it meant that young people don't know what they are doing in the same way as adults? That they lack the capacity of adults (of what age?) to control their behavior? That they should not be burdened with the same weight of guilt as adults? That they should not be made to suffer punishment of the same severity as adults? When these questions are asked about adults, the answers at best have been contradictory or unintelligible. Such questions seem never to have been systematically raised about young offenders. In practice, they are answered by action rather than by analysis. Young offenders above a specified age are treated like adults and proceeded against in criminal court; offenders below that age are proceeded against in juvenile court, where their acts are attributed to them but categorically mitigated in some unstated way. The underlying question of responsibility remains unexplicated, either to the court or to the child.

The second modification of assumptions concerns punishment. Ostensibly the juvenile court does not punish but only "treats" or "corrects." To the extent that this displacement occurs or is believed to occur, it means that the punishments which legal process can impose are ineffective or inappropriate when applied to the young offender. This is a major difference in position. The difference is so great, indeed, that the arguments made in support of it inevitably raise serious doubts about the effectiveness and appropriateness of punishment applied to adult offenders. At the same time, the disposition of cases in juvenile court does resemble adult sentencing, certainly in the mind of the offender.

The issue of punishment is indeed central to the jurisprudence of the juvenile court. At least formally, and to some degree substantially, juvenile court sanctioning practice represents an abandonment of the goal of general deterrence. No child may be "punished," and so no examples of punishment may be made to deter others. At the same time, juvenile court "sentencing" practices depart from the principle of proportionality of punishment. Juvenile offenders can be held in "treatment" as long as eight to ten years for a nonheinous offense, while the maximum severity that they can suffer is a period of incarceration equal to the difference between their age at commitment and the age of compulsory discharge, which is also about eight to ten years. Ultimately, a scheme of punishment that does not generally reflect the principle of proportionality is inexplicable and therefore arbitrary and unjust. Calling a scheme "treatment" which amounts to punishment does not alleviate the injustice; whatever treatment is actually received may moderate but does not erase the injustice, at least from the viewpoint of the person who is subjected to it. At the same time, the substantial resemblance between juvenile court schemes of disposition and adult sentencing is embarrassing from a political viewpoint. It compels juvenile court advocates to make claims for the effectiveness of treatment that simply cannot be substantiated. It permits the advocates of "hard-line" criminal law policy to acquiesce in a dispositional scheme that they probably would work to repeal if its punitive character were not so obvious. In addition, the persistence of a dual dispositional scheme, punitive for adults but nonpunitive for juveniles, raises a persistent question about what is wrong with imposing legal punishment on both younger and older offenders.

The third respect in which the assumptions of juvenile law are modified from those of the criminal law is the most indefinite but perhaps most important. This is the way in which it looks at the offenders' state of mind, their emotional and social development, their fixedness of purpose in life, and their prospects for somehow growing out of their inclination to commit crime and get caught at it. The outlook expressed in juvenile law tends to be more sympathetic, more optimistic, more tentative, and less judgmental than in the criminal law. This quality is no doubt chiefly the product of a kind of hopefulness and sentimentality with which most people view children and adolescents. These sentiments are shared not only by the court and its personnel but by the legislature and the general public. The attitude is not as strongly or consistently expressed across class and ethnic group lines, and is also subject to exceptions where "young hoodlums" are concerned—they are perceived to be somehow different. Even so, positive expectations for the young offender generally temper the outrage and desire for retribution that are aroused by the specter of a serious criminal act. The result is an ambivalence toward the juvenile offender that is less often displayed toward his adult counterpart. The ambivalence in turn gives the juvenile court opportunity to exercise a breadth of policy and program that is hesitantly and only grudgingly permitted to the agencies handling adult offenders. The critical question for juvenile law is whether the most has been made of this opportunity, given the severe constraints under which any program of legal intervention must operate.

JUVENILE COURT POLICY AND PROGRAM
It would be impossible to recapitulate the experience of the juvenile court in the compass of this paper. Yet it is essential to establish some common understanding of what that experience has been. Fortunately this formidable undertaking was assumed by the Task Force on Juvenile Delinquency of the 1967 President's Commission on Law Enforcement and Administration of Justice (1967), whose report is hereby incorporated by reference. Moreover, Edwin Schur (1973) of New York University has completed an incisive, thoughtful, and even more up-to-date analysis of the theory and practice of juvenile court law. Professor Schur's study says so much so well that I shall simply use it as a point of departure.

The policy and program of the juvenile court, despite recurrent retreats and circumambulations, have been animated by two more or less distinct ideas about criminal deviance and how to respond to it. One of these ideas, which Professor Schur calls "individual treatment," is that the deviant child differs from nondeviant children in his psycho-social orientation. The difference is relatable to psychological factors such as intelligence and sociability and also to structural factors such as family solidarity and peer and school relationships. These factors can impel the individual to commit antisocial acts that may include criminal misconduct. Commission of these acts is not regarded as having an invariable or systematic relationship to social class and ethnic identity or to economic status and environment. To deviance, as thus interpreted, the appropriate response is diagnosis and personally focused therapy—hence the term "individual treatment." The function of the juvenile law is to facilitate this response by ordering it directly or providing legal reinforcement for other agencies that can provide it.

The other principal theory of deviance is implicit in what Professor Schur calls "liberal reform." According to this idea, delinquency is a product of social setting—poverty, bad neighborhood, corrupting peer and adult associations, lack of vocational opportunities and incentives, and the like. The influence of these circumstances is regarded as inevitably adverse and as more or less independent of the psychological characteristics of the individuals involved. The strategy of the juvenile law is to reform the environment by providing counterinfluences and opportunities in the form of constructive clubs and neighborhood activities, job programs, and positive adult involvement through, for example, street gang workers. More comprehensively, the required strategy is to reform the social and economic structure of the environment in which delinquency-prone youths find themselves, that is, a broad program of social justice directed toward the socio-economic classes and ethnic groups among which criminal conduct is highly evidenced.

The role of the juvenile court in the liberal reform interpretation of deviance is problematic. The court lacks the legal authority and administrative competence to intervene on the scale required by the theory. The court also lacks the political and fiscal resources necessary to commission other institutions to intervene. The role of the court under liberal reform is therefore either peripheral or merely exhortative. This may help explain why, even among those in the juvenile law field who espouse the liberal reform interpretation of deviance, there remains a commitment to the program of individual treatment. Even if the latter theory is dubious, it implies a program that can be operated on the small, case-oriented scale on which the judicial branch of government is organized.

The sources marshaled by Professor Schur point out that both individual treatment and liberal reform are infirm bases for policy and program. The individual treatment approach rests on assumptions about causal relationships, diagnostic accuracy, and therapeutic capabilities that are tenuous at best. To implement it beyond the level of sporadic intervention would require program resources that have never been made available and never will be. Similarly, the liberal reform approach rests on dubious assumptions about causes and curbs for criminal deviance, and following it in more than a token way would require even larger resources. Indeed, in any fully explicit version, liberal reform would require a reconstruction of society and could not even then guarantee a substantial reduction of crime by adolescents.

At this point it is necessary to offer some faint praise of individual treatment and liberal reform after all the criticism leveled by Professor Allen, Professor Schur, and others. This is that these approaches are no more infirm in their assumptions or dubious in their prospects of success than whatever is the theory underlying the hard-line approach to controlling criminal deviance. Hard-line theory is not often articulated, perhaps because it is shared mostly by people not disposed to discourse on theory but to quest for practical results. Underlying the hard-line quest, however, is in fact a highly complex theory. It embraces a set of notions about the effects of family structure, early subjection to strict discipline, respect for authority symbols, and imposition of relatively severe punishments, combined with an implication that the incidence and seriousness of criminal deviance has worsened in recent years for reasons other than the automobile, the gun, the age structure of the population, and the adverse treatment accorded ethnic minorities. The theory has going for it the point that there would be a lot less criminal deviance if people behaved themselves. Unfortunately, it does not pursue the question of what it takes to get people to behave themselves under the conditions of human interaction that exist in contemporary society, especially in the inner city. The bleeding hearts and knee-jerk liberals may have no provable theory for dealing with youthful criminal deviance, but neither do their antagonists.

Some of the reasons that the hard-line approach to deviance has a poor record and poor prospects are essentially similar to those explaining the inadequacy of the individual treatment and liberal reform approaches. At the political level, the hard-line would be virtually impossible to implement in a fluid society such as ours. At the administrative level, it is no more possible to predict criminal deviance among a population subjected to strong doses of authority than among a population subjected to ego-threatening influences, other things being equal. Nor is it any more possible to reshape society on the model of a patriarchal tribe than on the model of distributive justice and participatory democracy. The hard-line approach to deviance among the young, like any other approach, must cope with the fact that there is a great deal of deviance, that its incidence is largely unpredictable, that most of it is undetected or ignored, and that the character of any official response is to some extent fortuitous. Furthermore, under the hard-line approach the juvenile law is just as capricious from the viewpoint of the young people to whom it is applied as it is under any other approach.

In this connection it seems appropriate to take notice of a variation of both soft and hard lines that often finds expression among judges and lawyers. It may be called the "procedural" response to deviance. The liberal version of this theory is that a demonstration of due process will have of itself a reformative effect on offenders. (This view is at odds with the pre-*Gault* juvenile court doctrine that procedural formalism had an alienating and destructive effect on juvenile offenders.) The hard-line approach is that a no-nonsense procedure, stripped of the delays and quibblings inherent in elaborate procedural protections, will inculcate a healthy respect for authority that will carry over to offenders' behavior out of court.

The trouble with both approaches is that they assume a correspondence between the population of offenders to whom the procedural demonstration (of whichever kind) should be made and the population to whom it is in fact made. There is no such correspondence under either type of procedural demonstration. Those who are fully proceeded against are a small and more or less arbitrarily selected fraction of those who legally are eligible. This basic randomness in selection of candidates for the adjudicative process would seem to vitiate the lessons in fairness or firmness that the process is supposed to teach.

REDEFINING AIMS

If the program and policy of juvenile law regarding criminal deviancy are judged by their effectiveness in achieving presently professed aims, juvenile law is ready for receivership. That is so whether the aim is individual treatment, liberal reform, hard-line, or procedural justice. Nor does there appear any prospect of rescuing juvenile law by purifying its policy and pursuing one of these aims more relentlessly. On scientific grounds, there is no reason to suppose that a purified policy would be much more effective than the amalgam now in force. On practical grounds, it must be recognized that legal control of deviance inevitably involves programs with conflicting aims: they must elicit conformity while preserving a substantially open society, attempt to intercept dangerous behavior while keeping program costs within reason, effectively enforce the law while observing procedural fairness, and so on. Finally, on political grounds, there is no real possibility of forming a coalition of sentiment around any better vectored policy than the one we have now. There is therefore little hope of realizing the professed aims of juvenile law to any greater degree than at present, whatever those aims are understood to be.

Realization of this situation strongly suggests that all present theories of legal response to juvenile deviance are simply too ambitious. This was Professor Allen's thesis concerning the individual treatment program of juvenile law. It is the conclusion suggested by Professor Schur for liberal reform as well. It also may be true of the "war on crime." Hence, if no intellectually defensible and politically feasible policy dealing with juvenile deviance will "work," the question arises, why should we suppose the law will work in the first place?

The question posed for juvenile law is the same as that posed, for essentially similar reasons of program failure, for the criminal law as a whole. Yet the question penetrates even more deeply when posed about juvenile law, because the legally admissible policy alternatives in juvenile law cover a wider range of possibility than in criminal law. In procedural matters, notwithstanding *Gault,* the range of permissible variation is much greater because so many of the procedures for prosecution of adult crime are constitutionally specified. In legally defining various forms of deviance, juvenile law could, if it were feasible and wise to do so, provide for intervention at a lower threshold of deviance—as it has in the case of protocriminal behavior. In enforcement policy, children and adolescents can be given the full range of treatments derivable from the concepts of legal irresponsibility on their part and *parens patriae* on the part of the state. Available to support all such alternatives is the more optimistic and forbearing public attitude toward young people previously alluded to.

With all these supporting circumstances, however, the prospects for improving the effectiveness of legal controls of juvenile deviance appear modest, indeed bleak. (The same is true, *a fortiori*, for the prospects of improving the effectiveness of legal controls on adult crime.) In short, we must recognize that the law will not "work" as a device to control "real" crime. No doubt improvement can be made in the various elements of the law enforcement "system," and quite properly a major effort is presently being made to do so, but the net gains will be modest.

To say that the law will not work to control criminal deviance is to say that no manipulation of the elements of the legal system will drive down the rate of serious deviancy, that is, "real" crime. These elements include the legal definition of deviance, the sanctions imposed on it, the resources of law enforcement, the techniques of adjudication, and the dispositional alternatives. These legal devices are utilitarian in conception, but now appear to have only a marginal utility, one that is very limited. This realization is difficult to accept. It not only casts doubt on the practical value of reforming particular legal devices for the control of deviance but also on our very assessment of the value of law. If the age of Bentham is over for the criminal law, what now?

Perhaps we should begin by recognizing that most of the deviance that the law seeks to control is simply inaccessible from any external position. To the extent it is caused by psychological factors in the individual, we now know those factors are hard to identify and harder to modify through legal and governmental processes. To the extent it is caused by the actor's immediate social environment (family, peers, neighborhood), we now know such environments are largely impervious to the intervention of planners. To the extent it is caused by breakdown of self-control, we now recognize that inculcating self-control through legal compulsion is essentially a contradiction in terms. To the extent it is caused by chance opportunity, we now know that the state cannot establish controls on the exigencies of everyday life. Put differently, it is possible for society to create government of sorts, but it has proved impossible for government to create society.

Just as government cannot create the social order, so also law—which for this purpose is government expressed in specific rules—cannot create subordinate systems of social order, such as conformity to the norms implied by criminal proscriptions. The law can memorialize society's values and reiterate them on the more or less random occasions when the law is enforced by official intervention. It can validate its seriousness of purpose by imposing punishments in the most serious cases that come to its attention. If it conserves its resources, it may be able to do something in the way of individual treatment in selected cases where the subject is receptive. It can incarcerate some offenders to interrupt their preying on others, and possibly to teach them basic literacy and job skills. In the procedure it employs, the law can display concern for truth and the capacity to withhold judgment in the face of inadequate evidence. It can display its valuation of human life and welfare by social reforms selected for their symbolic rather than their material significance.

These seem to be the limits of the law's effectiveness. To reach beyond them, the social processes of exemplification, reaffirmation, and expression of community disapproval will have to carry the load, as they always have. The law's role is thus auxiliary, exemplary, and educative, rather than instrumental. Still, to perform those functions well is a large order to which we need to give renewed response.

BIBLIOGRAPHY

Allen, Francis A. 1964. *The Borderland of Criminal Justice.* Chicago: University of Chicago Press.
President's Commission on Law Enforcement and Administration of Justice. 1967. *Task Force Report: Juvenile Delinquency and Youth Crime.* Washington, D.C.: U.S. Government Printing Office.
Schur, Edwin M. 1973. *Radical Nonintervention: Rethinking the Delinquency Problem.* Englewood Cliffs, N.J.: Prentice-Hall.

2 Isolationism in Juvenile Court Jurisprudence

J. Lawrence Schultz
and Fred Cohen*

The purpose of this paper is to examine the impact of *In re Gault* (387 U.S. 1 [1967]) on the conceptual and policy foundations of the juvenile justice system. In brief, *Gault* held that juveniles charged with delinquency and facing possible incarceration are constitutionally entitled to notice, counsel, confrontation and cross-examination, and the privilege against self-incrimination. Since 1967, reams of paper have been expended on empirical assessments of *Gault*: Is counsel actually provided? What influence is exerted by the presence of counsel? Does counsel actually alter the result in delinquency cases? Of what consequence is the extension of the privilege against self-incrimination?

Our aim is neither to duplicate nor attempt to improve on such efforts. Rather, we seek to examine the underlying premises of *Gault* and some of its better-known offspring in order to understand better the current directions of the juvenile justice

*This paper was begun by Larry Schultz before his untimely death. It was reworked and completed by Fred Cohen who acknowledges that the major contribution is Larry Schultz's and hopes that in the revision Larry's brilliance and insight have not been lost.

system. We ask whether *Gault* disagreed in any fundamental way with earlier judicial statements of the premises which support the unique attributes of juvenile justice, whether a body of legal doctrine is emerging which demonstrates either a new or more sharply defined understanding of why young people should be subject to a different jurisprudence than adults, and whether a coherent model has emerged which might help explain the substance and procedure of juvenile justice.

It may be helpful to identify the major themes of this paper before examining them in detail. We find the juvenile court to occupy a sort of conceptual no man's land lying vaguely between the models of criminal law and of the civil commitment law applicable to the mentally ill and some others "in need of treatment." Juvenile court law has some of the characteristics of each but also possesses unique attributes. The court has oscillated between concern for violations of the criminal law, the amelioration of supposed harmful conditions (for example, waywardness), and the rescue of the child as victim. At the same time it has consistently claimed therapeutic objectives as the desideratum of any official intervention.

Juvenile justice occupies a no man's land. But it is not completely sealed off from related legal processes. Juvenile justice is affected by the enforced adoption of some criminal law processes and a dubious rejection of others. In the main, however, it is almost totally isolated from the conceptual foundation of criminal law and the constitutional principles (such as fair warning of proscribed conduct and the "void for vagueness" doctrine) which surround that body of law. In this regard, juvenile court theory is artificially cut off from analogous areas of law and from sustaining intellectual resources.

To be a bit more concrete, we may think for a moment about the very term "juvenile delinquency." Juvenile, of course, is a reference to the age base of the entire process and as such refers to a status. But what of the term delinquency? Is it simply shorthand for a criminal violation by a youth or does it denote a pathological condition—yet another status—of a youth who has violated the criminal law? The answer, it seems, is that it all depends. *Gault,* and *Breed* v. *Jones* (421 U.S. 519 [1975]) most recently, view a delinquency proceeding as the counterpart of a criminal proceeding for the purpose of mandating certain trial-

centered procedural safeguards. On the other hand, preadjudication procedures and, even more plainly, postadjudication procedures and goals of juvenile justice are dominated by the
pathological condition–therapeutic response view. To compound
the confusion of conceptions of delinquency, in twenty-six states
so-called status violators (like truants or runaways) are not
differentiated from criminal law violators and are classified as
delinquents, subject to the same dispositions as juveniles who
violate the criminal law (Levin and Sarri 1974).

Let us turn now to a more specific inquiry into these general
themes.

Gault: BACKWARD AND FORWARD

Many commentators on the *Gault* decision, including Justice
Black in his concurring opinion (387 U.S. at pp. 59–64), thought
that *Gault* heralded the destruction of the juvenile court as a
special institution with unique attributes. Empirical evidence
aside, the accuracy of that estimate turns, in large part, on
whether the *Gault* decision incorporated a view of the juvenile
court and its processes that is basically inconsistent with what are
understood to be the basic foundations of that court.

When *Gault* was handed down, enthusiasts and detractors
alike announced a victory for the adversary model over the
traditional *parens patriae* view of juvenile courts. It was thought
to overturn the premises of more than a half-century of judicial
decisions dating back to the font of those decisions, *Commonwealth* v. *Fisher* (213 Pa. 48 [1905]), decided by the Pennsylvania
Supreme Court. By comparing *Fisher* with *Gault,* however, we
are able to deflate both the claims of victory for *Gault* and the
suggestion that a new era had dawned for juvenile courts.

The *Fisher* court was faced with four central objections to the
constitutional validity of the juvenile court. The court's responses
to those objections can be framed in the following propositions:

1. It is not true, as was argued, that the juvenile court act is
invalid as a constitutionally prohibited single law containing
multiple subjects—that is, dependent, neglected, and incorrigible
children as well as delinquent children. Its unitary purpose, the
court held, was to provide state protection for children who
needed it.

2. Children are not denied equal protection of the law, al-

though subjected to more stringent controls than adults, since the
juvenile court act is merely one of many laws properly protecting
children who need help in ways that adults do not.

3. The absence of the procedural safeguards afforded in criminal cases does not deny due process because children are not
"harmed" by the juvenile court act. In the court's view, the act
simply provides how children who ought to be saved may reach
the juvenile court to be saved. It should be noted, however, that
the court did not claim that informal procedures were essential to
the act nor did it claim that children would be harmed by
formality in the juvenile court, a premise which is at odds with the
current thinking of some justices on the Supreme Court of the
United States.

4. Specifically, children are not deprived of the right to jury
trial guaranteed in criminal cases since the court, in placing
children under proper guardianship, exercised a form of equity,
or chancery, jurisdiction historically unencumbered by jury trial
requirements. (Equity developed in England as a separate court
[chancery] and a separate body of law in response to the rigidity
and limitations of the common law.)

Pervading the Pennsylvania court's opinion was the assumption
that the juvenile court exercises only a "natural" restraint over
children, derived from the natural control normally exercised by
parents. This proposition is expressed in slightly altered form
when courts speak of a child having a right not to liberty but only
to custody.

Our approach to clarifying *Gault* is to ask which of these
propositions the Supreme Court disagreed with. The answer is
simple. Justice Fortas, writing for the majority, did not disagree
with any of these propositions. Indeed, the only clear difference
between *Gault* and *Fisher* seems to be the empirical evidence on
outcomes available to the two courts. Central to the holding in
Gault is a finding that the juvenile court simply has not been able
to deliver on its promises: promises of confidentiality, reduction
of recidivism, reduction of stigma, and bona fide (if not effective)
treatment. If the *Fisher* court had possessed the evidence available to Justice Fortas, it would not have violated its principles to
require the limited adjudicatory safeguards adopted in *Gault*.
Conversely, if the *Gault* court had been convinced that children
appeared in juvenile court only to be saved, there is little in *Gault*

that is antithetical to the *Fisher* court's proposition that "[t]he act simply provides how children who ought to be saved may reach the juvenile court to be saved" (213 Pa. at p. 53).

The clamor over *Gault* clearly has more to do with its sweeping rationale and its broad indictments of the system than with its limited prescriptions and still more limited conception of the juvenile and the juvenile court. There is no hint concerning how juvenile courts exercising delinquency jurisdiction differ in principle, if they do, from adult criminal courts. *Gault* purports to abandon decision making by labels, at least by civil as contrasted to criminal labels, but in the process provides no new label reflecting a fresh juridical conception of what it means to be a juvenile. If anything, *Gault* accepts the failure of juvenile justice as a failure in operations and resources, not as a failure in concept and theory.

Adversarial tissue from one small portion of adult criminal justice has been grafted on to a similarly small portion of juvenile justice, but the major questions of purpose and process remain unanswered and in some ways confounded.

From *Gault* to *McKeiver* to *Breed*

In the years since *Gault,* numerous decisions of lower courts have reflected its inherent ambiguity and lack of clear concepts. *Gault* expressly did not concern itself with police procedures, preadjudication processes, or the dispositional process (see also *In re Winship,* 397 U.S. 358 [1970]) at p. 366). Nor did it touch on the juvenile court's all-embracing jurisdiction over troubled and troublesome children or the lack of articulable objectives for the court's versatile and potent remedies.

While *Gault* clearly has prodded lower courts to apply more rules of criminal procedure to various phases of the juvenile court process, the tendency is by no means uniform and the rationales offered reflect *Gault*'s confusion. The further we come from the narrow confines of the delinquency adjudication process, the more likely we are to find inconsistency of result and confusion of concept.

Illustrative of this point is the question of the extent to which traditional notions of criminal responsibility apply in delinquency proceedings involving charges as serious as murder. In *In re H.C.* (106 N.J. Super. 583 [1969]) a New Jersey court was confronted with the post-*Gault* question of whether the insanity defense applied in the case of a fifteen-year-old accused of a double homicide. This defense recognizes the impropriety of affixing accountability for criminal acts upon offenders who, by reason of a mental disorder, lack the mental capacity that the law defines as requisite to being held responsible for criminal acts. In light of the evidence presented, the court was satisfied that if an adult were on trial a complete insanity defense would have been made out. The court ruled, however, that the defense of insanity does not bar an adjudication of delinquency so long as no penal sanctions are imposed on the juvenile. That the philosophy of the juvenile court supposedly precludes the imposition of penal sanctions on any juvenile not only failed to deter the court, it was not deemed worthy of mention.

The court's solution was to focus on the fact that the acts as charged had been proved and to conclude that it was in the best interests of the child that he be committed to a state hospital for psychiatric treatment. In actual result, the disposition of *H.C.* does not differ substantially from cases of adults who successfully plead insanity. In the rationale employed, the court simply could not decide whether a delinquency proceeding involving a murder charge requires proof of criminal responsibility in the traditional sense of *mens rea,* or "guilty mind." But, if insanity is not a defense, it might be asked why, in other cases, self-defense or even coercion should be a defense? The "best interests of the child" might dictate a coercive intervention in each instance, never mind that an adult would be freed.

Thus, the fundamental question remains: Is a delinquency proceeding an analogue to a criminal proceeding in substance and procedure, or is it at bottom a search to identify a condition requiring treatment or rehabilitation? If it is the latter, then even a concern for overt conduct may seem overly restrictive. That is, if an important objective of juvenile justice is to prevent a harmful condition, then the earlier the condition can be identified and treated the greater the chances for success.

Shifting our focus to the front of the juvenile justice process, police interrogation in particular, we may note that virtually all courts that have considered the question hold that *Gault,* by necessary implication, requires that a juvenile be given the *Miranda* warnings (*Miranda* v. *Arizona,* 384 U.S. 436 [1966]; see cases cited in Paulsen and Whitebread [1974]). These call for informing persons subject to in-custody interrogation of their right to remain silent (that is, to invoke the privilege against self-incrimination), of the fact that statements made under questioning may subsequently be used against them, and of their right to the advice of counsel, appointed or retained. Prior Supreme Court rulings had established that involuntary confessions by juveniles—as opposed to those that are defective only in that the *Miranda* rights were not given or observed—are inadmissible (*Haley* v. *Ohio*, 332 U.S. 596 [1948]; *Gallegos* v. *Colorado*, 370 U.S. 49 [1962]). In determining the voluntariness of a confession, the inquiry is into the totality of circumstances surrounding the confession, including any special characteristics of the person confessing. Youth—with its lack of experience, susceptibility to suggestion and authoritarian influences, and, often, a lack of physical stamina—is a constitutionally recognized special characteristic and requires that courts examine closely any confession of a youth.

We do not quarrel with the general extension of *Miranda* to delinquency proceedings. Rather, we ask whether even strict compliance with *Miranda* is adequate to assure the juvenile of a free and informed choice. If youths are considered more susceptible to pressure when the question is the voluntariness of a confession, then why does this conception not carry over to *Miranda* issues with the result, for example, that a juvenile may not waive the right to counsel unless first advised by counsel? Moreover, if it is important that juveniles act voluntarily and with knowledge of the possibly adverse consequences of giving preadjudication information, then why is it not equally important that the juvenile act similarly when giving information relevant to disposition? After adjudication, however, juveniles not only have no protection regarding interrogation relating to disposition—even questioning as to unadjudicated offenses—it is expected that they will cooperate. Given the fact that such information can influence the disposition, the juvenile's full awareness of the consequences must be equally important at this stage.

Gault will not aid in answering these questions precisely because it involved an inquiry into the parallels between delinquency and criminal procedure and not an inquiry into the distinctions between juveniles and adults. As such, it is little help to courts facing the type of questions posed above.

The ambiguity and indecisiveness of *Gault* were made starkly apparent when the Supreme Court decided *McKeiver* v. *Pennsylvania* (403 U.S. 538 [1971]), holding that the due process clause of the Fourteenth Amendment did not require that states provide juveniles with jury trials in delinquency proceedings that may result in incarceration. Justice Blackmun's opinion for a sharply divided Court is itself a model of confusion, displaying what appears to be a random selection of authorities supporting his views. Summarily dismissing several centuries of thought about juries, the Court advanced two reasons for rejecting a right to a jury trial: (1) requiring juries would somehow inhibit states from experimenting with juvenile court procedures; and (2) juries, in some unspecified manner, would bring the curse of adversariness and of the criminal court in their wake. Most revealing is Justice Blackmun's apparently approving recital from the opinion by the Pennsylvania Supreme Court that of all possible due process rights it is the right to a jury which would be most likely to alter the practice in juvenile courts (403 U.S. at p. 540).

The Court's opinion in *McKeiver* seems to be remarkably isolated from general theories about the role of juries in American jurisprudence. The simple answer to the Court's two basic policy arguments is that the juvenile justice system has no greater need than does the adult criminal system for experimentation and flexibility, and for the avoidance of such supposed by-products of adversariness as court delay and clamor. Indeed, Supreme Court decisions permitting juries of less than twelve (*Williams* v. *Florida*, 399 U.S. 78 [1970]) and nonunanimous verdicts (*Apodaca* v. *Oregon*, 406 U.S. 404 [1972]) have introduced considerable flexibility into the criminal courts. Had *McKeiver* been decided differently, more flexibility would still have been possible through the use of dual calendars: formal (juries available) and informal (no juries, no chance of coercive removal from home). Delay and expense in the use of juries could be minimized by improving administrative practices. The introduction of six jurors into a court system already swarming with probation officers, lawyers, referees, and assistants would hardly constitute a breach of the fictional secrecy so highly prized by spokesmen for the status quo.

Ultimately, *McKeiver* is striking not for its failure to answer the Court's own arguments supportive of the jury in *Duncan* v. *Louisiana* (391 U.S. 145 [1968]), but for its *Gault*-like failure to place the juvenile court system into some coherent framework of jurisprudence governing processes whereby the state deprives persons of liberty. *McKeiver* continues the tradition of conceptual oscillation when juvenile court procedure is at issue and, like *Gault*, adds nothing to our understanding of what it is about being young that causes the extension of some rights and the denial of others.

Notably, *McKeiver* does not directly overrule *Gault* in any way. It does, however, accept a theory that *Gault* rejected, namely, that informality in court procedure—meaning the absence of criminal procedure safeguards—is desirable itself. As we noted earlier, even the prototypical *parens patriae* court in *Fisher* did not adopt this notion.

The Supreme Court has most recently addressed the area of juvenile delinquency in *Breed* v. *Jones* (421 U.S. 519 [1975]). There it held that the prosecution of a seventeen-year-old in a criminal court following an adjudicatory proceeding in a juvenile court violated the Fifth Amendment's double jeopardy clause as applied to the states through the Fourteenth Amendment. In result, *Breed* is in the *Gault* line of decisions, leaving *McKeiver* in constitutional limbo. Once again, we are left with no clear understanding of the jurisprudence of juvenile courts, the objectives of juvenile court proceedings, or what model of dispute resolution might ultimately apply.

Jeopardy, Chief Justice Burger tells us, denotes risk, a "risk that is traditionally associated with a criminal prosecution" (421 U.S. at p. 528). What risks did the respondent face when adjudicated in the California juvenile court? The risks, we are told, are both the stigma inherent in the determination of delinquency and the deprivation of liberty for many years. Concerning potential consequences, the Court also found little to distinguish the adjudicatory hearing held here from a traditional criminal prosecution. Given the identity of risks faced in the juvenile court and in subsequent criminal prosecution, the Court ruled that the task of twice marshaling resources and twice being subjected to the heavy personal strain of trial is constitutionally forbidden.

Breed arose under a particular California response to a recognized problem among drafters of juvenile court acts, namely, that of dealing with the juveniles "who cannot benefit from the specialized guidance and treatment contemplated by the [juvenile court] system" (421 U.S. at p. 535). The great majority of jurisdictions provide for transfer to a court of general criminal jurisdiction under certain circumstances. The California procedure at issue was a provision for transfer after the adjudicatory hearing, when the juvenile had been found delinquent, and the Court recognized it as such. In no sense does *Breed* preclude the result sought by the California authorities, that is, access to adult criminal sanctions. *Breed* merely requires that transfers be sought before evidence is taken at an adjudicatory hearing. In the earlier decision of *Kent* v. *United States* (383 U.S. 541 [1966]) the Court had mandated that transfer hearings meet essential due process and fair treatment standards. At first glance, therefore, *Breed* appears to paint itself into a corner. On one hand, the Court rules that double jeopardy forbids successive adjudications and prosecutions while on the other, it already has mandated a more than ceremonial hearing before a juvenile may be transferred to face a subsequent prosecution. Indeed, in a footnote, the Court states, "We note that nothing decided today forecloses States from requiring, as a prerequisite to the transfer of a juvenile, substantial evidence that he committed the offense charged, so long as the showing required is not made in an adjudicatory proceeding" (421 U.S. at p. 538, nt. 18). Backing out of its corner, the Court decided that, while transfer hearings require some attention to procedure, there are no prescriptions concerning criteria, the nature and quantum of evidence, nor, presumably, what findings must be made.

If *McKeiver*'s manifest inconsistency with both *Gault* and *Breed* disturbed the Court, the opinion in *Breed* managed to hide it quite well. *McKeiver* is dispatched in a sentence: "We deal here, not with the 'formalities of the criminal adjudicative process' [citing *McKeiver*], but with an analysis of an aspect of the juvenile court system in terms of the kind of risk to which jeopardy refers" (421 U.S. at p. 531). Since *Breed* characterized those risks as scarcely distinguishable from the risks of criminal prosecution, and since in *McKeiver* "the Pennsylvania juveniles' basic argument is that they were tried in proceedings 'substantially similar to a criminal trial' " (403 U.S. at p. 541) we are at a loss to comprehend this terse explanation.

The Scope of Jurisdiction: PINS, MINS, CHINS,
and Other "Nonstigmatized" Undesirables

Since *Gault,* commentators, litigators, and would-be reformers
have followed the trend in adult criminal law and adult civil
commitment toward proportionately less concern with court
procedures and more with substance: with the jurisdiction,
dispositional powers, and correctional programs of the courts. In
the juvenile area, something of a crusade has emerged from
efforts to curtail sharply, and eventually to eliminate altogether,
the role of juvenile courts in the troubled middle ground between
child protection proceedings (neglect, dependency, abuse) on one
side and youth crime on the other.

So far, these efforts have had little effect. The minority of states
that have separated noncriminal misbehavior by juveniles into a
different jurisdictional category from juvenile crime have restricted juvenile courts' powers in dealing with the former—the
class of noncriminal offenders—very little or not at all. It is
commonly argued that being labeled a PINS, MINS, CHINS
(person, minor, or child in need of supervision), or unruly child is
only marginally less stigmatizing than being adjudicated a
delinquent, although it must be admitted that there is little
empirical evidence on the point.

The recent experience in New York State with persons in need
of supervision (PINS) is worth recounting as an example of the
general futility of seeking systemic change through the expedient
of changing labels. New York established the PINS category as
early as the New York Family Court Act of 1962. While confinement in state training schools was at first proscribed, it was not
long before the Act was amended to render PINS eligible for
training school placements. A 1974 decision by the New York
Court of Appeals, *In the Matter of Ellery C.* (32 N.Y. 2d
588 [1973]), involving the permissible disposition of PINS, created
a minor flurry in the state and stimulated a fairly comprehensive
study (initiated by coauthor Schultz) of the impact of that
decision (Institute of Judicial Administration 1975).

The Legal Aid Society of New York City brought the appeal,
contending that the state training school placement of Ellery C.,
adjudicated as a PINS, violated the juvenile's statutory and
constitutional right to adequate care and treatment. What came
to the court as a form of "right to treatment" challenge emerged

in the opinion as a rather garbled holding susceptible to many interpretations. The lack of clarity in the opinion caused many problems of implementation that might easily have been avoided. The court concluded that the appellant's confinement with juveniles found guilty of committing criminal acts could not realistically be considered as appropriate supervision or treatment. The decision went on to mandate that proper facilities be made available to correct this deficiency. What facilities or program would suffice and what schedule of compliance was required were not dealt with. Indeed, the opinion was so imprecise that some argued that PINS no longer could be dealt with except under some form of community supervision.

The *Ellery C.* study wanted to know what would happen to the 400 PINS then in state training schools, how the Division for Youth (the statewide agency for juveniles) would interpret and then respond to the ambiguous mandate, what the impact on programs might be, and whether there would occur a post-*Ellery C.* alteration in the characteristics of juveniles appearing before New York Family Courts.

Put succinctly, practically nothing of consequence occurred. The eight New York State training schools were divided into PINS and delinquency institutions. Questionnaires and interviews were used to determine how PINS and delinquency institutions differed. On most of nine categories (ranging from physical living conditions to education and treatment to legal status of residents), the two sets of institutions were found to be very much alike, except for heightened security in the delinquency institutions. Nothing indicated a greater potential for treating the PINS cases. The Division for Youth took the position that *Ellery C.* was not retroactive and thus was inapplicable to PINS currently under confinement. Continued legal efforts, especially in New York City, resulted in obtaining the release or parole of some while others were transferred to different training schools. What is significant is that these alternative dispositions were not determined by any assessment of the juveniles' needs but rather by the accident of geography, litigation, or varying juvenile court interpretations of the decision.

In the study it was postulated that *Ellery C.* might have an impact on the personal and social characteristics of the juveniles appearing in family courts after the decision. That is, if *Ellery C.*

really mandated treatment and if treatment was unavailable in training schools, then persons charged only with status offenses might be expected to be diverted from court. By all the factors investigated, however—including age, ethnicity, family income, education, school records, and previous treatment for mental disorders—no significant differences were found between the populations appearing before the courts after the *Ellery C.* decision and those appearing previously.

It is difficult to know just what went wrong since the decision was unclear on what would be right, but if reasonable speculation is in order, the following observations may be made. The Division for Youth held strongly to the view that treatment needs are not determined by legal statuses. Thus, in equating a PINS determination with a right to treatment, legislative and judicial policy directly conflicted with a firmly held contrary view by the agency charged with implementing the program. The agency did engage in some administrative reshuffling. Training schools were redesignated, mingling of delinquents and PINS cases was prohibited (although one PINS school was designated as a secure facility to which PINS who could not be otherwise controlled would be transferred), a regionalization program was launched, and coeducation was instituted. But all of these measures seem either peripheral or unrelated to the "vital distinction" between PINS and delinquents referred to in the *Ellery C.* opinion (32 N.Y. 2d at p. 591).

A *Gault*-like ambiguity of concept and objectives characterized the *Ellery C.* opinion. Where *Gault*, at least, was clear on the adjudicatory procedures required, *Ellery C.* was fatally flawed on the question of remedy.

For those who seek treatment for PINS, to say nothing of those who seek to remove them from the coercive jurisdiction of the juvenile court, the *Ellery C.* experience is indeed a melancholy one. Putting aside the question whether the trend toward excluding noncriminal "offenders" from the legal category of delinquents is anything more than a verbal exercise, we note that advocates of more thorough reform press two lines of attack: that present laws are unconstitutional and that they are bad policy. We will deal with these attacks separately, while recognizing that they tend toward the common perception, valid or misguided, that more harm than good is done by the courts' use of coercion in response to problems not classifiable as either criminal problems or child neglect.

Constitutional Challenges

The constitutional attack follows well-worn lines. Statutes permitting courts to enter orders seriously interfering with children's freedom on the basis of noncriminal misbehavior are said to be overbroad, to punish a status rather than an act, and to deny children equal protection of the laws. There is a fundamental problem with the adequacy of the first two arguments if they are intended ultimately to lead to the judicial destruction of the noncriminal offender category. It is certainly true that most juvenile court laws include jurisdictional language that is blatantly overbroad under the most permissive test of the adequacy of a criminal statute. These laws also include categories that permit courts to premise dispositions on the adjudication of a status: that the child is unruly, ungovernable, beyond control, or the like.

In *Gesicki* v. *Oswald* (336 F. Supp. 371 [1971]), a three-judge court in New York fastened on such a typically overbroad status definition contained in a statute permitting the state courts to commit so-called wayward minors to adult prisons. It would be difficult to see how the language in question could have survived scrutiny, and in fact the decision was subsequently affirmed summarily and without dissent by the Supreme Court (406 U.S. 913 [1972]).

Like *Gault,* however, *Gesicki* was fatally ambiguous and noncommittal on the key issue raised by the case: was it the fact that wayward minors could be sent specifically to an adult prison that mattered, or was it that they could be dealt with in ways indistinguishable from those used with adult criminals, regardless of what institutions they could be sent to?

The basic problem can be traced back to the flaw in *Gault* described earlier in this chapter. Courts in the past seven years have continued to make their constitutional judgments depend on their own assessment of whether juvenile institutions are basically good or bad, or, like *McKeiver,* on whether they are potentially good or bad for children. The implication of this approach is that if a court faced with a constitutional problem is convinced that children found to be delinquents or PINS will not be treated as harshly as adult criminals, it will tend to relax constitutional safeguards. In other words, courts have continued to dissociate their thinking about juvenile courts from their thinking about the jurisprudence of criminal courts.

That this is so can be illustrated if we imagine a statute permitting courts to incarcerate adults adjudicated "unattractive and eccentric" to a new class of institutions designed to restore them to attractiveness and normality. It is submitted that no judge sitting today capable of understanding the problem and writing an opinion about it would find that such a statute was constitutional, even if the state could show that the average person committed to such an institution came out happier, healthier, and with 50 percent greater earning power (cf. *O'Connor* v. *Donaldson,* 422 U.S. 563 [1975]). Constitutional protections against serious and coercive governmental intervention in the lives of adults based on their undesirable behavior have never been thought to vary according to how good or bad a particular state's prison system may be. Constitutional safeguards have been concerned with how seriously the state interferes with the freedom of the individual—that is, the extent to which it attempts to substitute its will for that of the adult—and not with the qualitative results of that interference. The freedom to decide whether the result is good or bad is the very freedom that is sought to be protected.

This is not to imply that the freedom of adults can be seriously curtailed only if they violate a reasonably precise criminal statute. In striking down a criminal statute in California that punished narcotics addicts for their addiction, the Supreme Court in *Robinson* v. *California* (370 U.S. 660 [1962]) was careful to preserve governmental power to provide a treatment program for narcotics addiction. Still, it is necessary for courts to develop rules for deciding what is and what is not a valid treatment statute. For instance, courts cannot be permitted broadly to commit anyone adjudicated as "ill" to an "appropriate treatment facility." To protect against abuses of treatment statutes, constitutional minima would suggest that the treatments must be specifically tailored to a disorder concretely defined by the statute. Further, there must be hard evidence that the treatments permitted under the statute do in fact ameliorate the defined disorder in some reasonably high percentage of cases. Finally, there must be

controls to see that people committed for treatment under such
statutes do in fact receive it and to see that those who are not
helped after a reasonable period of commitment are then released. The point of this discussion is not to elaborate the need for
controls over civil commitment. That is being done with increasing vigor by advocates, commentators, and some courts (Harvard
Law Review 1974). Yet courts faced with challenges to juvenile
court jurisdiction over status offenders have managed to seal
themselves off from the impact of these views. Courts analyzing
juvenile court laws not only largely ignore criminal law jurisprudence, they also ignore the developing jurisprudence of civil
commitment statutes.

And well they might, if for some unarticulated reasons they
want to preserve these statutes. Status offense definitions could
not pass any of the minimal tests for civil commitment statutes
suggested above. Being an unruly child is not, any more than
being an obnoxious adult, a treatable condition. Status offense
definitions simply do not isolate a special class of people with an
identifiable disorder treatable by specified means. Because they
do not, and because they permit removal from home and
incarceration, they are indistinguishable by any meaningful test
from criminal statutes.

Policy Implications

If these statutes are so vulnerable to any reasonable constitutional
analysis derived from obvious analogies in adult jurisprudence,
then why are they so remarkably resistant to attack? The answer
may be that judges, including those who decided *Gesicki, Gault,*
and *Breed,* were afraid to confront the most difficult legal
dilemma of juvenile court laws—how to defend them against a
challenge to their validity on the grounds that they deny juveniles
equal protection of the laws.

It is a measure of the trepidation felt by courts confronted with
this problem that they have only recently struck down statutes
providing different age limits for juvenile court jurisdiction over
girls and boys (see *A.* v. *City of New York,* 81 N.Y. 2d 83 [1972]).
Once these cases have been litigated, the states have been able to
muster virtually no credible defense of these statutes, which
courts have rightly perceived as anachronistic manifestations of a

double standard of morality based on indefensible assumptions about inherent differences between the sexes.

Courts may have perceived that they would be entering dangerous and unmapped territory if they ever tried to go further with equal protection analysis and fashion a principled, coherent, and workable justification for each of the many ways that juvenile court acts (and many other laws) treat juveniles differently from similarly situated adults. In some ways, juveniles seem to be treated better, in some ways worse. Definitions of who is a juvenile vary for different purposes within individual states as well as among different states. These differences are never, to our knowledge, satisfactorily explained in the legislative history or in any preface to the laws themselves.

What is the key? Is it psychological dependency or immaturity? The best contemporary knowledge indicates that moral and intellectual development does not change dramatically after about age fourteen, which is well below any state's definition of a juvenile—although, interestingly, it corresponds to the common law rule presuming that children younger than fourteen were not responsible for their criminal acts. Furthermore, there are many adults of all ages who are the moral and intellectual inferiors of most older juveniles, and even of some young children. Conversely, there are many juveniles who are the superiors of most adults. The level of people's moral and intellectual development varies widely (Piaget 1965; Kohlberg and Gilligan 1971). How is it that states can treat all "juveniles" or "minors" differently from all "adults," so that dramatically different consequences are experienced by otherwise similar persons who happen to fall into different classes?

If the key is not psychological development, perhaps it is social or legal development. The problem with this approach is that social and legal dependency may be artificial products of a social structure defined, to an immeasurable but substantial degree, by the very laws in question (see Bittner, this volume). That is, if states impose social restrictions on residents until they become sixteen, eighteen, or whatever—for instance, limiting their capacity to contract, to drive a car, to read sexually explicit books, or to choose not to attend school—then such residents are likely in fact to be dependent and it is perhaps logical to subject them to parental control. (Reinforcing parental control, as so many statutes in point illustrate, is the essence of status offense jurisdiction.) But can the state justify one form of discrimination by reference to a whole complex of other kinds of legal discrimination, on the grounds that the social structure of the state has come to reflect and reinforce the system of legal discrimination?

Even assuming that in general many differences between state treatment of adults and juveniles can be justified on some such grounds, the question remains whether those grounds are sufficient to support status offenses. A negative answer would imply that states are prohibited from using the force of government to reinforce and, if necessary, supplant the "natural authority" (in *Fisher's* telling phrase) of parents over their children. It is doubtful that courts will be willing in the near future to work so drastic an interference with the traditional structure of the family.

A MISCELLANY AND FRAMEWORK FOR CHANGE

Straddling the juvenile process, as we did earlier with insanity and police interrogation-confession issues, we will now look briefly at detention and corrections and conclude with some recommendations for change. No issues in juvenile justice better portray its compartmentalization and provincialism, its worthy and unworthy characteristics.

It is estimated that nearly one million youth are detained annually in the United States, with about 500,000 held in jails and the others in specially designated juvenile detention facilities. In raw figures, the number of youth jailed or otherwise detained is about ten times the number of youth in all public training schools, halfway houses, camps, group homes, and the like (Sarri 1974). The figures alone are staggering but when seen in context with the conditions of confinement, the absence of procedural safeguards, and the multiplicity of objectives, detention may well be the area of highest priority for sweeping reform (see P. Wald, this volume; cf. Schultz 1973).

While adult detention struggles to be minimally effective at assuring the appearance of adult defendants, juvenile detention accepts this as only one of its goals. Remarkably, the controversy over the legality or desirability of preventive detention for adult defendants has thus far passed by the juvenile courts. Juveniles always have been liable to preventive detention under all juvenile court laws with which we are familiar and that situation is only now being frontally challenged in the courts. In addition to seeking to assure the appearance of juveniles in court and to preventing them from committing offenses while awaiting court action, juvenile detention embraces what in the adult system is imperfectly attempted through various medical care, observation, and civil commitment statutes. Thus, the vagueness and breadth of the law allow children to be detained because they need medical help, or to protect them from their parents or their parents from them, or because they have no parents, or to keep them from harming themselves, or to keep them off the streets, or simply to give them a taste of jail—all in the name of "detention."

That the scope and complexity of juvenile detention has not been commonly recognized may be due to the prevalent but unjustifiable distinction between what is labeled "detention" and "shelter care." Shelter care can involve involuntary removal of children from their homes for periods even longer than if they had been officially detained and under conditions that would not be tolerated even in detention. The supposed distinction between shelter care and detention puts far more importance on a single aspect of detention—the degree of security—than is warranted. A "home-away-from-home" without locks can be just as miserable or as inappropriate a place for children as an institution with locks.

Future analysis of juvenile detention must take into account practices designed to serve the same purposes among adults and must seek some order among the artificial categories and multiple objectives in the juvenile detention system. The goal must be to reduce the vast numbers of children under lock and key. Procedural and substantive safeguards must be related to the objective sought rather than to the incidental matter of the kind of petition that has been filed against the juveniles involved.

Unlike juvenile detention with its potpourri of objectives, juvenile corrections—the process that follows an adjudication of delinquency—at least marches under a single banner, rehabilitation in the best interests of the child. Every decision by the Supreme Court, whether it has imposed procedural safeguards like *Gault* and *Breed* or denied them like *McKeiver*, assumes like *Fisher* that the child is to be saved and not punished. Indeed, again and again it is said that the commitment to individualization and treatment is the unique cornerstone of the juvenile court process. This commitment is, in fact, an important source of the isolation and fragmentation of juvenile court jurisprudence. This being so, let us now examine the area of corrections and look there for a framework of reform. We will ask, How might correctional policy be reformed to eliminate its sole reliance on the "best interests of the child" theories and to incorporate other jurisprudential insights as well?

Corrections and Liberty

There are books to be written on the question of how far any coercive intervention works, whether that intervention is community treatment, supervised release, or a form of confinement. Our reading of the literature, or our bias (if that is more palatable), may be stated as follows: there is little reason to believe that any effective way to reduce recidivism through coercive rehabilitation has been found. The few instances of full or partial success are isolated and show no clear pattern of efficacy attributable to any particular method. Evaluation is primitive and often self-serving. The one hopeful item is that the reduction of coercion—for example, preferring probation to confinement—is currently less expensive and produces results that are at least as good and probably better. Apparently, success is not related to the casework dynamic in probation but rather to avoiding the more destructive effects of incarceration (Martinson 1974).

Given our skepticism about the efficacy of rehabilitation, we feel a certain distaste for a system built around that objective. Our problem is to suggest a suitable alternate focus. There are perhaps no simple answers—such as abandoning the juvenile justice system, sending young offenders into the adult criminal courts and relying on the existing welfare–social services network for rehabilitation; or keeping a separate juvenile justice system but dealing out punishment rather than therapy to those juveniles (at least those who are thirteen or fourteen and above) who commit serious offenses. As lawyers, our initial concern is with the procedural and substantive consequences in law of the rehabilitation model. The exchange theory—the juvenile is given help in exchange for giving up some procedural safeguards—simply does not hold up on analysis and *Gault,* for all its shortcomings, partially recognized that.

We propose, instead, a procedural law of deprivation of liberty, a law that turns on the interest at stake—liberty—and not on good intentions or even good results. Juvenile justice need not slavishly imitate either criminal law or civil commitment law; but both have something to offer. It can take from criminal law recognition of the legitimate state interest in responding to criminal misconduct by youth, and from civil commitment law recognition of the youth as a competent participant in a process which may affect a precious individual interest, liberty.

Concerning sanctioning principles, we believe that the nature (confinement, probation, fine, and so on) and duration of a sanction imposed on a juvenile for criminal misconduct must in the first instance be limited by the seriousness of the predicate offense. That is, "just deserts" should replace indeterminate dispositions, limited only by the attainment of the age of majority. The "just deserts" (or equity) model is a principle of equivalency between the juvenile's culpability (harm caused plus the mental state of the actor at the time) and the nature and duration of the sanctions available to the state. Operationally, this would mean scaling acts of delinquency—like immoral conduct—according to severity and limiting available sanctions by this severity scale.

To this equity approach must be added further limitations on state power. While the state should attempt to equate the severity of a sanction with the seriousness of the offense, there should be definite restrictions on what the state may do (such as inflict corporal punishment, bread and water diets, prolonged isolation) and how it may act (for example, there should be no form of discipline without procedural safeguards, no enforced "consents," or the like) while it exercises authority over the juvenile offender.

Let us stress that these proposals do not mean that no efforts may be made to resocialize, to educate, or to provide vocational skills. We argue only that the methods and substance of juvenile justice can no longer turn on what we view as the discredited premise of rehabilitation. Within the limits of our equity–justice model, all manner of services and programs can be offered. Juveniles under state supervision would be subject to the same laws (such as compulsory education) that apply to other youth. In short, the state can and should continue to classify youth generally as a class deserving of special legal treatment, different

from that accorded the adult offender. The mere absence of
experience in the child, the recognition that children are persons
incomplete in their development, and the near-universal support
for a social moratorium for youth—all these favor a separate
classification before the law.

Thus, we are not led to conclude that the juvenile court as a
separate institution with distinctive legal characteristics need be
abandoned. What does need to be abandoned is whatever isolates
the juvenile court from the mainstream of jurisprudence, which
includes criminal law and civil commitment law. Without offering
any detailed program for change here, we would add the following to what already has been said.

With all of its shortcomings, *Gault* may still be applauded for
stimulating legal thought and analysis of juvenile justice. It is now
time, however, for courts, legislatures, and standard-setting
projects to go further—to think through the legal and psychological bases for affixing responsibility for crimes by juveniles and
to devise procedures that recognize the harsh reality that liberty is
at issue, not good intentions or dashed hopes. It is time for
juvenile courts to become courts and not hybrid institutions
unable to help and hard-pressed to provide justice.

We seek visibility and accountability in decision making
throughout the process, a participant role for juveniles which
turns on their actual competence and not on a blanket presumption of incompetence, and we seek to minimize the basis for state
intervention and to minimize and control (through monitoring,
for example) state intervention which does occur.

It is time to recognize that the juvenile justice system can and
often does cause harm rather than provide help. To reduce the
amount of harm caused even by the well-intentioned may not be
the most stirring battle cry for reform, but it just may comport
with reality.

BIBLIOGRAPHY

Harvard Law Review. 1974. "Developments in the Law: Civil
Commitment of the Mentally Ill." 87:1190–1406.
Institute of Judicial Administration. 1975. *The* Ellery C. *Decision: A Case of Judicial Regulation of Juvenile Status Offenders.* New York: Institute of Judicial Administration.

Kohlberg, Lawrence, and Gilligan, Carol. 1971. "The Adolescent as Philosopher: The Discovery of Self in a Postconventional World." *Daedelus* 100:1051-86.

Levin, Mark M., and Sarri, Rosemary C. 1974. *Juvenile Delinquency: A Comparative Analysis of Legal Codes in the United States.* Ann Arbor: University of Michigan.

Martinson, Robert. 1974. "What Works? Questions and Answers about Prison Reform." *The Public Interest* 35:22-54.

Paulsen, Monrad G., and Whitebread, Charles H. 1974. *Juvenile Law and Procedure.* Chicago: National Council of Juvenile Court Judges.

Piaget, Jean. 1965. *The Moral Judgment of the Child.* New York: Free Press.

Sarri, Rosemary C. 1974. *Under Lock and Key: Juveniles in Jails and Detention.* Ann Arbor: University of Michigan.

Schultz, J. Lawrence. 1973. "The Cycle of Juvenile Court History." *Crime and Delinquency* 19:457-76.

3   Notes on Helping Juvenile Nuisances*

Margaret K. Rosenheim

It seems safe to say that reformers of juvenile justice do not ordinarily regard the mission and scope of the helping services as a primary concern. I suggest that they should. There is a symbiotic relationship between the juvenile justice system and the helping services—call them "social" or "welfare" or "community" services, as you please. The proclamation of new goals for juvenile justice is as momentous for the child-oriented service agencies as it is for the more obviously concerned agencies of law enforcement and justice. Failure to understand this fact may thwart the reform impulse of the late twentieth century as surely as other errors have frustrated other good intentions in the past.

Commentators on juvenile justice have recently proposed non-judicial handling of a large proportion of its cases as one way to repair the shortcomings of the system. The phrase "nonjudicial handling" refers to diversion of cases from formal process within the agencies of juvenile justice, either at various stages of

---

*A previous version of this chapter appeared in *Social Service Review* 50 (1976): 177-94. © 1976 by The University of Chicago.

the process or at the stage of juvenile court intake (Nejelski, this volume).

Typically, the advocates of nonjudicial handling focus on the population I have termed "juvenile nuisances" (Rosenheim 1969). Best defined by exclusion, they are minors who are neither seriously criminal nor severely disturbed. They include petty thieves, playground assailants, raucous loiterers, runaways and truants, and many more. Their proportionate representation in the caseloads of juvenile justice agencies appears to vary somewhat by location and circumstance (that is, by race, socioeconomic status, density of population, specific public targets of concern), but whoever they are exactly, they are ubiquitous. They probably comprise the majority of all children dealt with by the juvenile justice agencies of most communities.

Although there have been many proposals for nonjudicial handling, few have been specific about either the content of service or structural possibilities under the new approach. Nonjudicial handling is certainly an idea whose time has come, but an idea, one suspects, that takes as many different forms as it has adherents. What we find in the proposals, on the whole, are recommendations for substitute organizations to take on certain kinds of juvenile problems hitherto routinely routed through the justice system. Seldom is rationale related to detailed pictures of these preferred nonjudicial methods. What would happen? Who would do what?

Since the call for nonjudicial handling is so pervasive in contemporary reform, I propose to take it as the starting point of inquiry, rather than the finish. It is my purpose in the following notes to sketch the assumptions that underlie the preference for nonjudicial handling of juvenile nuisances and to identify some of the difficulties inherent in the present course of reform. A major source of difficulty is our failure to appreciate the interconnections between the juvenile justice and the service sector. It is my contention that, if helping services are not constructed on principles very different from those governing the substance and process of juvenile justice, they will fail to provide help and also fail to advance the reform of the justice system. I conclude by suggesting what some of these principles might be.

THE REFORM APPROACH

The endorsement of nonjudicial handling as one of the reforms of juvenile justice is an outgrowth of a "revised conception" of the juvenile court. That conception, as advocated in 1967 by the President's Crime Commission (President's Commission . . . 1967a, 1967b), means "channeling the principal rehabilitative effort [toward children] into community-based dispositions that occur prior to assumption of jurisdiction by the court, narrowing the reach of juvenile court jurisdiction to cases of manifest danger either to the child or to the community, and infusing in the court itself procedures designed to assure fair and reliable determinations for those who reach the point of judicial action" (1967b, p. 9). For several reasons the nuisance population contains prime candidates for the proposed substitute of nonjudicial handling. It might be said that the juvenile nuisance stands, in theory, at the junction of two important streams of thought regarding the juvenile court.

One stream can be summarized as "New Ways of Thinking about Delinquency" (Schur 1973, chap. 4). Among the ways cited by Schur, three are particularly pertinent to the growing disenchantment with the juvenile court as a major vehicle of juvenile control. Schur reports evidence in support of the view that delinquency is normal and transient, by and large; that affixing the label "delinquent" may very well deleteriously influence the "self-concepts and long-term behaviors of rule-violators" (Schur 1973, p. 119; cf. Mahoney 1974); and that the rhetoric of rehabilitation has masked a real world where harm is often done and organizational needs prevail over the child's. These findings obviously counsel caution in invoking the authority of juvenile justice. Admittedly, where serious crime is involved, there is nowhere else to turn. But for many routine cases of the police or courts, better alternatives are thought to exist. Juvenile nuisances provide a population ready-made for diversion to alternative modes of response.

Another influential body of thought is contained in the legal writing on due process in juvenile justice. There is now general acceptance of the juvenile's need for constitutional protection against imposition of coercive measures of control. Animated by the general modern concern for rights and strengthened by Justice Fortas' opinions in *Kent* (383 U.S. 541 [1966]) and *Gault* (387 U.S. 1 [1967]), the movement to secure observance of due process in the juvenile court is indebted to the persuasive arguments earlier propounded by Tappan (1949) and Allen (1964). Advocates of substantive and procedural regularity in this court, as in any court, insist upon observance of certain standards of fairness that incorporate and honor the basic values of our legal system.

In the wake of the due process revolution, efforts have been made to work out standards of fairness appropriate to a court with a special clientele and to determine how these standards should influence the activities of other officials who are placed downstream from the court, like police, or upstream, like correctional authorities. Even more significant is the continuing search for coherent theory on which to build a juvenile jurisprudence (Hazard, and Schultz and Cohen, this volume). This takes the form, among others, of questioning the substantive authority of the court. What type of behavior should fall within its purview? What is the underlying rationale for state intervention in juvenile cases, and—more important—should that rationale differ from the one normally accepted as conferring authority for coercive handling of adults? While definitive answers are certainly not yet in sight, their absence should not—and, realistically, cannot—impede the pursuit of partial solutions.

Nonjudicial handling is best seen, then, as an outgrowth of attempts to rethink the problem of delinquency and the function of the juvenile court. The new approaches to delinquency and the insistence on due process influence conceptions of the juvenile justice system and agencies external to it. Followers of the new approach to delinquency would support narrowing the court's jurisdiction and make the court's main business "real" crime (and juvenile nuisances would be out). The reawakened concern for due process is consistent with a narrower role for the court; the cost of the due process model is high—so high that only by substantially reducing caseload can a sharp rise in overall costs be avoided. Diversion of cases from the coercive authorities to nonjudicial agencies has the additional merit (as some would see it) of perpetuating the "rehabilitative ideal" (Allen 1964), but relocating its organizational expressions in voluntarily sought services, where many think they rightly belong.

A revision of the juvenile court mission to emphasize non-judicial handling shifts substantial responsibility from the justice system to somebody else. Few people would advocate ignoring the misconduct and problems subsumed under the label of juvenile nuisance. Debate centers on means, not ends. There is general agreement on the desirability of some amount of schooling, on the undesirability of taking many kinds of drugs, on the risks in wholesale defiance of adult advice and counsel, on the impropriety of shoplifting, and even on the danger of "habitually wander(ing) about any railroad yards or tracks or jump(ing) . . . onto any moving train" (Laws of Illinois 1905, p. 153, §1)! Though current discussion seldom addresses the issues head on, the consensus seems to be that the social problems posed by juvenile nuisances are real and cannot be solved by ignoring them or by trying to define them out of existence.

Nonjudicial handling not only promises to avoid the rigidities or drawbacks of formal justice-system process; commentators also find in it particular virtues all its own. For one thing, it is able to ameliorate social problems that are ongoing, or relatively trivial. Such difficulties are miscast as justiciable issues. They do not yield to one-shot solutions or, if they do, they scarcely warrant invoking the power of the state. Community agencies or informal organizations are (at least in theory) better able to deal with chronic problems and low-level disturbances than are the police (that high-visibility authority) or the courts (who are encumbered by ceremony and procedure).

Another potential advantage of nonjudicial agencies is their ability to utilize a set of diverse responses. The officials of juvenile justice are poorly equipped in this regard. Their range of dispositions is formally laid down by law. Practical constraints also affect both choice of response and its timing and duration. One agency, the police, is typically under pressure to act quickly and decisively (see Bittner, this volume). For the police, kids as trouble are trouble to be disposed of by a particular officer during a particular shift. Courts, by contrast, are constrained by the rhythms of calendar and procedural requirement. Even the first court appearance often takes place weeks after detection, when shame and anxiety have passed; the final hearing may occur at months' remove.

Community agencies should be able, better than police or courts, to implement a crisis-relief approach (Caplan 1964; Rapoport 1962). The helping services can (though I concede they often don't) mobilize energies for a nearly immediate response aimed, first, at relief of symptoms. Only then, according to crisis theory, should there be more protracted attempts, client-initiated, to search for insight and new ways of coping. In this view of human behavior, the crisis is not necessarily a sign of illness. It is instead "an upset in a steady state" (Gerald Caplan, as cited in Rapoport 1962) and, as a rule, is temporally self-limiting. Runaway houses and some of the recent diversion projects (for example, Baron, Feeney, and Thornton 1973) offer instances of crisis intervention theory put to work in the interests of juvenile nuisances.

Another advantage of the helping services, already noted above, is their voluntary character. Help voluntarily sought and rendered is a welcome alternative to the exercise of police power. The conventional wisdom is that all service relationships, apart from obvious ones involving persons "sentenced to treatment" (such as criminal offenders or committed mental hospital patients), are voluntary. And so they are, in many instances.

The new learning suggests we may have made too much of this feature, however. It can be shown that "social service agencies are capable of exerting great control over the lives of people" (Handler 1973, p. 157). Sometimes they acquire their power from control over benefits in a continuing relationship. Sometimes it inheres in contingencies of choice, as, for example, when local policy makes diversion from the juvenile justice system contingent upon the juvenile's acceptance of a referral for services. But whatever the source of its power, the service sector is bound to have more control over situations than does its clientele. It has knowledge, money, and commodities. The agencies are in the driver's seat.

Granting all this, common sense still compels us to distinguish between the police power of the state and the capacity of community agencies to overreach their clients or take arbitrary action. The promotion of nonjudicial handling is a product of this recognition. There are, after all, severe limits to what service agencies can do to people. At their most arbitrary they can hardly compete with the sorry examples of overkill reactions by juvenile justice officials to nuisance behavior. And the danger of arbitrary exercise of power by service agencies can be reduced.

All things considered, nonjudicial handling affords rich opportunities for help in crisis. Juvenile nuisances, especially, stand to gain from expansion of community dispositions. But we have still to begin the task of recasting the objectives of these helping agencies that are not part of a modest, modern juvenile jurisprudence even while they have become indispensable to it.

HELPING SERVICES: THE WELFARE MODEL

If there are limits to what service agencies can do to people, there also seem to be severe limits to what they have been able to do for them. The shortcomings of agency service are especially visible when we consider juvenile nuisances. It is widely accepted that the petty offenders and other incorrigibles who have somehow escaped the notice of police or court have generally been ignored by other organizations carrying a youth service mandate. There are conspicuous exceptions, of course. The street work movement illustrates a countertendency, and there can always be found individuals and community centers where help is given generously, flexibly, and continuously to troublesome youngsters and where some success is achieved in redirecting their energies into more socially acceptable forms of behavior.

Nevertheless, the reform strategy has not relied on existing groups to provide nonjudicial handling. The President's Crime Commission plainly doubted that such groups would be willing or able to do the job and recommended establishment of new agencies—youth services bureaus. Judging by the proliferation of the bureaus, community after community (doubtless encouraged by the availability of federal funds) has apparently agreed with the Commission's conclusions that:

An essential objective in a community's delinquency and prevention plan should . . . be an agency that might be called a youth services bureau, with a broad range of services and certain mandatory functions. . . . A mandate for service seems necessary to insure energetic efforts to control and redirect acting out youth and to minimize the substantial risk that this group, denied service by traditional social agencies, would inevitably be shunted to a law enforcement agency (1967a, p. 83).

So far, the record of the bureaus is unimpressive (Lemert 1971; Seymour 1972), and there are grounds for concern about their programs (see Nejelski, this volume). They may be serving a less deviant group at the expense of the nuisances for whom they were intended to provide nonjudicial handling; and the group actually served may become labeled stigmatically as a result. On the other hand, the bureaus may be reducing the volume of cases handled by the police and courts, and they may well be rendering services that are otherwise unavailable. We do not know. In any event, it should be stressed that definitive assessment is not yet possible. In the perspective of bureaucratic timekeeping, a decade of discussion of reform (let alone the far fewer years of actual service effort) is but yesterday. While youth services bureaus clearly deserve to be evaluated, a measured judgment of success or failure will take time.

Notwithstanding this plea to avoid premature conclusions, I admit to the suspicion that there is something wrong with what youth services bureaus are doing. It is true that their rationale is not unambiguous (Schur 1973, p. 62). Are they supposed to emphasize individual treatment or social reform, or to use the new ways of thinking about delinquency? These new views, subsumed under the term "radical nonintervention," would imply

policies that accommodate society to the widest possible diversity of behaviors and attitudes, rather than forcing as many individuals as possible to "adjust" to supposedly common societal standards. This does not mean that anything goes, that all behavior is socially acceptable. But traditional delinquency policy has proscribed youthful behavior well beyond what is required to maintain a smooth-running society or to protect others from youthful depredations (Schur 1973, p. 154).

In my opinion, youth services bureaus can be run in a way consistent with a radical nonintervention perspective. But I doubt that this potential is currently being exploited. Rather, it appears from an examination of bureau programs that "old ideas [are] being recycled" (Lemert 1971, p. 93). There is reason to fear that the bureaus are perpetuating some of the drawbacks to judicial response to juvenile nuisances and perhaps the shortcomings of the welfare model as well.

The Welfare Model of Helping Services

The welfare model of helping services, like the medical model of health provision, takes an approach to human needs that stresses pathology. The pathology that concerns the helping services is social deviance ("social-behavioral sickness"); the pathology addressed by the medical model, physical and mental illness. Obviously the two overlap to some degree. I will use "welfare model" to refer to services that are based on an individualistic social-pathological perspective and that rely on individual treatment to restore healthy social functioning. While able to accommodate different strategies of help—such as socialization and educational approaches, group treatment and environmental manipulation—the helping services primarily use counseling. The welfare model presently dominates the nonjudicial handling provided through diversion projects. As a result, these projects "involve singling out, and doing something with or for, specific individuals; they are programs for dealing with delinquents, rather than dealing with delinquency in some broader sense" (Schur 1973, p. 62).

This is unfortunate. It is unfortunate because there is little chance that nonjudicial agencies committed to a welfare model will have more success in individualizing the juvenile nuisances who abound in every community than the juvenile court has had over the past seventy-five years. Herein lies a great weakness of the welfare model. To individualize is expensive. It probably takes skill and training, but it certainly takes time. And time costs money. To implement the individualistic perspective seriously in the human services demands an infusion of people and money on a scale we have yet to approach.

Failure to achieve individualization of juvenile nuisances in the service sector could well destroy reformers' hopes and expectations. It is wholly possible that the shift from reliance upon one set of mechanisms (such as law enforcement) to another (such as nonjudicial agencies) will prove not to produce the grand differences that doctrinal contrasts imply. If managing an overwhelming burden of cases becomes the daily experience of the service sector, perhaps the important theoretical differences between the due process and welfare models will have minor practical effects. However stark the contrast between the aims and methods of courts and service agencies, if routinization of response dominates over individualized disposition, the consequences (given the minor character of nuisance behavior) to the child may be much the same: "Be good." "Be home on time." "Go to school." The overload of the systems vitiates the force of theory.

Have we been tilting at windmills, debating the merits of

alternatives neither of which is realizable in any ideal way? It is clear that the recent reorientation of juvenile justice systems has placed expectations on the helping services that are yet to be met (compare Zimring 1974, pp. 240–41). Does this simply indicate a lag in shifting funds from justice officials to service agencies and a need for a larger pool of resources overall?

I believe there is more at stake. Questions about helping services should be asked before a role is given them. The demands being made of them betray ignorance of what specialists employed in these agencies can, and most like to, do. The attempts to reform the handling of juvenile nuisances seem to me to illustrate more general shortcomings of the helping services.

"Problemization"

I suggest we have been hampered in reform by the prevailing conception of helping services. As I see it, their basic emphasis runs counter to the new learning about delinquency, which urges upon us the wisdom of "normalizing" as much delinquent conduct as we possibly can.

Generally, neither courts nor helping services act as if low-level deviancy among children is normal. Even if they acknowledge it, this point of view does not appear to be a major influence upon their operations. Yet self-report studies of delinquency and other pieces of evidence inform us that various kinds of juvenile misconduct are best understood as the endemic and transient phenomena of youth. Why have program administrators and other officials apparently resisted the implications of these findings? Why do they persist in relying on the individualistic approach as a general strategy, rather than reserving it for instances of severe pathology (crime or illness)?

One clue to understanding the persistence of old ways is found in the phenomenon I call "problemization." By this term I mean to suggest something different from the treatment (or pathological) perspective just discussed. Although related to the pathological perspective—which focuses on the deviance or illness of a person—problemization refers to the activity of individuals and agencies in organizing and applying their particular apparatus of classification and cure. Problemization refers to the organizational context in which a view of man is being interpreted and acted upon.

Problemization is by no means unique to the service sector. Specialists commonly appear to define the needs of an individual in relation to their own technologies and bodies of learning. Jerome Frank long ago summed up the tendency by saying that, "to a dentist, a man is a body surrounding his teeth" (1949, p. 399). It is easy to dismiss his comment as caricature. It is particularly tempting for professionals who take pride in being generalists to shrug off its applicability to them. Yet none should be quick to do so, for having command of the knowledge thought useful for solving a group of problems is likely to be a potent influence on the expert's perception of the conditions or problems presented to him for help.

Problemization is a natural outgrowth of specialization, itself a product of growth in knowledge and technology. Obviously, at the pathological extreme, personal troubles fall readily into professional or specialty categories. A carcinoma is a medical problem; a homicide, grist for the legal system; a problem of child placement, appropriate for the service sector. Experts, it seems, find most interesting and challenging the most extreme sorts of cases, to the neglect of the less "pathological" which may well be far more numerous. The theories supporting intervention and the rules of doing business give disproportionate attention to the bizarre troubles that come to attention in a particular specialist area.

We can understand why problemization takes place more readily on the extremes of human need or misbehavior. The unique contribution of the specialist is readily discerned, and the severity of the trouble legitimizes the expert's intervention. This is crucial when the intervention is coercive: the state must justify the expert's contribution. It remains important when the service is voluntary since someone, often the public, pays the expert for the help he renders.

The organization of professional/specialist activities presumes that each group of experts knows what lies within its competence and has established procedures to assure an appropriate intake. It presumes, as well, that problem-identification and problem-solution will form a perfect match. The importance of this point can be seen in the fact that boundaries of specialization frame not only the diagnostic process but also the structure of service. It is this latter feature which so profoundly influences the helping services' capacity for response to juvenile nuisances. What I am suggesting is that a problem orientation has preempted the field of thinking about organized helping activities. Problemization influences officials of helping services; it has influenced the policy strategies of political leaders as well. Contemporary approaches to extending services to more people, especially the poor, are not moving toward a normalizing commitment; the more and better services are implicitly intended for "problem" people. To a striking extent, widely applauded strategies of decentralizing and "deprofessionalizing" services are essentially strategies of specialist response. Changes have not jeopardized professional or specialist hegemony over services.

Reflection on these points leads to the question of what specific significance problemization holds for social planning for the needs of juvenile nuisances. First, there is the irony that juvenile nuisances may not be a severe enough problem for the services sector. Because their participation in relatively mild, transient misconduct marks them, by current thinking, as candidates for nonjudicial handling, they are not thereby established as the business of another field of specialization. Even if the field concedes the suitability of juvenile nuisances as recipients of its services, they seem destined to be placed low on the priority list. The problems most readily identified as "belonging" to the helping services are those that are more severe. Child abuse, protracted or intense marital conflict, and dire want are high among their acknowledged priorities. The moderate cases can readily become anybody's business—which, of course, risks their being no one's.

The second significance of problemization for the helping services concerns the structure of service. The conventional programs of service agencies are ill-suited to restraining or redirecting the actions of nuisances. For the agency, it probably seems poor practice to spend much time dealing individually with problems so likely to be outgrown. Besides, agency technology employs the treatment approach. Counseling is of doubtful merit as a sole or predominant service, and many agencies lack other resources commonly offered to ebullient miscreants—space and equipment for sports, machine work and repairs, crafts and so forth; educational supplements of a creative character; staff experienced in dealing with defiant, potentially threatening clients. The juveniles need things ranging from job preparation and placement to recreational opportunities, from learning household and child care routines to getting started in rewarding hobbies. The range could be as broad as the diversity of the young. (Parenthetically, it occurs to me the problemization view may explain the relative popularity of one new form of service— runaway houses; it fits more closely into accustomed ways of doing business than do some of the other desirable responses to juvenile nuisances.)

There are such formidable problems to overcome before nuisance "control" can be shifted *en masse* to service agencies that it is suprising to find so little attention has been given them. (It is not surprising that the President's Commission recommended a new agency to do the job!) Juvenile nuisances need a whole range of responses that no single field of specialization contains and that no single group of experts comfortably dispenses. The needs of nuisances call for a service structure quite unlike those we are familiar with. At the same time, obviously or not, the difficulties being encountered in implementing the nonjudicial handling of juvenile nuisances point up broader issues. These are not yet widely recognized.

BRIDGING THE WELFARE–DUE PROCESS DICHOTOMY: THE CASE FOR THE "UNDISTRIBUTED MIDDLE"

The experience with reform directed at juvenile nuisances can usefully inform our thinking about concepts underlying the helping services in general. Juvenile nuisances merely serve to illustrate more broadly applicable propositions.

Problemization has a particular sting for the poor. All of us— young and old, rich or poor—have problems, by which I mean personal troubles. It is the experience of the middle class, who can buy time to sort out their troubles, that problems are often short-lived and minor and they go away. For the poor—always in trouble of some kind (see Sheehan 1975)—this opportunity is a luxury. To get help they must frequently participate in some kind of "problem formulation" process. And many of them need help on more than one occasion. Then they become known for having several problems. The "multiproblem family" is an artifact of these reports. The term can be misleading by implying that the multiproblem person is beset with unusual troubles usefully labeled law, medicine, vocational counseling, psychiatry, *ad infinitum*. A juvenile nuisance whose "problems" include truancy, psychological impairment, petty offending, and low school achievement is a candidate for the problem-remedies of several systems.

Why are we so insistent on pinning labels to personal difficulties? Most human troubles are just what juvenile misconduct shows itself to be—protean, endemic, and transient. Many troubles quickly yield to practical measures of "palliation" (I fear "solution" would strike the reader as claiming too much). If we thought about personal troubles this way, I suspect that the preoccupation with professional boundaries, which has so long dominated discussion and organizational plans (possibly nowhere more than in the social services), would be relegated to a minor role. We would, instead, be looking for organizational models which hold hope of uniting a humane response to personal troubles with an epidemiological perspective on incidence, growth, and severity. We would, to borrow from C. Wright Mills (1959), be looking for arrangements to join, not sever, personal troubles and political issues in long-term efforts to reduce human misconduct and misery.

The Contributions of a Normalizing Perspective

For too long we have talked about the dichotomy between the due process model and the welfare (or medical) model, between coercive intervention and voluntary helping, as if these antitheses exhaust all available choices. In truth, they do not so much represent a range of choice as extreme points on a wide spectrum. As is often the case, we see the end points much more clearly than those in between. Yet these models capture only two possible approaches to social policy toward the juvenile nuisance. The fact that intermediate models are poorly defined and bear none too meaningful labels (like "educational" or "socialization" or "recreational") is persuasive evidence of the primitive state of discourse; it is not proof of limited choice.

If we think about the situation of juvenile nuisances as essentially normal, new policies and programs are likely to augment, if not replace, the traditional models. A normalizing approach would assume that much juvenile misconduct is minor, although annoying or troubling, and rarely persistent or deeply alarming. (Remember your own youthful missteps.) It follows that the major task of public policy is not to develop diagnostic and remedial strategies for exotic cases. The "success" of policy must not be measured by such criteria. Instead, the task of public policy is to ease for all (and certainly not to augment) the pain of growing up, and to ease for some the special pain of growing up poor or disadvantaged.

Classification and Problemization

This policy posture turns its back on the conventional wisdom about juvenile courts. Classification of proscribed behavior is considered essential to due process in juvenile courts. The courts were flawed, before *Gault*, not only for their failure to observe "fundamental fairness" but for failure to specify the precise reason for state assumption of power. Francis Allen (1964) gave currency to the criticism in his remark that there is an important difference between doing something for a person and doing something to him. The courts, by and large, had glossed over which reason was the basis for their intervention. Joel Handler (1965) has also spoken of the need, in the name of substantive fairness, to break up the unity of delinquency, neglect, and dependency. Under the unity view of juvenile court jurisdiction, a child's being in trouble was no different in theory or consequence from a child's causing trouble. This view of juvenile court law is now widely rejected, and law reform in the sixties insisted on the importance of making distinctions between jurisdictional categories.

This is all to the good. Classification is of the essence of law. Surely neglect is a different ground for asserting jurisdiction than is crime-delinquency. There is no disputing the legitimacy of distinguishing mental illness from robbery for purposes of asserting state power over adults; there is little debate over the same basic proposition as applied to juveniles in court.

But what of juvenile nuisances? Is it necessary or desirable to differentiate sharply among the many possible bases of misbehavior? If the remedies for nuisance misconduct are to be neither stigmatic nor coercive, what is the justification for seeking diagnostic precision? One plausible response is that differentiation leads to the right solution; that is, without the label we cannot know what the answer is. This argument is persuasive if we are addressing severe pathology where, presumably, a great deal rides on diagnostic judgment. If, on the other hand, nuisance behavior is transient, endemic, protean—what then? Symptomatic response, palliation, and crisis support would provide more flexible help than the limited purpose formula of diagnosis-prescription-and-(we hope)-cure.

Thus, in my opinion, the preferred position is this: on a continuum between the extremes of court or clinic, the farther the nuisance behavior falls from either end, the less important it is to distinguish the class of problems being handled. The unity of nuisance behavior is a tolerable fact of life outside the courtroom (or the hospital). In fact, it may do youthful nuisances a favor not to classify their misbehavior too explicitly, because diagnosing them may produce labels that prematurely confer problem status on an occasional or short-tenured "problem" child.

A more important reason to avoid classification is to counteract the tendency of officials and professionals to problemize. If we see juvenile nuisances as going through something which is reasonably normal, presumably we who have gone through the phase have the wisdom to respond. This opens up a potential reservoir of helpers, with experts no longer dominating the service response. The problems of juvenile nuisances are redefined as falling initially within almost anyone's competence—that is, within the competence of many persons with many different kinds of skill or experience. Experts occupy a second line, rather than the front line, of response.

Resisting classification and its attendant problemization at an early stage also affects the relationship of helper and helped. It tends to free the help-seeker to define the problem for which help is sought. Typically, problem definition has been the prerogative of the helper. In his area of competence he knows what is best. The helper's influence is further enhanced when juveniles are involved by the general assumption that what is best for them is something only adults know. This combination of expertise and age-specific authority is imposing.

From the juvenile's vantage point, a normalizing perspective on the control of nuisance behavior entails a relationship that is less one of expert-dependent than of authority-subservient. The distinction may seem trivial but is not. In the latter instance the spotlight is on misconduct. That is something juveniles can control. Treated as nuisances rather than as problems, they retain control over other dimensions of their lives. The helper seeking to eradicate nuisance behavior is not licensed to alter other "properties" of the child. It appears to me that adults choose helping agents with a keen appreciation of how their choice will affect the definition of their problems. It seems no less something that concerns children.

The Principles of Helping

Up to this point my discussion has centered on the shortcomings of present policy and particular weaknesses of the problemization perspective. I have recommended a policy of normalizing personal troubles. Yet a pledge of allegiance to normalization merely conveys philosophical preferences. It does not provide a plan of action. It will be asked, What structural models are consistent with a normalization approach? I submit the question is premature. Structure should flow from agreement on content and technology; here, as elsewhere, form should follow function.

Moreover, the very nature of the normalizing perspective and all it implies would make it unproductive, it seems to me, to stress structure. Various models, I am confident, would evolve out of the experience of communities (small neighborhoods). I suspect they would display a variety that mirrors the diversity of interests, ways of life, and priorities of groups that are geographically, ethnically, and otherwise distinctive. It is foolhardy to expect that one or two models, released full-panoplied from a reformer's brain, will accommodate the wide existing variations in social needs and preferences. If government is incapable of creating society (Hazard, this volume), and has so far even failed to strengthen society (Glazer 1971), perhaps it is partly because of its premature insistence on structural formats for governmentally supported or operated services.

Nevertheless, I must consider what the normalization view of juvenile nuisances might mean in practice. As I have earlier suggested, a statement of principles could offer a useful start in thinking about practical applications. Let me begin by noting the result I am striving for. It is one of "service"—broadly conceived, close at hand geographically, responsive and flexible and speedy in addressing individual needs, and equipped to deal with common, repetitive episodes of local concern or with personal distress. I see these services occupying the front line of response, having appropriate links to better equipped specialized facilities. For juvenile nuisances such an aim could be translated into provision of a place to hang around, young adults (role models) to associate and talk with, a place of information (on jobs, on transportation, on negotiating bureaucratic organizations, and the like), a place of counsel and concrete aid in crisis. The range of functions is limited only by resources and imagination.

In my mind's eye I see a place that is modest in appearance and modest in ambition. It should not try to serve large areas or large populations. It should try to be a place of help, often inventing its responses ad hoc; a place where information and advice are available, where intelligent, dispassionate analysis of human troubles is possible, and where the concrete supports of life can be obtained by those who need them. Above all, the attitude of the enterprise should be humane, taking each day's events seriously as personal troubles, but not as "problems."

Normality

Several principles may provide useful guides to action. The superordinate principle is that of normality. It should dominate the approach to helping services. It is to be expected—it is normal—that people will have trouble finding their way about the labyrinthine corridors of organizations and coping with the inevitable crises of life. It is to be expected that juveniles will sometimes break the bonds of social decorum, that they will experiment with forbidden fruits, that they will test the values of the adult world surrounding them. Some misconduct and some crises are, to be sure, more "normal" than others, and some are more normal in certain neighborhoods (Sheehan 1975). But the view that dominates helping services at the moment is that most such events (if not all) portend future pathology, whereas a normalization approach assumes that personal troubles and low-level misconduct are common and transient, if lamentable.

Presumed normal, the individual's difficulties would be approached in the context of a group sharing similar weaknesses or deviance. The normality principle rejects the problem focus on the individual; it runs contrary to the problemization perspective of professionals. The starting point for the helping agency is: what do persons experiencing normal troubles expect and require? At least five considerations come to mind.

1. Immediate response. If we consult our own experience, we know that members of the middle class who define themselves or their families as being in trouble expect action. Being in pain, or threatened, or ignorant of the answer to pressing questions leads them to seek someone to do something for them. Those who are fortunate enough to command professional services at the end of a telephone are in a position to secure immediate palliation of their painful circumstance. Even if they have only been assured that a cure is possible after a long intermediate process, they still have been responded to; someone has listened and suggested something.

Those who are not so fortunately situated require no less, even if they dare not expect as much. Crisis intervention theory supports the commonsense importance of rapid action. The chances of a healthy resolution to a crisis are enhanced by quick help. The prescription of choice calls typically for simple remedies. The action desired may be as straightforward as information, room and board for the night, or solace. If thought of as first aid for personal troubles, it will not demand time-consuming expensive professional diagnoses. Speedy and simple response will be feasible. Of course, the first aid given by the helping services in certain cases will be the first step to sources of highly expert assistance. The point is that helping procedures should assign priority to first-aid response rather than to careful, formal diagnosis. In short, we should be able to expect speedy action from helping services as we do from our major social agency, the police.

2. Authentic response. A speedy response, however, must be authentic. This means more than a perfunctory report, recorded or otherwise; it means, at least, a substantively helpful referral. This need not protract the contact unduly, as police experience proves. In many communities the police have become a near-universal information service, to their distress (Gupte 1975). Even if an incoming request seems to staff grossly inappropriate under their services' charter, they should not be absolved of the duty to identify an appropriate course of action. It is encouraging, in this connection, to note that a number of state departments administering social services are, under Title XX of the Social Security Act, assigning to their information units the task of answering all questions that come their way.

3. Respect for the help-seeker's "problem formulation." Allied

to the legitimacy of speedy response is the point that the help-seekers' definition of their troubles should dominate the agency's. I am not suggesting it should invariably prevail, but without derogating the importance of professional knowledge and competence, I am eager to lessen the tendency on the front line of services to problemize. This is consistent with a preference for the normality view of human troubles. Acknowledging that the help-seekers know what they are talking about is recognition that, while the trouble may be a first in their experience, it is sufficiently typical (normal) for them to recognize it for what it is.

4. Proximity. If we want to promote helping services in disorganized, anomic neighborhoods populated by residents of low income and often of low skills as well, then we should take the principle of proximity far more seriously than we have so far. There is nothing either "grassroots" or comfortingly familiar about a service center that covers an area many blocks square and is intended to serve a "neighborhood" of 100,000. By contrast, the local dry cleaner or tavern or grocery has greater potential for responding to difficulties with flexibility and knowledge of both the troubled person and the area; these virtues may well outweigh their limitations as sources of help. Models of service structure should take realistic account of how distance affects productive use of available counsel and resources. This is a sound criterion for planning in general. It acquires added significance when we are considering low-income people forced to walk or rely on public transportation as their means of access to services.

Given the modest, first-aid character of the helping services recommended here, the entire approach to planning deserves revision. If our intent is to respond quickly and humanely to diffuse common personal troubles, leaving to more remote centers of specialization the solution of severe pathology, then the whole strategy of catchment areas should be revised. To date, the usual approach to planning presumes specialist—that is to say, inevitably expensive—resources at the hub of the wheel. Planning strategies move outward from this specialist focus. But to recognize that efficiency and economy dictate, say, a catchment area of 500,000 for highly specialized types of medical facilities does not inevitably lead to the conclusion that thinking about how to distribute the centers of first aid and palliation should start at the same point. First-aid centers need not necessarily conform to the catchment criteria that frame the planning of more specialized service. 5. The use of technology. To reach and serve people calls for creative use of human technology. Specifically, I am thinking of three basic, everyday types of technological support for effective social first aid: training, telephone, and transportation. To operate a social first-aid outpost, the staff members must receive some initial orientation and have access to consultation. This is often summed up as training, but the word unhappily connotes an activity that occurs before taking up the duties of the job, never to happen again. Obviously, the principle of immediate response to anything dictates a staff eager for continuous learning. This desirable orientation is best nurtured through imaginative consultative patterns.

Which leads to the telephone. Why not exploit the consultation possible through the telephone by organizing panels of experts (volunteeers, perhaps?) to be on call to the service outlet at regular intervals in the month for 24 hours a day? A rota of lawyers, housing experts, psychiatrists, and so forth could provide concrete advice to staff as well as bolster their self-confidence. They would supplement, not replace, more conventional patterns of regular staff meetings and consultations.

Finally, there is transportation. Implementing the proximity principle is likely to result in numerous local outposts modestly endowed with equipment and staff. Certainly some of the personal troubles that walk through their doors will call for immediate specialist help. This help is generally found at a considerable distance. As helping services are now arranged, people who need help also need large amounts of persistence and endurance to get it. Not only must they "broker" and translate specialist responses to achieve their ends, they must often do so on foot or by irregular public transportation at their own expense. Circulating mini-buses would provide a useful link to specialist centers.

What might application of these principles mean to juvenile nuisances? One example comes to mind: a multipurpose center I have visited in Denmark. There a new four-story building was designed to serve a host of functions: all-day child care as well as care of school children before and after school; a meeting place for the aged; crafts for all interested parties; study facilities for students with skillful advisors sometimes on hand; provision of game room, snack bar, dance floor and soundproof rock-and-roll practice rooms for youths' recreation; and hostel accommodation (on request, not on court commitment) for a handful of adolescent girls. There were also staff assigned to handle general inquiry, give advice and counsel, and make referrals. (Lest you think this center sounds too good to be true, let me ruefully admit that during one of my visits it was closed for lack of funds—and this during the summer holiday from school.)

Each reader will have his own examples, drawn from past or present, on which to test the principles. How would Jane Addams' Hull House measure up? Or Mobilization for Youth? Could the most successful antinuisance programs we know of be accommodated within a service enterprise comforting to these principles? Obviously I think so or I would not be proposing principles for helping services. But my vision is cloudy. Who would sponsor such centers? The principles are silent, though I visualize private sponsorship as well as public. They are silent on methods of funding and accountability, yet both are essential. There is much thinking and work to be done.

CONCLUSION

Future discussion of the helping services and of services to juvenile nuisances in particular would profit, I have said, from a shift in emphasis. Problemization should give way to the normalization perspective. But perhaps I should add that the normalization perspective, above all, requires heavy emphasis on giving. This means that the helper is more appropriately seen as taking part in a "gift relationship" (Titmuss 1971) than in a professional one (though, of course, the two may coincide). This concern for giving, in our day, provides a way to value and freely serve what Titmuss terms the "universal stranger." In this world of strangers (Lofland 1973), helping efforts are misplaced if they do not center on the universal stranger.

Juvenile nuisances appear to be examples of the strange and the alienated. Their transient nonconformity sets them apart today from their more conforming peers. Tomorrow the groups may be reversed, and for several years generational distance will separate them from the adult majority. Yet neither cause of separation is constant or enduring; neither will yield to approaches that are purely clinical, still less purely punitive. New principles for helping services should proceed from premises other than those of either due process or welfare, for juvenile nuisances hold the promise of becoming energetic and productive adults. Social policy should, above all else, respect and encourage that promise.

BIBLIOGRAPHY

Allen, Francis A. 1964. *The Borderland of Criminal Justice*. Chicago: University of Chicago Press.
Baron, Roger; Feeney, Floyd; and Thornton, Warren. 1973. "Preventing Delinquency through Diversion: The Sacramento County 601 Division Project." *Federal Probation* 37:13-19.
Caplan, Gerald. 1964. *Principles of Preventive Psychiatry*. New York: Basic Books.
Frank, Jerome. 1949. *Courts on Trial: Myth and Reality in American Justice*. Princeton, N.J.: Princeton University Press.
Glazer, Nathan. 1971. "The Limits of Social Policy." *Commentary* 52:51-58.
Gupte, Pranay. 5 September 1975. "Non-urgent 911 Calls Rising Despite Urgent Police Plea." *New York Times*. P. 27.
Handler, Joel F. 1965. "The Juvenile Court and the Adversary System: Problems of Function and Form." *Wisconsin Law Review* 1965:8-51.
———. 1973. *The Coercive Social Worker: British Lessons for American Social Services*. Institute for Research on Poverty Monograph Series. Chicago: Rand McNally.
Lemert, Edwin M. 1971. *Instead of Court: Diversion in Juvenile Justice*. Chevy Chase, Md.: National Institute of Mental Health, Center for Studies of Crime and Delinquency.
Lofland, Lyn H. 1973. *A World of Strangers: Order and Action in Urban Public Space*. New York: Basic Books.
Mahoney, Anne Rankin. 1974. "The Effect of Labeling upon Youths in the Juvenile Justice System: A Review of the Evidence." *Law and Society Review* 8:583-614.
Mills, C. Wright. 1959. *The Sociological Imagination*. New York: Oxford University Press.
President's Commission on Law Enforcement and Administration of Justice. 1967a. *The Challenge of Crime in a Free Society*. Washington, D.C.: U.S. Government Printing Office.
———. 1967b. *Task Force Report: Juvenile Delinquency and*

Youth Crime. Washington, D.C.: U.S. Government Printing Office.

Rapoport, Lydia. 1962. "The State of Crisis: Some Theoretical Considerations." *Social Service Review* 36:211–17.

Rosenheim, Margaret K. 1969. "Youth Service Bureaus: A Concept in Search of a Definition." *Juvenile Court Judges Journal* 20:69–74.

Schur, Edwin M. 1973. *Radical Nonintervention: Rethinking the Delinquency Problem.* Englewood Cliffs, N.J.: Prentice-Hall.

Seymour, John A. 1972. "Youth Service Bureaus." *Law and Society Review* 7:247–72.

Sheehan, Susan. 29 September 1975. "A Welfare Mother." *New Yorker.* Pp. 42 ff.

Tappan, Paul W. 1949. *Juvenile Delinquency.* New York: McGraw-Hill.

Titmuss, Richard M. 1971. *The Gift Relationship.* New York: Random House.

Zimring, Franklin E. 1974. "Measuring the Impact of Pretrial Diversion from the Criminal Justice System." *University of Chicago Law Review* 41:224–41.

II

JUSTICE FOR THE DELINQUENT CHILD

4   Policing Juveniles: The Social Context of Common Practice

Egon Bittner

When one asks on what terms police service is made available in society, two significantly distinct answers are possible. The police mandate may be said to derive wholly from codes, statutes, ordinances, or case law. These authorizing norms are taken as determining the scope of substantive responsibility and of proper procedure, and thus also as furnishing all relevant categories for the description, analysis, and critique of observed activities. Or the police mandate may be considered to consist of a readiness to respond to a vast array of recognized service needs. Although it is possible to anticipate the types and volume of such needs and to prepare to deal with them, categories of problems and procedures remain permanently open, and their description, analysis, and critique must emerge from observations of police work.

Neither of the two answers ought to be taken as doing full justice to the question. They are both relatively plausible starting points for further inquiry. Choosing the first option means that inquiry will focus on problems of authorization, and observed facts will be seen and assessed in relationship to it. The second option will give priority to the description and analysis of pressures that arise from exigencies and of practices oriented to them, and matters connected with authorization will be treated as part of the factual circumstances.

In the following I will deal with the policing of juveniles as a need-responsive practice, following the second of the two study options. In particular, I shall attempt to review, and to assess the consequences of, two sets of considerations that frame the ways in which policemen recognize and cope with juvenile problems. Both sets of considerations—one concerning the status of youth in modern society and the other concerning certain routines of police practice generally—tend to be subsumed under *ceteris paribus* clauses in most modern police studies. I must add that in talking about needs I shall refer solely to actually perceived needs. While questions concerning the desirability of these perceptions are obviously implicit in the discussion, I do not undertake to advance explicit answers to them. I shall weigh *what is* against *what ought to be* only by employing criteria that are internal to the problems under consideration.

THE STATUS OF YOUTH
From Middle Ages to Modern Times

The historical understanding of our times centers heavily on three trends originating in the period between the Renaissance and the Reformation, which constitutes the break between the Middle Ages and the following Modern Age. The first subsumes the complex of events connected with the formation of the nation states. The second consists of the rise of the commercial-industrial system that goes under the name of capitalism. The third encompasses the growth of secular culture with special emphasis on the development of science. There is also a fourth trend with a claim to equivalent social significance. It concerns the evolution of the concept of the family and of the idea of childhood from the seventeenth century on.

Of course, neither childhood nor family were wholly discovered in the seventeenth century. But since that time both have been undergoing profound transformations, which have culminated only in our times. Approximately four hundred years ago, "the family began to hold society at a distance, to push it back beyond a steadily extending zone of private life" (Ariès 1962, p. 398). The withdrawal of the family from the hustle and bustle of wide open sociability became possible with the development of a relatively closed urban, family household. In this newly constituted home, "the child ... had won a place beside his parents to which he could not lay claim at a time when it was customary to entrust him to strangers. This return of the children to the home was a great event: It gave the seventeenth-century family the principal characteristic, which distinguished it from the medieval family. The child became an indispensable element of everyday life, and his parents worried about his education, his career, his future" (Ariès 1962, p. 403).

It would lead too far afield to go into the details of this momentous revolution, but it seems clear that the encapsulation of child raising in isolated families would have far-reaching consequences for opportunities for interaction among various age groups, and that this would have further impact on the age-grading system and on age-related status in society.

In the European Middle Ages, the "ages of man" were still recognized, but available evidence indicates that these distinctions were maintained and the transitions between them were celebrated only with regard to certain special considerations. Life in its more mundane aspects was a matter for all the people to partake in without regard to age, virtually from the time a person had left the physical dependency associated with early childhood. Children of a rather tender age, in terms of our values, had uninhibited access to participation in adult work and fun, and their manners and morals were not subject to special adult solicitude. In contrast, among ourselves the lives of young people are structured, often well past adolescence, by the prominence given to dealings with either their parents or with close age-mates. Coupled with these prolonged childhood relationships is the strict segregation of young people from adult work and fun while interactions between young people and adults are generally regulated on both sides by a special code of decency and decorum. Where everyday life in the Middle Ages consisted of indiscriminate intermingling of persons densely distributed on an unbroken age-continuum, being a young person in the Modern Age, up to the age of eighteen or even later, appears to call for a radically separated form of human existence.

It is important to note that the segregation of family life from general sociability, and of young people from adults, is strongly class-related. At its outset the trend was reflected only in the lives of a narrow elite. During the Industrial Revolution it permeated the propertied middle classes. The people who made up the peasantry and the urban proletariat of the nineteenth century were still untouched by it and their children were drawn into the vortex of adult misery and pleasure in ways that scandalize contemporary consciousness. Moreover, the classbound culture of the urban ghettos and of certain "backward" parts of the United States does not yet reflect the degree of protectiveness toward the privacy of the family and of the sheltering of youth that has become the dominant social norm of our time. These ideals determine the orientation of the political, educational, and economic institutions toward young people. And the norm hangs over the heads of people who have not spontaneously adopted it, or who have not succeeded in accommodating to it because of the intractable realities of their existence. Compliance with the norm does depend upon the attainment of a certain level of material well-being.

This brief allusion to cultural history would not be complete without mention of circumstances peculiar to the American past. The conditions in the United States were auspicious for the ascendance of a strong and independent nuclear family unit because of the immigrant origin of its people and because the trend was not impeded by the survival of medieval institutional culture and polity. As de Toqueville said, "Whereas the European tries to escape his sorrow at home by troubling society, the American derives from his home that love of order which he carries over into affairs of state" (de Toqueville 1969, pp. 291–92). But the expectation that the family would be able to take care of its own weakened around the turn of the last century with the influx of large numbers of immigrants from non-English-speaking parts of Europe. In response, the child-saving movement came into existence to aid in the Americanization and embourgeoisiement of their offspring. Though this movement issued from philanthropic and charitable impulses, it involved the use of those coercive measures that are now associated with the administration of juvenile justice (Platt 1969).

The American picture thus consists of the interpenetration of (1) the general evolution of the ideals of the family and childhood which have come to be embodied in the standards of middle-class culture (Parsons 1942, 1943) and (2) a well-established set of

mechanisms for externally and forcefully imposing these standards on those segments of society that do not measure up to them
(cf. Rainwater and Yancy 1967). In this way American expectations have been tempered by realism. The common attitude seems
to have been that the place of children was the parental home and
the duty of parents was to turn them into useful citizens, but that
in the case of many people, especially people who spoke in foreign
tongues or were dark-skinned, something had to be done about
their children by their betters. Therefore, although the juvenile
problem today is not limited to dealings with these populations,
the methods of coping with it are tainted by this background.

The Seamless Dome of Control

There is probably nothing quite so revealing of American attitudes toward children as the nervous amusement caused by
W. C. Fields's unabashed assertion of distaste for them. Underlying the response is a deep unease about the immense responsibility each set of parents separately bears for the raising of their
offspring. Our feelings about children are confused by an
ambivalence that recognizes in them both a source of great joy
and a heavy burden, by a doubt whether children betoken a
bright future or decadence for our civilization, and by fear of
being overtaken by them and sent into premature and undeserved
retirement. Unable to face the problem of youth, Americans have
mounted an attack of mind-boggling complexity to cope with it.
Not only are more parents than ever before well-instructed and
considerate in their dealings with offspring, but their strenuous
efforts are augmented by the services of an army of professionals,
including pediatricians, teachers, child psychologists, recreation
specialists, clergymen, authors of children's books, athletic
coaches, and many others. While all this makes the burdens of
parenthood somewhat easier to bear, the common view is that it is
arranged entirely for the benefit of children, with all its costs
charged to adults. But it is not too difficult to recalculate the
credits and debits of this arrangement by taking a close look at
what is being asked of children in return for all the benefits
bestowed upon them. They are expected to be good. Let us take a
look at what this expectation means in practice. For clarity's sake,
I will overdraw certain features of the demands made of young
people. Furthermore, I must stress that I shall be talking about

the demand-in-effect without necessarily implying that adults mean it that way.

Perhaps the most important and least appreciated norm governing the lives of young people is that they are in every aspect of their presence, demeanor, and appearance *accountable*. Unlike adults, who can hold each other to account only on the basis of certain special entitlements and only to a limited extent, young people must answer fully to their parents. Adults are, mercifully, not methodical in applying the norm. They invoke it most often in the breach but regularly enough to remind young people about its availability, a fact to which young people refer to as "the hassle." Even psychologically sophisticated parents who recognize the child's need for privacy retain the right to limit its scope, determine its occasions, and revoke it peremptorily.

The condition of "watched freedom" for the child binds children and parent alike. Parents are not merely entitled to know everything, they are obliged to find out. The presumption of total parental control colors the meaning of a young person's presence everywhere in society. The question, "Do your parents know where you are?" is never wholly impertinent. Both the assumption of functioning parental control and the suspicion that it may have lasped create a peculiar asymmetry in the dealings between young people and adults. It is difficult to overestimate the advantage any adult has over a young person, an advantage that is often buttressed by the claim that the interest advanced by the adult is social, rather than merely personal. For example, people who put up with a great deal of adult outside interference in their work or any other activity are characteristically free to say, "Beat it, kid!" Because young people are socially incomplete persons, it is possible to deal with them as tractable nuisances. Policing juveniles is not a task created by or for the police; it merely devolves upon the police when juveniles are, or are thought to be, beyond the reach of primary supervisory control.

The seamless dome of control over youth is supported by the adult conceit according to which everything in the life of a young person is in some sense only propaedeutic and devoid of any inherently valuable significance. Since young people cannot be counted on to have a proper appreciation of whatever they are being prepared for, they cannot be trusted to know what to do. This is not, however, a simple matter of lack of foresight or knowledge. It must be remembered that children do not grow up amid those circumstances of human existence over which they will later be expected to exercise mastery. Rather, they are confined to a world apart, one specially constructed for them from nursery to college, whose pedagogic design they are specifically held incompetent to participate in. It is true that the design includes opportunities for choice within it, and young people have succeeded in constructing within the reservation a form of human existence all of their own. Outside observers call it youth culture.

It is generally agreed that this culture regulates certain of the activities young people engage in, certain understandings they have among themselves, and certain modes of expression that have developed spontaneously in their midst and distinguish them from the rest of society (Berger 1971). The most interesting part of the youth culture concept is that it has—compared with similar uses of the term "culture," as in "culture of poverty"—an extraordinarily narrowly defined scope of relevance. In fact, it might be considered more correctly as a distinct form of esthetic appreciation of leisure. As far as adults are concerned, in any case, it carries a charge somewhat akin to that formerly associated with the "culture of slaves"—it is capable of getting out of hand if not watched and of conflicting with the interest of the ruling class, but within its proper bounds it touches only the nonserious aspects of life.

Now, it is a serious matter that young people do what they are told, particularly that they go to school and study faithfully. Even so, it is clear that nothing young people do has the seriousness, necessity, or importance attached to practicing medicine, fighting wars, or making money. Accordingly, any adult interest enjoys a claim of precedence over any youth interest that is nontraversable. That many adults are quite generous and tolerant and that many more seek to avoid confrontations creates more uncertainty than freedom. And so young people find it expedient to resort to guile, concealment, and extortion to get their way, acting on the well-founded assumption that adults do not understand anyway. At the very least, young people face the hazard that any claim of interest they may advance will be assessed by standards extraneous to their own lives. That is, the judgments will reflect either pedagogic considerations and adult conceptions of wholesomeness or the constraints and conveniences of the adult order of society.

The seemingly nonserious nature of the concerns of young age is romantically aggrandized by attributions to youth of innocence and freedom from adult responsibility. The notion of childhood innocence has a long history, dating back to the Sermon on the Mount and continuing into modern advertising. But innocence has its correlate in irresponsibility, and there also exists a long tradition representing the dangerous and amoral character of the child, extending from the myth of Oedipus to Golding's fable, *Lord of the Flies*. Freedom from adult cares, on the other hand, is darkened by the expectation that in return children will at all times live up gratefully to an extraordinarily high standard of decorum. Thus risks are controlled and the trade-off is brought into a just balance, all at once, by requiring young people to be unconditionally nice and surrounding young people with walls of censoriousness. Of course, not only children are supposed to be well-mannered, but their manners draw a vastly greater amount of attention than the manners of adults. An adult can be considered a diamond in the rough, or a coarseness of demeanor may be mitigated by the seriousness or pressure of the business at hand. The general unavailability to young people of such dispensations is evident in the dismissal, during the so-called youth revolt of the sixties, of many of their arguments solely on grounds of the offensive manner of presentation. Without ignoring the harm caused by campus revolutionaries, commentators have noted that most of the outrage and many of the reprisals were brought forth mainly by symbolic indecencies. Hence the paradoxical situation: young people can get away with anything, but their breaches of etiquette are wholly unforgivable (Slater 1970, chap. 3).

Because their concerns are not accepted as mattering in the way such concerns matter in the adult world, young people find their transactions with adults permeated with formalism, ritual, and drama rather than with substance—all of which abets evasion, deceit, or provocation. Adult emphasis on etiquette does not stand alone. There is an academicism that pervades formal education, which accepts, say, a young person's espousal of communism as merely preparatory to becoming a good capitalist. By not taking what young people say or do as real coin, adults feel relieved of the obligation to pay attention to it and thereby push the social existence of young persons to the edge of nonexistence. How well this confinement is sealed off! We do not even become aware that young people might want to break out of it. When they do, we are stung by the insult of their intention, and even then the most enlightened adults tend to view the assault as a mere phase in their development (Feuer 1969).

The principal way of judging how well young people are growing up is how well they do in school. But even the rigors of education in our society are interlarded with substantial amounts of recreational activity. Now it may seem difficult to conceive that fun could be visited by troubles. But this is a singularly shortsighted view, however, which could gain acceptance only in a wholly secularized society in which the value of any human activity is determined by its relationship to the paramount interest in "making a living." The inadequacy of the usual negative definition of recreation—merely time away from the stresses of making a living—is easily realized by considering the threat of tragedy lurking in virtually every form of fun. To understand the structured potential for conversion of fun into trouble, to understand the nonadventitious nature of the frequent outbreaks of serious disturbance and violence in connection with dances or athletic events, we must understand play and games as independently serious activities.

In archaic, tribal, and peasant societies all occasions of recreation stood under sacred auspices. Fairs and holidays had the patronage of deities and saints, and were, like everything done in connection with the supernatural, highly structured even when they included orgiastic excesses. As long as the doings were kept within the set limits, they were seen as boding well for those who participated in them; they "recreated" the unity and harmony between man and the powers in the cosmos. Breaches of order, time, and place, on the other hand, caused forebodings of evil. In secular society, the whole penumbra of the supernatural fell away and recreation acquired the primarily psychological significance of character building and tension release (Huizinga 1950; Caillois 1961). Even in its secular form, recreation activity incorporates canons of morality, fair play, and esthetic appreciation. That is why it is considered wholesome. Yet, while proprieties of order, time, and place remain recognizably significant, the absence of ritual sanctions weakens their force. Thus, the momentum of having fun tends to overshoot the boundaries set for it, turning recreation into scandal. Since this is quite common, there are special dispensations for it, as implied in the expressions, "boys will be boys" or "feeling one's oats." There is, however, no assurance that a breach of limits will receive the benefit of dispensation, especially if it conflicts with adult convenience or is seen as having causes beyond the case at hand, such as, for example, "typical" lower-class licentiousness which portends even greater scandal. Things do not need to go that far for reaction to set in, however. Because the boundaries of recreation are ill-defined, there is a tendency to overcontrol it. The absence of patent evidence of strict control worries adults even while fun is still well within accepted limits. It is only a short step from worry to seeing any aggregation of young people having fun as betokening trouble.

Before moving on, I should like to repeat the warning I gave at the beginning of this paper. It has not been my desire to render a well-rounded picture. Instead, I attempted to present a tendentious sketch of the unintended but inevitable consequences of certain good intentions. Above all, it is important to emphasize that the status of young people is not simply a function of adult pigheadedness. The condition is part of a general social, economic, and political order that entraps the parent no less than the children. Moreover, I have discussed those aspects of the problem which are, in my view, generally neglected but crucially relevant to consideration of police-juvenile relations. These aspects constitute background conditions to which the police are responsive when they deal with young people.

POLICE WORK WITH JUVENILES

For several reasons, we must begin the discussion of policing juveniles with some observations concerning crime and crime control. In the first place, the public and the police share a common conception, that the control of crime is at the center of police work. Regardless of the substantive merit of this presumption, it colors the perceptions and procedures of police officers. Second, a large and increasing proportion of all serious crime reportedly is committed by young people. The demographic distribution of crime suggests that criminality reaches its peak early in life and declines progressively in older age (President's Commission . . . 1967). This finding can be disputed, to be sure, because it rests in the statistics of cleared crimes and may merely indicate that young people are less adept at, or less interested in, evading arrest than are their older counterparts. But discounting rates still leaves the absolute numbers intact, and there is no getting around the fact that alarmingly large numbers of young people steal and commit assaults of all degrees of seriousness.

The seriousness of the crime problem notwithstanding, and with all due regard for police concern for it, it is important to note that crime control and policing are not coextensive activities. It has been widely acknowledged that the preponderant part of police work has nothing to do with crime control (Niederhoffer 1967), and that this is especially true of police work involving juveniles (Goldman 1963; Rubinstein 1973). Accordingly, to keep things in their proper place and to assess their actual practical significance, the matter of policing juveniles must be considered in the context of routine police practice, only part of which is concerned with crime control.

One further presumption deserves to be mentioned at the outset. In keeping with the general cultural view of the young as a separate species, the police allow that working with juveniles constitutes a special police activity. Modern departments have, resources permitting, juvenile officers who are presumed to draw on special skills and resources in their work (Kenney and Pursuit 1970). While the institution of this specialty is a very important innovation in police work and has impact on the lives of some young people who run afoul of the law or otherwise come to the attention of the police, it must be remembered that virtually all contacts between young people and the police initially involve members of the uniformed patrol, and most never progress to the point of involving a juvenile officer (Reiss 1971). Aside from dealing with far more cases, patrolmen also deal with a considerably wider range of cases than do juvenile officers. Still more important, the work of the patrol is fully exposed, which makes it difficult for patrolmen not to see what they are supposed to see and not to do what they are supposed to do. In contrast, the juvenile officers' less public situation somewhat protects them from both external popular pressure and internal police constraint; they therefore have much greater control over what they elect to see and do. Hence, the following several characterizations of police work with juveniles refer principally to members of the uniformed patrol, but what will be said applies, *mutatis mutandis,* to the police as a whole.

The Low Status of Juvenile Work

However broad, varied, and ambiguous a conception of the police mandate patrolmen may have, they assign a low priority to working with troublesome juveniles. Their experience teaches them that the majority of cases in which they are called upon to act are trivial, that most of these cases allow no good solutions, and that even a successful treatment of a case is not considered an accomplishment of note in the hierarchy of police values. The risk of frustration and the absence of credit lead patrolmen to shun assignments involving young people, to get involved as little as possible when they cannot be avoided. Consequently, skill in the handling of juvenile problems is less well developed than skill in other areas of police work, such as the handling of mentally ill persons (Bittner 1967a).

In no other aspect of police work is the inherent irony so poignantly apparent as in the patrolmen's aversion to work with juveniles and its unavoidability. Always pursuing the elusive "big pinch," forever hoping to solve important crimes for which they lack both skill and means, patrolmen unhappily accept its necessity. This circumstance is fundamental for understanding the policing of juveniles.

The crucial reasons that the police are disinclined to work with juveniles are, first, the internal police organization and, second, the personal career interest of patrolmen. No points are gained by careful and considerate handling of a juvenile problem, and there is some risk that attention given to it will be judged excessive in relation to problems deemed more important. Moreover, juvenile problems are more likely than other kinds of police problems to have untoward consequences, about which grievances will be posted with patrolmen's superiors, thus spoiling their performance records. Against this background, patrolmen feel compelled to minimize their involvement and structure it to avoid troubles. And they will have to be guided by these considerations even if they must employ solutions they know to be less than commensurate with the problem at hand. Minimizing involvement includes, indeed favors, resorting to strongly coercive measures without first assaying the feasibility of alternatives, except in cases where violence or arrest might produce protests from politically powerful parents.

The Function of the Police

Three expectations define the specific function of the police in modern society more than anything else. First, it is expected that they will do something about any problem they are called upon to deal with; second, it is expected that they will attack problems wherever and whenever they occur; and, third, it is expected that they will prevail in whatever they undertake and that they will not retreat in the face of opposition. This does not mean that the police cannot occasionally refuse to deal with some matters or that they cannot advance good reasons for such refusals. Nor does it mean that policemen can never refer some problems presented to them to be dealt with by someone else at some other place and time. Nor, finally, does it mean that policemen can never be brought to desist from carrying out their decisions by pleading or suasion. It does mean that when people call the cops they do so with the above expectations, that when policemen are mobilized to act they reckon with these expectations, and that these expectations are uppermost in the minds of the persons against whom policemen proceed.

Police power to impose solutions in the natural habitats where problems emerge is restricted, of course, by the supposition that solutions are provisional and subject to review. Nevertheless, many provisional solutions have lasting consequences, and the police emphasis on prevailing often impedes other avenues of recourse. Further, to make it possible for policemen to prevail in a wide range of circumstances, they are uniquely authorized to use physical force in an amount measured not to exceed the requirement of the situation, but they are given no guidelines to what the proper measure of force might be and are largely without effective external control in this regard (Bittner 1970).

The requirement of active and immediate intervention does not appear to present any special problem in situations involving individual juveniles. Even in relatively serious cases, patrolmen tend to avail themselves of the option of returning a young person to parental control because they consider it the right solution, and because it happens to be the easiest thing to do. Where detention is required, the detained youngster is, where possible, taken to a special facility. But in the majority of juvenile cases, patrolmen do not confront individuals. In matters ranging from riotous and destructive conduct, to noisy and boisterous behavior, to groups of youngsters hanging around some street corner, patrolmen must deal with aggregations of young people in which individual culpability cannot be easily determined. Where alleged deeds cannot be associated with doers and the business at hand cannot be readily defined by what has happened, patrolmen's attention tends to focus on what is taking place during the intervention. The decision of what has to be done takes shape in relationship to how the young people act toward the intervening patrolmen. Within a considerable range, police judgment of substantive misconduct will be mitigated by expressions of diffidence on the part of young people and aggravated by their arrogance (Cicourel 1968; Piliavin and Briar 1964; Sullivan and Siegel 1972).

Three factors complicate this situation. First, though it is true that policemen tend to be sensitive concerning respect, they are not interested in the show of good manners for their own sake, but see in rudeness the portents of more serious opposition. They apparently believe that anyone who would risk being rebellious and unruly in their presence can be counted on to go even further if left alone. Second, the expectation of doing something is joined with the desire to gain tactical advantage over resistance even before it is manifest. Thus, patrolmen tend to take an approach they consider aggressive but which others may call "overreacting." Third, the signs of contrariness detected by patrolmen are often exceedingly subtle. For example, policemen are accustomed to people not returning their gaze and they sometimes take being stared at as a sign of provocation (Rubinstein 1973).

Almost all juvenile disturbances occur in public places. Thus the duty to deal with them at the time and in the place of their occurrence combines with policemen's concern for maintaining dominion over the public space (Rubinstein 1973). Since, in a manner of speaking, patrolmen host the presence of young people on the streets, in the parks, and elsewhere in the city, they not only act whenever and wherever incidents happen, they actually decide at what times and places the presence and manner of youngsters jeopardize their ability to control ongoings in public places.

I have already mentioned that the duty to prevail must be understood in connection with the expectation of doing something. It deserves mention that prevailing and overcoming the resistance of youth are subject to peculiar distortions. In many instances policemen must proceed on no more than an allegation of misconduct. Since they assume that if the allegations were true the young people would not admit it, they cannot credit denials. In accepting the allegation as their working hypothesis, they can only make errors of judgment that weigh against young people. The likelihood of such errors is enhanced by the often nondescript character of citizens' complaints and the possibility that the youngsters who become the target of police intervention are not the ones whose misconduct occasioned the complaint. Even when witnesses are present the onus of the accusation is frequently placed on "the whole bunch of them." It is not surprising, therefore, that young people feel that policemen accuse them of doing things they have not done and force them to submit to arbitrary restrictions and commands (Bouma 1969).

In the light of the foregoing it does seem somewhat off-base to complain that police dealings with youngsters do not conform to the latest insights of child care. In fact, what is commonly expected of the police leaves them with little choice but to make certain that young people cannot have their way in the city, and this is what many encounters with young people are reduced to, whatever the occasion. Moreover, in placing great emphasis on manners, in considering the use of public space to be an occasional privilege rather than a right, and in invoking ambiguous rules about proprieties of time and place to limit juvenile fun arbitrarily, the police are simply doing society's dirty work. Police activity alone clearly does not explain how it is so amazingly easy for an innocent young person to get into trouble, quite aside from (and without disregarding) the many instances in which the trouble is far from innocent. It is probably right, however, to say that standard police procedure contains no safeguards against unwise and improvident action and that the expectation of having to prevail induces the police to employ measures that might be appropriate in some circumstances to cases where they are not.

"Proactive Intervention" in the Field

Several factors shape the policing of juveniles beyond specific incidents of encounter. Because behavior in the public spaces of the city tends to be structured around exigencies of adult life, and because the police jealously guard their right to control public spaces, the mere conspicuous presence of young people can cause concern. They are, as it were, off the reservation and, lacking justification for being abroad, they are subject to preventive regulation. Moreover, juvenile trouble is patterned, partly because of large numbers of youths in certain neighborhoods and partly because school and other facilities cause regular aggregations. Hence, incidents can be anticipated and are watched for with a wary eye. Finally, because young people are unable or unwilling to respond to contradictory expectations—for example, that they accept as normal the filth in the neighborhoods in which they live but refrain from littering in certain other places—the police face the perennial disciplinary task of holding young people to arbitrarily high standards of conduct. Much more could be said to show that for the police the juvenile problem exists long before it takes the shape of an incident. Indeed, it is not too much to say that as far as a working patrolman is concerned kids do not so much make trouble, they are trouble.

The strength of this assumption varies, but it applies in full force to young people from race- or class-disadvantaged segments of the society. These youngsters are made to feel the whole burden of race and class inequality, and in turn they express the pain of this burden in ways that violate the usual boundaries imposed on such expressions. It is superficial to say that policing imposes unwanted and unwonted middle-class standards upon them. It would be more to the point to argue that the struggle between the police and race- and class-disadvantaged youngsters, into whose family life the "new" ideals of family and childhood have not descended, is one of the few overt manifestations of class struggle in our society. Their elders may have settled for what society has in store for them and the "lower-class ways" are part of this lot. But the life of young people is not supposed to reflect the divisions of society because young age is lived in a domain in which the relevance of the factors determining these divisions is suspended. However laudable and absorbing the aspiration might seem to others, the police are attuned to the dark threats emanating from the "dangerous classes" (Silver 1967), which they find contained in the nuisances and harm created by the offspring of people from the lower depths of society.

To forestall lurking danger, to gain advantage over what might happen, patrolmen engage in what is euphemistically called proactive intervention. They consider it especially necessary to engage in this practice in blighted areas of the city simply because the young people there are very often found in places where they are not supposed to be—other places being in short supply. Moreover, they act in this way because there has grown up a stabilized relationship of conflict, or at least contest, between the police and kids who feel that they have nothing to lose in giving the police a hard time because they would not be left alone under any circumstances (Werthman 1967). Some of the efforts of young people to bedevil police attempts at preventive surveillance are undertaken in the spirit of fun and adventure. But often the resentment at being hassled is bitter enough to produce the more serious reactions associated with overly strict controls of all kinds (Taylor and Walton 1971). Thus the proactive approach, far from preventing troubles, is a source of them. Aside from occasionally leading to ugly flareups, the patrolmen's gratuitous poking around in their affairs causes many young people to grow up accepting hostility between cops and kids as a natural fact of life (see Brown 1965). Believing that cops always accuse and insult people for no good reason, they search anything a policeman says for the accusation or insult supposedly contained in it. The result comes to be a pervasive atmosphere of distrust on both sides, and a free-wheeling search for opportunities to get at each other.

Transfer of Cases to Juvenile Authorities

Though the bulk of police work ends where it begins, in the field with only the patrolmen involved, certain cases do move on to the care of juvenile police officers, juvenile probation officers, and the juvenile court. Many of these cases involve child neglect rather than misconduct. Though such activities are not celebrated as achievements, in these cases, as in most instances where policemen deal with people plainly in need of help, they take care of neglected children with conspicuous consideration and often do much more than is generally expected of public officials. Though such consideration certainly does not characterize every patrolman, the humane and resolute attitude toward the helpless is, broadly speaking, more often found among the police than in any other official agency of society, including the schools, public health, and probably also the religious institutions (Bittner 1967b; Cumming, Cumming, and Edell 1965).

The rest of the cases involve formally labeled delinquency. The concept of juvenile delinquency refers to the fact that the state is empowered to proceed coercively against young people (in some states on grounds that would not be sufficient to justify such process vis-à-vis adults) and to remove from the criminal process young people who are alleged to have violated provisions of the penal code. Juvenile delinquency shares one formal feature with adult criminality, namely, that persons to whom the designations are applied are removed from the context in which they have done what they are said to have done into a separate institutional context where the facts are reviewed and judged (Bohannan 1965). Though this process differs in the two instances, in both it is based on specially formulated accounts of facts. This would be too obvious to mention were it not for the circumstance that police decisions concerning both crime and delinquency are based partly on considerations that do not enter into the subsequently reviewed and judged accounts. What these police-specific considerations are is a huge and poorly investigated topic which I must treat here in the briefest possible manner (LaFave 1965).

Though it is of course true that policemen receive accounts of events and treat them with due regard for their schematized significance (that is, knowing that they are never told the whole story), the determination they make about a case also always draws on aspects of context that elude formulation. It is possible to argue proof of the connection between the presence of a young person and of a broken window, but the full force of the directly intuited conclusion cannot be revived in the way it presented itself and appeared to matter in the realities of the occasion. In other words, what informed persons can plainly see they cannot always tell in ways that will make the matter "visible" to others. It is a peculiarity of police work that policemen are not supposed to act on considerations they cannot place into evidence but they are not supposed to disregard them, either.

Whatever formal significance may be attributed to the concepts of crime and delinquency, their actionable sense is always colored by the work situation of those who invoke them. The work situation of the judges and law professors who define the meaning of these concepts is not the work situation of policemen. While it is easy to overstress this point, it is important to remember that to understand how and why policemen charge people with delinquency, one must see the decision to charge in the context of police work rather than court work. While policemen are informed about the subsequent fate of the charges they file and take this information into account, they may treat it as merely one fact in a matrix of facts on which their decisions are predicated. One way of explaining this is to say that the matter mentioned in the charge might have been no more than the proverbial last straw. The decision to arrest someone may have had more to do with routines of police work rather than with accountable merits of the case. Now, I do not mean to argue that the substantive reasons advanced in the charge always lack merit in such cases (although this is often enough true in fact), only that the decision was not actually based on these merits. For example, a fellow may have broken the window and his past may have been suffused with all sorts of trouble making, but the decision to refer him to the juvenile court on that particular occasion may have been wholly dependent on a combination of factors located in *that* particular situation and on the constraints of expectations to which the policeman was responsive, namely the expectations to do something and to prevail in doing it.

Because the policeman deals with matters in vivo while those to whom he refers them deal with them in vitro, and because the practicalities of his work situation influence what he does, there is a communication gap between him and officials of the administration of justice that is possibly unbridgeable. The police are distressed by what they consider excessive permissiveness on the part of juvenile court judges and believe that the judges do not sufficiently appreciate the seriousness of juvenile delinquency. Convinced that they arrest young people only when it is utterly unavoidable, policemen feel betrayed when sanctions are not applied and the arrested youngster is set free even before they return to their beats. They conclude that the courts, more than anything else, must be blamed for the proliferation of lawlessness and for the scorn heaped upon the police for attempting to control it. Whether these views are justified matters little; the bitterness they reflect interferes with the development of a fully reasoned approach to the policing of juveniles in concert with other public agencies (Ferster and Courtless 1969).

CONCLUSION

This paper was written to draw attention to some facts not generally known or sufficiently appreciated. In a way, its task is accomplished by furnishing grist for the mill. Still, some concluding remarks are in order.

Over a quarter of a century ago there appeared a book on the changing American character that enjoyed some popularity before it became a classic (Riesman, Glazer, and Denney 1950). Its principal thesis was that in our society the ideals and aspirations connected with work, industry, and production have begun to yield precedence to ideals and aspirations connected with leisure, life style, and consumption. Official homiletics still place work before pleasure, but the work of large and increasing numbers of people no longer possesses compelling necessity, seriousness, and importance (Mills 1953; Goodman 1962), while others, especially persons in executive and professional occupations, import added interest into their work through the search for psycho-social adjustment and personal gratification. Coincident with this change, people have ceased to rely on the resources of inner strength of character and the material evidence of achievement to feel justified, and have begun to search instead for approbation and validation from others.

This early pall of doubt about the value of work acquired new life in recent debates on the future of work (Bureau of Labor Statistics 1966). The question now is whether there will be enough work in the future to justify the common assumption that gainful employment of some sort is indispensable to normal human life, and whether, accordingly, work can remain the paramount calling of man. While the debates concerning work are exciting and fruitful, they give short shrift to one question, perhaps because raising it is considered premature. The question is, How is society without work possible? I do not mean, of course, work as a source of wherewithals, but work as a foundation of order. There have been societies founded on other principles—indeed, it seems that virtually all other societies were founded on other principles—but with us what a person does for a living determines who he is, what he can do, what he is entitled to, with whom he lives and interacts, where he lives, and how he dies. By extension, the occupational system and the social organization of work determine the proper place and weight of all things—such as, whether we wage war, how we distribute wealth, and how we locate our holidays—more than any other factors. With us the division of labor in society is the most general framework for the distribution and maintenance of trust among ourselves (Durkheim 1933). Moreover, it is integral to this order that it contain allocative mechanisms by which those "minorities" of persons who do not work are somehow incorporated into society.

The purpose of this digression is to lay the foundation for a brief animadversion concerning these mechanisms. Our economic system is based on formally free labor, as opposed to systems where the duty to work is politically enforced, as in slavery, villeinage, or serfdom (Polanyi 1957). In return for working, people earn wages and leisure, which they are free to spend as they choose. If for the moment we ignore people of independent means, this means that only people who work earn their freedom to do as they please and be left alone, while people who do not earn income and leisure cannot do as they please and should not be left alone. Their lives are subject to being policed in ways the lives of working people are not. When work is the basis of order and freedom, people who do not work cannot be expected to lead orderly lives and be trusted with freedom.

But young people do not have that option. I suggested earlier that being young means living under continuous supervisory control and having to live up to higher standards of decency and decorum than are required of one's supervisors. Normally, parents and teachers are in charge of young people, but those youths who elude their erratic mastery fall into the laps of the police. And thus the police become the final cutting edge of the society that has liberated young people from the necessity to work gainfully without giving them freedom, and without even considering that it is one thing to say that one must earn what one gets but quite another that what one cannot earn one must do without. Even though the policing of juveniles is rooted in the condition of young age as an unfree status in our society, and not in the existence of policemen, the police do play an important part in the lives of the young.

During the past decade the modern police have received a far

greater amount of attention than during the entire century and a
half of their previous existence, dating from the institution of the
Metropolitan Police for the City of London. As a result of this
recent study, it has become clear that police work is not a
low-grade occupation in which men do what they are told and
may be said to attend to their task well enough as long as they stay
honest. Many people now say that police work is a complex,
serious, and important public service, perhaps even deserving the
dignity of being called a profession. But I believe that such
sentiments do not begin to do the case justice. The matter is quite
simple: policemen have truly awesome powers and what they do
can have irreversible effects on the most vital interests of the
people with whom they deal. I would even say that anyone who
feels fully adequate for the job is thereby disqualified from it.
There exist, after all, virtually no norms of judgment and
procedure, no body of technical knowledge, and no standards by
which to judge performance, that policemen can refer to in their
work. Judges hear motions and pleadings before deciding what to
do, physicians discuss their recommendations with their patients,
and both may postpone resolution of the problem they confront
until they are ready to take steps. But policemen must do what
needs to be done alone and may not desist in the face of either
argument or opposing force, regardless how critical a problem
they face. It seems paradoxical, to say the least, that we do not
insist on recruiting policemen from the most gifted, the most
aspiring, and the most equipoised among us.

All this may seem to be an outrageous exaggeration to those
who know the police as they are. It is one thing to say that
policemen ought to be better educated, but it is quite unrealistic
to suggest that we recruit from among the cream of youth. Surely
those who could be physicians would not want to go into an
occupation in which they may have to direct traffic, transport
prisoners, type their own reports, work under the control of a
sergeant, and so on. But suppose being a physician required
doing the work that nurses, secretaries, and orderlies do, and
following the orders of hospital administrators, in addition to
saving lives? Would the choice be still clear-cut? Somehow, in
appraising police work, "realism" drives us to judge policing at
the level of its most menial aspects and, in consequence, to
entrust it to people who are deemed competent to operate at that

level. We then hope that the more serious and important tasks will somehow get done with the least possible amount of trouble.

BIBLIOGRAPHY

Ariès, Philippe. 1962. *Centuries of Childhood: A Social History of Family Life.* New York: Knopf.
Bell, Daniel. 26 August 1965. "The Bogey of Automation." *New York Review of Books.* Pp. 23–25.
Berger, Bennett M. 1971. *Looking for America: Esays on Youth, Suburbia and Other American Obsessions.* Englewood Cliffs, N.J.: Prentice-Hall.
Bittner, Egon. 1967*a.* "Police Discretion in Emergency Apprehensions of Mentally Ill Persons." *Social Problems* 14:278–92.
———. 1967*b.* "The Police on Skid-Row: A Study of Peace Keeping." *American Sociological Review* 32:699–715.
———. 1970. *The Function of the Police in Modern Society.* Washington, D.C.: U.S. Government Printing Office.
Bohannan, Paul. 1965. "The Differing Realms of the Law." In *The Ethnography of Law,* ed. Laura Nader. Special Publication of *American Anthropologist.* 67, no. 6, pt. 2: 33–42.
Bouma, Donald H. 1969. *Kids and Cops: A Study in Mutual Hostility.* Grand Rapids, Mich.: Eerdmans.
Brown, Claude. 1965. *Manchild in the Promised Land.* New York: Macmillan.
Bureau of Labor Statistics, U.S. Department of Labor. 1966. *America's Industrial and Occupational Manpower Requirements, 1964–1975.* 6 vols. Prepared for the National Commission on Technology, Automation, and Economic Progress. Washington, D.C.: U.S. Government Printing Office.
Caillois, Roger. 1961. *Man, Play, and Games.* Glencoe, Ill.: Free Press.
Cicourel, Aaron V. 1968. *The Social Organization of Juvenile Justice.* New York: Wiley.
Cumming, Elaine; Cumming, Ian; and Edell, Laura. 1965. "Policeman as Philosopher, Guide and Friend." *Social Problems* 12:276–86.
de Toqueville, Alexis. 1969. *Democracy in America.* Garden City, N.Y.: Anchor Books.
Durkheim, Emile. 1933. *The Division of Labor in Society.* New York: Macmillan.
Ferster, Elyce Z., and Courtless, Thomas F. 1969. "The Beginning

of Juvenile Justice, Police Practices, and the Juvenile Offender." *Vanderbilt Law Review* 22:567-608.

Feuer, Lewis A. 1969. *The Conflict of Generations.* New York: Basic Books.

Goldman, Nathan. 1963. *The Differential Selection of Juvenile Offenders for Court Appearance.* New York: National Council on Crime and Delinquency.

Goodman, Paul. 1962. *Growing up Absurd.* New York: Vintage.

Huizinga, Johan. 1950. *Homo Ludens: A Study of the Play Element in Culture.* New York: Roy.

Kenney, John P., and Pursuit, Dan G. 1970. *Police Work with Juveniles and the Administration of Juvenile Justice.* Springfield, Ill.: Charles C Thomas Publisher.

LaFave, Wayne. 1965. *Arrest: The Decision to Take a Suspect into Custody.* Boston: Little, Brown.

Mills, C. Wright. 1953. *White Collar Worker: The American Middle Classes.* New York: Oxford University Press.

Niederhoffer, Arthur. 1967. *Behind the Shield: The Police in Urban Society.* Garden City, N.Y.: Anchor Books.

Parsons, Talcott. 1942. "Age and Sex in the Social Structure of the United States." *American Sociological Review* 7:606-16.

―――. 1943. "The Kinship System of the Contemporary United States." *American Anthropologist* 45:22-38.

Piliavin, Irving, and Briar, Scott. 1964. "Police Encounters with Juveniles." *American Journal of Sociology* 70:206-14.

Platt, Anthony M. 1969. *The Child Savers: The Invention of Delinquency.* Chicago: University of Chicago Press.

Polanyi, Karl. 1957. *The Great Transformation.* Boston: Beacon Press.

President's Commission on Law Enforcement and Administration of Justice. 1967. *Task Force Report: Crime and its Impact: An Assessment.* Washington, D.C.: U.S. Government Printing Office.

Rainwater, Lee, and Yancy, William L. 1967. *The Moynihan Report and the Politics of Controversy.* Cambridge, Mass.: Massachusetts Institute of Technology Press.

Reiss, Albert J. 1971. *The Police and the Public.* New Haven: Yale University Press.

Riesman, David; Glazer, Nathan; and Denney, Reuel. 1950. *The Lonely Crowd: A Study of the Changing American Character.* New Haven: Yale University Press.

Rubinstein, Jonathan. 1973. *City Police.* New York: Farrar, Strauss and Giroux.

Silver, Allan. 1967. "Demand for Order in Civil Society: A

Review of Some Themes in the History of Urban Crime, Police, and Riot." In *The Police: Six Sociological Essays,* ed. David J. Bourdua. New York: Wiley. Pp. 1–24.

Slater, Phillip. 1970. *The Pursuit of Loneliness: American Culture at the Breaking Point.* Boston: Beacon Press.

Sullivan, Dennis, and Siegel, Larry J. 1972. "How Police Use Information to Make Decisions: An Application of Decision Games." *Crime and Delinquency* 18:253–63.

Taylor, Laurie, and Walton, Paul. 1971. "Industrial Sabotage: Motives and Meaning." In *Images of Deviance,* ed. Stanley Cohen. Hammondworth, England: Penguin. Pp. 219–45.

Werthman, Carl B. 1967. "The Function of Social Definitions in the Development of Delinquent Careers." In *Task Force Report: Juvenile Delinquency and Youth Crime.* President's Commission on Law Enforcement and Administration of Justice. Washington, D.C.: U.S. Government Printing Office. Pp. 155–70.

5   Diversion: Unleashing the Hound of Heaven?*

Paul Nejelski

> I fled Him, down the nights and down the days;
> I fled Him, down the arches of the years.
>
> Francis Thompson
> *The Hound of Heaven*

The term "diversion," made popular by the 1967 recommendations of the President's Commission on Law Enforcement and Administration of Justice, has been used so often to justify such a wide response to children in trouble that its value has become seriously debased. A recent study noted that diversion has been used to describe "almost any discretionary action available to a public or private agency dealing with children and youth" (Department of Health, Education, and Welfare 1973*b*, p. 15).

Part of the problem lies in the term itself, for a diversion is merely the turning or redirection of something from its normal path. In the juvenile justice system, diversion takes place at each stage. The archetypal form is the diversion performed by probation intake, but diversion is practiced by virtually every official in the system. In this chapter I will focus on children charged with delinquency and status offenses, although diversion is also an issue in dealing with problems such as mental retardation or illness, child neglect or abuse.

*A previous version of this chapter appeared in *Crime and Delinquency*, October 1976. © 1976 by The University of Chicago.

There is much that is new about juvenile diversion—new screening procedures, new programs, and new incentives from federal funding. Diversion is the overture to the "new corrections," with its emphasis on deinstitutionalization and purchase of services (Miller and Ohlin, this volume). On balance, however, diversion is striking not for its novelty but for its substantial historical roots and some very traditional shortcomings. Most children in trouble never have a judicial hearing of the facts surrounding their plight. Sheer volume guarantees that in delinquency cases, the system is a filter where, of every 500 possible juvenile arrests, it is estimated that there are 200 police contacts, resulting in 100 arrests. Of these, only 40 youths are taken in, only 20 appear before a judge, and only 2 or 3 are sent to a correctional institution (Nejelski and LaPook 1974, p. 14). The juvenile justice system is a continuous disposition process, starting with police, schools, and welfare, continuing through probation and social services, ending in treatment and correctional institutions. The designation of only one stage of the process as "adjudicatory" or another as "dispositional" is misleading if it suggests there is only one proceeding which determines guilt and another which diagnoses and prescribes the treatment. The whole system embodies a continuous use of the state's coercive power—with the juvenile court as a final resort—to force a disposition on a child and his parents.

The fluid procedures of the system—before, during and after adjudication—are tolerated because every child who enters it is presumed to need some service or to be guilty of some evil. To many people in the juvenile justice system, it is inconceivable that a "client" could be innocent or not need their help.

One reason for the omnipresence of the presumption of guilt is the knowledge that, if a delinquency case cannot be proven, a petition alleging that the minor is a "person in need of supervision" (PINS) can usually be sustained. PINS jurisdiction may be divided into four parts: (1) school matters—truancy or disruptive behavior; (2) parental discipline—running away and disobedience; (3) violation of general laws which may have special provisions or harsh consequences for children—curfews and morality; and (4) a catch-all category that the child is in danger of becoming a delinquent or is incorrigible (for example, N.Y. Family Court Act §712(b), [McKinney Supp. 1971]). Champions of the juvenile court rightly see this last amorphous category as a key to the power of the juvenile court, for any child may be a "predelinquent." At their 1967 annual meeting, the National Council of Juvenile Court Judges resolved, "The fundamental right of a child is not to unrestrained liberty, but to custody.... [The Council] is opposed to any narrowing of the jurisdiction of the juvenile court which would eliminate any traditional jurisdictional grounds which generally are and have been found in the juvenile court statutes of the several states" (National Council of Juvenile Court Judges 1967, p. 107). The enormous power of the juvenile court is particularly visible in those instances where it is asserted that the child is beyond parental control.

Diversion provides the necessary flexibility in a system overburdened with requests for service. The official system could not survive if every case followed the procedures contemplated by statute or appellate decision. Self-reporting studies suggest that most juveniles commit an offense that would bring them within the court's jurisdiction (President's Commission ... 1967, p. 55). If the "illness" of juvenile crime and misbehavior is universal, treatment is selective. Police officers, welfare investigators, intake officers, and correctional administrators constantly make final, unreviewed decisions about children and about their relation to their parents.

The pressures that have given rise to the diversion of juveniles from court are not unique. For decades, arbitration and administrative agencies have been taking over the work of the judiciary. It is useful (or at least sobering) to note that criminal and civil adjudication is undergoing a similar evolution. Writing over a decade ago, two commentators emphasized the dramatic extent to which disputes in American society are no longer litigated in courts or by judicial process:

It is timely to see and to state how far reality deviates from the American myth that a prescribed mode is available when controversy remains unresolved or when government threatens personal freedom. It is no less timely to ask whether the inevitable continuance of the discernible trend away from the courts and their complement of judges, juries, lawyers, advocacy and rules of evidence and procedure will not just as inevitably erode the integrity of the trial process as we know it today (Botein and Gordon 1963, p. 99).

In criminal cases, plea bargaining resolves approximately 90 percent of the cases filed (American Bar Association 1967).

The rising importance of an administrative class in and around the juvenile court—service agencies and "plea bargainers" and the like—raises questions about the distinction between administrative and judicial decisions. Arguably, the "administrative hegemony" about which Paul Tappan warned in 1962 cannot be removed from the juvenile justice system (Tappan 1962, pp. 145–49). As noted below, in many instances the administrative alternative may be properly delegated by the courts. In any event, the large number of cases to be processed, the crucial role of probation officers from the beginning of the juvenile court, the diminishing role of judicial fact finding in civil and criminal cases, and the growth of the administrative classes serving the courts—all suggest the permanence of nonjudicial routing for most of the children vulnerable to intake into the system. The challenge is two-fold. First, the proper boundaries between judicial and administrative decision making must be defined. Second, judges and other participants must develop new ways to supervise the total operation of the justice system.

For the purposes of this discussion, diversion is defined as the channeling of cases to noncourt institutions, in instances where these cases would ordinarily have received an adjudicatory (or fact-finding) hearing by a court. In some instances, the child may be merely returned to his preintervention status. Labeling theorists and critics of existing correctional programs would generally argue that this is the most salutary result (Schur 1973, pp. 153–71). The only issue here is differential selection. For the defense attorney: "Why wasn't my client found to be divertable?" For members of minority groups: "Why are blacks, Puerto Ricans, Native Americans, and so on, not diverted out of the system on the same basis as whites?"

But often youths are not just diverted from the juvenile court, they are diverted into a treatment program. The problems stemming from the coercive treatment of children in diversion programs are a central concern of this chapter.

Another way of defining diversion is to emphasize that it is not prevention. In diversion, the child has been designated as an immediate candidate for court adjudication and formal processing; the child has committed an antisocial act which could bring him or her within the court's jurisdiction. In prevention, services are made available to a broad range of children to keep them from being designated as court clients; the child might in the future commit an antisocial act.

This distinction is emphasized by a national survey which found that 63.8 percent of the directors of youth service bureaus thought that diversion was the primary objective of their organization (Department of Health, Education, and Welfare 1973*b*, p. 14). However, only 25 percent of the youths in their programs were "in immediate jeopardy of the juvenile justice system" (p. 11)—a term undefined in the report but presumably meaning that the child would have been the subject of an adjudicatory proceeding in juvenile court but for the intervention of the youth service bureau. These figures suggest that youth service bureaus may be following the established pattern of service agencies which, suffering from the battle fatigue of dealing with the hard-to-treat recidivists they were set up to help, increasingly turn their attention to more malleable children whose only offense is an administrative determination of predelinquency.

The distinction between diversion and prevention is important. Diversion presumes a *prima facie* case to invoke the juvenile court's jurisdiction. Coercive intervention by administrators can therefore be justified as "saving" the child by diversion from court action. In prevention, in contrast, the court lacks the statutory jurisdiction to intervene. A good test of the effects of the new diversion programs, therefore, is whether the number of juvenile court adjudications is reduced as a result. To illustrate, a court may be handling fifty cases a week before a diversion project. After the project, it is still handling fifty cases and an additional twenty cases are receiving coercive treatment in the diversion program. Instead of a reduction of court cases, the number of children coercively treated merely rises in proportion to the money spent on diversion. In fact, no one is diverted. The subjects of diversion would never have been adjudicated under the previous system; their cases would have been dismissed.

In summary, the purpose here is neither to praise nor to condemn diversion as a general proposition. Diversion, like discretion, is inherent in a system where decisions are made by individuals about other individuals. The question is not whether diversion should exist, but when and under what circumstances it is best employed.

PAST DESCRIPTIONS AND PRESENT PROGRAMS

At least three approaches have been taken in describing the diversion of juveniles from court. The first considers the decision points in the process: diversion by police, diversion from pretrial detention, pretrial (or prosecutional) diversion, and a postconviction (or correctional) diversion (Vorenberg and Vorenberg 1973). The second focuses on models from different parts of the system: schools and welfare, law enforcement, and community organizations (Lemert 1971). The third studies specific diversion mechanisms, such as youth service bureaus (Duxbury 1972; Norman 1970; Rosenheim 1969).

This section looks at diversion from court at pretrial (or prosecutional) intake. Intake was one of the distinctive features of the American juvenile court system and it remains the hub of diversion. Consequently, it may be useful to describe briefly some current programs which start at intake: the New Jersey Juvenile Conference Committees, the Sacramento 601 Diversion Project, the "Van Dyke" Youth Service Bureau, and the Bronx Neighborhood Youth Diversion Program.

These programs, while indicating the broad range of approaches to diversion, also contain elements common to most pretrial diversion projects:

1. The use of paraprofessionals typically drawn from the same social or ethnic community as the juveniles being served by the program.

2. The use of crisis intervention techniques to substitute immediate, short-range aid to juveniles and their families for the long, cumbersome procedures of the judicial system.

3. A reliance on administrators or arbitrators, rather than judges, with a view to conflict resolution rather than determination of guilt.

4. The attempt to avoid the stigma of the juvenile court process by not keeping records or by restricting their availability to outsiders.

5. A policy of limiting the population served to status offenders and minor delinquents.

6. Another common characteristic of most diversion projects is the lack of evaluation by people outside of the program.

New Jersey Conference Committees

The New Jersey plan (see Goff 1966) has committees of representative citizens sitting to hear minor complaints against children and working out solutions on the basis of a voluntary agreement between the complaining party and the offending child and his parents. It grew out of the so-called Monmouth County Plan devised in 1945. The plan proved so successful in Monmouth and in other New Jersey counties that the state supreme court adopted a statewide rule in 1953 permitting juvenile court judges to appoint committees in each municipality. There do not appear to have been any systematic studies of how many and what kind of cases have been referred, but a 1974 telephone interview with the Administrative Office of the New Jersey courts revealed that approximately 10 percent of the cases statewide are diverted at intake to these committees.

Ordinarily only first offenders charged with minor offenses are referred to the committee, though the types of referrals are within the discretion of each juvenile court judge. Following the referral, the committee must obtain the voluntary submission to its jurisdiction of the complainant, the child, and the child's parents. Otherwise the committee has no power to act. If the parties all agree to submit to the committee's jurisdiction, a hearing is held "in a spirit of friendship" to decide the case (New Jersey Supreme Court 1959, p. 10). After all sides are heard, the committee can dismiss the case; or, if they are "convinced to a moral certainty" that the child committed an act of delinquency, they have broad authority to determine a suitable disposition (p. 18). Dispositions often require youths to make repairs where they caused damage or to apologize to the complainant where personal injury occurred.

In *Report of the New Jersey Supreme Court's Committee on Juvenile Conference Committees* (Goff 1966), the study committee unanimously concluded that Juvenile Conference Committees serve a useful purpose and should be continued. But this study called for closer supervision of the committees, noting that some of them had become courts both in name and in practice. Instead of facing one judge, the juvenile and his parents faced nine, all leaders of the community—such as the head of the PTA, the local bank president, and the police captain. These committees were on occasion dealing with serious offenses—serious homosexual attacks or repeated burglaries. Juveniles were frequently put on probation, although there was no authority for this form of disposition. In one county, the committees were illegally assessing fines. Another common practice was ordering psychiatric or psychological tests and evaluations. All of this activity was without statutory authorization or any form of judicial review.

Critics of the New Jersey Juvenile Conference Committees complain that the conference committees are effective in some communities in diverting middle-class white youths, but in the urban ghettos they have not been very successful. The juvenile courts in those areas continue to be flooded with poor kids from minority backgrounds (Chused 1973, p. 575).

Sacramento County 601 Diversion Project

In October 1970, the Sacramento County Probation Department in California initiated an experimental diversion project designed for predelinquents (see Baron, Feeney, and Thornton 1973). At the time of the study, complaints falling within Section 601 of the California Welfare and Institutions Code—alleging that a youth consistently refuses to obey, is beyond the control of parents, or is a habitual truant—constituted over a third of all juvenile court cases in Sacramento County. The cases typically involved conflict and lack of communication within the family. The Sacramento County 601 Diversion Project is an experiment designed to test whether juveniles charged with such offenses can be better handled through short-term family crisis therapy administered at intake by specially trained probation officers than through the traditional procedures of the juvenile court.

Probably the key feature of the project is the provision for immediate, intensive family counseling rather than extended, piecemeal court proceedings. When a Section 601 referral is made—whether from police, school, parents, or any other source—the project arranges a family session to discuss the problem. Project staff make every effort to hold the sessions immediately. Most are held within the first hour or two after referral. Through family counseling techniques, the project counselor urges that solutions to the problem be sought by the family as a whole. These sessions rarely last less than an hour and often are as long as 2½ hours. Since first sessions take place when the problem arises, the project has stayed open until two o'clock in the morning to finish an evening's work.

The first session is mandatory. In Section 601 cases, the project staff members are functioning in place of probation intake officers. Instead of calendaring cases for a judicial proceeding, they schedule an immediate family counseling session. After the first session, families are encouraged to return for a second discussion with the counselor and, depending on the nature of the problem, for a third, fourth, or fifth session. The later sessions are voluntary.

Preliminary results indicated that project cases were referred to court much less frequently than control group cases in which traditional probation techniques were used (project 2.2 percent, control 21. 3 percent). Recidivism rates for the project were lower (35 percent vs. 45.5 percent). Overnight detention was dramatically reduced: project cases required detention only 10 percent of the time compared to 60 percent of the control cases (Baron, Feeney, and Thornton 1973, p. 24).

Van Dyke Youth Service Bureau

The Van Dyke diversion program operates as an alternative to detention booking for predelinquent young women, freeing them entirely from involvement in judicial proceedings (see Cressey and McDermott 1973). In this program the probation department secured an arrangement with a Good Neighbor Agency that happened to own an empty twelve-bed cottage on the same street as the juvenile detention center.

Using flexible criteria but emphasizing a girl's willingness to cooperate, intake officers screen girls before they enter the detention center. If a juvenile appears acceptable and willing, the officers then obtain verbal parental permission for her to go into the Good Neighbor Agency program. This process avoids any official booking; no official record of the transaction is kept, although an unofficial card is kept for accounting purposes. The girl is completely out of the juvenile justice system. The probation department, in making the placement, forfeits its right to file a petition for a hearing or to place the girl on probation. Thus, cases in the project have never officially been opened. No conditions are attached to participation in the program. Counselors are available throughout the recommended five-day stay at the agency, but the girl is free both to leave the agency and to refuse counseling. She is not locked, guarded, or observed. Only 5 of 250 girls have run away.

The program had only been in existence four months at the time of its description, but there was already some indication of a lower recidivism rate among participating girls than among those detained in juvenile hall or placed on probation.

Bronx Neighborhood Youth Diversion Program

This program operates in the predominantly black and Puerto Rican sections of the Bronx, New York. The program works with youths between twelve and fifteen years of age, and is run by residents of the community. It was started in 1971 by the Vera Institute of Justice and Fordham University. The following description relies on a personal visit to the program in September 1972, and subsequent discussions with the project director, Warren Williams, as well as a reading of Jones and Bailey (1973).

Cases are referred by probation intake officers and the family court judges. Unlike many diversion projects, the focus here is on juveniles charged with delinquency and not on cases which would normally be adjusted at intake. The program represents an attempt to divert young people only from the family court and not totally out of the juvenile justice system, since they are not free of the threat of further state intervention when they go to the program. If their performance is unsatisfactory, they can be referred back to intake for formal court proceedings.

When a case is diverted to the project, the juvenile is assigned an advocate, generally a person under thirty years of age who lives in the youth's neighborhood. The advocate counsels the young person and helps to obtain outside referrals such as temporary homes, school, or part-time work. The referrals are then reviewed periodically (usually every two or three weeks) to make sure that something is being done for the youth.

One of the most innovative aspects of the program is the "forum," in which a panel of community residents address the problems evolving from minor offenses committed by neighborhood juveniles and help resolve problems between parents and children. The members of forum panels are nonprofessional members of the community who have received training in mediation and conciliation.

Almost all cases go to a forum hearing at some point, and there two or three volunteer forum "judges" attempt to bring disputing parties together to settle difficulties without referral to the juvenile justice system. Referrals are hardly ever necessary, but the possibility remains part of the program.

A PROPOSED BALANCE SHEET

An assessment of diversion is difficult because we know so little about the process and its impact on clients. In addition, the criteria for evaluation are often subjective. Lack of treatment is favored by laissez faire liberals, abhorred by interventionists. A lack of procedure is decried by civil libertarians, applauded by champions of treatment. Often a proposed advantage will be cancelled by an inherent countervailing pressure.

The following issues appear relevant either to diversion in general or to specific projects. They raise questions that should be considered in weighing the merits of diversion. The issues center on the client and the treatment program, the coercive role of the state and fairness, and resources and evaluation.

The Clients and Their Treatment

Proponents of diversion programs emphasize that, like community correctional methods such as halfway houses, diversion avoids placing people in closed institutions. It emphasizes the value of putting the burden on the children for their own salvation. Diversion keeps them in the community and does not force them to adjust to an institutional setting.

Opponents of these views argue that there must be reasons why the delinquent got into trouble. The best help that society can provide may be separation from an undesirable environment, including parents who failed to prevent misconduct, bad friends, poverty, drugs, or other unfavorable influences. As a minimum, a positive goal of court intervention may be just to keep recidivists under supervision or out of circulation during a difficult period when they could be dangerous to themselves and others.

A hallmark of the juvenile court has been its attempt to shield its clients from adverse labels or stigma. The creation of a special vocabulary (such as hearing instead of trial), the nonpublic nature of the proceedings, and the confidentiality accorded to records attempt to protect juveniles from a negative social reaction to a court involvement. Diversion is often endorsed because it is supposed to reduce stigma even more. However, the charges of juvenile court labeling may have been overstated and, in any event, the actual effects of being diverted have not been studied. Mahoney (1974, p. 583) has noted that the persons concerned with labeling include the child, parents, peers, and prospective schools and employers. The provisions for secrecy and confidentiality in the court are largely irrelevant to the child, parents, and peers. They know that the delinquent has been in court, and they will know if he or she is in a diversion project. As Cressey and McDermott (1973) have pointed out:

So far as we know, no one has shown that the juvenile offender and his family perceive their handling as materially different under the auspices of a diversion unit than under a more traditional juvenile justice agency. The question is rarely formulated, let alone asked (p. 59).

However, diversion may offer less stigma than court for employers and schools. Lemert (1969) indicates that juvenile court records are not as secret as champions of the court would like to believe. But, as Mahoney also notes, this source of stigma may be overrated, since juvenile offenders often bear other labels such as bad school records (Mahoney 1974, p. 588).

The situation noted in discussing the New Jersey Juvenile Conference Committees highlights another range of problems: the diversionary system itself may operate on the basis of labels with discriminatory results (Herbert 1971). For example, white middle-class youths and black ghetto youths may commit the same act. The tendency for the administrators in the juvenile justice system is to absolve the former through diversion but to deny ghetto residents the benefits of diversion because they are already stereotyped and, therefore, not deemed to be proper subjects of administrative grace.

Whether children follow the court or the diversion route, swift resolution of their problems is to be encouraged. Contrary to popular assumptions, the courts can on occasion be fast, as the Rapid Intervention Project in New York City suggests. The Rapid Intervention Project is an experimental crisis intervention project of the Family Court of New York. It provides an immediate psychiatric evaluation and report to the court regarding the need for remand for hospitalization, or the existence of suicidal or homicidal tendencies, and the presence of drug or alcohol abuse. The project makes and implements recommendations regarding juvenile offenders, family referrals for full evaluation, outpatient psychiatric care, family agencies, and other forms of treatment (Rapid Intervention Project [1973?]). Nevertheless, diversion programs are generally quicker to reach decision and briefer in duration of contact. The Sacramento 601 Diversion Project and the Bronx Neighborhood Diversion Project both emphasize crisis intervention. The emphasis is on doing as much as possible within a short time, usually no more than three months. In the Bronx project, short-term goals are fixed for the child and his advocate. Every two weeks, the case is reviewed. Progress or failure to meet the goals is determined. If necessary, new goals are established.

Diversion projects also attract a different kind of staff. They generally employ paraprofessionals, ex-offenders and members of the indigenous community. Blacks, Puerto Ricans, or members of other minorities are given a chance to deal with their own people. But the use of paraprofessionals also raises the traditional debate about professionalism in the helping services.

Advocates point out that the use of paraprofessionals facilitates empathy between helper and client. Community self-help and self-reliance are also fostered. A burst of pride and energy appears on the scene, in contrast to the apathy of tired bureaucrats. At least the paraprofessional and the juvenile speak the same language. In the area served by the Bronx Neighborhood Diversion Project, none of the city probation workers speak Spanish, although a large number of the juveniles in the court are Puerto Rican. Consequently, one of the most basic contributions of the project is placing Spanish-speaking advocates at the courthouse to aid in intake and at hearings.

Critics argue that children in trouble need professional assistance. More than enthusiasm is needed to deal with intractable problems. Paraprofessionals do not keep records and have high turnover. Members of minorities also may be harsher than outsiders in dealing with their own troublemakers.

Diversion projects which emphasize short-term intervention and use of paraprofessionals cost less to operate. Paraprofessionals usually receive less compensation than traditional probation officers or social workers. The shorter time in processing is another saving, provided that there is not a significantly higher rate of recidivism or other need for services. The Sacramento project reported an average total cost of $29 for project handling of single-contact cases, compared to $222 for control cases. In the case of repeated bookings, the average project cost was $170 compared to $405 for the average control group case (Baron, Feeney, and Thornton 1973, p. 18).

A strong pressure for the continued growth of diversion programs is generated by federal, state, and local officials who believe that extrajudicial resolution of juvenile problems should be encouraged. Armed with the national crime commission reports of 1967 (President's Commission ... 1967, pp. 83–84) and 1973 (National Advisory Commission ... 1973, pp. 51–55) which strongly endorsed diversion, bureaucrats at all levels can safely substitute action for thought. Whatever the real merits of diversion, it is fashionable. Consequently, diversion has become a new and up-to-date label under which new federal funds are spent without much recognition of the problems—both traditional and unique—resulting from this kind of state intervention in the life of the individual.

Fairness and the Power of the State

Where the child is merely released from the system, we have noted that the only question is one of differential or discriminatory selection. But where the child is diverted into a treatment program, the role of the state in forcing this decision on the child and his parents needs careful examination.

Where participation in some program or treatment is required, voluntary diversion is a contradiction in terms. The coercive power of the state and the court is always present in diversion. The child and his parents "agree" to enter a particular program "recommended" by some state official—because they can be ordered by a judge to accept this same program or one that is substantially more unpleasant.

Some programs, especially those dealing with children alleged to be status offenders, may entail less coercion than court-ordered dispositions because the stakes are lower for all concerned. But even welfare programs are seen by the recipient as bringing the full weight of the state to bear on a subject population:

Welfare workers, in the pictures ghetto children draw, stand near the police like dogs, with huge piercing eyes, ears that seem twisted as they are oversize, and mouths noticeably absent or present as thick lines enclosing prominent and decidedly pointed and ragged teeth. To ghetto children, as to their parents, the welfare worker is the policemen's handmaiden, and together they come, as one child put it, "to keep us in line or send us away" (Coles 1971, pp. 599–600).

The coercive potential of diversion programs raises basic questions about corrections and treatment in general. Does the individual have a right to refuse treatment? Can children be forced to accept treatment for their own good or for the good of society (for example, be required to learn a trade so they will not be a drain on society)?

Diversion raises the problem that "less may be more." That is, by emphasizing preadjudication diversion instead of postadjudication institutionalization, society will be spending fewer resources on each individual but "helping" many more people than before.

Under a diversionary scheme, the persons who will be making decisions in such agencies as welfare, schools, or youth service bureaus are less visible and have less training than the intake officers and the judges of the juvenile court. For example, diversion is not a substitute for diagnosis. Diversion merely redesignates or shifts the responsibility for making such determinations. Fundamental questions remain: By whom are these individuals to be judged and upon what evidence? One of the most serious needs in the administration of criminal and juvenile justice in recent years has been to rationalize and make visible the discretion that exists at all levels (Davis 1969). It is ironic that the National Advisory Commission on Criminal Justice Standards and Goals (1973, p. 45) recommended the abolition of plea bargaining for adults at the same time that it encouraged diversion for juveniles.

Probation officers and others along the route of diversion make decisions that, if made by a judge, would require some show of due process. The juvenile justice system has demonstrated considerable adaptability in avoiding the impact of *In re Gault* (387 U.S. 1 [1967]) and other pressures for increased formalization. After genuflecting to the formalities of the adjudicatory and dispositional hearings, it has delegated decisions to its extremities—police and intake at the beginning, correctional institutions and aftercare agencies at the end.

Where the state coerces children into programs which usually restrict their liberty and attempt to modify their behavior, important questions are raised about the fairness of the procedures and the substance of the mandated programs. Much of the diversion literature seems to assume that the juvenile court is unredeemably bad and that any substitute is preferable. The following program description unconsciously summarized a central problem in diversion. An undefined mixture of delinquency cases, status offenses, and child protective problems are transferred for the sake of convenience directly from police to treatment, without the benefit of judicial proceedings:

[In] the youth services project in San Antonio, Texas . . . (t)he police chief has ordered all officers to deliver juveniles picked up for such offenses as glue or paint sniffing, liquor violations, runaway, ungovernable and disorderly conduct, truancy or loitering to one of three project neighborhood centers in the city. . . . The immediacy of service and convenient physical locations of the bureau saves police a long drive to the juvenile hall. . . . (Department of Health, Education, and Welfare 1973b, pp. 16–17).

While the juvenile court may have some negative effects such as labeling, court proceedings also have positive aspects which should not be overlooked. They provide a measure of accountability and formality in decision making.

Although appeals from the juvenile court have been rare, they are at least possible and are probably increasing with the rise in defense lawyers, transcripts, and improved appellate procedures (Bowman 1965, p. 63). In the juvenile system, machinery does not exist for the review of administrative decisions about stationhouse release or dismissal at probation intake.

Decisions about deprivation of liberty and forced behavior modification have traditionally been made by judges or at least under their supervision (Tappan 1962, pp. 153–59). In communist countries, community councils composed largely of local residents decide most family problems, including delinquency, incorrigibility, and neglect (Feifer 1964). In Orwell's *1984,* diversion reigns supreme. Trials and courts have been abolished in that picture of the not-too-distant future; administrators make all the decisions.

Resources and Evaluation

In assessing diversion, it should be remembered that, traditionally, resources for juvenile justice have been meager. Will diversion provide an answer to society's chronic unwillingness to be more generous? In shifting from adjudicative to administrative models, we should be careful not to mistake motion for progress. Neither intended solution may have been given the resources— especially in large urban areas—to be viable.

Even if there were resources, we know little about how to change behavior. And there is little indication that diversion projects will be significantly more successful than their predecessors. There are labels now under which little or nothing is being done. Probation may be one such label; diversion, another. Seen in this light, diversion is a minimum courtesy offered by society to the complaining witness or to the child in trouble or to concerned parents. The public conscience is propitiated.

Unless diversion is adequately tested and verified, it may merely be a placebo which helps the system struggle through another decade. But it may be impossible for diversion projects to be studied in a rigorous empirical fashion and, thus, to demonstrate any "success." The Vorenbergs complain that not enough has been spent on evaluation (Vorenberg and Vorenberg 1973, p. 182), where Cressey notes that we may never know about diversion because of serious methodological problems (Cressey and McDermott 1973, pp. 56-62). The Department of California Youth Authority noted, "Based on the available data accumulated in this study, it is impossible to prove that any significant number of youth have been diverted from the juvenile justice system by Youth Service Bureaus.... It is not that diversion is not a desirable goal for youth service bureaus; it is just that it is virtually unmeasurable" (Department of Health, Education, and Welfare 1973a, pp. 129, 135). Zimring cautiously concludes, "Diversion programs, if designed and executed humanely, are probably a healthy reform in the present state of American criminal justice. As a result of uninformed evaluation efforts, they are oversold and widely misconceived" (Zimring 1974, p. 241). Diversion projects, like the juvenile court, may appear to prosper only if they enjoy very little public scrutiny.

This uncertainty about the result of diversion projects raises a problem concerning the burden of proof. If the project is coercive, it must show success. If voluntary, it need only be shown not to be a failure in order to protect the public purse.

THE FUTURE OF DIVERSION

Diversion in the context of the juvenile court is not without its ironies since the court itself was created to divert cases from the adult system. It is doubtful that diversion can avoid the problems which plague the juvenile court itself, such as difficulty in making diagnoses and lack of client satisfaction. In the short run, diversion programs will probably suffer a kinder fate only because they avoid the public scrutiny to which the court has lately been subjected.

The juvenile court movement has suffered a split personality concerning its mission. On the one hand, its most distinctive rationale has been rehabilitation—the child needs help and the state has therapeutic remedies. This approach is characterized by medical, welfare, or administrative models. Mental health experts, social workers, and probation officers are seen as the agents of salvation. Its theology was aptly summarized by Judge Paul Alexander's comment that to deny the child in trouble access to the juvenile court is like denying the sick child admittance to a hospital (Alexander 1962).

On the other hand, there has always been the requirement that the child or his parents have committed an act that lies within the jurisdiction of the state's power. People should not be "treated" at random. In some formulations of the court's mission, guilt must be proven. The 1967 Crime Commission (President's Commission ... 1967, p. 81) recognized punishment as an articulated rationale for the court's jurisdiction. Under this view of the juvenile court mission, judges and lawyers predominate.

The split creates a tension in determining the court's jurisdiction. In examining a delinquency petition, the court is primarily concerned with whether the child has committed an act which would be a crime if committed by an adult. In examining dependency and neglect, the court is more concerned with whether it can offer a unique service to the child or whether the case might better be handled by informal and nonjudicial means. Significantly, the court is more willing to cede jurisdiction to administrative agencies in child protective proceedings.

This dichotomy betwen the welfare and the due process models exists in almost every phase of the juvenile court proceeding (see Schultz and Cohen, this volume). The controversy since *Gault* about how formal and legalistic the adjudicatory hearing shall be is only one manifestation. Another is the criteria for transfer or waiver of jurisdiction to the adult court: not only should it be shown that a serious offense has been committed, but it is equally relevant to show that the juvenile cannot be rehabilitated by the juvenile court and its services (Department of Health, Education, and Welfare 1969, §31). This dichotomy was reflected by the 1967 Crime Commission. On the one hand, the commission suggested a more formal adjudicatory hearing for cases which progressed to that stage. On the other hand, it emphasized diversion to youth service bureaus for treatment and service of children who need help. The Crime Commission at once predicted and was a force for realizing fewer, more formal trials and an emphasis on diversion (President's Commission ... 1967, pp. 78–89).

The original mixture of the welfare and due process models in the creation of a separate juvenile court represented a reaction against two nineteenth-century trends (Schultz 1973, p. 457; Rothman 1971, pp. 206–36). First, reformers rebelled against the practical consequences of children being given the same trials (softened only by rules of diminished responsibility) and prisons (although some had separate but equally severe facilities) as adults. Second, they objected to children being administratively determined to be in need of a changed life style and coercively placed in apprenticeships or, in the most dramatic instances, shipped off to distant states or on whaling voyages to begin life anew—all without the benefit of judicial deliberation.

Seen in this light, the spirit of 1899 arose from a desire to increase the services available to children within a framework of due process. While later generations have tended to view the separate juvenile justice system as either all welfare or all due process, the founders sought to combine these equally laudable objectives. If not properly managed, the pressure to legitimate existing diversion procedures and create new mechanisms will perpetuate, rather than bridge, the dichotomy.

Because it focuses almost exclusively on the therapeutic or rehabilitation goal, diversion may be an unhealthy tendency. A typical diversion project takes up individuals who are charged with crime or misbehavior and, if it can rehabilitate the individual within a relatively short time before trial, the court will simply dismiss the charges. Concern about establishing the guilt or

innocence of the individual is overriden by the desire to rehabilitate. Absolution, though informal, is deemed to be complete. The
cure is presumed to be adequate.

The reformers who established the juvenile court rejected either
a purely administrative or a purely treatment agency. As Pound
noted, they purposely created a court, albeit a rather special
court, to determine the extent and nature of state intervention in
the life of the child and his parents:

It was a fortunate circumstance that the statute creating [the first
juvenile court] was drawn by a committee of the Chicago Bar
Association and so by lawyers in a state which had preserved a
separate equity procedure. It was set up as a court of equity, with
the administrative functions incidental to equity jurisdiction, not
as a criminal court, and not, as might have happened later, as an
administrative agency with incidental adjudicating functions
(Pound 1945, p. 5).

Each approach offers a limited truth. Past attempts to combine
the two approaches have resulted in the uneasy compromise
which currently exists. But the answer is not necessarily to route
more cases through the juvenile court. Rather, due process should
be insured at each point where the state exercises coercive power
over the juvenile and his family.

An initial observation is that some cases, because they involve
serious offenses, should not be diverted. The review of the New
Jersey Juvenile Councils, for example, found that they were
handling some serious burglaries and sex offenses informally. We
need better criteria for determining which cases should receive
the ceremony of a hearing before a judge and which should be
directed for informal treatment.

There is no need to copy the exact rituals of the adult criminal
trial in every juvenile case. We need to revitalize old and create
new methods of insuring due process (Skoler 1974). These
concerns are not limited to juvenile justice but have analogues in
mass production courts such as those handling traffic violations,
divorce petitions, public drunkenness arrests, and lesser misdemeanors (Barrett 1965). Significantly, most of the criteria for
evaluation are concerned with the outcome of treatment, especially recidivism. Few measurements for the fairness of a proceeding exist outside the requirements of an adult criminal trial—

such as right to counsel or a hearing. While these are important, they may be irrelevant or economically impossible to provide at every stage.

There is a continuing need for judicial review of the administrative decisions inherent in diversion. This review, however, may take a variety of forms:

1. Courts might act, as they have in the past, to review administrative agencies—that is, to protect against abuses of discretion rather than provide a new hearing.

2. Masters of the court might serve as ombudsmen and report their findings to the court and the public.

3. Courts might develop a research capability to monitor the performance of the various agencies on a systematic basis.

In each of these ways, the court would shift from a fact-finding forum to an instrument for testing the fairness of extrajudicial fact finding (Nejelski and LaPook 1974).

The rise of administrative agencies and arbitration tribunals to handle business that formerly was the subject of court litigation provides a historical antecedent for such changes. Central requirements are formalized criteria for decisions, such as written guidelines approved from above, and a mechanism for review of administrative decisions, such as written reports from below. Rather than pretend that the problem of delegation does not exist, we can attempt to gain control over the diversion process through various means of formalization. At least three Supreme Court justices have suggested that the Administrative Procedure Act is arguably broad enough to reach a prosecutor's discretion in unilaterally deciding to charge certain offenses which automatically transfer a juvenile to adult court (*Bland* v. *U.S.* [denial of certiorari], 412 U.S. 909, 912-13 [1973]).

The justification for due process in the juvenile justice system is simply that coercive state intervention must be tempered with fairness. This notion runs counter to the "social contract" theory espoused by Judge Orman Ketcham (Ketcham 1962, pp. 22-43) and suggested by Justice Abe Fortas in the *Gault* decision. That theory may be interpreted as arguing that the juvenile court could dispense with due process if in fact the court were treating and correcting its clients. As Fortas suggested, the lack of due process in the juvenile hearing might be excused if recidivism rates or other criteria of success were improved. In its most extreme form, this theory would permit the total elimination of ceremony and due process if the system resulted in a completely favorable evaluation of the treatment aspects, such as recidivism. A sounder basis for according due process is simply the fact that the state is coercively intervening in the life of its citizens.

A final problem with diversion is that it diverts attention from fundamental reform by reducing the visibility of coercive state intervention. In the adult system, society is coming to realize the impracticability of processing drunks or alcoholics as criminals. In contrast, where there is case by case diversion of minor cases, especially in the so-called status offenses, there is little pressure for radical change; sentiment for the repeal of the statutes which form the basis for state intervention does not develop. Instead, an administrator is deciding privately that some "juvenile offenders" are better treated in noncourt systems. Such a scheme currently calls for ad hoc decisions in individual cases by someone in the large system which deals with children in trouble. This discretion has low visibility and may be exercised in a discriminatory or arbitrary fashion.

Discretionary screening of cases, which has the most serious impact on the poor and minorities, may have the unfortunate result of postponing more basic reform. In calling for the abolition of jurisdiction over all juvenile status offenses such as incorrigibility, a California legislative committee found the section to be "notoriously vague and ambiguous":

It has often been suggested that almost any child alive in America could, if the court so desired, be found to come within the provisions of this statute. . . . Trying to define an idle, dissolute, lewd, or immoral life is like trying to define art. It is impossible. It can only be assumed that the courts are expected to know it when they see it. . . . [A]s a result of the absence of objective standards the application of Section 601 throughout the state is anything but evenhanded. What one judge might view as trivial behavior will elicit an angry reaction from another judge (California Legislature 1970).

Outright abolition, and not passing the buck to anonymous administrators, may be a more appropriate solution in dealing with status offenses.

In sum, diversion has always been a part of the juvenile justice system. As a result of the increasing formalization of the juvenile court, there is a danger that diversion will become a means of expanding coercive intervention in the lives of children and families without proper concern for their rights. The challenge of the next decade will be to determine when diversion is appropriate and to monitor diversion programs to insure that they deliver their considerable promise.

BIBLIOGRAPHY

Alexander, Paul W. 1962. "Constitutional Rights in the Juvenile Court." In *Justice for the Child: The Juvenile Court in Transition,* ed. Margaret Keeney Rosenheim. New York: Free Press of Glencoe. Pp. 82–92.

American Bar Association, Advisory Committee on the Criminal Trial. 1967. *Standards Relating to Pleas of Guilty.* Chicago.

Baron, Roger; Feeney, Floyd; Thornton, Warren. 1973. "Preventing Delinquency through Diversion: The Sacramento County 601 Diversion Project." *Federal Probation* 37:13–19.

Barrett, Edward L., Jr. 1965. "Criminal Justice: The Problem of Mass Production." In *The Courts, the Public and the Law Explosion,* ed. Harry W. Jones. American Assembly, Columbia University. Englewood Cliffs, N.J.: Prentice-Hall. Pp. 85–123. .

Botein, Bernard, and Gordon, Murray A. 1963. *The Trial of the Future: Challenge to the Law.* New York: Simon and Schuster.

Bowman, Addison M. 1965. "Appeals from Juvenile Courts." *Crime and Delinquency* 11:63–77.

California Legislature, Interim Committee on Criminal Procedure. 1970. *Juvenile Court Process.* (Hearings held in Los Angeles, 14 and 15 September 1970.)

Chused, Richard H. 1973. "Juvenile Court Process." *Rutgers Law Review* 26:488–615.

Coles, Robert. 1971. *The South Goes North.* Boston: Little, Brown.

Connecticut Juvenile Court. 1969. *Annual Report.*

Cressey, Donald R., and McDermott, Robert A. 1973. *Diversion from the Juvenile Justice System.* National Assessment of Juvenile Corrections. Ann Arbor: University of Michigan.

Davis, Kenneth Culp. 1969. *Discretionary Justice: A Preliminary Inquiry.* Baton Rouge: Louisiana State University Press.

Department of Health, Education, and Welfare. 1969. *Legislative*

Guide for Drafting Family and Juvenile Court Acts. Children's Bureau publication no. 472-1969. Washington, D.C.: U.S. Government Printing Office.

———. 1973a. *Youth Service Bureaus: A National Study.* Department of California Youth Authority. DHEW publication no. (SRS) 73-26025. Washington, D.C.: U.S. Government Printing Office.

———. 1973b. *The Challenge of Youth Service Bureaus.* Youth Development and Delinquency Prevention Administration. DHEW publication no. 73-26024. Washington, D.C.: U.S. Government Printing Office.

Duxbury, Elaine. 1972. *Youth Service Bureaus in California.* Youth Authority Progress Report no. 3. Sacramento, Calif.

Feifer, George. 1964. *Justice in Moscow.* New York: Simon and Schuster.

Goff, Donald. 1966. *Report of the New Jersey Supreme Court's Committee on Juvenile Conference Committees.*

Herbert, Robert M. 11-16 July 1971. "Justice for Jersey Juveniles." 6 pts. *Newark Star Ledger.*

Jones, James A., and Bailey, Linda. 1973. *Second Year Evaluation Report: Neighborhood Youth Diversion Program.* Center for Research and Demonstration, School of Social Work, Columbia University. (Mimeographed.)

Ketcham, Orman W. 1962. "The Unfulfilled Promise of the Juvenile Court." In *Justice for the Child: The Juvenile Court in Transition,* ed. Margaret Keeney Rosenheim. New York: Free Press of Glencoe. Pp. 22–43.

Lemert, Edwin M. 1969. "Records in the Juvenile Court." In *On Record: Files and Dossiers in American Life,* ed. Stanton Wheeler. New York: Russell Sage Foundation. Pp. 355–87.

———. 1971. *Instead of Court: Diversion in Juvenile Justice.* Chevy Chase, Md.: National Institute of Mental Health, Center for Studies of Crime and Delinquency.

Mahoney, Anne Rankin. 1974. "The Effect of Labeling upon Youths in the Juvenile Justice System: A Review of the Evidence." *Law and Society Review* 8:583-614.

National Advisory Commission on Criminal Justice Standards and Goals. 1973. *A National Strategy to Reduce Crime.* Washington, D.C.: U.S. Government Printing Office.

National Council of Juvenile Court Judges. 1967. "National Council Matters Resolutions." *Juvenile Court Judges Journal* 18:106-7.

Nejelski, Paul, and LaPook, Judith. 1974. "Monitoring the Juvenile Justice System: How Can You Tell Where You're Going, If You Don't Know Where You Are?" *American Criminal Law Review* 12:9–31.

New Jersey Supreme Court. 1959. *Manual for the Guidance of Juvenile Conference Committees Appointed by the Juvenile and Domestic Relations Court.*

Norman, Sherwood. 1970. *The Youth Service Bureau: A Brief Description with Five Current Programs.* New York: National Council on Crime and Delinquency.

Pound, Roscoe. 1945. "The Juvenile Court and the Law." In *The 1944 Yearbook.* New York: National Probation Association.

President's Commission on Law Enforcement and Administration of Justice. 1967. *The Challenge of Crime in a Free Society.* Washington, D.C.: U.S. Government Printing Office.

Rapid Intervention Project, Family Court, State of New York. N.d. [1973?] *What Is R.I.P.?* N. 33.

Rosenheim, Margaret Keeney, ed. 1962. *Justice for the Child: The Juvenile Court in Transition.* New York: Free Press of Glencoe.

———. 1969. "Youth Service Bureaus: A Concept in Search of a Definition." *Juvenile Court Judges Journal* 20:69–74.

Rothman, David. 1971. *The Discovery of the Asylum: Social Order and Disorder in the New Republic.* Boston: Little, Brown.

Schultz, J. Lawrence. 1973. "The Cycle of Juvenile Court History." *Crime and Delinquency* 19:457–76.

Schur, Edwin M. 1973. *Radical Nonintervention: Rethinking the Delinquency Problem.* Englewood Cliffs, N.J.: Prentice-Hall.

Skoler, Daniel L. 1974. "Protecting the Rights of Defendants in Pretrial Intervention Programs." *Criminal Law Bulletin* 10:473–92.

Tappan, Paul W. 1962. "Judicial and Administrative Approaches to Children with Problems." In *Justice for the Child: The Juvenile Court in Transition,* ed. Margaret Keeney Rosenheim. New York: Free Press of Glencoe. Pp. 144–71.

Vorenberg, Elizabeth, and Vorenberg, James. 1973. "Early Diversion from the Criminal Justice System: Practice in Search of a Theory." In *Prisoners in America,* ed. Lloyd E. Ohlin. Englewood Cliffs, N.J.: Prentice-Hall. Pp. 151–83.

Zimring, Franklin E. 1974. "Measuring the Impact of Pretrial Diversion from the Criminal Justice System." *University of Chicago Law Review* 41:224–41.

6   Pretrial Detention for Juveniles

Patricia M. Wald

For years, critics of our juvenile court system have deplored the horrors of juvenile detention before trial. The statistics are dreary: over half a million juveniles annually detained in "junior jails," another several hundred thousand held in adult jails, penned like cattle, demoralized by lack of activities and trained staff, often brutalized. Over half the facilities in which juveniles are held have no psychiatric or social work staff. A fourth have no school program. The median age of detainees is fourteen; the novice may be sodomized within a matter of hours. Many have not been charged with a crime at all. From New York to California, the field reports repeat themselves depressingly (Sarri 1974).

Generally critics agree about where the fault lies and what ought to be done. They have scored the police, intake officers at the juvenile court, and the courts themselves. They have shown that too little money is spent on recruiting and training good staff and on mounting constructive programs in detention facilities. They have called for alternatives to detention for juveniles who "can't go home again" but are not really dangerous to anyone. Still, progress is painfully slow. While several of our larger cities report that fewer juveniles are being detained before trial than in previous years, in other cities overall estimates continue to grow (Sarri 1974; U.S. Congress, Senate 1973). When a situation as unsavory as juvenile detention persists as long as it has, reappraisal is essential. Any new look at the problem requires an assessment of what has been done or attempted in the past.

How the System Works

Under traditional juvenile law and practice, children facing juvenile court proceedings can be placed in detention when someone in authority—police, intake worker, or judge—decides that it is not safe for them or society to permit them to remain at liberty in the community pending a final disposition by the court. Generally children brought to court because of neglect or abuse by their parents are placed in shelters, not detention facilities, although in some localities all juveniles are commingled and many shelters are as secure, and as dreadful, as detention facilities.

Police may detain an arrested juvenile for any reason although juvenile laws generally state a preference for release of the juvenile to his parents unless it is "undesirable," "impractical," or "not in the best interest" of the child or the public. Police detain juveniles arrested for serious offenses; juveniles who are "uncooperative," "rebellious," or "antagonistic"; juveniles with previous records or currently on probation or parole; juveniles whose parents are not available to take immediate custody. In many localities, this results in initial detention for one-third to one-half of all juveniles who are arrested.

Interim detention, despite its brevity, contributes enormously to overcrowding at detention facilities. In most jurisdictions a police decision to detain can be reversed by intake workers at the juvenile court. In fact, studies show that up to half the juveniles detained by police are released by court intake workers either because they disagree with the police or because the child's parents eventually appear and are willing to take the child home. Juveniles detained for court appearance may be released, or their detention confirmed, by a juvenile judge, with or without a hearing. Criteria for detention include a likelihood that the juvenile will flee, commit a new crime before trial, or have inadequate supervision at home (President's Commission . . . 1967; Ferster, Snethen, and Courtless 1969; National Advisory Commission . . . 1973, pp. 257–60).

CURBING OVERDETENTION

The experts are virtually unanimous that we detain too many juveniles too long. Estimates of overkill range from 25 percent to more than 75 percent. The juvenile justice system is subject to the same irrational skewing as the adult criminal system. More juveniles are locked up before trial than afterward, and the majority of those detained are released into the community after, sometimes even before, adjudication. There is no logic to widely disparate detention rates in neighboring communities; habit and local custom are the apparent explanations (Sarri 1974).

Efforts to cut down on the numbers of detained juveniles have focused on defining more precisely the classes of juveniles who should be detained, providing court personnel around the clock to review police detentions, and ensuring a court hearing before a child can be detained. (Most juvenile arrests occur at night or on weekends when courts are not usually in session.) Some advances have been made in hearing procedures, less in substantive efforts to narrow the categories of detainables. Probably the greatest hope for reducing detention lies in placing limits on the kinds of juveniles who can be detained.

Detention Hearings

Reform efforts aimed at ensuring that a juvenile detained by police obtains a prompt detention hearing, usually within twenty-four hours of arrest, have succeeded in only a dozen or so states. A detention hearing should be a constitutional necessity, although few courts have so held. Admittedly, there is as yet little hard evidence that detention hearings, where they exist, substantially reduce overdetention. The salutary potential of a hearing also may be largely wasted unless the juvenile is represented by counsel at such hearings and the counsel has time to investigate and prepare alternative dispositions. Still, a judge's oversight of police or intake worker detention can act as a necessary check on arbitrary decisions to detain (Ferster, Snethen, and Courtless 1969; *Cooley* v. *Stone,* 414 F. 2d 1213 [D.C. Cir. 1969]).

Criteria for Detention

Critical to any detention hearing are the criteria the judge uses in making his determination. If the criteria are loose enough to permit him to interpose subjective judgments about the child's best interests, or his own predictions about possible danger to the community, the results are bound to vary with the judge's philosophic disposition and will be unpredictable on a juris-diction-wide basis. Even now, in those states with detention hearings, judges differ as to whether it is necessary to show probable cause that juveniles committed the offense before they can be detained. Statutory criteria typically sanction detention for any law violation or status offense where it is anticipated that the juvenile will flee, commit a new offense before trial, or is not subject to adequate home supervision. There are, moreover, no statutory guidelines to what makes a flight risk or a danger to the community, or what constitutes an inadequate home for pretrial supervisory purposes. Youths need not have previously run away to be a flight risk; a serious charge or past record of trouble with the law usually suffices to make them dangerous enough to detain. Most troublesome juveniles who are runaways or beyond control have committed no crime but are combatants in a chronic war with their parents. As a rule, they are more likely to be detained than the juvenile law violator (Sarri 1974; Ferster, Snethen, and Courtless 1969; Beale 1973).

Response to Flight Risks

In reformulating detention criteria, one of the first obstacles is a lack of reliable statistics on the nonappearance rate of juvenile defendants. Is it higher or lower than in the adult criminal system? Which classes of juvenile defendants are most apt to flee? In the absence of empirical field data, juvenile laws should at the very least require the judge to specify on the record why he is detaining a juvenile as a flight risk, and probably should limit such detention to juveniles who have a record of "no-shows."

There are valuable lessons to be learned from the adult bail reform movement in the last decade (P. Wald 1972). Arguably, under the Eighth Amendment to the Constitution, and certainly under a majority of state constitutions, adult defendants (except where capital crimes are alleged) have a right to bail, or more accurately, a right to have conditions set for their release. These conditions are, in theory, fixed for the sole purpose of discourag-ing flight. Historically, judges either intentionally or unthinkingly imposed high money bail as a condition of release, and indigent defendants who could not afford a bondsman's fee were caught in the detention net. Beginning in the sixties, under mounting pressure for bail reform, money bail began to be supplanted by release on promise to return for defendants with family and job ties in the community or by release in the custody of a reliable third party. Bail projects were established in a number of jurisdictions, rating defendants on a point system as good or poor flight risks, based on their community ties. The Bail Reform Act of 1966 (18 U.S.C. §3146) and its state counterparts legislated a presumption in favor of release for all defendants under a variety of conditions: promise to return, third-party custody, restrictions on travel, residence rules, limits on associations, forfeitable cash deposits, commercial surety bonds, daytime or weekend release. The judge must pick the "least restrictive" conditions that will assure the defendant's appearance at trial. While implementation has been imperfect and high money bonds still hold many defendants in jail, the principle that some release conditions can be set for virtually every defendant deserves legislative and judicial recognition in the juvenile field (see National Advisory Commission ... 1973, Standards 4.4–4.5, pp. 120–25; 16.9, pp. 573–75; American Bar Association, Project on Minimum Standards for Criminal Justice 1968, §5.3, pp. 58–59). Indeed, the juvenile system, historically unencumbered by money bail, provides a more favorable environment than the adult system for bringing practice close to principle. Minibail reform acts and objective screening of flight risks deserve serious consideration for juveniles.

Experience with adult bail systems shows that an objective point system results in significantly higher proportions of release recommendations than do subjective recommendations by adult probation officers. The same would probably be true for juveniles. We have no reason yet to believe that a juvenile's flight potential is any greater than an adult's. Indeed, it should be less: the median age of detainees is fourteen, and they are unlikely to have money, transportation, or working papers. A child with no history of escapes or runaways is entitled to a considered presumption that pretrial conditions for release can be formulated.

It should not be difficult to fashion a set of daily checks on a youth who lives at home or in a supervised setting, goes to school or works, and can be required to report to a probation officer by telephone or in person. Even money bail may have a place among the conditions of release in the juvenile court. Approximately a dozen states now give juveniles a right to have bail set if they are not released on other conditions, but several prohibit money bail. Model acts and rules have traditionally eschewed it on the theory that it would make release dependent on family wealth, not on the best interests of the child and society (see, for example, President's Commission . . . 1967; *Vanderbilt Law Review* 1965). But in fact a cash deposit system requiring the juvenile to post his own money may serve as an insurance of appearance. Many teenagers make, spend, and have a true regard for their own money. If the real aim of release conditions is to guarantee juveniles' presence in court, compelling them to turn over their own funds or personal bank accounts until trial may indeed be a substantial inhibition to flight. It should, of course, be their money and not a compensated surety bond or even the parents' money. And it should never be set in an amount the juveniles cannot meet, lest we repeat the abuses of money bail in adult courts.

Response to Dangerous Juveniles

There is no responsible evidence to indicate that we know how to predict dangerous or violent behavior in a juvenile any more than we do in an adult. Yet juvenile courts have operated on the premise that they are authorized to detain for possible future criminal behavior. Typically, the kind of illegal behavior that warrants detention is not even specified; it could be any offense, from murder to marijuana. What few statistics we have show that only a small majority of juveniles in detention are charged with serious crimes involving violence to the person of others.

In the adult criminal courts a battle has raged over the past decade whether any defendant—and if so, who—can be "preventively detained." Only a very few jurisdictions—notably the District of Columbia—have a preventive detention law. After an initial flurry of activity in the District following enactment, the law has been used very sparingly. Its utility (aside from its constitutionality) is dubious. The law restricts detainable defendants to those accused of crimes of violence and requires for most a past crime of violence as well. The government, moreover, must show not only a "substantial probability" that the accused committed the charged offense but also that the subject will be a future danger to the community and that no conditions short of detention will avoid that danger. Detention, in any event, is limited to thirty days, and the law calls for speedy trials (*Harvard Civil Rights, Civil Liberties Law Review* 1971; Bases and McDonald 1972).

At an absolute minimum, analogous standards should govern preventive detention of juveniles. Crimes permitting detention should be the equivalent of a serious felony involving violence to others and the juvenile should have a past record of similar violence. Plainly there are dangerous juveniles; even the most ardent advocate of deinstitutionalization will concede that. Their numbers, however, are small. Juvenile courts should be compelled to define their criteria and to attempt to justify their determination that a juvenile is dangerous, even as we acknowledge the imprecision in any prediction of future dangerous conduct.

Handling of Status Offenders

In almost any detention facility, the majority of juveniles will be charged with no criminal conduct at all; they will be runaways, incorrigibles, PINS (persons in need of supervision)—youngsters beyond control. These status offenders are also held for the longest periods in detention. It is ironically and bitterly true that most lawbreakers can go back home but those who offend against their parents usually cannot. For years juvenile authorities have decried commingling of serious lawbreakers with merely wayward juveniles and recommended that the latter be placed in separate, open shelter settings (see National Advisory Commission ... 1973, p. 259; National Conference ... 1968; Uniform Juvenile Court Act, §16(a), pp. 258-59).

More recently, the effort has been to legislate or judicially rule status offenders out of secure detention homes and jails. There are pending proposals to remove status offenders from juvenile court jurisdiction altogether (Gough 1976). Realistically, this may be the only way to achieve the most desired result. Most runaways and children beyond control are victims of family malfunctioning; they and their families need counseling and, sometimes, a brief respite from one another. There are services that can be provided by a network of family crisis intervention facilities, small group residences, and runaway houses. We also know that PINS cases can be kept out of detention without adverse effect. Experience shows that runaways from their own homes do not automatically run away from a group or foster home. The incorrigible at home may become cooperative away from home, or even at home with help from knowledgeable family therapists. Three years ago, between 50 and 60 percent of New York City's detainees were PINS. Since then the city has moved aggressively to place PINS in open settings such as foster and group homes; now fewer than 5 percent of detainees are PINS (U.S. Congress, Senate 1973, pp. 304–5; see also Juvenile Justice and Delinquency Prevention Act of 1974, 42 U.S.C. §3723(10)(H)).

OVERLONG DETENTION

Long delays from arrest to trial, from trial to disposition, and from commitment to actual placement—these engender detention overloads. Half of all detained juveniles are held more than two weeks; some are detained for months (U.S. Congress, Senate 1973, p. 299; Ferster, Snethen, and Courtless 1969, pp. 187, 196). Detention will persist as a stagnant holding action until the subsequent stages of the process—trial and disposition—are reformed. It is not enough to reduce the time between the juvenile's arrest and trial if long delays continue from adjudication to disposition and from disposition to permanent placement.

Hard to place juveniles (retarded, hyperkinetic, brain-damaged, and emotionally disturbed) suffer the worst abuses of detention. For them, detention often is an easy substitute for permanent placement. Some courts, alert to this repugnant prospect, now apply the same "right to treatment" standards to long-term detention as they do to training schools (*Martarella* v. *Kelley,* 389 F. Supp. 478 [S.D.N.Y. 1973]).

The curse of juvenile courts has always been their lack of appropriate disposition resources for the variety of problem children they handle. The availability of detention facilities for holding juveniles indefinitely in lieu of a proper final placement thus has proved a convenient device for avoiding reform. Therefore, postadjudication and postdisposition detention must be strictly limited. After detention of (at most) a few weeks, release or transfer to a permanent placement should be mandatory. If a juvenile justice system in fact has no resources to treat or rehabilitate a juvenile, the dilemma ought to be faced in open court and the juvenile released, if no proper placement is possible. A juvenile judge should not be allowed to feed the illusion, by recommending a placement or committing to an agency, that something is actually going to happen if it is not. Deadlines and absolute bars to detention may seem arbitrary, yet it is striking how frequently detention personnel ask for such limitations, realizing that they cannot cope with an unending stream of detainees. Particularly if the traditional views of detention resist drastic reform, the best hope of reducing the detention over-population appears to be (1) substantive reformulation of the criteria applicable to flight risks and dangerous juveniles, (2) a flat ban on detention for status offenders, and (3) a time limit on pretrial and posttrial detention. The underlying assumption behind such efforts—one proved by experience—is that detention has no demonstrable salutary impact and should be limited to that irreducible minimum of juveniles who present a serious threat to the community or themselves.

Standards Relating to Interim Status: The Release, Control, and Detention of Accused Juvenile Offenders between Arrest and Final Disposition (Freed, Terrell, and Schultz 1976), approved by the IJA-ABA Juvenile Justice Standards Project, provides that detention be limited to cases of juveniles accused of serious crimes that would be punishable as an adult by over a year's imprison-ment and for which the juvenile is likely to be sent to a secure institution. In addition, the juvenile would have to have a recent record of willful failures to appear in court, serious threats to witnesses, or tampering with evidence or a recent record of serious personal violence while under court jurisdiction.

Detention would be limited to fifteen days from arrest to adjudication and fifteen days from adjudication to carrying out of disposition. Detention hearings would be held within twenty-four hours after arrest, and the juvenile must be represented by an attorney. The judge must file written reasons for detaining any child. At the end of seven days another hearing shall be held if the juvenile is still in detention. Prosecutors and judges who recom-mend and order detention must make periodic visits to the facility to assure that they know where they are sending juveniles. Weekly lists of juveniles who remain in detention and the reasons therefore must be given the court.

CONDITIONS OF DETENTION

The conditions under which juveniles are detained have peren-nially been the target of justified outrage (Sarri 1974; U.S.

Congress, Senate 1973). Hundreds of thousands of juveniles are still detained in local adult jails, sometimes segregated from adult offenders but often not. Over 90 percent of the jurisdictions have no separate juvenile detention facility at all. State laws may forbid juveniles in the same jail cell with adults, but only nine states, by statute or regulations, forbid juveniles in jail at all (National Advisory Commission . . . 1973, p. 258). The latter restraint is essential. A few courts have ruled that juveniles cannot be jailed, but the practice stubbornly persists, portending more juvenile suits under the Eighth Amendment ban on cruel and unusual punishment. In the words of one judge:

If the state cannot obtain the resources to detain persons awaiting trial in accordance with minimum constitutional standards, then the state simply will not be permitted to detain such persons (*Hamilton* v. *Love,* 328 F. Supp. 1182 [E.D. Ark. 1971]).

Most juvenile facilities, of course, are not significantly superior to jails. For decades, the National Council on Crime and Delinquency and other national organizations concerned with child welfare have been promulgating physical, program, and staffing standards for detention facilities (National Council . . . 1961). The most recent set of standards cut recommended populations down to thirty or less, and prescribed that they be coeducational and located within the community (National Advisory Commission . . . 1973, Standard 8.3, pp. 269–70). But "practical" needs and "lack of money" typically block implementation of standards. One reason for the blight in these facilities is that detention is almost entirely a local business (U.S. Congress, Senate 1973, p. 27) and resources to reform detention facilities are traditionally low on the list of priorities.

In recent years, despairing of success from citizen oversight commissions, national child care standard-setting groups, legislative committees, and even juvenile judges' pleas, the lawyers from legal service offices have taken to the courts demanding judicially mandated minimum standards for physical structures, staff, education, recreation, medical care, and programs in any facility holding children. Judicial decrees have banned censorship of mail, set flexible visiting hours, allowed access to lawyers, mandated education and recreation programs, medical and psychiatric care and adequately trained staff, and defined standards for isolation, discipline, and corporal punishment (see *Martarella* v. *Kelley,* 389 F. Supp. 478 [S.D.N.Y. 1973]).

Yet under ideal circumstances, detention will be difficult to administer constructively because of the transient population and the comparatively short duration of stay. Recruiting high-grade personnel to staff detention programs is not easy because staff-"inmate" contacts are brief and no long-term therapy or treatment is feasible. Good physical care, a program of productive activities, and some crisis counseling probably comprise the best attainable detention regimen. A few facilities have experimented with contracting for medical and psychiatric services from universities and training hospitals. These arrangements lessen isolation and allow more community surveillance of conditions inside the facilities. It is a truism that efforts to run a closed detention facility, providing all needed services from within, result in inferior personnel and services. Most educational and medical programs in detention facilities are poor in quality and isolated from the mainstream of services in the community. Affiliation with the professional and lay community and purchase of service arrangements offer some promise of improvement (U.S. Congress, Senate 1973, pp. 352–75).

Where the juvenile justice system is funded locally, the juvenile can usually anticipate regressive pretrial detention procedures. Since jail is the cheapest option, jail too often it is. At the least, state supervision and state subsidies are required to assure that juveniles are not penalized simply because of where they live (see National Advisory Commission ... 1973, Standards 9.2–9.3, pp. 292–95; Freed, Terrell, and Schultz 1976; Juvenile Justice and Delinquency Prevention Act of 1974, 42 U.S.C. §3723(10)(H)).

Experience strongly suggests that control over detention of a juvenile should be exercised by the same agency which has supervision over pretrial release. While secure detention, almost inevitably, will be a holding action, pretrial release has infinitely more possibilities. Where juveniles cannot be released unconditionally to their parents, it can provide the opportunity to test various living arrangements, to begin voluntary counseling and peer or family therapy, to diagnose and correct medical and dental defects, and to construct a package of services the juvenile needs and wants so that the court at disposition will have practical and realistic alternatives to incarceration in most cases.

Although such a juvenile pretrial services agency could be administered by the courts or by an independent executive agency, there is a case to be made for integration of pretrial and corrections processes in a single agency where the agency is committed to a program emphasizing deinstitutionalization and community-based services. A few states, such as Massachusetts and Florida, already are testing this joinder of functions. In Massachusetts, detention cannot exceed fifteen days without court approval; shelter care units housing from ten to twelve juveniles have been set up or contracted for (several in YMCAs) throughout the state; foster care for detention cases has been enlarged; court liaisons from the state agency have been placed in the juvenile courts to institute community planning from the point of arrest (Massachusetts Department of Youth Services 1973; Ohlin, Coates, and Miller 1974).

This strategy of course presupposes that the state correctional agency is prepared to trust or hazard placement of juveniles in noninstitutional settings in their own communities, using daytime programs, small group and foster homes, purchase of service arrangements for individual, group, and family therapy, specialized vocational and academic programs, and the like. In such a "new corrections" system, control over pretrial services means simply that the process of matching juvenile to program begins at the earliest possible stage. Rationally administered, bringing the full range of community resources to bear, the process should be able to reduce to a minimum the number of juveniles committed to secure detention.

A NEW CONCEPT OF DETENTION

It can also be argued that the conventional concept of juvenile pretrial release and detention is overdue for reexamination. We have too often and too long applied the adult postarrest model to juveniles. We assume that the period preceding trial is one in which the status quo is not to be altered; activity is devoted primarily to preparation for trial; the accused is presumed innocent and any attempt at rehabilitation is thus postponed. Yet the statistics of the juvenile justice system show that only a minute percentage of juvenile arrests ever go to trial or disposition at all.

What would happen if those at the head of the system—police, intake workers, judges at detention hearings—accepted the fact that, in the vast majority of cases, their actions and their decisions will be the only real help (or sanction) that the system will inflict on or offer to the juvenile? Would they then conceive of their roles differently and make different decisions? Police who now berate the rest of the system because the juveniles they arrest "are right back on the street again within an hour" would have to face up to the reality that in all but the very serious cases, the function of their arrest was itself merely to be a form of crisis intervention to cool an immediate situation. They should not expect it to initiate a process of removal and judicial sanctioning of the juvenile for individual behavior. The buck would then be passed to the communities in which they serve to find other means to discourage unacceptable behavior and to create ways of preventing such behavior or guarding against its effects. Such an acknowledgment runs the risk, of course, of producing vigilantism or illegal police behavior "to teach the kid a lesson" (some of which goes on today), but it might also divert police energies and talent from lamenting the acknowledged inefficiencies of the rest of the system to working with communities to handle all but the most serious offenders on their own turf.

As to other participants in the system, assuming the aim of juvenile justice is still therapeutic and not punitive, the postarrest period might also be considered as crisis intervention rather than as merely a pretrial period.

The arrest or apprehension is the crisis; its immediate aftermath is a crucial event for most juveniles and for society in dealing with their problems. A crisis-intervention model would, with the juvenile's consent, use this postarrest period to assay endemic problems of school, family, or peer relationships that may have triggered the incident that culminated in arrest. Such an approach echoes the venerable (if currently challenged) juvenile court philosophy that it is not the offense but the child's underlying problems that must concern society. The old model, however, contemplated that the juvenile court hearing itself would be the therapeutic agent. The working of the system betrays this model: either the hearing never materializes or it is an episode, concluded in moments, occurring weeks or even months after the trauma of arrest. It is a haunting experience to watch the shock of juveniles who have been caught up in routines following arrest, perhaps for many months, when they are finally punished for something which, in their perspective, happened long ago to a different person. Any perception of cause and effect is lost, and so is the opportunity to change the juvenile under the stress of crisis.

Perhaps it is time to alter the system like this: to use the postarrest period to help juveniles in the same way that we, in theory, now help them after adjudication—if they want help. Thus juveniles, on advice of counsel, might of course prefer to go down the legal track all the way, betting on ultimate vindication. If they did not so choose, however, the system might just as well attack their problems sooner rather than later, on the assumption that in all but a small minority of cases there will be no trial or disposition at all. Even if there is, the juveniles should, except in a small number of extreme cases, stay in the community and be provided the services needed to stay out of future trouble.

If we were to shift to this kind of crisis-intervention model, the most skilled and best trained interveners and therapists (including lawyers) ought to be on the spot at police stations and in places where juveniles are taken following arrest. Their numbers should be sufficient to provide personalized attention to juveniles and their families. In no event would juveniles be shut away in isolation for hours after the high-tension incident of arrest. They and their families should be worked with intensively.

In such a setup, crisis intervention would still have to accommodate due process. Juveniles still have legal "rights" to release if they are not substantial flight risks or dangerous to others according to the stricter criteria proposed here, regardless of their needs for therapy (except, possibly, for a brief counseling interview). Plainly, most juveniles can be worked with better if they are released to their homes or community-based substitutes rather than locked up. Even where the juveniles meet *prima facie* detention criteria, trained crisis personnel would have the discretion to release them pending a prompt court hearing.

There are dangerous juveniles. There are panicked and psychotic juveniles. Anyone's reactions in a crisis may be bizarre and violent. Yet many of these same juveniles, if handled expertly, can quickly be calmed. Skilled counselors can sense within a short time whether the juvenile has settled down and can be safely released to parents or into an open setting of some kind. They can relay this information (but nothing about the alleged offense itself) to the judge at a detention hearing held within twenty-four hours, or they can release the juvenile with a summons to appear in court at a certain time. They can also advise the judge on what kinds of controls or supports they think are necessary to hold the juvenile in line until trial or for a finite probationary-diversionary period (after which discharge will presumably follow) and how these supports will be given if the youth is released into the community. The judge still decides at the detention hearing whether to release the juvenile into the community or whether she or he must stay in a controlled setting. And in any instance when the juvenile is detained, a definite trial date should be set. Most important, to satisfy due process, the judge should determine whether there was probable cause for arrest. Society has not yet given juvenile courts the power to gratuitously treat juveniles who have not committed an offense!

Under this crisis intervention model, if a juvenile is detained, the remand should not hold until trial; it should expire whenever the counselor, or whoever supervises the case, feels the child can be released. The court should obtain a tentative time frame from the counselor at the outset and weekly progress reports. The juvenile's defense counsel should have access to the reports and opportunity to challenge them. To test dependability, the juvenile can be given daytime and weekend release, home visits, work and school release. The juvenile would receive, if they were needed and wanted, services during the pretrial period with a goal of successful adjustment within the community without major eruption or flight.

The alternatives to judicial process (diversion) would be investigated, and charges against the juvenile could be formally dropped if there appeared to be real progress solving the problems that led to delinquency. The crisis intervention model should require, as well, that counselors work with the juvenile's family and other community contacts to structure a plan that would reduce new risks of flight or repeat offenses.

The runaways, beyond control cases, PINS, and status offenders, as long as they remain in the system (cf. Andrews and Cohn 1974), would be the most obvious beneficiaries of a crisis intervention approach. The police typically do not feel threatened by these children—rather they tend to sympathize with them. The police resort to detention only because they have no safe place to take such juveniles. In some jurisdictions, the law requires the police to deliver all young offenders who cannot be released to their parents to the detention home where the court probation worker is on duty. A crisis intervention model would give the police more leeway by allowing them to deliver juveniles to any one of a number of approved crisis intervention centers, runaway houses, temporary lodgings, shelter residences, hospitals, or drug abuse centers. In these places, personnel would take charge of juveniles and arrange to interview their families as well as to make further decisions about temporary home substitutes, family counseling, drug treatment, or other procedures designed to overcome the crisis. If the proposed course were opposed by the juvenile or the parents, the case would be dropped altogether or scheduled for court. If no petition were filed, the court worker could not involve the juvenile or the parents in any programs against their will. If there were a petition, the crisis plan would have to be approved by the juvenile's counsel or the judge. The goal should always be to solve the problem before resort to trial.

It is difficult to predict how much improvement would result from such a crisis intervention model. The process does propose a major change by allowing the police a more differentiated response at the beginning of the crisis; it introduces treatment where the juveniles and their families desire it—at the earliest possible stage; it involves skilled crisis interveners in postarrest settings. As could happen with any system, its fundamental objective could be aborted by lack of skilled people and resources. Moreover, if a full-scale trial was likely, defense counsel might object to any form of pretrial therapy, not only because of the possibility of incriminating disclosures to therapists, but also because of possible conflict in the child's loyalties between therapist and counsel. Confidentiality would have to be guaranteed.

The crisis intervention model admittedly continues a treatment orientation of the juvenile process. This orientation is currently under attack by juvenile court revisionists who, on the basis of past failures to treat and abuses of juveniles' civil rights in the name of treatment, would prefer to conform the process more nearly to the adult criminal model. They want finite sentences to be served in secure settings or in the community on a punishment rationale; no obligation to offer juveniles special rehabilitative help; no pretense of individualization of disposition. If such an approach were adopted, it would focus pretrial programs primarily on due process rights to release or bail, rather than on individual help for any crisis.

While I recognize that the system has indeed been guilty in the past of sins of overreaching and unnecessary intrusions into family life, I am not yet convinced that it is preferable to abandon any attempts to assist juveniles, especially at the beginning of the process, when it may be possible to avoid adjudication. The problem of monitoring help so that it does not become tyranny will always be with us, but punishment-oriented personnel and systems seem to offer the same potential for abuse of juveniles as do insensitive helping personnel and systems—without much benefit in exchange for the risk.

The crisis intervention model suggested here might help to resolve the days following arrest into a more focused and con-structive period, one tailored to the juvenile's needs and not simply dead time before a trial that may never come. And in the event of a trial, the suggested pretrial procedures would give the judge a record of real experience to draw upon at the time of final disposition, and would, I hope, make a dispositional decision a part of a process of change already begun. Whether the change in orientation would amount to more than juggling concepts is impossible to predict. We do seem to need a theory and function for the postarrest period that more nearly accommodates the reality that the vast majority of juveniles will never go to trial, as well as one that fits better into a community-based corrections program.

CONCLUSION

Juvenile detention needs a new focus and a new rationale. The detention period ought to be used to begin to draw together resources necessary for constructive change, whether or not the juvenile is adjudicated. There is abundant evidence that detention has failed as an isolated interlude between those more dramatic parts of the juvenile justice system—arrest and trial or dis-position.

The juvenile judge still has a vital function to fulfill in detention. The judge is charged with the solemn determination whether to deprive juveniles of liberty or whether they can be released in their parents' custody or to a third party and, if so, what conditions should apply to the release. In making such a decision the judge should follow due process hearing procedures and the legal presumption should favor release. If the decision is to detain, the judge must make a record to support that decision. The legality of preventive detention in the juvenile court needs to be tested. If the power is upheld, the procedural safeguards should be as precise as they are for adults. We should abandon the notion that secure detention is good for the child.

Some legal absolutes seem imperative: jail for juveniles should be outlawed; status offenders should not be put into secure detention; finite limits should be set on how long a child can be detained before or after adjudication; minimum standards for physical structure, staff, and program should be enforced by the courts. Even then, we should not cease inquiring whether there are yet better and more enlightened ways to use the interlude after arrest to help juveniles so that, unless they are innocent, or so blighted that removal from the community before or after trial is an almost indisputable necessity, there may be no need for the rest of the process at all.

BIBLIOGRAPHY

American Bar Association, Project on Minimum Standards for Criminal Justice. 1968. *Standards Relating to Pretrial Release.* New York: Office of Criminal Justice Project, Institute of Judicial Administration.

Andrews, R. Hale, Jr., and Cohn, Andrew H. 1974. "Ungovernability: The Unjustifiable Jurisdiction." *Yale Law Journal* 83:1383–1409.

Bases, Nan C., and McDonald, William F. 1972. *Preventive Detention in the District of Columbia: The First Ten Months.* New York: Vera Institute of Justice.

Beale, David. 1973. *Juvenile Justice in New Jersey.* Princeton, N.J.: Center for Analysis of Public Issues.

Ferster, Elyce Zenoff; Snethen, Edith Nash; and Courtless, Thomas F. 1969. "Juvenile Detention: Protection, Prevention or Punishment?" *Fordham Law Review* 38:161–96.

Freed, Daniel J.; Terrell, Timothy; and Schultz, J. Lawrence. 1976. *Standards Relating to Interim Status: The Release, Control, and Detention of Accused Juvenile Offenders between Arrest and Final Disposition.* Cambridge, Mass.: Ballinger.

Gough, Aidan R. 1976. *Standards Relating to Non-criminal Misbehavior.* Cambridge, Mass.: Ballinger.

Harvard Civil Rights, Civil Liberties Law Review. "Preventive Detention: An Empirical Analysis." 1971. 6:300–96.

Massachusetts Department of Youth Services. 1973. *Annual Report.* Boston.

National Advisory Commission on Criminal Justice Standards and Goals. Task Force on Corrections. 1973. *Corrections.* Washington, D.C.: U.S. Government Printing Office.

National Conference of Commissioners on Uniform State Laws. 1968. *Handbook of the National Conference of Commissioners on Uniform State Laws and Proceedings of the Annual Conference Meeting in its Seventy-Seventh Year, Philadelphia, Pennsylvania, July 22 to August 1, 1968.* Chicago: National Conference of Commissioners on Uniform State Laws. Pp. 248–89.

National Council on Crime and Delinquency. 1961. *Standards and Guides for the Detention of Children and Youth.* 2d ed. New York.

Ohlin, Lloyd E.; Coates, Robert B.; and Miller, Alden D. 1974. "Radical Correctional Reform: A Case Study of the Massachusetts Youth Correctional System." *Harvard Educational Review* 44:74–111.

President's Commission on Law Enforcement and Administration of Justice. 1967. *Task Force Report: Corrections.* Washington, D.C.: U.S. Government Printing Office.

Sarri, Rosemary C. 1974. *Under Lock and Key: Juveniles in Jails and Detention.* Ann Arbor: University of Michigan.

U.S. Congress, Senate. 1973. *The Detention and Jailing of Juveniles.* Hearings before the Subcommittee to Investigate Juvenile Delinquency of the Committee on the Judiciary, 93d Cong. 1st sess.

Vanderbilt Law Review. "The Right to Bail and the Pre-'Trial' Detention of Juveniles Accused of 'Crime.'" 1965. 18:2096–2109.

Wald, Patricia M. 1972. "The Right to Bail Revisited: A Decade of Promise without Fulfillment." In *The Rights of the Accused in Law and Action,* ed. Stuart Nagle. Berkeley Hills, Calif.: Sage Publications.

7   Perspectives on Juvenile Probation

Charles H. Shireman

Intellectual revolutions tend to break out in the United States at the point in history at which they become safe. Then only modest courage on the part of dissidents—including the present writer—is required to mount bruising attacks upon major, previously invulnerable institutions. So it is at the present time with juvenile probation, a daring innovation in the decades just before and after the opening of the last century helped usher in the modern era in child welfare. The succeeding years have seen probation become a dominant reality in the lives of many thousands of the nation's young people.

During the 1960s and the early 1970s, however, probation and other institutionalized helping services have fallen under widespread attack as being futile at best, and possibly detrimental in their impact upon the child. Perhaps it is in the nature of things that the most severe condemnation of the practice comes from those who view the system from without—those who have never known and thus would disavow the existence of the enormous richness that (in at least some cases) can pervade the helping relationship in probation. Nonetheless, not even its most ardent defenders can deny that probation service to a juvenile court clientele remains, after some seven decades of practice, a concept lofty in intent but still lacking either a clear definition of its reasonable goals, an adequate theory and knowledge base, or a methodology that is generally agreed and understood, much less one that has been subjected to systematic empirical verification. New and competing theories about intervention in the lives of human beings constantly arise. Differences of opinion among the proponents are met by the erection of ever more dazzling pyramids of intellectual analysis resting upon vague and impressionistic data, or by superior advocacy and competing charismas. Such methods of debate may be appropriate to theological issues; they are not likely to lead to resolution of empirical questions such as whether, or under what circumstances, a given model for intervention with a child and family does or does not produce a desired result. It is the purpose of this paper to suggest some of the dimensions of the mission of juvenile probation, and to examine the degree to which an appropriate methodology is at hand.

Recent critical analysis of the American juvenile court has focused mainly on jurisdiction, due process, and procedural fairness. These are issues of great import, but it may well be that further clarification of questions of justice must await the solution of problems concerning probation and probation-related services. Procedural fairness is essential to protect the child and to preserve the integrity of the juvenile system. But preoccupation with this goal may obscure the issue that most determines the welfare of the child—what happens as a result of the jurisdictional ruling. It is true that some scholars have considerable faith that evident, scrupulous fairness at the court hearing will assist in bridging the gap between the child and the demands of conforming society, but, realistically, such contribution must be modest.

At the gut level, children before the court (usually quite correctly) perceive their behavior as the product of a tangled network of circumstance dominated by long years of injustices. But they alone are hauled before the bar of justice. The sins and crimes that produced them are left untouched. They can hardly be expected to regard as anything but a cruel hoax an elaborate system that places its entire emphasis upon whether they did commit an illegal act. At best, such a system will seem to provide only the barest beginning of justice. The problem dominating all

others is to find a way out of the entangling network of circumstance of which the alleged offense is only part.

Recognizing these facts, the early framers of the juvenile court
arrived at pertinent legal postulates that rest to a considerable
extent on assumptions that the socio-psychological task defined
by almost all juvenile court statutes can be performed. Thus the
errant child will be helped to grow toward responsible citizenship.
The provision of help, under the enabling authority of the court,
is the task of a wide range of community services. Proponents of
the court early recognized, however, that juvenile court judges
required more than the voluntarily provided—or in the case of the
delinquent, all too often withheld—services generally available in
the community. They needed agents at their disposition who
could carry out programs calculated to change the children and
their life situations. In short, juvenile court judges needed a
probation arm. That arm is now generally supplied. The question
whether the court may be reasonably expected to accomplish its
loftily defined goal depends largely on how far the faith placed in
probation's potential is justified.

A HIERARCHY OF PROBATION MISSIONS
The assumption has been that the probation caseload consists
almost entirely of a hard core of youngsters whose violative
behavior demonstrates their personal or social maladjustment
and the need for aggressive intervention in their lives. The
existence of some unknown proportion of such youngsters within
the probationer group cannot be doubted, but the notion that
their existence proves that all identified delinquents can use
services calculated to impose radical change upon their personal
or social adjustments simply does not survive close scrutiny.
Indeed, if violative behavior indicates the need for such intervention, we would have to step into the lives of most of our
country's young people, for most of them have violated the law.
In a recent careful survey of a national probability sample of
thirteen- to sixteen-year-olds, 88 percent of them reported having
committed violations for which they could have been adjudicated
delinquent, although only 3 percent of such acts were detected by
police and only 2 percent of the youngsters had ever been under
judicial consideration (Williams and Gold 1972). Such data
suggest the wisdom of using a variety of responses to the

delinquent child involved with the juvenile and criminal justice system, from a carefully disciplined hands-off policy to a range of more active interventions.

Probation's Latent Function

It is possible, of course, that probation's major contribution to the child lies in its unacknowledged but enormously important latent function: the provision to the court of a dispositional resource giving the appearance that something has been done without the necessity of committing the juvenile to an institution. The hurt and therefore hurtful child is all too often the object of community fears, anger, and desire for retribution. Thus, in the name of "help" or "rehabilitation" he or she may be separated from the mainstream of society; branded as "sick," "deviant," and frightening; used under theories of general deterrence as an object lesson to frighten others; and subjected to punitive assaults that disregard the child's very humanity. There may be pressing necessity for a device whose major function is simply to limit the penetration of the child into the juvenile or criminal justice system—and in so doing to offer protection from a vengeful society. This latent function perhaps could not survive public scrutiny, but it may well operate whether or not a more active service to the child is provided. After all, while the limited evidence suggests that probation may achieve success rates as high or higher than those achieved by incarceration, it is not at all clear that even less active intervention—fines, suspended sentences, or even simple discharge—would not yield equally favorable results (Hood and Sparks 1970; Klapmuts 1973). But the need to take some action as a means of retaining public confidence in the juvenile justice system remains.

A Peacemaker Role

A few veteran practitioners have, in recent years, suggested a further mission for probation, more active than benign neglect but still short of trying to reconstruct the child's basic life patterns. In a significant proportion of cases, the probation officer may operate simply to help the child and community learn to tolerate each other. Most juvenile lawbreakers—or, in other words, most juveniles—do get along without justice system intervention. Although they may not be wholly at peace with their communities, they are not at war with them, either. The creation or restoration of such detente may be a reasonable goal for many youngsters drawn into the juvenile justice system. In at least a part of their endeavors, veteran probation officers seem to be engaged in a series of Kissinger-like excursions between two hostile camps—the youngster and the dominant social institutions of the community. One goal of such endeavors is to help the youngster avoid bugging the police, the school, and the community quite so much. Old hands at probation and parole speak of helping the child "slide"—slide between the conflicting demands of family, school, police, the frequently highly delinquent peer group, personal gratification needs, and a variety of other competing pressures. At the same time, officers may be engaged in helping teachers, police, and others either tolerate youth more readily or assess with more realistic humility the sufficiency of available resources to coerce behavioral change. The possible benefits of such endeavors should not be lightly dismissed. It is at least possible that positive personal or institutional change may take place if energies are not exhausted in the sort of warfare that can bring victory to no one.

More Positive Intervention

For all the foregoing, no social institution charged with doing something to or about youngsters can rest content with a definition of its function as "benign neglect" or with seeing itself as a sort of smoke screen protecting the child from society's primitive retributive urges. Something more will be done—and for many of our charges a great deal more needs to be done. It is the further definition of that "something more" that must preoccupy us. Presumably, most students would agree that the generally agreed mission of probation—as of other elements of the criminal justice system—is intervention sufficiently active to protect the community against further law violations. However, the juvenile court is under the strongest injunction to accomplish this end, whenever possible, so as to enhance the best interest of the child, and many would argue that accomplishing the social protection goal is generally impossible unless the helping goal can first be achieved.

It is largely in its responsibility to provide positive help that the juvenile court differs from other courts dealing with law violators. The criminal court has long been charged to dispose of the violator so as to produce behavioral change, but the mechanisms available to the law have traditionally been those of incapacitation and deterrence. Either individuals are detained or supervised to make their continuing law violations impossible, or such behavior is deterred by creating in the individual and in other potential violators a perception that it will result in discomfort. The major change process relied upon is that of compliance, resulting largely from fear. The juvenile court, on the other hand, has long considered itself charged to develop other change-producing mechanisms. The child is to be helped to identify with the law-abiding community, to internalize new value systems, and to achieve perceptions of nonviolative life styles as being inherently more appealing and satisfying. Such children, and usually their families, are to be helped to increase their abilities to cope with the problems confronting them. At the same time, they are to be provided increased opportunity for legitimate success.

The desirability of the court's arranging for help to enhance the child's capacity to cope is contested by few students of the juvenile court, either pre- or post-*Gault*. This also holds for the notion that society should provide the child an opportunity structure bringing gratification for desired behavior. What is ever more insistently questioned is the feasibility of assigning such a task to a court probation service.

It must be admitted that the realities of much present probation practice suggest that the feasibility has not to date been convincingly demonstrated. While practice varies enormously, many courts seem to operate on an assumption that meaningful service to youngsters is assured simply by including them in the unmanageably large caseload of a staff member without discernible qualifications for intervening usefully in the lives of other human beings. Thus the national study of corrections made in 1966 for the President's Commission on Law Enforcement and Administration of Justice (1967) revealed that in a national sample of probation departments, median caseload size (cases actually under supervision) was between seventy-one and eighty. This would obviously allow an average of only a few minutes a month for meetings between officer and the child and family. Only 4 percent of the departments in the sample required any sort of graduate professional training as a condition of employment. Agreement upon any other qualifications—other than "good moral character"—is far from universal. Such a situation may present a facade of service but it will not make for much substance. Yet we continue to punish with increased severity the recidivist who violates probation "in spite of all the help given."

The most common response to such criticisms of probation's performance is a demand for more staff to lower caseloads. Occasionally, this is accompanied by a vague assertion that intensified staff training might also be desirable. Seldom is an even more fundamental problem elucidated: we do not now have a clearly expressed and generally accepted conceptual framework for probation practice. The injunction, "Help the child achieve a nonviolative, productive way of life," is no more useful a guide to action than is the exhortation of the army officer, "Overwhelm and annihilate the enemy." In probation, there is little agreement upon basic strategies, much less upon how to implement them. Strong goal expectations without ways to achieve them can result within probation staffs, as elsewhere, in normlessness, frustration, defensiveness, and aggressiveness toward presumed detractors.

Most present proposals for restructuring probation practice seem to cluster at one extreme or the other of a continuum ranging from concern with changing the attitudes, understandings, and behavior patterns of the individual offender, to preoccupation with the need to change society generally. Realistically, a position at either of these extremes is untenable. A concern for change solely between the two ears of the offender simply fails to recognize the vital role of external reality in determining behavior. An exclusive focus on change in the environment fails to take account of the wide variety of ways in which individuals cope with given situations. It also fails to consider how effective juvenile courts and probation departments are likely to be as launching pads for the revolution. As underfunded and uninfluential parts of the established order, they have no footing from which to attack social injustice, even though delinquent behavior often seems to be a response to society's failings.

The tendency for practitioners and theorists to cluster at the extremes of "individual therapy" or "social change" seems to stem partly from the state of theory about origins of delinquent behavior (Schur 1973). One group of theorists stresses its intrapsychic and intrafamilial etiology, while another points to the injustices and deprivations arising from a social system which denies many young people achievement of societally implanted success goals. Each of these positions points to important facets of truth, but in their prevalent forms they are little help to the practitioner in the field. As usually stated, they are mutually contradictory, probably because each is based on observations of only part of the whole. In attempting to understand behavior, the practitioner is obliged to draw eclectically upon various theories. In addition, contemporary delinquency theory provides few guidelines for action. Most is etiological, not practice theory. In fact, to the extent that it does suggest active goals, it tends to reinforce a common practitioner failing: it seems to point to intervention on an almost Messianic scale, calling for frontal assault on the total personality structure, or on fundamental socio-economic problems, or on the whole human condition.

The present need, then, is for a conception of the probation mission that does not require assault upon all the life problems of the enormous number of young people annually referred to the American juvenile court, but one that would manage to contribute to the child's nonviolent reintegration into the community. The task is not easy. In the present state of conceptual development, it is important not to move prematurely toward forming a grand theory of probation practice. But more modest steps toward the definition of goals, tasks, and methods would seem possible. Taking them may contribute to the long period of empirical research and validation that inevitably lies ahead.

An Intervention Model

The term "probation" is used in two widely differing ways—as a legally created status imposed by a court, and as a service system provided by a probation officer or department. Clarification of both meanings is necessary to constructing any helpful model for contemporary practice. Thus, the model suggested here would include the following elements.

1. A probation status. The imposition by the court of a probation status should be seen not as the assumption of major responsibility for intervention on the part of the court but rather as a simple formalization of the fact that legally defined limits upon behavior have been transgressed, that the individual (and, in

the case of the child, her or his family) have been apprised of the results of further such transgression, and that the responsibility for avoiding further violations is the child's and family's. The prime necessity is for honesty in the manner in which the court and its staff help children perceive the nature of society's concerns for them and for social protection, the precise nature of the demand imposed upon them, and the probable consequences of failure to respond to such a demand. A degree of surveillance may be ordered. The realistic limits of this device must be recognized, but it should also be clear that some degree of surveillance may actually represent—and may be seen by the child as representing—a positive concern for the child. It has long been evident to sensitive practitioners that many young people quite logically expect such a function to be performed and interpret lack of surveillance as lack of concern for them or as a sign that the social institution with which they are dealing is impotent and to be disdained.

2. An offer of further help. Under the model here suggested (which owes much to Reid and Epstein 1972), from the very beginning of the probation process, society's concern about children would be further manifested by the offer of any pertinent help available to them. Such an offer will involve the exploration of the degree to which the children perceive problems for which they wish help. But probation service (other than that of the more limited sorts earlier suggested) would revolve about the help, if any, that children and their families say they want after having had the opportunity to think through their needs and deliberate regarding available services. As a part of this process, the probation officer's responsibility most certainly includes the expression of concern and of professional judgment concerning the alternative courses of behavior available and their probable consequences. Confrontation with reality is a part of the decision-making process, as is the challenging of seemingly unwise decisions. But the ultimate decision to engage or not to engage in problem-solving effort is the probationer's. Further, when and if it is decided that a problem exists upon which work is needed, the nature of that work will also be arrived at by a process shared between the helper and the helped. Here the concept of the performance contract may be valuable: early in the process, an attempt will be made to arrive at (and perhaps even to reduce to

writing) a clear statement of the nature of the problem to be tackled, the specific problem-solving task accepted by each partner to the endeavor, and the precise outcome to be striven for.

The model here presented finds its justification in part on ethical grounds noted in later paragraphs of this chapter, but it also derives from the general inadequacy of our track record to date in coercing attitudinal and behavioral change. Dedication to healthy realism demands reexamination of what often seems to be a widely prevalent, uncritically accepted illusion of omnipotence. Somehow, this illusion suggests that the court, the probation officer, or somebody, should be able to produce major changes in the personalities, the life situations, and the behavior of almost anybody, if only enough resources and will were addressed to the problem. All available evidence suggests that this is simply not true. We may help many individuals to assess the reality of their situations and the probable consequences of their behavior. We may bring some resources to bear on their problem-solving efforts. But we can compel very little change. Thus, expectations that we should cover a department's caseload with intensive and protracted services to all clients at all times, accepting responsibility for all outcomes, do not accord with reality.

It appears realistic, however, to accept an assumption that many acting-out, delinquent youth (including those from inner-city areas from whence the majority of the court's caseload comes) are quite aware of their problems of social functioning and that they want help. It further appears that they will accept and use such help from institutions of conventional society. It is almost fashionable in recent years to question this. It is said that representatives of the court will inevitably be perceived as allied with the enemy and that the probationers' ideal solution would be to get the authorities off their backs. There is at least some empirical evidence that this assessment is quite wrong. Two small-scale studies by Shireman and others (Shireman et al. 1972, 1973) of randomly drawn samples of adolescent male probationers from deprived inner-city areas revealed a high degree of awareness of problems for which help was wanted and needed, and showed generally favorable opinions among the boys of their probation officers as helping persons. Similarly, Maher and Stein (1968) report in a larger study that adjudicated delinquents from an inner-city area tended to perceive their probation officers positively as persons interested in and sympathetic to them. In a third quite ambitious study reported by Gottesfeld (1965), another large sample of inner-city delinquents included among their choices of treatment methods the provision of help with concrete problems and the use of an almost parent-surrogate approach stressing true concern about them combined with realistic confrontation with the probable results of violative behavior. These findings come as no surprise to experienced, thoughtful practitioners, one of whom has remarked to me, "The kids want help all right—they are going down for the third time, and they know it."

3. Problems in social functioning. In the model here suggested, it is contemplated that most problems presented can best be perceived as problems in social functioning impeding individuals in their strivings to secure normal and necessary life gratifications. Such problems lie at the intersection between personality and environment. They are approachable not solely as matters of psyche or social environment, but as a field of interaction where personality and environment intersect. Thus, for example, a target problem may be school functioning. The problem-solving tasks may include change both in a youngster's school-related behavior and in the way the educational system confronts the child. It is the person–environment transaction that is of concern. Further, the emphasis is upon the behaviors of the participants in such interactions, with feelings, attitudes, and intrapsychic processes becoming a target for change only as they emerge in the particular behaviors that are of concern.

Also involved is the realization that the helping process in probation goes far beyond the sort of dyadic relationship traditionally envisioned. Basic to probation's methodology are techniques for (1) service brokerage, or the skilled mustering of all available resources pertinent to the target problem; (2) advocacy, calculated to help the clients achieve equity in their interrelationships with community institutions and services; and (3) counseling of various sorts, individual or group, to help identify and explore the problem, to help decide on tasks necessary for its resolution, and to enhance and make use of the fullest capabilities of the individual. Such patterns will necessarily involve providing help from a much broader platform than is possible for a single probation officer assigned sole responsibility for carrying a caseload. Group and family counseling may be provided; the probationer may attend day care centers, some of which provide remedial education or vocational training or both; and juveniles for whom continued residence with families does not seem wise may be placed in foster or group homes.

Probation Diagnosis

Under the sort of reality-based model here envisioned, probation diagnosis will focus first not on the intrapsychic life of the child, not on the etiology of behavior, not on culture-group identifications and pressures, but on the person to be helped as a potential partner in a process of problem solving. The diagnostic questions thus become, as Ripple suggests (Ripple, Alexander, and Polemis 1964), Can the helper and the helped arrive together at a common definition of a problem to be worked upon? Do the probationers have, or can they be helped to achieve, the motivation necessary to the problem-solving effort? Do they have the physical, mental, and emotional capacities necessary to problem solving? Are the resources necessary to realistic opportunity structure for problem solving at hand, or can they be made available?

To illustrate, under "motivation" we assess (1) the degree of discomfort probationers experience about the problems and the degree of hope that solutions may be possible (we speak of the push of discomfort and the pull of hope); (2) the extent to which probationers perceive their own role in problem-creation and thus the necessity for playing a role in its solution; and (3) the degree to which possible solutions envisioned are realistic. In considering "capacity" we are concerned with whether the requisite physical energy and intellectual ability are available to cope with the problem at hand. Also important is emotional capacity, as indicated by ability to perceive, talk about, and deal realistically with the emotional components of the problem. "Opportunity" includes the external economic, educational, and similar sources of support or stress, and the degree to which necessary support systems exist (or can be developed) in the family, in the peer group, and in the services of the community.

Short-term, Crisis-related Service

While some youngsters require and others can use the sort of long-term, sustaining relationship with fairly intensive contacts over a considerable period of time, such cases are probably infrequent exceptions in probation service. Great emphasis will be placed upon short-term, intensive help, rather than long-term, open-ended treatment. Considerable use will be made of emerging concepts of crisis-related casework service (Cunningham 1973). The probation officer often makes contact with his clients at a period of extreme crisis, when their usual adaptive abilities may prove inadequate. At such point, response to an offer to restore equilibrium may be particularly positive. Successful crisis resolution may lead to new coping abilities and new person-environmental relationships. What is contemplated here is the probability of long periods during which the client may be on probation but with infrequent and less intensive contact. For many probationers, however, there will be periods of intensive worker–client engagement when real and pressing problems can be agreed on and given concentrated effort.

The Need for Knowledge and Theory

Admittedly, the realities of practice that will arise from the proposed probation model have not been systematically explored. Like other critics of prevailing practice, the writer has yielded to the temptation to present an ideal, pristine and free from the complexities, irrationalities, and bureaucratic inanities that inevitably appear when any theoretical formulation emerges into large-scale operation in the real world. But bits and pieces of the sort of practice here suggested have long existed, and the model probably describes much of what many probation officers now are doing, often with great dedication and true practice wisdom. Such doing must find its way into the literature and provide the basis for the long, hard accumulation of empirical research that will replace doctrine with knowledge. The theoretical base that presently exists to support the proposed model is incomplete and undeveloped. It assumes that providing assistance toward the immediate solution of urgent problems in social functioning may be one way (or perhaps the only available way) of approaching whatever the life problem of the individual may be. But it leaves undefined the nature and etiology of such life problems and does not ask whether such etiology lies in cultural or psychological phenomena. Nor does it specify a theory of attitudinal and behavioral change. Such specification would be desirable, of course. As Reid and Epstein (1972) so cogently observe, it may be true that there is nothing so practical as a good theory, but in this field a good theory is hard to find. The model does suggest a focus for the problem-solving endeavor and indicates possible reasonable limits for it. In doing so it may contribute to the beginning of a true practice theory.

A VALUE BASE
Fundamental to the position taken in this chapter is a postulate that the state should intervene authoritatively in the lives of children and families only when imperative. This limitation is in part pragmatic, because positive change in the attitudes, behavior, or social situations of offenders is generally difficult to impose, and attempts to do so seem tragically often to do more harm than good. But reticence rests upon an ethical base, as well. Human dignity and human freedom are paramount values, to be curbed for the individual only when necessary to the preservation of the freedom of all. Coercion can be justified only to support the social protection purpose, not the treatment goal, of the juvenile justice system. It may well be, however, that the most pressing and challenging questions confronting the system are those that arise from attempts to put into operation so noble a philosophy. Under what circumstances, if any, are sanctions justified to achieve or preserve deterrence of wrongdoing? Does such action use human beings as objects, and sacrifice their rights in pursuit of an ephemeral common good?

Questions even more poignant suggest themselves when one addresses the problem of "the best interests of the child." Is there never a time when, out of love and compassion, children should be placed in coercive situations known to be for their best welfare? Well, yes, but the response must be offered hesitatingly. The imperfect state of our helping technology contributes to the difficulty of the ethical problem. Let those who escape the troubled midnight without anxiety about this problem suggest answers to inevitable but agonizing questions such as these: What degree of danger to the child's welfare should balance what degree of imposed suffering or loss of freedom? Who, or what profession, is to be trusted to assess the reality and extent of such danger? What available methodology can assure help and not harm? To what extent, and under what circumstances must the rights of the child to self-determination be weighed against the rights of the parent? Who is the client in the process, the parent or the child?

No comforting answers to these questions are available. To the first three, the "clear and present danger" principle offers some very general guidelines. Beyond that, only with great humility can any of us venture to intervene coercively in the lives of children and families. The final form of such intervention is institutionalization. We can only be shaken by cautions like this from the director of a major state division for youth:

With the exception of relatively few youths, it would probably be better for all concerned if young delinquents were not detected, apprehended, or institutionalized. Too many of them get worse in our care (quoted in Samuels 1971, p. 146).

BIBLIOGRAPHY

Cunningham, Gloria. 1973. "Crisis Intervention in a Probation Setting." *Federal Probation* 37:16–25.
Gottesfeld, Harres. 1965. "Professionals and Delinquents Evaluate Professional Methods with Delinquents." *Social Problems* 13:45–59.
Hood, Roger, and Sparks, Richard. 1970. *Key Issues in Criminology.* London: Weidenfield and Nicholson.
Klapmuts, Nora. 1973. "Community Alternatives to Prison." *Crime and Delinquency Literature* 5:310–12.
Maher, Brendan, and Stein, Ellen. 1968. "The Delinquent's Perception of the Law and the Community." In *Controlling Delinquents,* ed. S. Wheeler. New York: Wiley. Pp. 187–221.
President's Commission on Law Enforcement and Administration of Justice. 1967. *Task Force Report: Corrections.* Washington, D.C.: U.S. Government Printing Office.
Reid, William J., and Epstein, Laura. 1972. *Task-Centered Casework.* New York: Columbia University Press.
Ripple, Lilian; Alexander, Ernestina; and Polemis, Bernice W. 1964. *Motivation, Capacity, and Opportunity: Studies in Casework Theory and Practice.* Social Service Monographs. 2d ser., no. 3. School of Social Service Administration. Chicago: University of Chicago Press.
Samuels, Gertrude. 5 December 1971. "When Children Collide with the Law." *New York Times Magazine.* Sec. 6, pp. 44 ff.
Schur, Edwin M. 1973. *Radical Nonintervention: Rethinking the Delinquency Problem.* Englewood Cliffs, N.J.: Prentice-Hall.

CHARLES H. SHIREMAN   153

Shireman, Charles; Dolin, Gary; Fagin, Elise; Hawkins, William; and Lisiak, Jean. 1972. "Probation Officer-Probationer Perceptions of the Probation Process." Unpublished report to the Juvenile Court of Cook County, Illinois.

Shireman, Charles; Anselmo, Lewis; Benedetto, Andrew; Bone, Bruce; Boyd, Timothy; Debevec, Linda; and Murphy, Donna. 1973. "Probationers' Perceptions of the Probation Process in a Community Center." Unpublished report to the Juvenile Court of Cook County, Illinois.

Williams, Jay R., and Gold, Martin. 1972. "From Delinquent Behavior to Official Delinquency." *Social Problems* 20:209–29.

8 The New Corrections: The Case of Massachusetts

Jerome Miller
and Lloyd E. Ohlin

Among academic and professional authorities in the United States, there is a rapidly growing consensus that major reform of the system for dealing with the problems of youthful offenders is long overdue. A measure of this consensus is the consistency with which recent national crime commissions have called for abandoning large training schools (President's Commission ... 1967; National Commission ... 1969; National Advisory Commission ... 1973). Next to the probation services attached to juvenile courts, these traditional training schools and their aftercare services are still the principal treatment resource in most states (Department of Justice 1974). These schools emerged in the first half of the nineteenth century from the efforts of private, charitable organizations to provide for the vocational and moral retraining of delinquent or wayward youth. The first state-supported training school in the United States, the Lyman School for Boys, was located in Westborough, Massachusetts, in 1847 and the first public training school for girls at Lancaster, Massachusetts, in 1856 (Mennel 1973). Appropriately enough, therefore, Massachusetts is the first state publicly to adopt and quickly implement a policy of closing down the traditional training schools and to shift to a diversified structure of community-based services.

This chapter offers a personal perspective from the standpoint of an insider and an outsider on the events in Massachusetts and their implications for youth corrections. The reforms discussed here were undertaken under the direction of Jerome Miller as Commissioner of the Department of Youth Services; a six-year evaluative study of the process and impact of the reforms is still going on under the direction of Lloyd Ohlin at the Center for Criminal Justice, Harvard Law School. Here we shall examine the justifications for the new policy in Massachusetts, the alternatives available to the traditional training schools, the principal barriers to change, and the strategies employed to overcome them.

THE PREREFORM DEPARTMENT OF YOUTH SERVICES

The passage of legislation in August 1969 reorganized the former Youth Service Board and the Division of Youth Services into a new Department of Youth Services. The new legislation gave centralized authority to the new commissioner, a deputy commissioner, and four assistant commissioners, each in charge of a newly created bureau: institutions, education, clinical services, and aftercare. Passage of the legislation was quickly followed by the appointment of the new commissioner, Dr. Jerome Miller, in October 1969 to implement the reform mandate (Ohlin, Coates, and Miller 1974; Rutherford, 1974).

These changes had been preceded by a period of considerable turbulence and public criticism of practices and policies within the former Division of Youth Services. Six major investigations of youth corrections, undertaken at the instigation of either the governor or of legislative committees, paved the way for the changes of 1969. Perhaps the most detailed recommendations for change came from a study by technical experts from the U.S. Department of Health, Education, and Welfare (1966) Children's Bureau at the request of Governor John A. Volpe. A blue-ribbon committee of local experts, appointed by Governor Volpe a year later in 1967, confirmed the findings of the HEW study and helped to concentrate pressure for change.

These investigations pointed to the failure of the Division of Youth Services to give priority to treatment over custodial confinement, to provide centralized direction of child care, to raise the level of professional competence, to establish desirable diagnostic and classification procedures, and to assure proper parole supervision. Further public charges of brutality and mistreatment of youth at the Institution of Juvenile Guidance at Bridgewater in 1968 finally led to the resignation of the long-time director of the Division of Youth Services, Dr. John D. Coughlin, in March 1969. The Massachusetts Committee on Children and Youth under the chairmanship of Dr. Martha Eliot, a former director of the Children's Bureau in HEW, had mobilized the liberal coalition for reform. They applauded the appointment of a professional social worker as the new commissioner and promised the support of the professional community to back impending reforms within the department.

In 1969, most of the 800 boys and girls committed to the department were housed in five institutions: the school for preadolescent boys at Oakdale, a school for adolescent boys at Lyman, the industrial school for older boys at Shirley, an institution for rebellious or emotionally disturbed boys at Bridgewater, and an industrial school for girls at Lancaster. In addition, the department maintained four detention and reception centers, a forestry camp, and a newly acquired facility at Topsfield. The department also operated a unit for delinquency prevention and an office for supervising boys and girls on parole.

These Massachusetts institutions implemented the ideology of the traditional training school that is still the prevalent type of facility for adjudicated delinquents throughout the country. They provided residential custody for an average period of eight months during which the boys and girls were required to perform chores and attend school or vocational training. A small clinical staff carried out diagnostic testing and provided some counseling to disturbed youth. However, these efforts at reeducation and psychological treatment reached only a very few of the boys and girls in any effective way (Pappenfort, Kilpatrick, and Kuby 1970; Ohlin 1973). A rhetoric of rehabilitation thinly veiled the basic organizing principles of these institutions, custody and punishment. The committed youth were regarded as rebels against authority in the home, the classroom, the police station, the juvenile court, and the probation office. Believed a danger to themselves and others, they needed confinement away from the community in order to be taught obedience, respect for authority, and self-discipline. Their treatment was paternalistic and often harsh when they disobeyed established routines or regulations. Inmates at Lyman were threatened with transfer to the institution for older boys at Shirley. Those who violated rules or ran away were subjected to the enforced silence of the punishment cottage, physical coercion, and confinement to isolated strip cells in the punishment cottage. Those who continued to be rebellious were transferred to the maximum security and highly disciplined Institution for Juvenile Guidance at Bridgewater. Thus, training schools were conceived as a final resort of the courts for reinforcing adult authority. Confinement and the threat of punitive deprivation were the sanctions to be employed when all else had failed to teach obedience and responsiveness to adult instructions.

Rationale for a New Policy

The reform administration felt strongly that the basic ideology of the traditional training schools was destructive and doomed to failure. Such a system might elicit a surface conformity from youth in the presence of adult authority—but only there. Such coerced conformity could only obscure identification of the real problems preventing a more constructive social adjustment. The punitive sanctions of the training schools simply displaced the blame on individual youth for the failure of staff and programs. The availability of sanctions reduced staff motivation to cultivate other forms of authority in dealing with youth, ones based on loyalty, knowledge, emulation, respect, and affection. The sanctions also constituted a punitive threat which other authorities could employ in dealing with the adjustment problems of children in their homes, schools, or neighborhoods. By providing a custodially secure dumping ground for rebellious youth, the training schools encouraged communal authorities to weed out recalcitrants in order to induce greater conformity in others and to divert attention from basic defects in family life, the school system, the church, the employment market, and other essential socializing and control agencies.

Perhaps most important of all, the new administration felt that the punishment system built into the model of the traditional training school alienates essential adult support and dramatizes and consolidates socially destructive definitions of youth in trouble. From the traditional institutions, stigmatizing definitions of youthful offenders were picked up and reinforced by other socializing agencies. This correctional atmosphere closed off opportunities for youth, made reintegration more difficult, increased recidivism and serious crime, and led youthful offenders into adult criminal careers (Schur 1971; Coates, Miller, and Ohlin 1974).

Finally, research had shown that the traditional training school system alienates the youth exposed to it and generates anti-authority, peer group subcultures (Street, Vinter, and Perrow 1966). Within these institutions, peer groups develop allegiance to deviant roles, norms, beliefs, and values that best serve to thwart efforts to change them through coercive treatment policies. The available evidence in Massachusetts seemed to confirm this appraisal of the self-defeating impact of the traditional training school model for youth corrections. Fragmentary studies placed the recidivism rate at from 40 percent to 90 percent, depending on the length of follow up, the measure of recidivism, and the age group involved (Ohlin, Coates, and Miller 1974).

As the commissioner began to humanize and close the institutions, he found that a number of staff members were deeply committed to their work with children and capable of establishing supportive and helpful relationships with them. He also found widespread preoccupation with mere job security and the routinization and simplification of work demands. Many of the practices more commonly associated with maximum security adult prisons were still to be observed—silent marching in formation from one assignment to another; silence while eating in the mess hall; close haircuts and the issue of institution uniforms on admission; initial orientation by peer groups rather than staff; the withholding of privileges like smoking, television watching, and recreation for minor disciplinary infractions; the use of solitary isolation cells, shaved heads, enforced day-long silences, and sometimes punitive physical exercises for more serious rule violations; an organized system of alarm and pursuit of runaways; and the staff manipulation of informal agreements with peer group leaders to enforce disciplinary control. The oppressiveness of this system was evident in the sullen and hostile attitudes of many youths and in the frequent exploitation of some youths by others, shielded by the informal peer group subcultures and the strongly enforced norms against informing.

Alternatives to the Traditional Training Schools

The traditional training school model for youthful offenders is deeply rooted and will prove hard to dislodge. These facilities have been built and staffed for over a century to provide secure residential care for children whom community agencies feel they can no longer serve effectively or without disruptive effects to others in their program. Since the definition of which youth are dangerous or uncontrollable cannot be stated precisely, these state facilities can easily be filled with young people defined as least desirable within the community. Little change can be expected in the established system of training schools for youthful offenders unless the barriers to change are clearly confronted. The first requirement in effecting such changes is to envision what the alternatives to the traditional training school may be.

Initially on taking charge of the Massachusetts Department of Youth Services, the new administration believed that reform should aim to humanize the existing institutions, to change programs and staff assignments, and to create decentralized therapeutic communities in self-contained cottage programs. The reorganized institutional services could be backed up by newly created group homes and halfway houses based in local communities and integrated into a more effective system of aftercare services.

For reasons noted more fully below, these changes proved extremely difficult to accomplish and there gradually emerged a new set of plans for the reorganization of the department. By spring 1971, the administration and planning staff evolved a seven-point plan to guide reforms. This plan called for (1) the creation of seven regions within the state to coincide with the existing mental health regions, (2) the development of a network of community-based residential and nonresidential treatment services, (3) expansion of the existing forestry program, (4) organization of shelter care facilities and other placements to phase out existing detention centers, (5) an increase in placement alternatives through the use of privately purchased services, (6) delinquency prevention grants-in-aid to cities and towns, and (7) acquisition of a new, small, intensive care, security unit.

It was contemplated that committed youth would gradually move to the new community-based services by transfer from institutional confinement and by direct placements from department reception centers for the courts. Again, strong resistance to change slowed the development of the new system. The commissioner and his top aides finally decided that only a rapid closing of the existing training schools could generate the pressure needed to convert the department programs to the new system. By February 1972 the Oakdale, Lyman, and Shirley facilities had been closed and the population greatly reduced at the girls' school at Lancaster.

BARRIERS TO CHANGE

It is predictable, if not self-evident, that an entrenched system of correctional services, based primarily in large institutions, would have a variety of vested interests intent on maintaining the status quo, virtually unrelated to the effectiveness or propriety of the existing system. These interests soon become obvious to any administrator determined to introduce major changes in a correctional agency. They include staff resistance to change, civil service protection, union agreements, fiscal and personnel constraints, ideological differences, and public inertia. Surprisingly, perhaps, a number of social service professionals, such as psychiatrists, psychologists, and social workers, join with judges, police, and probation officers in resisting major change. Some of these professionals work within the juvenile correctional system itself and others within an array of mental health and private child care agencies. They are highly critical of traditional institutions but have developed at the same time a symbiotic relationship with them.

Staff Interests

The staffs of traditional juvenile correctional institutions are usually the most obvious and immediate opponents to basic change of that system. They exemplify in a sense the ambivalence of the larger society about youth corrections. There is public demand for innovative rehabilitation programs which at the same time do not significantly threaten existing arrangements, commitments, and protected interests. It is undoubtedly for this reason that most so-called reform strategies in juvenile corrections have consisted of new means for manipulating inmates or clients while demanding relatively few changes of the staff or the social and economic arrangements which provide structural support for correctional institutions. It is also probably why, for example, the frankly manipulative approaches to inmates of many new so-called behavior modification programs have been readily accepted recently as "reform" or "rehabilitative" measures by staff members of traditional juvenile and adult institutions. These methods commonly demand very little of the staff but very much of the inmate population. There is danger here once again that the rhetoric of reform will be co-opted by the custodial tradition and create a new treatment ideology that will sustain the existing institutions during the present assaults upon them. This pattern has been repeatedly enacted over the last century as "reform" programs provided new hope for rehabilitation (such as vocational training, remedial education, individual counseling, group therapy, and on and on) while allowing the basic institutional structure to ride out the criticism without succumbing to basic change or dissolution.

To achieve major reform of a system of corrections, there must be radical and definitive changes on the part of those who define and maintain that system—primarily, the administration and the staff. Unfortunately, a new administrator pursuing a policy of abandoning large correctional institutions ordinarily has limited resources and very few points of leverage to create motivation for change against the active resistance or apathy of older staff. Most juvenile correctional institutions have relatively low custodial staff turnover, long-standing traditions, and numerous unwritten agreements and roles for staff members. These arrangements are often buttressed by civil service and union protection of staff, political patronage, and economic considerations crucial to the small rural communities in which training schools are typically located. This powerful blend of interests is not easily broken. In less "progressive" states, these arrangements are clearly defined for the outsider to see. In more "progressive" states, they are less clearly outlined but just as surely in place. It is in the latter states that liberal professionals often provide support and the gloss of reform for existing systems by urging the addition of more "trained" staff, better educational resources, and new treatment ideologies, hoping that such additions can make the traditional training school effective as well as more humane.

Professional Interest Groups

Perhaps one of the most disappointing and unexpected lessons from the Massachusetts experience was the failure of the liberally oriented "helping professions" (such as social workers, psychologists, and psychiatrists) to support fully the department's efforts to close down the traditional training schools. It was expected that there would be resistance to this change by the older generation of correctional workers whose professional lives had been committed to making the training schools work. However, the initial widespread support for reform from the mental health and social service professions changed in many instances to resistance and criticism as the process of closing the institutions and creating community-based alternatives reached critical points.

For a number of years, the helping professions have been critical of the juvenile correctional systems for giving primacy to custody rather than to treatment and rehabilitation goals. There are two basic problems here, however. First, the service professions maintain strong convictions that professionally qualified personnel should operate rehabilitative programs for delinquent offenders (Weber and Haberlein 1972). Though recent research studies are increasingly questioning these assumptions, professionals insist that work with offenders would prove successful if the right conditions for the provision of services were available (Martinson 1974). They are therefore constantly seeking new resources to demonstrate, in pilot or experimental programs, the effectiveness of their techniques under control conditions. Such experimentation is desirable, but one unfortunate by-product is a visible gloss of treatment-oriented programs over what remains for most offenders a punitive system of custodial confinement.

Second, and a more serious problem in its way, the idea is widely accepted that juvenile and criminal offenders must be motivated to participate in treatment programs by some element of implied threat or coercion (Pray 1951; cf. Shireman 1973). Because of this belief, professional personnel have perhaps inadvertently helped to maintain the existing system under a facade of new nomenclature, techniques, and justifications for existence. The old, oppressive parts of the system are perceived as integral to the success of the more progressive-appearing parts. On the one hand, the private professional service agencies carefully define characteristics of those offenders they regard as most amenable to treatment in their programs. The normal result is that they treat the most compliant offenders and leave the most recalcitrant, disturbed, or socially disorganized offenders to public institutional care. Such a procedure is likely to produce higher success rates in treatment from the more cooperative and responsive offenders who have been "saved" from prison. But these treatment facilities implicitly rely on the symbolic threat of the more repressive correctional system of prisons, jails, or training schools. It is striking to observe the number of privately run group homes or self-help drug centers that publicly condemn the regimen of traditional correctional institutions but nevertheless see it as crucial for their program. The intensive security of custodial institutions serves as a threat to frighten or cool persons overly resistant to their treatment program.

It is hard to escape the conviction that the viability of professional treatment programs is in part dependent, or is felt to be dependent, on higher rates of failure in the traditional training schools. As long as coercion is deemed both feasible and necessary to treatment, the professional services are likely to continue to support the existence of some type of graduated system capable of providing greater or lesser amounts of punishment and deprivation. It is recognition of this fact which has increasingly led articulate spokesmen for basic reform in adult corrections to argue for separating treatment efforts from the other ends served by a correctional system—those of retribution, deterrence, and community protection (American Friends Service Committee 1971; Fogel 1973). They believe that treatment can be successful only if the individual seeks it on the basis of a voluntary, uncoerced choice and this, we would argue, should apply to juveniles as well. They also believe that a frank recognition that imprisonment serves ends other than the "best interest" of the offender would lead the courts to resort to this final sanction less often, especially if smaller, more benign and humane community-based residential programs were available to serve much the same ends with less destructive consequences.

Other criminal justice professionals, such as juvenile court judges, police, and probation workers, are even more explicit in their conviction that some type of punitive, maximum-security facility, however small in capacity, is essential to induce greater conformity in those offenders spared this type of commitment. This is perhaps the single most difficult issue raised by the closing of the training schools in Massachusetts. Such an institution would serve as a symbol of general deterrence, community protection, and retribution. Even successful treatment in a community-based program would not achieve this symbolic objective (Motley 1973). It is not treatment so much as visible and symbolic confinement in a secure institution away from the community that is desired. Most professionals agree that cases requiring such security represent a small number, but they are the most troublesome for the local juvenile justice system to manage. There is, of course, wide disagreement about just which offenders merit this type of treatment. We fear that the concept of the "dangerous offender" is readily expandable and would soon convert the small, intensive, secure unit into a large, traditional, training school.

Financial and Personnel Constraints

Another serious barrier to change in Massachusetts has been the inflexibility of financial arrangements for funding new reform programs. The Department of Youth Services was assigned line-budgeted funds for the operation of each institution. It was impossible to transfer funds from one institution to another, from one personnel category to another, or from institution to community-based programs, even when some institutions showed a surplus.

Such budgetary constraints make it very difficult to move away from an institution-based model of corrections without legislative changes in the penal code or appropriation procedures. The common pattern throughout the country, therefore, is for states to move slowly into a few "pilot" community programs added to the normal operating budget. Consequently, reform administrators must continue to operate large institutional facilities and programs even though they regard them as worthless and destructive. The same constraint exists in some measure on the new federal funds now being made available to the states by the Law Enforcement Assistance Administration of the U.S. Department of Justice. These funds tend to be channeled into a search for new, innovative programs on an experimental basis rather than to be available to support a massive shift from institution- to community-based programs. Similar problems, of course, confront programs in mental health, mental retardation, and other service approaches to social deviance that traditionally have been carried out in large institutions.

Practices of hiring, firing, transfer, and reassignment of staff are also closely tied to the needs of the existing, outmoded system of institutions, rather than to the community-based system being proposed and developed. Actions to transfer or reassign staff in Massachusetts have to go through the legislative process and the delay involved more often than not insures that no action will be taken. Civil Service constraints on hiring, firing, promotions, and job classification were also designed to serve institutional needs. A challenge to the established order calls into play a network of alliances between the legislature, the Civil Service Commission, the governor's office, the personnel office, the Bureau of the Budget or Department of Administration and Finance, the patronage office, and a variety of special interest groups. Staff resources cannot simply be reassigned to more productive or effective programs. Even if there were the real possibility of effective staff training, the structural constraints on making such moves are well-nigh insuperable.

The reform administration is therefore placed in an absurd situation: either it must begin small "pilot" programs involving a negligible number of new staff, or it must somehow create a system outside of bureaucratic constraints parallel to the existing one. To do the former insures little basic change in the system and to do the latter insures accusations of administrative and fiscal mismanagement. It is a classic double-bind guaranteed to induce administrative schizophrenia in the best intentioned reform efforts. Thus, in Massachusetts and elsewhere, recent experience suggests that opposition to new programs stems not so much from whether such programs work, but from the degree to which they threaten the existing arrangements for staff.

Public Inertia and Ideological Conflict

Public inertia, ignorance, and ideological conflicts about appropriate treatment systems for delinquent youth are additional obstacles to change. The public is rarely fully and properly informed about operations of a correctional system by the administrators of that system or by the legislators or executive officers who sustain it (Miller 1973). It is difficult to change a system if those who are responsible for running it, or funding it, are satisfied with it. Critics of the existing system are not likely to be promoted within it or to achieve positions of responsibility from which to change it. The juvenile correctional system is vulnerable to constantly being exposed by "outsiders"—legal aid attorneys, reform groups, journalists, and so on—a situation which only puts those responsible for the system on the defensive.

This is what happened in Massachusetts in 1969 and it may be an inevitable part of preparation for major change (Ohlin, Coates, and Miller 1974). We wonder, however, whether useful reform might also result if the chief administrator of an essentially unproductive and harmful system were to expose his own system. This undoubtedly would cause great turmoil within the agency and bring public charges that the administrator was "scapegoating" the staff, legislators, and others for his own deficiencies. It is a difficult path to walk—to point out the inadequacies of the system without at the same time denigrating individuals responsible for that system.

Yet we believe, based on the Massachusetts experience, that if the public were fully informed of the conditions, problems, and routine handling of youngsters in large institutions under state auspices, it would support basic and even radical change. Providing such information, however, is itself disruptive to the system. At this point it becomes clear that it is impossible to change a correctional system significantly without creating a large amount of turmoil and disequilibrium within that system (Ohlin 1974). How that turmoil is explained to the public and how the public is involved in settling issues are crucial to effective reform. Most often the turmoil is blamed on loss of control over the inmate population and the administrator's inability to keep them in line. If the old system is not to be reinforced as a result, public attention must be redirected. Public awareness of the deficiencies of the system being administered might then be channeled toward effective reform.

It is apparent that basic ideological differences underlie such conflicts about the proper treatment of delinquent youth. Major change will result only if these differences are clearly exposed and a public coalition aroused to support more progressive policies.

STRATEGIES FOR CHANGE

Crucial to bringing about change in a system is mobilizing public support for the changes to be accomplished.

Mobilization of Reform Coalitions

From the beginning in Massachusetts, a number of interest groups mobilized to support the reforms. Involved were such groups as the National Council of Churches, the League of Women Voters, various professional bodies, the Massachusetts Council on Crime and Corrections, and the Massachusetts Committee on Children and Youth. Also important was the involvement of local chapters of service clubs, such as Rotary and Kiwanis. Staff were encouraged to speak about the need for change in the department and to seek to enlist helpful individuals and groups in accomplishing it. Staff members were regularly available as speakers at civic meetings, church affairs, and colleges. As a result, many thousands of persons were kept informed during the period of deinstitutionalization in Massachusetts. They were made aware of the various problems within the old system and the need for change.

One lesson became very clear after a series of skirmishes over closing of the institutions in Massachusetts: lay groups were often more supportive of radical change than many professionals. The lay groups active in corrections, such as the League of Women Voters, the Massachusetts Committee, and the National Council of Churches, also proved more effective and less likely to undercut basic reform under the guise of rational political compromise.

The groups enlisted in the reform coalition were able to keep constant pressure on the legislature and executive branch to support the new directions. During one particularly critical period, they were able to generate a large number of telegrams and letters to the Speaker of the House in favor of critical changes in the department. Thus, it proved valuable to keep them fully informed about the old system, the need for change, sources of resistance, and transitional problems. Reform groups were regularly invited into the institutions and made privy to the problems on the spot. They were also actively involved in seeking support for new programs, ranging from halfway houses and foster homes to the use of a variety of nonresidential counseling, training, and job placement programs. Problems anticipated with the legislature or the executive office were outlined publicly and clearly for the reform groups beforehand, so that these groups not only understood the problems of the department but became able to anticipate assaults upon progressive change in the correctional system.

A similar pattern was established with the press. Reporters and others were told that no institutions, buildings, or rooms were off limits to them at any time of the day or night. They were encouraged to observe any new or old programs, to identify problems and assess the need for effective change. In addition, regular background interview meetings were held with newspaper editors and television executives to explain the agency's difficulties and plans. As a result, the mass media became knowledgeable about the issues within the department and, with some exceptions, lent support and encouragement.

To achieve major change it is probably not enough to bring problems to the attention of small groups such as commissions, professional audiences, members of the executive branch and legislative committees. There must be a new public awareness of the need for change to get the proper legislative and community support. To communicate that need through the normal channels invites a "watering-down" of the brutality, the ineffectiveness, and the periodic insanity of the existing system.

The Dramatization of Past Failures

An initial problem in reform is to find a way to dramatize the need for change. The situation is somewhat easier for a new administrator brought in with a mandate to make changes than for an incumbent. However, the new person will also have to endure staff alienation and charges of scapegoating when attempting to arouse public indignation about destructive and dehumanizing practices of the old system. Nevertheless, such exposure is essential and some of the costs must be borne to achieve the benefits. No parts of the system can be allowed to hide behind passwords like "for the good of the youngsters in the program" or "for the protection of the public."

In Massachusetts, the commissioner and his aides found in department files records of the brutalities committed upon the inmate population at one of the training schools and distributed them to the press. These included reports of fingers broken, soles of feet beaten, youths being handcuffed in cold showers, and similar atrocities. These records were apparently accurate descriptions of a number of different cases. Attention of the press was also directed to the extremely high recidivism rates, and interviews were permitted with training school alumni who had gone on into the adult penal system to expose the impact of their early experience on their subsequent careers.

On one occasion a young college student volunteer was admitted to the department posing as a teenage inmate to gain information regarding treatment at one of the detention centers. During his four-day incarceration, he experienced staff dunking youngsters' heads in toilets, dousing them with pails of water, forcing them to march around with a pail over their heads, using one twelve-year-old boy as a mop and dragging him through urine in the boys' washroom, severely beating another boy, and finally forcing the student himself to stoop in an uncomfortable position for a long period because he had been observed reading in an area in which the staff felt he should not be reading. His report was made available to the press.

It became apparent that a large number of the escapes were being stimulated by staff in order to sabotage the reforms. The press were invited to interview the youngsters involved and were shown, on one occasion, a room intended for one occupant in which seven youngsters had been placed, given a steel bar, and left alone. One youth reported that when the staff member returned to the room and found a couple of youngsters still there, he asked them why they had not left. A host of such incidents made clear the need for change as well as the resistance to change.

The reform administration in Massachusetts also dramatized the need for change in the system in other ways. For example, early in the administration, a directive was sent to all the institutions outlawing mandatory haircuts. It stated simply that youngsters would not be given a haircut unless they so desired and that the only rule governing style of hair would be the necessity for cleanliness to avoid any danger of infection. This simple directive had almost revolutionary impact within the system because of staff contempt for the prevailing youth culture and their inclination to define youngsters in the institution as different from those outside, where long hair was becoming common. The directive also prohibited the dehumanizing initiation rite of shaving youngsters' heads on admission as an inmate. The haircut directive was a symbolic gesture, which had the advantage of striking at the institutional structure while at the same time diminishing the effect of the labeling process through which the youths were compelled to accept a definition of themselves as training-school inmates.

Furthermore, the closing of every institution was made a public event. The provision of alternatives was made public, with the press invited to inspect new developments such as the halfway houses, group residential and nonresidential activities, and the volunteer advocacy programs. In this way, comparisons could be drawn between the former institutional system and the new community programs. Also the elimination of the more repressive aspects of the institutions was deliberately dramatized. The closing of the solitary rooms in one institution was preceded by a banquet, after which a number of boys who had spent time in the solitary cells were given sledge hammers and allowed to break down the walls of these hated and feared instruments of repression.

As an alternative to the previous allocation of power, responsibility, and reward to the administration and staff of each institution, the department created seven new administrative regions within the state and assigned its administrators to an office in each of these regions along with parole and treatment staff. These regional offices became major decision-making centers for developing and contracting youth services and for receiving and placing youth committed to the department. Court liaison units were created to facilitate volunteer referral and placement of children by the courts into the residential and nonresidential services within the regions. This regionalization effectively moved the center of action and authority away from the old institutions to the new regional offices.

This redistribution of authority for organizing and providing services was further strengthened by adopting a new strategy of purchasing private services for youth committed to the care of the department. This represented an effort to create a more competitive climate among both private and public agencies to raise the quality of all treatment provided young offenders. The creation of a competitive service system in the private sector was slowed by a lag in the department's financial capacity to develop contracts with private service agencies. The legislative appropriation committees showed some reluctance to provide such funds, over which they would exercise far less control than they had over the former institutional budgets. The new system was also slowed by an elaborate rate-setting procedure involving several administrative levels before private placements or contracts could be fully validated. To some extent the availability of the new federal funds aided the process of transition, but the delays in payment proved very difficult for some of the newer agencies that had no other substantial resources available.

PROSPECTS FOR CHANGE

During the years 1973 and 1974, following Commissioner Miller's move to Illinois in January 1973, the Department of Youth Services entered a period of consolidation of the new regional, community-based network of services under the direction of Miller's former deputy commissioner, Joseph Leavey. At present the department seems to be making successful progress in developing and reinforcing the regional community-based system (Ohlin, Coates, and Miller 1974). The six training schools for committed youth have been closed and transferred from the jurisdiction of the department to other state services. The department continues to operate the forestry camp and the detention centers. Committed youth requiring intensive care are placed either in special units located in each of the three detention centers or with private services providing appropriate treatment (Harvard Center for Criminal Justice 1974). Creating these security units in the detention centers is expected to alleviate a major source of tension between the department and the juvenile courts. As presently planned, these units will house approximately eighty youth.

A number of problems remain to be solved. For example, the purchase of service from private vendors has created a serious problem of quality control. Many of the new private services were hastily created to meet an urgent need for both residential and nonresidential care as the institutions were closed. The department is expanding its evaluation unit to monitor these services more closely to ensure that delivered services are constructive and of high quality. Court liaison units have improved relations in a number of juvenile courts, but the department is seeking to develop these units further and provide more placement options. Commissioner Leavey also feels that more intensive treatment resources are needed for emotionally disturbed or dangerous boys in the secure facilities. A new program has also been launched to develop more and better services for girls.

Finally, however, the policy of shifting from an institutional system of youth services to a regional network of diversified, small, residential and nonresidential treatment programs has been successfully implemented. There appears to be a broad consensus among legislators and practitioners in the human services in Massachusetts, that the new program is desirable and will be permanent. There has been criticism of the speed with which the changes were brought about, the administrative and fiscal confusion attending the transition, the failure to develop adequate community placements for youth before closing the institutions, and the hardships imposed on institution-based staff members. Could the changes have been more carefully planned and carried out more slowly in order to avoid these criticisms? It is our view that deinstitutionalization would not have succeeded if it had been implemented in that way. Only a rapid, massive change could overcome the capacity of hostile staff to mobilize political resistance and to sabotage the new policy. It also took the pressure of a major crisis in youth treatment services to generate the present wide range of services from the private sector as well as the federal and state funds to purchase them. It may be that in other states staff-attitudes and political and financial support favorable to such a change will permit a more carefully orchestrated process of deinstitutionalization stretched out over a longer time period. A slower rate of change may also prove necessary in larger systems than Massachusetts', with more institutions, staff, and committed youth to be accounted for in the transition to new community-based services.

It should not be assumed that the new community-based system in Massachusetts is a final solution for youth correctional policy. As consolidation proceeds, there may well develop new vested interests in both public and private agencies that will become just as rigid and impervious to change as the old institutional system. Small group homes could grow larger. Intensive treatment and high-security facilities, even under private contract, could become minitraining schools in the old custodial mold. Private vendors of service might become more preoccupied with protecting jobs and favorable working arrangements for staff than with responding sensitively and creatively to youth problems. Unless these and other pitfalls can be avoided, the new system at some future date may in turn require radical reform. It may be that a logical outcome of the present mix of private and public services would be the development of a consumer voucher system as an alternative to the state purchase of services. Such a system would have its own problems of quality control and would presuppose, as a condition of success, the availability of different competitive forms of treatment which individual clients or their guardians might choose (Greenberg 1973).

For the present, the Massachusetts experience has demonstrated that major change in correctional systems can be brought about despite a variety of imposing barriers. Other states may encounter different obstacles, but many of them will be essentially the same. The lessons learned in Massachusetts should help reform administrators elsewhere to identify more clearly the problems they are likely to meet and some of the strategies that could be successful in overcoming them.

BIBLIOGRAPHY

American Friends Service Committee. 1971. *Struggle for Justice.* New York: Hill and Wang.

Coates, Robert B.; Miller, Alden D.; and Ohlin, Lloyd E. 1975. "The Labeling Perspective and Innovations in Juvenile Correctional Systems." In *Issues in the Classification of Children,* ed. Nicholas Hobbs. San Francisco: Jossey Bass. 2:123–49.

Department of Health, Education, and Welfare. 1966. *A Study of the Division of Youth Service and Youth Service Board, Commonwealth of Massachusetts.* Welfare Administration, Children's Bureau. Washington, D.C.: U.S. Government Printing Office.

Department of Justice. 1974. *Children in Custody: A Report on the Juvenile Detention and Correctional Facility Census of 1971.* Law Enforcement Assistance Administration, National Criminal Information and Statistics Service. Washington, D.C.: U.S. Government Printing Office.

Fogel, David. 1973. "The Model for Social Work in Corrections." In *Social Work Practice and Social Justice,* eds. Bernard Ross and Charles Shireman. Third NASW Professional Symposium. Washington, D.C.: National Association of Social Workers. Pp. 26–36.

Greenberg, David F. 1973. "A Voucher System for Correction." *Crime and Delinquency* 19:212–17.

Harvard Center for Criminal Justice. July 1974. *Quarterly Report.* Boston: Harvard University Law School.

Lerman, Paul. 1970. "Evaluative Studies of Institutions for Delinquents." In *Delinquency and Social Policy,* ed. Paul Lerman. New York: Praeger. Pp. 317–28.

Martinson, Robert. 1974. "What Works? Questions and Answers about Prison Reform." *Public Interest* 35:22–54.

Mennel, Robert M. 1973. *Thorns and Thistles: Juvenile Delinquents in the United States 1825–1940.* Hanover, N.H.: University Press of New England.

Miller, Herbert S. 1973. "The Citizen's Role in Changing the Criminal Justice System." *Crime and Delinquency* 19, no. 3: 343–52.

Motley, Constance Baker. 1973. "Law and Order and the Criminal Justice System." *Journal of Criminal Law and Criminology* 64, no. 3: 259–69.

National Advisory Commission on Criminal Justice Standards and Goals. 1973. *Corrections.* Task Force on Corrections. Washington, D.C.: U.S. Government Printing Office.

National Commission on the Causes and Prevention of Violence. 1969. *Crimes of Violence,* vol. 12. Washington, D.C.: U.S. Government Printing Office.

Ohlin, Lloyd E. 1973. "Institutions for Predelinquent or Delinquent Children." In *Child Caring: Social Policy and the Institution,* eds. Donnell M. Pappenfort; Dee Morgan Kilpatrick; and Robert W. Roberts. Chicago: Aldine. Pp. 177–99.

———. 1974. "Organizational Reform in Correctional Agencies." In *Handbook of Criminology,* ed. Daniel Glaser. Chicago: Rand McNally. Pp. 995–1020.

Ohlin, Lloyd E.; Coates, Robert B.; and Miller, Alden D. 1974. "Radical Correctional Reform: A Case Study of the Massachusetts Youth Correctional System." *Harvard Educational Review* 44:74–111.

———. 1975. "Evaluating the Reform of Youth Corrections in Massachusetts." *Journal of Research in Crime and Delinquency* 12, no. 1:3–16.

Pappenfort, Donnell M.; Kilpatrick, Dee Morgan; and Kuby, Alma M. 1970. *Institutions for Predelinquent or Delinquent Children: A Census of Children's Residential Institutions in the United States, Puerto Rico, and the Virgin Islands: 1966,* comp. Donnell M. Pappenfort and Dee Morgan Kilpatrick. 7 vols. Social Service Monographs, 2d ser., no. 4, vol. 3. Chicago: School of Social Service Administration, University of Chicago.

Pray, Kenneth L. M. 1951. "Social Work in the Prison Program." In *Contemporary Correction,* ed. Paul W. Tappan. New York: McGraw-Hill. Pp. 204–10.

President's Commission on Law Enforcement and Administration of Justice. 1967. *The Challenge of Crime in a Free Society.* Washington, D.C.: U.S. Government Printing Office.

Rutherford, Andrew. 1974. *The Dissolution of the Training Schools in Massachusetts.* Columbus, Ohio: Academy for Contemporary Problems.

Schur, Edwin M. 1971. *Labeling Deviant Behavior: Its Sociological Implications.* New York: Harper and Row.

Shireman, Charles. 1973. "The Justice System of the Future." In *Social Work Practice and Social Justice,* eds. Bernard Ross and Charles Shireman. Third NASW Professional Symposium. Washington, D.C.: National Association of Social Workers. Pp. 10–25.

Street, David; Vinter, Robert D.; and Perrow, Charles. 1966. *Organization for Treatment.* New York: Free Press.

Weber, George H., and Haberlein, Bernard J. 1972. *Residential Treatment of Emotionally Disturbed Children.* New York: Behavioral Publications.

9   Intervention with Juvenile Delinquents

Marguerite Q. Warren

Throughout this book, a variety of opinions are given concerning the extent to which the juvenile court, as well as other juvenile justice agencies, has a definable mission, whether that mission has been fulfilled, and whether that mission can be or should be fulfilled. This chapter will discuss the part of the juvenile justice mission that involves individualized handling of children. A way of conceptualizing the differences among children according to a theory of ego development will be described. The possibility of using developmental theory to specify the needs of individual children in a way leading to more rational decisions and programs will be presented. Further, research conducted on the use of ego development theories will be used to demonstrate that the picture concerning the effectiveness of treatment is not so bleak as sometimes painted.

HAS INTERVENTION FAILED?

Much of the current literature on juvenile justice, as well as much current activity, is based on the assumption that intervention with the juvenile offender has failed. Many would go further, arguing that intervention when not irrelevant is actually harmful to the child, increasing the chances of subsequent law violations or diminishing the general well-being of the individual. Such concerns are primarily ethical. They cluster around the potential negative impact of labeling, the almost inevitable juxtaposing of the naive child with the delinquent child in intervention settings, and the lack of rights or choices in treatment programs.

This chapter will not attempt to make the case for intervention with all juvenile offenders. The risk of negative impact of juvenile corrections suggests that society should (1) divert to community agencies outside the justice system all individuals who can be so diverted and (2) minimize the penetration of individuals into the justice system by always using the least drastic alternative possible under the circumstances. A major focus of criticism of correctional intervention is the overuse of incarceration; thus, to the above list can be added that, when intervening, the justice system should (3) normalize the intervention experience by placing as many juveniles as possible in community-based programs and keeping the remainder in as close contact with the rest of society as possible. Unfortunately, these recommendations make good sense as ideals but as scientific statements they only express our ignorance about how to deal with children's needs and problems.

In addition to ethical concerns, research findings have been used to support recommendations that rehabilitation be abandoned as a goal in corrections. Studies of the impact of treatment on offender populations have shown no change with treatment or have produced contradictory evidence about positive change. One possible explanation of these negative and contradictory findings is that in our current state of knowledge we do not know how to bring about significant change in human beings or their circumstances. Another possible explanation is that a masking or concealing effect occurs when all treated individuals are lumped together. The beneficial effects of an intervention program on some individuals, and the detrimental effects of the same intervention program on other individuals, may each mask and cancel out the other. The notion here is that any program element may have a positive impact on some kinds of individuals, a negative impact on other kinds of individuals, and be irrelevant to still others. A number of recent reviews (for example, Warren 1971; Glaser 1974) of correctional intervention have shown that it is necessary to classify offenders in ways relevant to the intervention before patterns of success or failure can be found.

Let me illustrate the issue by posing a series of questions. Is intervention in the free community always preferable to intervention in residential settings? Is behavior modification an effective program for juvenile offenders? Do adolescents do better if they enter parole through a short stay in a halfway house or a group home? Is psychotherapy passé? The point is that those questions cannot be answered yes or no. Psychotherapy, while certainly not appropriate across the board, may well be the most appropriate intervention for a certain proportion of juvenile offenders. Which offenders will do better if they enter parole through a stay in a halfway house? For which offenders is behavior modification the treatment choice? Who will do better in a community program and who will do better following a residential program?

If a study of an intervention program does not consider the program's impact on subgroups of the study population, it is very likely that more information will be concealed than discovered. This position can be given strong support with examples of differential research findings, mainly drawn from work with the California Youth Authority. (See appendix A following this chapter for a review of these findings.)

In his article, "Remedies for the Key Deficiency in Criminal Justice Evaluation Research," Daniel Glaser (1974) draws similar conclusions. Reviewing intervention research studies, he concludes that dividing offenders into subgroups, which he calls the "conflicted" type and the "committed" type, helps make sense of the findings. Glaser concludes that individual counseling and assistance emphasizing personal rapport will lead to reduced recidivism rates for conflicted offenders (those who can communicate fairly well, who have not previously had predominantly positive reinforcement from delinquent pursuits, and who have also not had predominantly negative reinforcement from legitimate alternatives to delinquency). Glaser concludes that committed offenders will become less recidivistic as a result of behavior modification procedures which provide them not just with staff talk but with tangible increases in their rewards from legitimate alternatives to crime and with less access to rewards from delinquent activity.

In a recent article, Palmer (1975) has reanalyzed Martinson's data (1974) from which Martinson concluded that correctional treatment doesn't work. Palmer's reanalysis shows the differential effectiveness of treatment programs as presented in Martinson's own data; when the type of offender, type of setting, type of worker, or type of treatment modality is taken into consideration, it is apparent that the effects of treatment programs vary. Palmer suggests that asking what always works with all offenders under all conditions is an inappropriate question.

The evidence indicates that looking at treatment programs without a system of identifying offender subgroups is, at best, wasteful. We must take seriously the concept that individuals entering the juvenile justice system differ from each other in their needs and in the ways that these needs can best be met. Global, across-the-board prescriptions are not only a disservice to the individuals subjected to them but also may give the erroneous impression that intervention programs have no impact on the individuals included in them.

THE THEORETICAL PERSPECTIVE

Let us consider a way of differentiating among persons by using a theoretically defined growth continuum. The theory, called the Development of Interpersonal Maturity (Sullivan, Grant, and Grant 1957), is best described as an ego development theory and is somewhat comparable to what has been described elsewhere as moral development (Kohlberg 1966), character development (Peck and Havighurst 1960), conceptual development (Harvey, Hunt, and Schroder 1961), and ego development (Loevinger 1966). As a way of differentiating among juvenile delinquents, it is quite different from the classification schemes of Argyle (1961), Gibbons (1965), Hurwitz (1965), Jenkins and Hewitt (1944), McCord, McCord, and Zola (1959), Quay (1964), Reiss (1952), and Schrag (1961).

The Development of Interpersonal Maturity theory (also known as I-level) originated with a group of psychology students in Berkeley, California, during the early fifties. It had antecedents in child development, psychoanalytic theory, Lewinian theory, phenomenological psychology, and social perception. The psychoanalytic approach having the greatest influence was that of Harry Stack Sullivan, with its emphasis on interpersonal interactions.

I-level theory is not a theory of delinquency but rather a general theory of personality development. It proposes that psychological development in all individuals can be meaningfully described in seven successive levels of interpersonal maturity. The levels range from the least mature, which resembles the interpersonal interactions of a newborn infant, to an ideal of social maturity which is rarely, if ever, reached.

Each of the seven stages or levels is defined by a crucial interpersonal problem that must be solved before further progress can occur. Not all individuals work their way through each stage; some may become fixed at a particular level. Interpersonal development is viewed as a continuum. The successive levels described in the theory are seen as definable points along the continuum. No assumption is made that delinquents will fall at any particular stage; rather it is assumed that individual delinquents will be found at a number of points along the continuum, as would the individuals of any other population. The point is not that individuals are delinquent because they are immature, but rather that one would know something about the meaning of an individual's delinquency, as well as the nature of the intervention strategies required, if the individual's maturity level is identified.

During the late fifties and early sixties, the theory served as a basis for a number of intervention studies with adult offenders. Beginning in 1961 and continuing through the present, a series of experimental studies collectively known as the Differential Treatment studies (Warren 1969) were conducted with juvenile offenders in the California Youth Authority. All these studies utilized a form of classification by I-level resulting from theoretical and empirical expansions during 1960 and 1961. Before that time, little systematic effort had been made to define subtypes within the I-level groups. As a result, little attention had been given to the implications of the differences within levels for treatment planning. The major impetus to this elaboration of the Maturity Level Classification was the need to develop rational treatment-control strategies for different types of delinquents in the Community Treatment Project (CTP).

The elaboration occurred in two areas—the definition of the subtypes within I-levels and preliminary descriptions of the differential treatment strategies. The assessment of I-level is based on individuals' ways of perceiving the world; for example, the complexity and differentiation with which they see themselves and others. The assessment of subtype within I-level represents an attempt to characterize the individuals' typical modes of response to their view of the world. Although the Maturity Level Classification was theoretically derived, as previously noted, the subtype categories were empirically derived; they were based on observations of patterns of response among delinquents occurring frequently within each I-level group. As a result, nine delinquent subtypes were identified.

With the beginning of the CTP, an attempt was also made to set down in an organized way the implications for treatment of the characteristics of each of the nine subtypes. The combination of the definitions of each of the nine subtypes and the corollary treatment strategies became the 1961 edition of the Differential Treatment model (Grant 1961).

During the sixties as the model was tried in the field, descriptions of the various subtypes, as well as of the treatment plans, were revised and further elaborated (Warren et al. 1966). The model appeared to be useful for intensive treatment with a delinquent population. The classification system and elements of the Differential Treatment model were used in a number of experimental programs. (See appendix B.)

The series of studies in differential treatment has been rather successful in teasing out some of the many complexities that interact in the correctional treatment process. A beginning has been made in sorting out the different contributions to success, or lack of it, made by offender characteristics, worker characteristics, treatment atmosphere, and treatment methods. Because a unifying theoretical orientation (I-level) guides the experimentation, each successive program grows logically out of the leads of the previous one.

CONCEPTS OF I-LEVEL

According to I-level theory, all individuals, young or old, have at any time some sort of relatively consistent or integrated way of looking at the world, including themselves. Individuals do not look out at their world and see chaos; whatever they see or experience is interpreted through their own social-perceptual frame of reference. The frame of reference changes over time in ways that have some structure to them and this structure can be described. The social-perceptual frame of reference—the integrated way in which individuals see the world—arises from an interaction between what they were born with and what they experience. Out of this interaction they develop a relatively consistent set of expectations and attitudes, a kind of interpreting and working philosophy of life. It is this nexus of gradually expanding experience, expectations, and perceptions that make up the core of the personality.

Interpersonal or social interaction is a crucial determinant in the development of this core, helping to expand and elaborate the basic potential with which a person is born. The core of personality cannot be considered to be stable in content, but it can reasonably be viewed as an organizational frame within which a variety of contents can be integrated. In this sense, consistency and stability in regard to the principles of organization can be hypothesized.

The normal pattern of psychological development follows a trend of increasing involvement with people, objects, and social institutions. These involvements generate new situations containing problems of perceptual discrimination in relationships between self and external environment. As these discriminations are made and assimilated, a cognitive restructuring of experience and expectancy takes place. A new reference scheme is developed; a new level of integration is achieved. The foundation for subsequent integrations is laid in the preceding levels. Each new level of integration may be regarded as the psychological counterpart of an increasingly efficient optical lens in the physical world. The more advanced the sequence of integration, the less the likelihood of perceptual distortion. With growth, persons can see themselves and the world more accurately and can operate more effectively.

The sequence of development along the continuum of interpersonal maturity is not age-specific. Because of differences in growth patterns, children at age four will not all have reached the same level of interpersonal maturity. As in the physical area, growth spurts occur at different times. Although the age at which a child will reach a particular integration level or milestone cannot be specified, the order in which the steps occur can be theoretically defined. It is assumed that all individuals will reach their stage of development by passing through each preceding step along the continuum, not by skipping steps. In this regard, the theory is similar to other ego development theories.

The dimensions used to describe these levels of interpersonal maturity include the way in which individuals perceive the world, the way in which they perceive themselves and others, and the relationships among all these. The following discussion describes the characteristics of individuals at each of these levels—what they have in common at that level and how it differs from the characteristics of individuals at the previous and subsequent points along the continuum. The focus will be on the whole individual, not isolated traits, behavior, or feelings. The individual's social-perceptual frame of reference will be described. What does the person "see" when looking out at the world?

Although many dimensions contribute to a description of this continuum, a major one concerns perceptual differentiation, how many and what kinds of distinctions the person tends to make in describing aspects of his or her world. The continuum represents an increasing capacity to look at the world complexly and abstractly. In many ways individuals who are higher on this continuum are better off than those who are lower, in their ability to function and cope within a complex society. For example, a junior high school student who does not make a distinction among vice principals, thinking that all vice principals are alike, will be less able to predict the reaction of a particular vice principal and thus be unable to individualize personal interactions with this person. If people assume that everyone looks at life in the same way they do, they will often not comprehend what is going on in their interactions with others. Children who are significantly retarded in this process of socialization are vulnerable because they are not able to anticipate the impact of their behavior on others or the impact of others' behavior on them. In this sense, there is an advantage to progressing along the developmental continuum as far as possible.

As previously stated, all persons do not work their way through each stage but may become fixed at a particular level. The persons who maintain a fixed point on the scale do so in a protective way, because there is something they cannot perceive or integrate. It may be too painful to grow. In other cases, a lack of stimulation for growth may result in the fixation.

The theory does not allow for regression in the usual sense. For example, a person does not retreat from I_4 to I_2 when sick and wanting to be babied. Having seen that people are somewhat complex and that they play roles, the individual does not lose this perception even when feeling bad. This is to say that behavioral regression may occur, but social-perceptual regression does not occur.

Behavior is not an index of I-level. Any bit of behavior may have several meanings, and it is the meaning rather than the behavior that is relevant to identifying I-level. This is not to say, of course, that behavior is irrelevant, but simply to say that it is not a referent for I-level. Behavior is, however, a major referent for establishing subtypes within I-level categories, as will be indicated below.

INTEGRATION LEVELS IN NORMAL DEVELOPMENT

The world of the newborn infant is made up primarily of physiological tensions and satisfactions. Physiological needs being met or not met constitute the only distinction being made by the newborn. Infants have not yet identified where they leave off and the rest of the world begins. Children's early exploratory movements will begin to establish that distinction. When they interact with different parts of themselves, it is a different experience than when they interact with the furniture. They bite the side of the crib and that is different from the experience of biting their own toes. These kinds of distinctions we call the self/nonself separation. In some childhood schizophrenics, this distinction has not been made. The integration of separateness from the world occurs theoretically at the first step along the Development of Interpersonal Maturity continuum: I_1.

The next step developmentally—I_2—has to do with the beginning distinctions between persons and objects. Having become aware of the distinction between self and nonself, developing personalities gradually focus attention on barriers to satisfaction, and they become concerned in a primitive way with the problems of how to control the rest of the world. Time and space are felt as delays to immediate gratification, and infants begin to become vaguely aware that elements in the world may also act as barriers to gratification. Meeting such resistance, the baby discovers differences in the way nonself elements interact with him. While continuing to deal with objects as if they were animate, the baby finds that interactions with objects are relatively predictable from experience to experience, while interactions with persons are more variable and therefore less predictable. He is not yet aware of feelings in others. Reality at this

stage of development is still totally related to his own needs. Even
though he is not the whole world, he is the hub of it. If his needs
are not being met, he is aware that something is wrong. Through
trial and error, children begin to solve this problem by attempting
to find particular people who can play the role of giver. If children
are continually deprived, they become baffled, helpless, and
fearful. In a home where children's needs are being met on a
fairly regular basis, they will feel secure enough to begin making
further differentiations.

Children who find their needs being met at the I_2 stage then
begin to observe that there is a part they themselves can play in
getting their needs met. Fairly young children who are starting to
talk begin to see that if they ask for things nicely, they are more
apt to get them than if they yell or stamp their feet. They may also
learn that if they stamp their feet a lot, they will get what they
want. In either case, they are learning that the way they behave
has something to do with whether they get what they want.

The assumption that a very few rules or formulas fit all
situations and are appropriate with all individuals is an I_3
characteristic. At this stage children, to some extent, see other
people as objects from which to get what they want, and rules are
seen as the magic talisman of control. They try to use the
formulas to obtain giving behavior from the external world. They
may test the limits of the rules, seeking to discover the un-
changing formulas that will help them to handle all problems
that arise.

Normally developing children who are growing up in an
atmosphere of love and support will begin fairly early in life,
probably by four or five years of age, to be aware that dealing with
the world is more complicated than applying simple formulas.
They learn this because the formulas do not work equally well
with all people or in all situations. One formula says that when
you behave in some disapproved way but say you are sorry,
everything will be all right. However, when in taking a toy away
from a new baby brother, a child injures the baby and makes him
cry, the "I'm sorry" formula may not dissipate all of the mother's
anger.

Assuming a general security for children in their families, such
incidents can lead to growth-producing anxiety, anxiety which
can promote further distinctions about what is going on inside the

individuals with whom the child interacts, as well as teach something about the differential appropriateness of the formulas. Children's behavior is still primarily influenced by their own needs, but as they move into the I_4 stage, they are becoming aware also of others' expectations. A child, by introjecting into his own reaction system the responses of others to his behavior, begins to develop an internalized value system. This is the stage of beginning identification with adult models, sometimes called superego development. Children at the I_4 stage discover through play activities and fantasy conversations that they can be like the powerful figures in their life. Such role playing is a safe kind of practicing, leading to greater differentiation and capacity for social integration. This is a stage we call "global identification"— an identification with an oversimplified model without any weaknesses or inadequacies. Small children, who admire courageous astronauts, want to be equally brave and may judge themselves quite harshly because they are scared when the light goes off in their rooms at night. They buy the global image as if it were the whole person, not knowing that astronauts sometimes cry. I_4 children evaluate themselves and others by dichotomous concepts of "good" and "bad." Neither ambiguities nor shades of gray are tolerated. Because of the rigidity of these standards, children at this stage may often feel self-critical and guilty when they fail to live up to their new standards.

Although, as we indicated earlier, signs of beginning movement from I_3 to I_4 may be seen in children as young as four or five, many children do not make this step until early adolescence. The next step, the movement from I_4 to I_5, does not appear to take place before middle or late adolescence. At the I_5 level, young persons begin to see that people are more complex than represented by the earlier frame of reference. They are able to perceive and handle ambiguities in people and situations, without the harsh judgments of the I_4. They are able to appreciate and respond to others as unit personalities—composites of needs, feelings, and behavior. They become aware of continuity in their own lives and in the lives of others. Instead of the earlier indiscriminant use of roles, they begin to differentiate roles for themselves and others which are appropriate for different situations. They come to comprehend what others are feeling, and this development frees them from some of the problems of overly intense identifications.

Empathy with a variety of other kinds of persons becomes possible. I_5 level persons may tolerate, and even enjoy, the complexity and ambiguity in others, but role ambiguities in themselves may still arouse anxieties. They may be bothered by the incompatibility of the roles they play; they may feel diffuse, wondering which of their roles is basic, which is the "real me."

As indicated earlier, children do not necessarily work their way through each stage but may become fixed at a particular level. The Community Treatment Project population during the sixties (ages 11-19) showed the following percentages at the various I-levels: 5 percent at I_2, 35 percent at I_3, 60 percent at I_4, and less than 1 percent at I_5. Populations of adult offenders have been shown to have a higher percentage of I_5s, especially populations of narcotics offenders being treated under civil commitment laws.

Developmental Stages among Adolescent Delinquents

As can be seen from descriptions of the normal developmental stages, an individual moving toward physiological maturity while remaining at the lower stages perceptually may appear increasingly odd or deviant to society's institutions. Social institutions assume that individuals have reached an I_4 stage, feeling personally accountable for their behavior, operating with an internal evaluator that tells them what is right and what is wrong, understanding that people are different from each other in their needs and motives as well as behavior, and so forth. Those individuals for whom these assumptions do not hold are at considerable disadvantage in understanding what is happening around them. The life of an I_2 at age nineteen still focuses on trying to maintain a position of comfort. The concern is still focused on getting needs met in an unpredictable and arbitrary world. During adolescence I_3s are still searching for structure in novel situations so that stereotyped rules for behaving can be applied. They continue trying to control their worlds with overly simple formulas and are still not tuned into the things going on inside people.

The reason for giving such a detailed description of the characteristics of the I-level groups is to make more meaningful the issue of differential intervention at various points in the juvenile justice system. The concept of limited responsibility in a court of law should have different meaning when dealing with an I_2, an I_3, or an I_4. Issues of consent and waiver, as well as court responsibility for special protection of youth, should have different meanings at different points along this growth continuum. In addition, making these kinds of distinctions among youth helps us to ask all of the correctional questions in a more meaningful way. What children should be diverted out of the juvenile justice system and to what? On what basis should a child be matched with a foster home or a group home? Who will benefit from residential programs? Many empirical questions about what kinds of programs are wanted for what kinds of children have not yet been the focus of careful research, but findings from the three phases of the Community Treatment Project can be used to sketch some possible responses. Before doing this, however, one further component of the I-level classification approach must be described.

Following classification by social-perceptual I-level, a further distinction is made according to the persons' typical way of responding to and dealing with their view of the world. Although the Maturity Level Classification system was theoretically derived, the subtype categories were empirically derived; they were based on observations of patterns of response which occurred frequently within each I-level group in a delinquent population. Thus, while the assumption is made that growth as described by I-levels will characterize the development of all individuals, subtypes identified are assumed to be specific to a delinquent population. It seems apparent that some of the subtypes described do characterize individuals beyond the offender population, but we will not pursue such possibilities here. While the labels characterizing the perceptual levels (I_2, I_3, I_4) have no value connotation, either negative or positive, the subtype labels do for the most part have a negative connotation (Conformist, Neurotic). These subtype labels reflect not only the general response characteristics of an individual but also the individual's path into the justice system. For example, the behavior typically leading an I_3 Conformist into the justice system reflects a conformity to the pressure of delinquent peers.

Most of the data of the Community Treatment Project have been reported for the nine originally defined subtypes at I-levels 2, 3, and 4. In contrast, some of the most recent CTP data reported by Ted Palmer (1974) are shown with several of the subtypes combined in order to simplify reporting. From these subtype combinations, three groups of youth together constitute 88 percent of the juvenile offender population: Passive Conformist, Power Oriented, and Neurotic. These groups are described by Palmer in the following ways:

1. Passive Conformist. These youths usually fear, and respond with strong compliance to, peers and adults who they think have the upper hand at the moment, or who seem more adequate and assertive than themselves. They consider themselves to be lacking in social know-how and usually expect to be rejected by others, however they try to please them.

The Passive Conformist category is found at the I_3 level and, in the original subtype descriptions, was called Immature Conformist.

2. Power-oriented. This group is actually made up of two somewhat different kinds of individuals, who nevertheless share several important features (they perceive the world as operating primarily on a power dimension, seek external clues for behavior, and so forth). Those of the first type like to think of themselves as delinquent and tough. They are often more willing to go along with others, or with a gang, in order to earn a certain degree of status and acceptance, and later to maintain their rough reputations. The second type often attempt to undermine or circumvent the efforts and directions of authority figures. Typically, they do not wish to conform to peers or adults; and not infrequently, they will attempt to assume a leading power role for themselves.

The Power-oriented category is found at the I_3 level of interpersonal development. This group includes two of the originally defined nine subtypes, Cultural Conformist and Antisocial Manipulator.

3. Neurotic. Here again we find two separate personality types which share certain important characteristics (they feel anxious and guilty regarding personal inadequacies, carry "bad me" self-images, and the like). The first type often attempts to deny—to themselves and others—their conscious feelings of inadequacy, rejection, or self-condemnation. Not infrequently, they do this by verbally attacking others, by using boisterous distractions, by playing a variety of "games," or by doing all these things. The second type often shows various symptoms of emotional dis-

turbance, such as chronic or intense depression, or psychosomatic complaints. Their tensions and conscious fears usually result from conflicts produced by feelings of failure, inadequacy, or underlying guilt.

The Neurotic category is found at the I_4 level of development and includes those subtypes originally identified as Acting-out Neurotic, and Anxious Neurotic.

DIFFERENTIAL FINDINGS BY I-LEVEL AND SUBTYPE

Palmer (1974) has reported on the overall results of the Community Treatment Project from 1961 to 1973. A large amount of very complex material is summarized in the publication and only highlights can be mentioned here.

Differences by Program

When the differential treatment-oriented community-based program was compared with the traditional training school program (1961–69), these results were noted. (1) Boys classified as Neurotic (53 percent of the population) performed much better in the intensive community program than in the traditional program. This was consistent when using criminal identification and investigation "rap sheets" showing arrests, recidivism rates, favorable and unfavorable discharges from the agency, and postdischarge convictions. (2) Boys in the Power-oriented group (21 percent of the population) performed substantially worse in the community program than in the traditional program. (3) Boys in the Passive Conformist group (15 percent of the population) performed somewhat better in the community program than in the traditional program, although the outcome criteria are not consistent.

For girls of the three groups, only small and inconsistent differences were found in their performance in the different programs.

During the 1961–69 period, despite the positive performance of the Neurotic group as a whole in the community-based program, a certain portion of this group, as well as some portion of most subtypes, was responding positively neither to the community nor the traditional program. During the 1969–73 period, these hard-to-reach youths were compared following programs involving either (a) a direct release to the intensive community-based program or (b) an initial assignment to a CTP-staffed differential treatment-oriented residential program and later assignment to the community program.

When this comparison was made with the hard-to-reach boys, (1) those classified as the more seriously disturbed Neurotics benefited most from the "residence-first" approach; (2) the hard-to-reach Power-oriented group benefited little from the residence-first program; and (3) the hard-to-reach Passive Conformist group did not benefit at all from the residence-first program, and did somewhat better with direct community release.

Combining these sets of findings, it appears that the Neurotic group responds very well to a differential treatment approach. It further seems that this group can be divided on the basis of extent-of-disturbance criteria (defined by Palmer 1974, and showing interrater agreement of 80 percent) in order to recommend either the direct community release or the residence-first program. The traditional training school program appears still to represent the best alternative for the Power-oriented group. The direct release into the differential treatment-oriented community program seems the most satisfactory alternative for the Passive Conformist group.

In addition to these three groups, the remainder of the CTP population is classified in four rarely occurring groups, two I_2 subtypes and two I_4 subtypes. Although too few cases were available to allow for definite conclusions, comments on some of these subtypes are important for other reasons. The I_2, Asocial Aggressive child was rarely declared eligible for the Community Treatment Project (even though a very large percentage of juvenile court commitments of other subtypes were eligible). This suggests that these children are seen as so damaged and as so difficult to deal with that they are unlikely prospects for diversion programs, probation, or other community alternatives. This subtype was the classification category of only 1 percent of CTP eligibles; C. F. Jesness (1974) found this group represented 2 percent of an institutional population. The second I_2 subtype, Asocial Passive, while equally damaged (usually by brutal life experiences), are easier to deal with in community programs.

As for the I_4, Situational Emotional-reaction subtype, this group should be mentioned because, although it represents only 2 percent of the CTP population, it represents a large percentage of some probation populations. These are children who have developed rather normally but have run into a crisis during adolescence that has resulted in delinquency. Youths in this group performed consistently well in CTP, whether incarcerated or placed in community programs. If such resources were available, these youths would be excellent candidates for diversion programs to aid in dealing with the crises.

Palmer, in summarizing the data on the issue of kinds of youth and preferred setting for intervention, concludes:

Delinquent behavior can probably be reduced in connection with community and residential programs *alike,* by means of careful diagnosis and subsequent placement of individuals into appropriate rather than inappropriate or less-than-optimal settings and programs. In short, it might be said that it matters which youths (or types of youth) are placed into *which* types of settings; and that careful selection may lead to higher rates of success for residential and community-based programs alike (Palmer 1974, p. 10).

Differences by Worker Style

An additional finding of the Community Treatment Programs, which should be mentioned because the data are so impressive, involves the concept of matching worker style to client needs. For more than ten years, research on this topic has been under way in CTP. Studies have involved the characteristics of treatment agents and the way in which these characteristics do and do not mesh with the needs of various I-level subtypes defined in the project. Five worker styles have been defined and methods of classifying worker specialists identified. The impact of a matched versus an unmatched worker on program outcome has been studied (Palmer 1973).

In the comparison of youth who were well matched with their worker versus those who were not well matched, all conditions were held constant except for the worker matching—both groups were in the differential treatment-oriented community-based program, on comparable sized caseloads with the same workers, and with comparable resources. Using a variety of outcome criteria (parole suspensions, revocations of parole, postdischarge convictions, and the like) matching was shown to make a significant difference for the total group of youths, for I_3 youths separately, for I_4 youths separately, and for a number of the individual subtypes. Matching of client and worker style made the greatest difference in the case of the subtype I_4 Acting-out Neurotic, with matched subjects having a revocation rate of 25 percent and the unmatched, 61 percent by the end of a two-year parole period. Not only does matching appear to make a difference during the period of actual contact between the worker and the client, but the data show a carry over of this impact four years beyond discharge from the correctional agency. Data for the subtype I_4 Anxious Neurotic show convictions for 60 percent of the unmatched group and only 33 percent of the matched group at this postdischarge point.

IMPLICATIONS FOR INTERVENTION

As noted earlier, there are many decision-making points along the juvenile justice continuum at which little empirical information is yet available concerning differential impact of decisions on different kinds of youth. During 1973 and 1974, staff of the Juvenile Justice Project of the State University of New York at Albany School of Criminal Justice studied children committed to the New York State Division for Youth, to determine the relationship between characteristics of youths (including I-level and subtype dimensions) and differential placement and planning in this agency (Paquin, Harris, Warren, and Hagel 1975). From 1974 to 1976, this staff asked comparable questions concerning characteristics of youth and decision making at the levels of police, precourt diversion, and the family court in Schenectady county, New York. These types of studies are providing base-line information concerning the relationship between decision making and characteristics of youths which will enable researchers to ask further questions concerning the differential impact of alternative decisions and programs on types of youth.

Early in this paper, it was suggested that there are two main criticisms of intervention with juveniles: (1) that it is unethical and (2) that it is ineffective. Data reported in this paper suggest that the impact of intervention programs is not so much negative as complex. A case has been made for the importance of recognizing the differences among children and their needs, and seeking one kind of program or another for meeting those needs according to their differential appropriateness for different kinds of children.

What then about the ethical question? It seems to me that,

once programs have been shown to be differentially successful with types of children, the ethical question takes on a different meaning. One now has to ask what are the ethics of *not* assigning a child to programs which have been shown to reduce chances of further law violation behavior?

Aside from keeping cognizant of the complexities of empirical findings, and perhaps rethinking the ethical issues involved, what is an appropriate stance regarding juvenile justice decision making and intervention which can be taken at this time? Two global suggestions can be made. The first is a strong recommendation that research in differential programming be continued and that comparable research be instigated at the levels of police, precourt diversion, and juvenile court.

The second recommendation is that decision makers in the juvenile justice system take into consideration at least the child's developmental levels. This recommendation is based on the assumption that the juvenile court should be concerned with the future development of the child and not just past behavior with its focus on assessing blame and its implications for punishment. The concern for the child's future development involves a "natural rights" definition of justice—a right for the child to grow up to a stage where society's assumptions of self-responsibility and free will (at least in the form of having behavioral alternatives) have a chance to apply. By I-level categories, this would mean the development of a child beyond the I_3 level.

Is there any evidence that we know how to restart this growth process, once it has stopped? In the paragraphs which follow an attempt is made to specify intervention decisions which could now be recommended, based either on the finding that the program involved brings about growth along the maturity continuum or the finding that the program reduces delinquent behavior.

Three sets of recommendations can be advanced. First, regarding those identified as I_2s, the most immature or unsocialized children, protection of the child is called for—protection of the child against society rather than the reverse. Even though delinquent children are at issue here, principles applying to the dependent and neglected child apply. Intervention by the court may often mean removal of the child from an impossible home situation. In the case of the more aggressive I_2 children, a residential program may be called for. Jesness has shown that I_2s in institutional programs benefit more (both with in-program measures and recidivism rates) from a behavioral modification program than from a more psychodynamic program (transactional analysis) (Jesness et al. 1972). It is unknown whether increase in I-level is also involved. In the case of the more passive I_2 children, a protective-style foster home or group home and an intensive community-based program may be appropriate. This approach for the passive I_2 children has resulted in lower recidivism as well as growth along the I-level continuum for 50 percent of the group (Palmer 1968). There is no reason to believe that punishment will help these children grow up.

Second, it is important to subdivide those classified as I_3s, middle maturity children, into the weaker (Passive Conformist) and the tougher (Power-oriented) groups. For the former group, research evidence supports referral to a community-based program with the child living in his own home or an appropriate foster or group home. Under such a program, these children show the largest percentage (other than the I_2s) growing to the next I-level stage (26 percent; Palmer 1968). Regarding further delinquency, children in this group do well during the period of matched worker contact with them; however, postdischarge convictions show the success rate not to hold up beyond agency contact (Palmer 1974).

Looking at both I-level growth and further delinquent behavior, less is known about how to bring about change in the Power-oriented group than in other I-level groups. Data on delinquent careers show this group (compared to other subtypes) to have the highest rate of assaultive behavior and felony-type offenses. As a result, incarceration is typically called for. In an institutional setting, Jesness has shown the Manipulator subtype of the Power-oriented group to benefit more (both with in-program measures and recidivism rates) from a transactional analysis program than from a behavior modification program (failure rates for this group after one year on parole were 26 percent following transactional analysis and 40 percent following a behavior modification program) (Jesness et al. 1972). It is unknown whether increase in I-level is also involved; however, the differences shown appear large enough to lead to program recommendations.

Of further interest regarding recommendations for youths

identified as I_2s and I_3s are recent analyses by Palmer showing the interaction among (1) treatment in the community-based differential treatment program versus the traditional training school program, (2) age at intake into the program, and (3) twenty-four-month recidivism rate. For I_2 and I_3 groups combined, subjects were divided into younger (ages 11–15) and older (16 and up) groups. Advantages for the community-based differential treatment program held only for the younger subjects. For them, the community program showed twice as many successes as failures, and the traditional program showed three times as many failures as successes (Palmer 1976). Such findings show the great importance of differential intervention with the younger delinquents who are classified at the lower ego development stages.

Third, the evidence is very strong and persuasive that if juvenile delinquents are identified as I_4s, a differential treatment program can be identified for them which will increase their chances of avoiding further law violation behavior. As noted earlier in this paper, a matched worker is crucial with the I_4 Neurotic group, and the extent-of-disturbance ratings are important in deciding on a direct community program or a resident-first program.

Little emphasis has been placed on movement from I_4 to I_5 in the delinquent population. Even though advantages to this movement would be reflected in a more complex, empathic, and flexible individual who could draw on a greater variety of behavioral alternatives, two reasons account for this lack of emphasis. First, little societal pressure exists for growth beyond I_4 and there may be social resistance to this movement as well. Second, it is likely that such growth, when it does occur, does not typically begin until late adolescence, thus making it less relevant to working with an adolescent delinquent group.

In an age comparison similar to that reported for I_2s and I_3s, advantages of the differential treatment program for I_4s held primarily for the older group (16 and up), in contrast to the lower maturity levels where the advantage lay with the younger children. Among I_4 subjects, the community program showed twice as many successes as failures, and the traditional program showed an equal number of successes and failures (Palmer 1976).

LEGAL AND ETHICAL CONSIDERATIONS

The findings which have been reported in this chapter are the

results of studies conducted with juvenile delinquents who were
committed to a state agency and who may be considered serious
or habitual offenders, having on the average more than five
arrests before commitment. Program decisions which were made
about them occurred subsequent to both the juvenile court
adjudication and disposition hearings. In proposing that these
findings have implications for decisions that could be made
earlier in the juvenile justice process, a number of questions
concerning legal and procedural issues arise.

Nothing in these recommendations suggests that the rights of
the child should be ignored in the judicial process. Programs and
services short of the juvenile court can be offered to as many
children as possible, and certainly to a majority of the status
offenders. If a child is to go to court, due process protections at
the adjudication hearing are appropriate. The issue of differential
handling arises primarily at the disposition hearing and involves
two aspects of one major question: When two youths commit the
same offense, is it ever appropriate to recommend different
intervention times (length of sentences) and is it ever appropriate
to recommend a greater restriction on one than the other (as in a
residential program versus a community-based program)?

Both aspects of this question—in the long run—will have to be
answered. For now, the first aspect may be relatively easy to deal
with, partly because of our ignorance. When considering intervention time for a child of particular developmental level, two
conditions may obtain: the data suggest that either we now know
how to help the child grow and to reduce chances for future
delinquency, or we don't. If we don't know (as in the case of the
older I_2s and I_3s), then a fixed time is certainly called for, except
for experimental programs aimed at furthering our knowledge in
the area. If our data now suggest that we know only how to make
a difference in a small proportion of the cases at issue or how to
make a difference for only a short time (as in the case of the I_3
Passive Conformist group), then again a fixed intervention time
appears appropriate, except for experimental programs. If data
are available suggesting that a particular kind of intervention
program will bring about a desired change and the resources
needed to conduct that program are not available, then a fixed
time is again appropriate. In all of these cases where no argument
can be made that the program for the child will bring about

desired change, the only possible rationale for intervention appears to be punishment by a restriction of freedom (not necessarily incarceration, of course) for a period of time limited by the offense committed. This punishment may be thought necessary, but it should not be defended on the basis of being good for the child.

It is only when our data indicate clear advantages to one intervention over another that the issue of duration of intervention arises. Even for subgroups where the data do indicate preferred interventions, a fixed intervention time may be appropriate. For the I_4 Neurotic subtypes, for example, it appears that the intervention program can accomplish a great deal within twelve to eighteen months. With an intervention time in that range, it is likely that for individuals classified in this group, a continuing relationship with a matched worker could be maintained on a voluntary basis, if the youth and worker both see it as useful.

Many arguments can be and have been made against the indeterminate sentence. It does seem that, at the present time, fixed intervention times could be given without serious violations of differential treatment thinking. That this is a temporary state of affairs seems likely. Knowledge about programs more successful with, for example, the Power-oriented group and issues of time will again be raised. As a general principle, it seems supportable that the case for indeterminate intervention times should depend on further knowledge, rather than fixed times being set only if and when data support this policy.

The concern over fairness in placing different degrees of restriction on the freedom of two youths committing the same delinquencies cannot be postponed for future resolution. An example of a case which can arise immediately involves two youths committing the same offense—both classified as I_4 Neurotic but differing in degree of disturbance. The recommended programs would be similar except that the preferred placement for the more disturbed youth would be a residence. There is no way of deciding this issue except to check the accuracy of the classification and then review the research data on the subject. To the social scientists involved in the Differential Treatment studies, the outcome evidence on this score is so persuasive that it would seem an injustice to either youth not to take the recommended course of action. But how strong should the research evidence be before individual case decisions can be based on it? This is clearly a matter of values, and dialog on this point between social scientists and officials of the juvenile justice system should continue.

APPENDIX A: REVIEW OF DIFFERENTIAL RESEARCH RESULTS

1. A study of Project Outward Bound (Kelly and Baer 1971; survival training in primitive areas) in Massachusetts showed that program to be effective with those delinquents who were "reacting to an adolescent growth crisis" and not to be effective with the more immature, emotionally disturbed, or characterologically deficient boys.

2. A number of studies (Havel 1963, and Berntsen and Christiansen 1965 of Denmark) showed individual counseling programs to be effective with cases in the midrange of difficulty (as measured by a base expectancy formula, for example) but not to be effective for either the easier or the more difficult cases.

3. In a large sample of delinquent youths participating in California Youth Authority institution programs, the recidivism rate at a fifteen-month community exposure point was 50 percent. If this population is subdivided into eight categories on the basis of a typology, one finds concealed in that 50 percent failure rate, one subgroup whose recidivism rate was only 14 percent, another whose recidivism rate was 68 percent, with other subgroups falling somewhere in between (Palmer et al. 1968).

4. Looking at the same subgroups of the delinquent population in a sample of experimental cases of the Community Treatment Project in California, one finds violation rates for subgroups ranging from 13 percent to 43 percent. Again these data were reported for a fifteen-month follow-up (Palmer et al. 1968).

5. In phases 1 and 2 of the Community Treatment Project, data over a number of years showed the benefits of treatment in a community setting to be greatest for three of eight subtypes of juvenile offenders (those identified as Acting-out Neurotics, Cultural Conformists, and Antisocial Manipulator youth). Also consistent over the years has been the finding that one subtype (the Cultural Identifier) is more successful following a program involving incarceration (Warren 1969).

6. In a study conducted by Carl Jesness (1971) at the Preston School of the California Youth Authority, it was found that homogeneity (by delinquent subtype) in the living units of the institution consistently decreased unit management problems, primarily for certain subtypes. Significantly fewer rule infractions and peer problems, as well as transfers out of living units for closer confinement, were found primarily for three of six subgroups (those identified as Antisocial Manipulator, Cultural Conformist, and Acting-out Neurotics).

7. In another study by Dr. Jesness and associates (Jesness et al. 1972)

at two Youth Authority institutions (O. H. Close School and Karl Holton School), evidence is accumulating concerning the differential impact of behavior modification and transactional analysis programs on different subtypes of offenders. Data which include such attitudinal assessments as taking responsibility for delinquency, alienation from adults, attitudes toward staff and toward self, academic progress while incarcerated, and recidivism rate, rather consistently show that the behavior modification program is particularly appropriate for two of six subtypes of delinquents (identified as "very low social maturity, asocial individuals," and "middle social maturity, cultural conformists"). On the other hand, transactional analysis programming appears to be particularly appropriate for one of the six subtypes (identified as "middle social maturity, antisocial manipulators").

8. A number of studies of guided group interaction have indicated a more positive impact of the program on those institutionalized offenders who were comfortable with confrontive interactions (Knight 1970). Similarly, data collected on guided group interaction within the Community Treatment Project supported this finding (Palmer et al. 1968).

9. Within the Community Treatment Project, intervention programs being conducted by workers whose style and stance (manner of working with clients) were well matched to the needs of the individuals assigned to them was a crucial factor in the success in some subgroups and less relevant in others. (Matching was especially crucial for Acting-out Neurotics) (Palmer 1973).

10. In phase 3 of the Community Treatment Project, the question asked was whether the likelihood of achieving specified treatment objectives with certain juvenile offenders would be considerably increased if treatment were to begin, not within the community proper, but within a differential treatment-oriented residential setting. Data from the study showed that the residential program offered considerable payoff for the more seriously disturbed Neurotic delinquents, but not for the Passive Conformist or Power-oriented delinquents (Palmer 1974).

APPENDIX B: CHRONOLOGY OF CALIFORNIA YOUTH AUTHORITY EXPERIMENTAL PROGRAMS

1. *Community Treatment Project, Phase 1.* A study of the differential impact of intensive community treatment vs. incarceration on the various subtypes of the delinquent population, 1961–63 (Grant et al. 1962–63).

2. *Community Treatment Project, Phase 2.* A study of the differential impact of the Differential Treatment Model program vs. a guided group interaction program on various subtypes of delinquents, 1964–69 (Warren et al. 1964–66; Palmer et al. 1967–68).

3. *Preston Typology Study.* A study of the differential impact of

homogeneous living units (that is, only boys of one subtype in a unit) vs. heterogeneous living units of various subtypes of the delinquent population, 1965-68 (Jesness 1971).

4. *Differential Treatment Environments for Delinquents.* A study of five types of group homes, each home representing a treatment environment specificially related to the growth and development needs of particular types of delinquent youths, 1966-69 (Palmer 1972).

5. *Northern California Youth Center Project.* A study of the differential impact of two specific treatment methods, behavior modification and transactional analysis, on various subtypes of delinquents, 1968-72 (Jesness et al. 1972).

6. *The Differential Education Project.* A study of the differential impact of homogeneous classrooms with matched teachers vs. the traditional school program, 1969-72 (Andre and Mahan 1972).

7. *Community Treatment Project, Phase 3.* A study of differential treatment begun in a residential setting vs. a community setting on various types of delinquents. This study also includes a comparison of "matched" or specialist workers with generalist workers, 1969-74 (Palmer 1974).

8. *Center for Training in Differential Treatment, Phase 1 and 2.* The development of a training model (including a video training package) for teaching Differential Treatment concepts to staff of a broad range of correctional agencies, 1967-74 (Warren et al. 1971, 1974).

9. *Cooperative Behavior Demonstration Project.* Training for probation and parole units in behavior modification techniques, and assessment of impact of resulting programs on various types of delinquents, 1972-75 (Jesness and McCormick 1974).

BIBLIOGRAPHY

Andre, Carl R., and Mahan, JoAnn A. 1972. "Final Report on the Differential Education Project." Educational Research Series, no. 11. Sacramento: California Youth Authority.

Argyle, Michael. 1961. "A New Approach to the Classification of Delinquents with Implications for Treatment." *California State Board of Corrections Monograph* 2:15-26.

Berntsen, Karen, and Christiansen, Karl O. 1965. "A Resocialization Experiment with Short-term Offenders." In *Scandinavian Studies in Criminology.* London: Tavistock Publications. Pp. 35-55.

Gibbons, Don C. 1965. *Changing the Lawbreaker.* Englewood Cliffs, N.J.: Prentice-Hall.

Glaser, Daniel. 1974. "Remedies for the Key Deficiency in

Criminal Justice Evaluation Research." *Journal of Research in Crime and Delinquency* 11:144–54.

Grant, Marguerite Q. 1961. *Interpersonal Maturity Level Classification: Juvenile.* Sacramento: California Youth Authority.

Grant, Marguerite Q., and Warren, Martin. 1962. *Community Treatment Project Research Report No. 1.* Sacramento: California Youth Authority and the National Institute of Mental Health.

Grant, Marguerite Q., and CTP staff. 1963. *Community Treatment Project Research Report No. 2.* Sacramento: California Youth Authority and the National Institute of Mental Health.

Grant, Marguerite Q.; Warren, Martin; and Turner, James. 1963. *Community Treatment Project Research Report No. 3.* Sacramento: California Youth Authority and the National Institute of Mental Health.

Harvey, O. J.; Hunt, David E.; and Schroder, Harold M. 1961. *Conceptual Systems and Personality Organization.* New York: Wiley.

Havel, Joan. 1963. *Special Intensive Parole Unit, Phase 4: A High Base Expectancy Study.* Research report no. 10. Sacramento: California Department of Corrections.

Hurwitz, Jacob I. 1965. "Three Delinquent Types: A Multivariate Analysis." *Journal of Criminal Law, Criminology and Police Science* 56:328–34.

Jenkins, R. L., and Hewitt, Lester. 1944. "Types of Personality Structure Encountered in Child Guidance Clinics." *American Journal of Orthopsychiatry* 14:84–94.

Jesness, Carl F. 1971. "The Preston Typology Study: An Experiment with Differential Treatment in an Institution." *Journal of Research in Crime and Delinquency* 8:38–52.

———. 1974. *Sequential I-Level Classification Manual.* Sacramento, Calif.: American Justice Institute.

Jesness, Carl F.; DeRisi, William; McCormick, Paul; and Wedge, Robert. 1972. *The Youth Center Research Project: Final Report.* Sacramento: California Youth Authority and American Justice Institute.

Jesness, Carl F., and McCormick, Paul. 1974. *Cooperative Behavior Demonstration Project: Progress Report to California Council on Criminal Justice.* Sacramento: California Youth Authority.

Kelly, Francis J., and Baer, Daniel J. 1971. "Physical Challenge as a Treatment for Delinquency." *Crime and Delinquency* 17:437–45.

Knight, Doug. 1970. *The Marshall Program, Part 2: Amenability* to *Confrontive Peer-Groups Treatment.* Research report no. 59. Sacramento: California Youth Authority.

Kohlberg, Lawrence. 1966. "Moral Education in the Schools: A Developmental View." *School Review* 74:1-30.

Loevinger, Jane. 1966. "The Meaning and Measurement of Ego Development." *American Psychologist* 21:195-206.

Martinson, Robert. 1974. "What Works? Questions and Answers about Prison Reform." *Public Interest* 35:22-54.

McCord, William; McCord, Joan; and Zola, Irving K. 1959. *Origins of Crime.* New York: Columbia University Press.

Palmer, Ted B. 1968. *Seventh Progress Report, Part 2: Recent Research Findings and Long-range Developments at the Community Treatment Project: Community Treatment Project Research Report No. 9.* Sacramento: California Youth Authority and the National Institute of Mental Health.

————. 1972. *Differential Placement of Delinquents in Group Homes.* Sacramento: California Youth Authority and the National Institute of Mental Health.

————. 1973. "Matching Worker and Client in Corrections." *Social Work* 18:95-103.

————. 1974. "The Youth Authority Community Treatment Project." *Federal Probation* 38:3-14.

————. 1975. "Martinson Revisited." *Journal of Research in Crime and Delinquency* 12:133-52.

————. 1976. *Final Report of the Community Treatment Project, Phases 1, 2, and 3.* Sacramento: California Youth Authority and the National Institute of Mental Health.

Palmer, Ted B., and Warren, Marguerite Q. 1967. *Community Treatment Project Research Report No. 8.* Sacramento: California Youth Authority and the National Institute of Mental Health.

Palmer, Ted B.; Neto, Virginia V.; Johns, Dennis A.; Turner, James K.; and Pearson, John W. 1968. *Seventh Progress Report, Part 1: The Sacramento-Stockton and the San Francisco Experiments: Community Treatment Project Research Report No. 9.* Sacramento: California Youth Authority and the National Institute of Mental Health.

Paquin, Henry; Harris, Phillip; Warren, Marguerite Q.; and Hagel, Susan. 1975. *Relationship between Characteristics of Youth and Placement and Program Decisions in the New York State Division for Youth.* Report to National Science Foundation, RANN Section.

Peck, Robert F., and Havighurst, Robert J. 1960. *The Psychology of Character Development.* New York: Wiley.

Quay, Herbert C. 1964. "Personality Dimensions in Delinquent

Males as Inferred from the Factor Analysis of Behavior Ratings." *Journal of Research in Crime and Delinquency* 1:33-37.

Reiss, Albert J. 1952. "Social Correlates of Psychological Types of Delinquency." *American Sociological Review* 17:710-18.

Schrag, Clarence C. 1961. "A Preliminary Criminal Typology." *Pacific Sociological Review* 4:11-16.

Sullivan, Clyde E.; Grant, Marguerite Q.; and Grant, J. Douglas. 1957. "The Development of Interpersonal Maturity: Applications to Delinquency." *Psychiatry* 20:373-85.

Warren, Marguerite Q. 1969. "The Case for Differential Treatment of Delinquents." *Annals of the American Academy of Political and Social Sciences* 381:47-60.

———. 1971. "Classification of Offenders as an Aid to Efficient Management and Effective Treatment." *Journal of Criminal Law, Criminology, and Police Science* 62:239-58.

Warren, Marguerite Q.; Palmer, Ted B.; and Turner, James. 1964. *Community Treatment Project Research Report No. 5.* Sacramento: California Youth Authority and the National Institute of Mental Health.

Warren, Marguerite Q.; Riggs, John; Underwood, William; and Warren, Martin. 1964. *Community Treatment Project Research Report No. 4.* Sacramento: California Youth Authority and the National Institute of Mental Health.

Warren, Marguerite Q., and Palmer, Ted B. 1965. *Community Treatment Project Research Report No. 6.* Sacramento: California Youth Authority and National Institute of Mental Health.

Warren, Marguerite Q., and CTP staff. 1966. *Interpersonal Maturity Level Classification: Juvenile: Diagnosis of Low, Middle, and High Maturity Delinquents.* Sacramento: California Youth Authority.

Warren, Marguerite Q., and Palmer, Ted B. 1966. *Community Treatment Project Research Report No. 7.* Sacramento: California Youth Authority and the National Institute of Mental Health.

Warren, Marguerite Q., and CTDT staff. 1971. *Center for Training in Differential Treatment: Final Report of Phase 1.* Sacramento, Calif.: American Justice Institute.

Warren, Marguerite Q.; Howard, George; Thompson, Edward; and McHale, James. 1974. *Center for Training in Differential Treatment: Final Report of Phase 2.* Sacramento, Calif.: American Justice Institute.

10   Privacy, Recordkeeping, and Juvenile Justice

Charles E. Lister

We have by imperceptible degrees become a nation of recordkeepers. Public and private institutions now devote important resources to collecting and maintaining detailed information concerning our individual abilities, conduct, and characteristics (see Wheeler 1969; Westin 1967; Karst 1966). New technologies have been devised to facilitate the handling and distribution of such information. Institutions have moved in different directions at different speeds, but there is evidence that more personal information now is being collected about more individuals and disseminated more widely than ever before in our history (Westin and Baker 1972). This gradual lengthening of our institutional memories has created significant issues of personal and civil liberties, to which the law has until recently given only occasional attention (Department of Health, Education, and Welfare 1973; Westin 1967; Lister, Baker, and Milhous 1975). Here, as elsewhere, the law arrives breathless and a little late.

Many of the law's difficulties in the resolution of recordkeeping issues arise from the absence of meaningful doctrinal guidance. The principal tool with which judges and legislators have come to work in this area is the doctrine of privacy. Despite the affection with which it is often regarded, privacy remains a notion of formidable obscurity. Partisans of every description find within it support for diverse and conflicting goals. At a minimum, however, privacy suggests that individuals should, as far as other social commitments permit, be assured an important measure of control over the release to others of information regarding their activities and attributes. Such control is intended to serve a variety of social and individual interests. Despite the importance of those interests, there is as yet little agreement on the scope or forms of protection to which privacy is entitled. The privacy doctrine now represents little more than an exhortation to more effective action. It provides a direction and goal for the law, but it offers neither guidance nor formulas for achieving that goal.

In these circumstances, it should hardly be surprising that the problems created by elaborate recordkeeping remain serious even where the law has long sought to protect interests of privacy and confidentiality. The juvenile justice system was among the first areas in which judges and legislators sought to control record-keeping activities. The drafters of the earliest juvenile court legislation obviously feared that the public might not share their belief that involvement with the juvenile justice process should confer no stigma. One method used to avoid stigmatization was the adoption of a new terminology, unrelated to that used by the criminal courts. Each subsequent generation of administrators and judges has made its own changes in jargon, in a continuing effort to emphasize the distinctive features of juvenile justice. A second method adopted in many jurisdictions was the imposition of an elaborate web of restrictive statutes and rules, intended to limit the dissemination of juvenile justice records. There can now be little doubt that both methods have failed. The general public has remained cheerfully unconvinced by the adroit juggling of terminology in juvenile justice. To the popular understanding, any involvement with the juvenile justice process raises a strong inference of misconduct. The stigma of such wrongdoing is supported and preserved by the widespread availability of juvenile justice records outside the system.

This chapter briefly describes the character, implications, and extent of recordkeeping in the juvenile justice process. Based upon the evidence of abuse of juvenile justice records, the chapter suggests a series of recordkeeping guidelines to protect privacy and other interests more effectively.

RECORDKEEPING PRACTICES

It is well to recall the scope of the recordkeeping activities that are involved here. The activities of the police and courts confirm that, as Philippe Ariès (1962) has suggested, this is the century of adolescence. Some 20 percent of the persons arrested in the United States in 1965 for crimes other than traffic offenses were under eighteen years old (National Advisory Commission ... 1973). In 1971, juvenile courts in the United States disposed of some 1,250,000 cases (Department of Health, Education, and Welfare 1971, p. 11). Even larger numbers of other children and young people are the subjects each year of pre-judicial inquiries and proceedings (Gough 1966; Tappan 1950; Handler and Rosenheim 1966). It is reported that in 1969 in New York City alone more than 50,000 Youth Division cards—on which police contacts with juveniles were recorded—were completed (Coffee 1972).

At each of the various stages of the juvenile justice process, extensive personal information may be accumulated (Cicourel 1968; Kahn 1953). Recordkeeping has, for example, become a principal activity of juvenile probation officers (Miles 1965). It has been estimated that they spend some 22 to 30 percent of their time at it. It is said that some case files concerning individual juveniles "contain more words than a substantial novel or textbook" (Lemert 1969, p. 356). A wide range of material may be included in such records. They almost uniformly include extensive identifying information and reports of each stage of the juvenile justice process through which the child has passed. They may contain reports of medical care or psychological counseling. They may include anecdotal and unverified appraisals of the young people involved, their behavior and their families. They may contain materials obtained from the juveniles' teachers and school records. They may provide a comprehensive portrait of the juveniles, their difficulties and perhaps their families.

Despite the extensive resources that are devoted to juvenile justice recordkeeping, there is strong evidence that such records have many deficiencies. It is reported that a juvenile may be "registered" as a delinquent in New York without the formality of an arrest. Whether or not an arrest occurs, a police record is created "without further opportunity for rebuttal or amplification." Since juveniles and their families are often not afforded access to the records concerning them, a useful method for eliminating errors and omissions is foreclosed. In many instances, pre-judicial records may not include the eventual disposition of an arrest or inquiry (Coffee 1972; cf. Project SEARCH 1970). The records are said to include "a vast amount of information" that is "seldom if ever used." Much of the information is reported to bear no "discernible correspondence" to the disposition of the cases to which they refer (Lemert 1969, p. 357; see also pp. 358, 359–60).

Notwithstanding the apparent deficiencies of the records, they are made available, at least in some jurisdictions, to a wide variety of agencies and individuals unconnected with the juvenile justice system. Two investigations conducted in New York City indicated that Youth Division reports may be disseminated to, for example, the Boy Scouts, Catholic Charities, and community antipoverty groups (Coffee 1972, p. 588). A New York decision, *In re Smith* (310 N.Y.S. 2d 617 n.4 [N.Y.C. Family Court 1970]), found that prospective employers, the military services, and even private investigators may have little difficulty in obtaining juvenile arrest records. The frequency and extent of such disclosures undoubtedly vary widely among agencies and jurisdictions, but there is persuasive evidence that records from the juvenile justice system are available to outside agencies and individuals in many, perhaps most, areas of the country.

The elaborate web of restrictive rules and statutes that has been woven about juvenile justice records in most jurisdictions has by no means proved effective. Those protective rules and statutes have been described as "so unsatisfactory" that they "may fairly be characterized as a failure" (*Harvard Law Review* 1966, p. 800). In some instances, such rules and statutes may even have served to increase the injuries produced by juvenile justice records. It has generally proved very much easier for prospective employers and others to obtain access to such records through police and other referral agencies than directly through the courts. Police and referral agency records often may not, however, indicate the disposition of arrests and other exculpatory information. Such records have all of the risks and deficiencies of investigatory and intelligence files. They are frequently incomplete and anecdotal. Some of their information may be unverified or unverifiable. They may include unsophisticated appraisals of the juvenile's family, environment, and needs. The designations of the juvenile's alleged conduct may be vague or misleading. Such records may not clearly indicate that the juvenile may have been the subject of a proceeding for protection or assistance unrelated to any misconduct (*Harvard Law Review* 1966). The careful efforts of many jurisdictions to regulate juvenile justice recordkeeping may thus have caused, at least in some instances, wider reliance upon the least accurate and most frequently injurious forms of such records.

There can be little doubt that the retention and availability of juvenile justice records may be injurious to young people and their families. The existence of such records, in which the juvenile's conduct may be inaccurately or unfairly characterized, or from which the ultimate disposition of the case may be omitted, may significantly prejudice the juvenile's subsequent contacts with the police and other agencies (Coffee 1972; Haskel 1973). A wide variety of pre-judicial decisions may be influenced to the juvenile's disadvantage. Even juvenile court records may be used to the juvenile's disfavor in various situations in the ordinary courts. Licensing and public employment agencies may deny a juvenile job and other opportunities on the basis of such records. In some instances, such agencies are expressly empowered to obtain such records from the police. The existence of an arrest or other juvenile justice record may limit a juvenile's opportunities for military service. In all of these situations, those who obtain access to the records are likely to accept them as regular and accurate.

There is extensive evidence that private employers frequently refuse to hire those who have been arrested or made the subject of police inquiries, even if no misconduct is found to have occurred. As one New York court observed, "Employers, like the general public, tend to conclude from a charge and an arrest that 'where there is smoke, there must be fire,' and they may automatically disqualify applicants with arrest records when there are sufficient untarnished applicants" (*In re Smith,* 310 N.Y.S. 2d 620 [N.Y.C. Family Court 1970]). It has been reported that 75 percent of the employment agencies in New York City will not refer an applicant with a criminal record, regardless of the absence of a conviction (Coffee 1972). Even if employers do not reject out of hand an applicant with a record, they may well conclude that an inquiry into the circumstances of the record would be unduly burdensome. Applicants are likely to have no effective remedy for such treatment. They may even be unaware that the facts of their records were the causes of their rejections. If, on the other hand, they seek to conceal their records, they may later be discharged as liars.

At a minimum, the availability of juvenile justice records to prospective employers, private investigators, and other outsiders may cause repeated embarrassment of the juvenile and family. The platitudes of custodial treatment and noncriminality offer little protection against such injuries. They represent, as a California court has emphasized, "a legal fiction, presenting a challenge to credulity and doing violence to reason." Viewed realistically, a juvenile justice record is both a blight upon the character of a child and a "serious impediment" to the future (*In re Contreras,* 241 P. 2d 633 [1952]). The harsh consequences of a juvenile record are particularly unfortunate because they are most often inflicted upon young persons who already suffer from the burdens of poverty, racial discrimination, and diminished social opportunities. The stigma of juvenile misconduct falls chiefly upon those who already bear, and who understand themselves to bear, the marks of society's neglect.

The objections to such uses of juvenile justice records are many and important (Gough 1966; Cannon 1973; Lister, Baker, and Milhous 1975). Isolated and insignificant misconduct, or even the accidents of dependency or neglect, may result in a severe and unfair blemish upon a juvenile's record. The creation and preservation of a stigma of wrongdoing may prevent the effective restoration of the juvenile's social status and opportunities, thereby defeating a principal purpose of separate systems of juvenile courts. The stigma creates a prophecy which often is self-fulfilling: it enhances the likelihood that juveniles will find themselves in new difficulties, and increases the pressures in the direction of adult criminal conduct. Much time and attention has been given in recent years to the unfairness created by current methods for handling and using adult criminal history records (Project SEARCH 1970, 1971). All the problems that have been identified in connection with those records also arise in connection with juvenile records. All the unjust and asocial results that demand a remedy there also warrant prompt and careful attention here.

RECORDKEEPING REFORMS
Rights of Access and Challenge

The first and most important possible step toward improved juvenile justice recordkeeping is to create for each juvenile and his or her parents and legal representatives the right to inspect and challenge the accuracy of records relating to her or him. (See generally Department of Health, Education, and Welfare 1973; Russell Sage Foundation 1970; Westin and Baker 1972.) Similar rights have recently been created for students by Section 513 of the Education Amendments Act of 1974 (20 U.S.C. §1232g) and for individuals generally by the Privacy Act of 1974 (5 U.S.C. 552a). The latter is applicable only to files maintained by federal agencies.

The reasons for the creation of such rights are several. First, such rights are among the most effective methods now available to assure the accuracy and completeness of records concerning individuals. Unlike the other available mechanisms, they are driven by the most consistent and reliable of motives, individual self-interest. Additional assurances of accuracy are particularly important for pre-judicial juvenile justice records, in which dispositions and other pertinent events may not be fully reported and the labels attached to conduct may be vague or even misleading. Second, the creation of such rights would help to restore a measure of public confidence in juvenile justice recordkeeping. A principal cause of fear and distrust of recordkeeping systems of all varieties has been the absence of clear information regarding what is in them. Those apprehensions have markedly increased as computerization has become more common (Russell Sage Foundation 1970; Project SEARCH 1970). The availability of records for inspection and challenge under reasonable conditions would do much to alleviate such apprehensions. Third, as shown above, juvenile justice records may have important consequences for the future opportunities of the juveniles to whom they relate. As a matter of ordinary fairness, such records should be available for review and verification by the children and their legal representatives.

If juveniles or their legal representatives believe that their records are inaccurate or misleadingly incomplete, they should be afforded reasonable opportunities to challenge them and to compel appropriate corrections and additions. A great variety of mechanisms might be used for that purpose. A particularly effective device might be small panels of professionals and private citizens who could conduct informal hearings, take evidence, listen to argument, and formulate specific recommendations. Such panels could be formed by or derived from the recordkeeping control committees recommended below. The decisions of such panels should be made subject to review in the juvenile courts or another appropriate forum. The panels should also serve as continuing mechanisms for evaluating juvenile justice record-keeping. They could for this purpose periodically report to the control committee, the juvenile courts, the legislature, or other appropriate authorities regarding the categories of abuse they encounter and the forms of remedy they find necessary.

Rights of access and challenge have little meaning unless juveniles and their legal representatives are also given accurate and timely notice of the categories of records maintained by the police, courts, and other juvenile justice agencies. Any young person who has contact with the juvenile justice system should routinely receive a concise description of the records maintained by juvenile justice agencies, the purposes for which those records are used, the lengths of time for which they are maintained, and the agencies to which they may be made available. The same information should be provided to the child's parents and legal representatives. A brief brochure might be prepared for these purposes. The brochure should be readily available to interested members of the public.

The notice afforded by a general brochure or comparable device should be supplemented by specific and timely notices given to all juveniles or their legal representatives on each occasion in which their records are released without their consent outside the agencies designated in the brochure. Such notices undoubtedly raise significant practical problems. Similar rules have, however, recently been adopted by many public school systems without evidence of extraordinary difficulty. Moreover, any practical problems will diminish in importance as computerization of juvenile records becomes increasingly widespread and as the dissemination of juvenile records outside the juvenile justice system becomes less common. Whatever those problems may prove to be, it is important that juvenile justice agencies acknowledge the genuine interest of young people and their parents in the proper usage and fairness of juvenile justice records.

Restrictions on Dissemination

A second step toward improved systems of juvenile justice
recordkeeping is to impose careful restrictions upon those to whom
juvenile justice records are made available. The severity of the
dangers created by any data system depends largely upon the
purposes for which, and agencies by which, the system's information may be used. Constraints upon the methods by which a
system collects and stores data, no matter how thorough, cannot
replace effective restrictions upon the uses to which those data are
put. Such restrictions have, however, proved extraordinarily
difficult to enforce. The history of criminal history recordkeeping
for both adults and juveniles provides vivid evidence that such
records almost irresistibly suffer abuse. Nonetheless, it remains
important to limit as far as possible the distribution of juvenile
justice records to those persons within the juvenile justice system
and ancillary public welfare agencies who genuinely need such
records to carry out their responsibilities.

When juvenile justice records are released, it should be clearly
understood that further dissemination is permissible only with the
prior authorization of the agency that originally provided the
records. Formal interagency agreements should be entered into
for this purpose. Licensing agencies, prospective employers,
credit bureaus, the military services, the communications media,
private investigators, and other outsiders should be forbidden
access to all such records by direct and unequivocal legislation.
No discretion should be given to police and other pre-judicial
agencies to distribute such records to such persons. Although the
release of certain general information from such records might
not in itself prove injurious, it would confirm that the child had
been involved in the juvenile justice process. Moreover, such
information is often readily available from other, less prejudicial
sources.

Such restrictions should be enforced by careful auditing procedures. Listings should be maintained of all persons to whom
juvenile justice records are made available, and samplings of
those listings should be periodically audited to verify that the
records have been distributed only for proper juvenile justice
purposes. If there is evidence that records have been misused or
improperly disclosed, sanctions should be available for imposition
upon those responsible. As suggested below, it may be necessary

for this purpose to adopt a series of internal and external control mechanisms.

Restrictions upon the dissemination of juvenile justice records to outsiders have little meaning if the juveniles involved may be compelled to authorize the release of their records. Such pressure is commonly used by the military services and many private employers to obtain access to juvenile justice records. Only a statutory prohibition can be expected to limit significantly the use of such methods, and even such a prohibition cannot be expected to prove wholly effective. A further response to the problem, and an essential ingredient of an improved juvenile recordkeeping system, is a statutory authorization to juveniles to respond negatively to inquiries regarding contacts with the juvenile justice system. It has been argued that such authorizations are undesirable because they are morally noxious and because they may deny information properly relevant to some inquiries (Gough 1966). It has, for example, been suggested that juveniles who have engaged in some forms of sexual or sex-related conduct should not be permitted to withhold that information from licensing agencies and prospective employers.

Despite the asserted moral deficiencies of such authorizations to withhold information, no other method adequately achieves a fundamental goal of the juvenile courts—the restoration of the juvenile's previous opportunities and social status. The history of our law consists in no small measure of the manipulation of fictions and equivocations, often for the service of interests less praiseworthy than the protection of young lives. It seems squeamish in the extreme to deny such authorizations on moral grounds. If licensing agencies and prospective employers genuinely need limited information from juvenile justice records, particularly concerning sexual or sex-related conduct, any such requirement could be fully satisfied by the creation of narrow statutory exceptions. To provide increased fairness in individual cases, such exceptions might be made subject to review in each instance by special petition to the juvenile court or other appropriate forum. Whatever mechanism might be preferred, the protection intended by the statutes and rules governing juvenile justice records should not be thwarted by the simple expedient of compelling responses from the juvenile.

Mechanisms of Internal Control

Another important step in the reform of juvenile justice record-keeping is the creation of appropriate mechanisms of internal control. Juvenile justice records are maintained under disparate conditions by a great variety of agencies. The adequacy of the rules by which those records are controlled varies widely. In some instances, an agency's recordkeeping practices may be ad hoc and even ad hominem. Information well protected at one stage of the juvenile justice system may be readily available to outsiders at another stage. The applicable rules are commonly not made known to juveniles or their legal representatives. Interested members of the public are rarely permitted to participate in the formulation or evaluation of these rules. More uniform and effective methods of regulation, which will help to increase public confidence in those records, are required.

A useful control mechanism has recently been suggested in connection with adult criminal history records. The Security and Privacy Committee of Project SEARCH, which included representatives of several state criminal justice agencies, suggested in 1971 that each state should create a criminal justice recordkeeping control committee, clothed with broad regulatory powers over adult criminal history records. Such committees would consist of private citizens, members of interested groups, and representatives of criminal justice agencies. They would be empowered to issue regulations to control all stages of the criminal history recordkeeping process. They would be responsible for formulating appropriate administrative standards, including methods for auditing the activities of recordkeeping agencies. Citizen complaints about the maintenance or use of criminal history records would be referred to the committees for resolution. Massachusetts already has created such a committee (Mass. Ann. Laws, chap. 6, 168 et seq.). Recent federal legislation has required the application of the SEARCH suggestions to a wide variety of state and local criminal justice agencies (42 U.S.C. 3771(b)). Other legislation has created a federal commission to regulate various forms of recordkeeping and to encourage the protection of privacy interests.

Similar state and local committees, drawn from the general public and interested professionals, could usefully be created to address the problems of juvenile justice recordkeeping. Such committees could formulate minimum standards for handling and using such records, audit the activities of juvenile justice agencies, and assess citizen complaints regarding the fairness and accuracy of juvenile recordkeeping systems. If they were given suitable statutory authority, such committees could enforce their administrative standards with appropriate sanctions. Individuals who are found to have abused juvenile justice records could be made subject to a graduated series of penalties, including termination of public employment. Agencies that abuse or acquiesce in the abuse of records could be made subject to a comparable series of penalties, including the denial of access to juvenile justice records compiled by other agencies. The committee might require, or recommend that others require, that custody of some records should be entrusted to an independent office or agency not directly subject to supervision by the police or social agencies.

Local control committees should also serve as focal points for continuing reform of juvenile justice recordkeeping. It should be their responsibility to ascertain what recordkeeping requirements will most effectively serve the various social and individual interests involved. They should for this purpose issue periodic public evaluations of recordkeeping practices within the state, identify the forms and occasions of abuse, and recommend any legislation that may be needed.

Mechanisms of internal control should be supplemented by an appropriate system of external remedies for those who are injured by recordkeeping activities. The legal history of this country provides elaborate evidence that administrative remedies are in themselves inadequate to guarantee individual interests. Juvenile justice recordkeeping systems will warrant public confidence only if they first provide tangible evidence of concern for the rights of those about whom they collect information. A meaningful system of external remedies would help to provide such evidence. The external remedies should be of several varieties. The juvenile's right of access, challenge, notice, and review should be made judicially enforceable. The juvenile courts might be entrusted with handling such enforcement actions. More effective civil remedies, including a right to obtain punitive damages, should be provided for persons who suffer injury to their reputations or other interests because of inaccurate, incomplete, or misused records. Criminal penalties should be imposed upon those who are found to have willfully abused juvenile records.

Record Use in Research

Juvenile justice records have increasingly been used in recent years for purposes of social and behavioral research. There is no reason to doubt that most such projects are genuinely in the public interest. Research projects involving juvenile justice records conducted without the consent of the juveniles or their legal representatives should not, however, be permitted without suitable safeguards. The public advantages of such projects may be satisfactorily accommodated with the privacy interests of juveniles if a series of minimum standards are adopted. The following standards closely parallel those suggested by Project SEARCH (1970) and Ruebhausen and Brim (1965):

First, no program of research utilizing individual records should be permitted unless a control committee or other appropriate body has investigated the proposed program, reviewed the professional qualifications of those involved, and approved the procedures included for the protection of individual privacy interests. Periodic audits should be made throughout the life of the research project.

Second, the control committee or other reviewing body should demand that the identities of individual subjects should be divorced as fully and effectively as possible from the data made available to the researchers. Anonymity of those whose records are reviewed should be regarded as an essential characteristic of all well-designed research programs. Any project not requiring anonymity should be examined with the greatest care. It should be assumed that such projects demand stringent supplementary protective measures designed to minimize the possibility that the identities of individual subjects may become known outside the research group.

Third, materials made available to research projects should be subject to security measures in the project which are not less extensive than those employed by the juvenile justice agencies from which the data were obtained. Any exceptions to the security measures approved for a project should be made only with the approval of the control committee or reviewing body.

Fourth, any code or key which identifies individual subjects should be given special protection and should be destroyed as soon as it is no longer essential for the research project.

Fifth, data released for one research project should not thereafter be used for any other purpose without the express prior authorization of the agencies which initially permitted the release of the data.

Sixth, these and other appropriate requirements should be embodied in a written agreement entered into by the research personnel, under which the juvenile justice agencies involved retain rights to monitor the project to assure adequate protection of the interests of the subjects. If materials are not properly used or protected, the agreement should authorize the agencies to terminate the project's access to juvenile justice records.

Expurgation

Another important ingredient of improved juvenile justice record-keeping systems is the creation of appropriate mechanisms for the expurgation of various categories of police and other juvenile records (Gough 1966; Baum 1965; Sheridan 1969). A variety of purposes may be served by such mechanisms. First, they help to eliminate inaccurate or unverifiable information from an agency's files. No objection can reasonably be made to expunging inaccurate information, although many might quarrel about timing and application. Regarding unverifiable information, the police or other nonjudicial agencies are likely to believe such materials to be essential tools in their efforts to identify juveniles who are thought to require their ministrations. The importance of retaining such materials may be assessed only as part of a broad reevaluation of the proper activities and goals of those agencies— an evaluation which cannot sensibly be made here. In general, however, the retention of unverifiable information may create severe hazards for the interests of juveniles, and a strong showing of social need should be demanded before it is permitted.

The second possible purpose of purging programs may be to eliminate information which, although accurate, is out of date or otherwise unreliable as a guide to a subject's present attitudes or behavior. Third, such erasures of institutional memory may contribute to the rehabilitation of juveniles, and their restoration to their previous opportunities and social status. A principal assumption of the juvenile justice system remains that juveniles should not be permanently disadvantaged by isolated or immature conduct. Society should instead undertake to ignore, and permit juveniles to ignore, relatively ancient involvements with the juvenile justice system. All of these purposes have also recently been urged as goals for adult criminal history record-keeping (Project SEARCH 1971, 1972).

A wide variety of time periods and other limitations might be adopted for purging rules. Modest programs of experimentation could usefully be undertaken to evaluate the relative advantages of such limitations. A sensible program might provide that the legal and social files of the juvenile courts, police, probation, and other agencies shall be closed two years after the final discharge of a person from custody or supervision, or two years after the entry of any other court order not involving custody or supervision. Where the juvenile has not been convicted, adjudged delinquent, or otherwide held to be in need of supervision, such records should be closed immediately after the termination of proceedings. Such rules already have been suggested by the Children's Bureau (Sheridan 1969, pp. 49-50).

When records are closed, they should be held under special controls in a central recordkeeping facility. As far as reasonably possible, such facilities should be independent of the agencies that originally compiled the records. Index and all other references to the proceedings should be treated "as if they never occurred" (Sheridan 1969, p. 50). Inspection of the records should occur only by permission of the juveniles and their legal representatives, or for purposes of any challenge to the accuracy of the records initiated by the juvenile. The records should not otherwise be available for inspection by any person or agency except under special order of the juvenile court or control committee. Where a conviction or adjudication of delinquency occurs in another proceeding after the records have been closed, the records might be made available to the juvenile court and supervisory agencies for purposes of that subsequent proceeding. Any such exceptions should, however, be carefully defined and limited by appropriate legislation, following the example of the recommendations made by Project SEARCH concerning adult criminal history recordkeeping.

CONCLUSION

The guidelines described here are intended to assist in creating juvenile justice recordkeeping systems that may more adequately protect the privacy and other interests of juveniles and their parents. They are no more than guidelines, and exceptions and variations will undoubtedly prove appropriate in many situations. Even without such alterations, however, none of the guidelines requires any fundamental changes in the character or organi-

zation of the juvenile justice process. I do not mean that such
fundamental changes are unnecessary. In an important sense, any
examination of juvenile justice recordkeeping begins at the wrong
point. Recordkeeping merely embodies and reflects the activities
and goals of the institutions by which the records are maintained.
The problems of recordkeeping properly should not be addressed
independently, as I have sought to do here, but as part of a broad
reassessment of the values and purposes of the juvenile justice
process. The guidelines described here are bits of odd carpentry,
designed to remedy a number of obvious deficiencies in the
juvenile justice process. They provide no excuse for delay in the
design and construction of a more nearly adequate structure.

BIBLIOGRAPHY

Ariès, Philippe. 1962. *Centuries of Childhood: A Social History
of Family Life.* New York: Knopf.
Baum, Terry L. 1965. "Wiping Out a Criminal or Juvenile
Record." *California State Bar Journal* 40:816–30.
Cannon, Joe A. 1973. "The Importance of Expungement of
Juvenile Records and the Execution of Private Slovik." *Clear-
inghouse Review* 6:38.
Cicourel, Aaron V. 1968. *The Social Organization of Juvenile
Justice.* New York: Wiley.
Coffee, John C: 1972. "Privacy versus *Parens Patriae:* The Role
of Police Records in the Sentencing and Surveillance of Ju-
veniles." *Cornell Law Review* 57:571–620.
Department of Health, Education, and Welfare. 1971. *Juvenile
Court Statistics.* National Center for Social Statistics. Washing-
ton, D.C.: U.S. Government Printing Office.
———. 1973. *Records, Computers, and the Rights of Citizens.*
Report of the Secretary's Advisory Committee on Automated
Personal Data Systems. Washington, D.C.: U.S. Government
Printing Office.
Gough, Aidan R. 1966. "The Expungement of Adjudication
Records of Juvenile and Adult Offenders: A Problem of
Status." *Washington University Law Quarterly* 1966:147–90.
Handler, Joel F., and Rosenheim, Margaret K. 1966. "Privacy in
Welfare: Public Assistance and Juvenile Justice." *Law and Con-
temporary Problems* 31:377–412.
Harvard Law Review. 1966. "Juvenile Delinquents, the Police,
State Courts, and Individualized Justice." 79:775–810.
Haskel, Peter B. 1973. "The Arrest Record and New York City

Public Hiring: An Evaluation." *Columbia University Journal of Law and Social Problems* 9:442–94.

Kahn, Alfred J. 1953. *A Court for Children.* New York: Columbia University Press.

Karst, Kenneth L. 1966. "'The Files': Legal Controls over the Accuracy and Accessibility of Stored Personal Data." *Law and Contemporary Problems* 31:342–76.

Lemert, Edwin M. 1969. "Records in the Juvenile Court." In *On Record: Files and Dossiers in American Life,* ed. Stanton Wheeler. New York: Russell Sage Foundation. Pp. 355–87.

Lister, Charles E.; Baker, Michael A.; and Milhous, Raymond L. 1975. "Record Keeping, Access, and Confidentiality." In *Issues in the Classification of Children,* vol. 2, ed. Nicholas Hobbs. Pp. 544–64. San Francisco: Jossey Bass.

Miles, Arthur P. 1965. "The Utility of Case Records in Probation and Parole." *Journal of Criminal Law Criminology and Police Science* 56:285–93.

National Advisory Commission on Criminal Justice Standards and Goals. 1973. *Report on Courts.* Washington, D.C.: U.S. Government Printing Office.

Project SEARCH. 1970. *Security and Privacy Considerations in Criminal History Information Systems.* Committee on Security and Privacy. Technical report no. 2. Sacramento, Calif.

———. 1971. *A Model State Act for Criminal Offender Information.* Committee on Security and Privacy. Technical memorandum no. 3. Sacramento, Calif.

———. 1972. *Model Administrative Regulations for Criminal Offender Record Information.* Committee on Security and Privacy. Sacramento, Calif.

Ruebhausen, Oscar M., and Brim, Orville G., Jr. 1965. "Privacy and Behavioral Research." *Columbia Law Review* 65: 1184–1211.

Russell Sage Foundation. 1970. *Guidelines for the Collection, Maintenance and Dissemination of Pupil Records.* New York.

Sheridan, William H. 1969. *Legislative Guide for Drafting Family and Juvenile Court Acts.* Children's Bureau, Social and Rehabilitative Services, Department of Health, Education, and Welfare. Washington, D.C.: U.S. Government Printing Office.

Tappan, Paul W. 1950. "Unofficial Delinquency." *Nebraska Law Review* 29:547–58.

Waterman, Nairn. 1969. "Disclosure of Social and Psychological Reports at Disposition." *Osgoode Hall Law Journal* 7:213–33.

Westin, Alan F. 1967. *Privacy and Freedom.* New York: Atheneum.

Westin, Alan F., and Baker, Michael A. 1972. *Databanks in a Free Society*. New York: Quadrangle Books.

Wheeler, Stanton, ed. 1969. *On Record: Files and Dossiers in American Life*. New York: Russell Sage Foundation.

III   JUSTICE FOR THE NONDELINQUENT CHILD

11 Developing Constitutional Rights of, in, and for Children*

Robert A. Burt

The Supreme Court has recently decided several cases challenging state substitute-parenting activities. The number of such cases on the docket is itself striking. Most likely, it reflects the Court's perception of widespread concern about family structure in the society. Taken together, these decisions appear to vest constitutional rights in both parents and children against state interventions and increasingly to curtail state authority to intervene against parental wishes on behalf of children. But the Court has not yet formulated a coherent rationale for this stance. Nor has it acknowledged that its application of constitutional norms in these cases yields some important generalizations about the permissible scope of state substitute-parenting activities.

This discussion will address that task. It will not consider state interventions to control juveniles who commit overtly antisocial acts. In principle, the justifications for these interventions are clear. In practice, the obstacles to successful interventions seem

*A previous version of this chapter appeared in *Law and Contemporary Problems* 39 (1975): 118–43. © 1976 by The University of Chicago.

the same as for adult corrections. Instead, the focus will be on state efforts exclusively intended, in the catch-phrase, to help troubled children rather than to punish children in trouble.

CONSTITUTIONAL BARRIERS TO STATE INTERVENTION
Protection of Parental "Rights"

Supreme Court decisions proclaiming rights of both parents and children to be free from state substitute-parenting have followed converging paths. Perhaps the most dramatic of the recent parents' rights decisions is *Wisconsin* v. *Yoder* (406 U.S. 205 [1972]). There the Court upheld the claims of Amish parents to exempt their children from state compulsory education laws following eighth-grade schooling. The Court rested its conclusion on intertwined principles of religious freedom and parental prerogatives, and suggested that parental claims which lacked an explicit religious content would command less deference (pp. 235–36). This application of the religion clause of the First Amendment is vulnerable to doctrinal criticism, and appears difficult to square with recent Supreme Court cases invalidating, for allegedly "establishing" state-favored religions, laws which assisted parents in sending their children to church-related rather than public schools (see *Committee for Public Education and Religious Liberty* v. *Nyquist,* 413 U.S. 756 [1973], and *Sloan* v. *Lemon,* 413 U.S. 825 [1973]).

But bypassing this objection, there is powerful good sense to the Court's result. Amish parents had a passionate belief that secondary schooling would expose their children to "modern" and "sinful" pursuits. The Court stated:

Modern compulsory secondary education in rural areas is now largely carried on in a consolidated school, often remote from the student's home and alien to his daily home life. As the record so strongly shows, the values and programs of the modern secondary school are in sharp conflict with the fundamental mode of life mandated by the Amish religion ... [and such school] carries with it a very real threat of undermining the Amish community and religious practice as it exists today ... (*Wisconsin* v. *Yoder,* 406 U.S. at pp. 217–18).

The state's justification for overriding the intense convictions of the Amish parents appears unpersuasive. It may be that Wisconsin school authorities appreciated the psychological stress, and even possible developmental risks, of forcing children into social settings that their parents saw as irredeemably sinful. But no such understanding was evident in the state's justification for this policy as it appears in the case record. The Court noted that the state school superintendent rejected a proposal offered by the Amish, and followed in several other states with Amish populations, that their children attend locally organized secondary schools with special curricula. The ostensible ground for rejection was that such arrangement "would not afford Amish children 'substantially equivalent education' to that offered in the schools of the area" (pp. 208–9, n.3). This attitude appears to ignore the fact that Amish children were not "substantially equivalent" to most school children in Wisconsin and that differences in rearing and parental attitudes required a different educational response.

This is not to say it was a clear-cut question whether Amish children should be exempted from compulsory secondary schooling. The choice between preparing Amish children for the circumscribed world of their parents or for entry into the more common community raises complex questions. But if the state is prepared to act against parental views, it must act with sensitivity to the conflicts imposed on the Amish children, or state action will have no reliable utility for them. As the state portrayed its purposes in the litigation, however, the special needs of these children seemed subordinated to the state's intention to do battle for Enlightenment against the Forces of Darkness.

This is a common characteristic of state interventions against parents purportedly on behalf of children—a generalized state self-righteousness, even punitiveness toward "difficult" parents, that takes little account of the individual needs of the affected child. This trait is as evident, and as harmful to children, in state interventions to rescue physically abused children from their parents, as in state efforts to save the less obviously needy Amish children (Burt 1971; see also *Prince* v. *Massachusetts,* 321 U.S. 158[1944]). Even where parents seem to be using children for their own ends, state intervention has little better to offer. The battle between state and parent in many cases seems remarkably like typical divorce custody disputes, in which neither adult is incontestably correct and each is locked in a power struggle with the other, using children as weapons and trophies while ignoring their needs (Watson 1969).

Protection of Children's "Rights"

This same analysis can be applied to recent Supreme Court decisions purporting to establish "rights of children" against state intervention without explicit reference to parental views. In *Tinker* v. *Des Moines School District* (393 U.S. 503 [1969]), the Court ruled that public schools could not discipline students for wearing black armbands to protest the Vietnam War. The plaintiffs were two children from the Tinker family, thirteen and fifteen years old, and a sixteen-year-old friend, Christopher Eckhardt. Justice Fortas, for the Court, resoundingly proclaimed that "students in school as well as out of school are 'persons' under our Constitution. They are possessed of fundamental rights which the State must respect ... " (393 U.S. at p. 511).

The Court did not mention, however, that two other children from the Tinker family (though not plaintiffs in the case) had also worn black armbands to school. These children were eight and eleven years old. Perhaps tactical reasons led to their exclusion from the suit. It does indeed seem incongruous to unfurl the First Amendment for the right of eight-year-olds to protest their government's war policy.

Further, the Court described, without any irony apparently intended, the way in which the plaintiff children decided to wear their armbands:

In December 1965, a group of adults and students in Des Moines held a meeting at the Eckhardt home. The group determined to publicize their objections to the hostilities in Vietnam and their support for a truce by wearing black armbands during the holiday season and by fasting on December 16 and New Year's Eve. [Plaintiffs'] parents had previously engaged in similar activities and they decided to participate in the program (393 U.S. at p. 504).

Justice Black, in dissent, noted that the Tinker children's father was "a Methodist minister without a church ... paid a salary by the American Friends Service Committee" and that Christopher Eckhardt's mother was an "official in the Women's International League for Peace and Freedom" (393 U.S. at p. 516). From this record, is it crystal clear whose political expression rights were being protected—the children's or their parents'? What of the concern stated by the Court earlier, in *Prince*, that "propagandizing the community ... create[s] situations difficult enough for adults" and that parents are not "free . . . to make martyrs of their children" (321 U.S. at p. 170)?

From this perspective, the *Tinker* decision is no different from the parental rights case considered earlier. In general, it is false psychology to portray a dispute between children and the state without acknowledging the direct (implicit or explicit) role of parents in that dispute (Freud 1964, 1965*a*). But the facts in *Tinker* suggest reasons why the Court was correct to favor the parents' position in both of the cases discussed thus far.

The state's error appears in the Court's narrative as follows:

The principals of the Des Moines schools became aware of the plan to wear armbands. On December 14, 1965, they met and adopted a policy that any student wearing an armband to school would be asked to remove it, and if he refused he would be suspended until he returned without the armband. . . . On December 16, Mary Beth and Christopher wore black armbands to their schools. John Tinker wore his armband the next day. They were all sent home and suspended from school until they would come back without their armbands. They did not return to school until after the planned period for wearing armbands had expired—that is, until after New Year's Day (393 U.S. at p. 504).

The Court noted that the December 14 school principal's meeting was originally called after a student told his journalism teacher that he "wanted to write an article on Vietnam and have it published in the school paper" (393 U.S. at p. 510). Following this meeting, school authorities dissuaded the student from that action. The Court also observed that "the school authorities did not purport to prohibit the wearing of all symbols of political or controversial significance" (393 U.S. at p. 510).

Even if *Tinker* is (as *Yoder* too may be) a symbolic battle between adults, each using children as sacrificial pawns, the Constitution clearly constrains the state more than parents in such matters. If the Des Moines school officials, that is, insist on one brand of ideological conformity, the traditions of the First Amendment amply justify a court ruling that this is impermissible state action in itself.

The *Tinker* case may be said to reach the correct result with inadequate theory. To supply a coherent constitutional rationale, the Court would need to acknowledge the potential educational and constitutional relevance of the facts in the case suggesting that the children's armbands reflected more their parents' convictions than theirs. The Court ignored the possibility that school officials might exclude parental political views from school in order to free children to think through these questions for themselves. As noted, that motivation was implausible on the face of the *Tinker* record. If the goal of the school was to bolster students' independence from their parents' political viewpoints, suspension from school and forced return home seems a strange instrument for that purpose. But this purpose is not an implausible educational goal nor should it be prohibited by the Constitution. The constitutional question would have changed complexion if the school officials had convincingly argued that they were acting not to impose their political views on students, but rather to protect the root values of the First Amendment—tolerance, diversity of thought, individual autonomy—against parental impositions on children.

A THEORY OF PERMISSIBLE STATE ACTIVITY
Whose Autonomy Does the Constitution Protect?

Commitment to individual autonomy is, of course, an ideology, but it is deeply a part of the American ethos. In extolling the virtues of the tightly conformist Amish society, the *Yoder* Court betrayed intellectual confusion by linking the parents' claims over their children with American individualistic tradition. The Court noted "the Amish qualities of reliability, self-reliance, and dedication to work" and asserted that

the Amish communities singularly parallel and reflect many of the virtues of Jefferson's ideal of the "sturdy yeoman" who would form the basis of a democratic society. Even their idiosyncratic separateness exemplifies the diversity we profess to admire and encourage (406 U.S. at pp. 225-26).

The Court was apparently not troubled by, or perhaps not aware of, the rigid intolerance of dissent reported among adult members of the Amish community (Hostetler 1968). It might surprise Jefferson or Thoreau to learn that a twentieth-century court found individualistic values incarnate in the Amish community. The school officials could equally well claim that Amish community self-determination is at war with the possibility that Amish children would develop toward autonomous individualism. They could point out that individualistic values are highly prized throughout this society and that small-group pluralism commands deference, in our tradition, only when it serves instrumentally to strengthen individualistic character traits alien to the Amish.

At heart, substitute-parenting authority has customarily rested on the claim that important social values were served if the state helped children toward self-reliant autonomy. The Court's recent skepticism toward this claim was given fullest expression in the celebrated juvenile delinquency case of *In re Gault* (387 U.S. 1 [1967]), which forced formalization of juvenile court procedures explicitly because that court system had failed to provide promised individualized helpful treatment to its charges. But procedures in that case can for the most part be seen as an attempt to produce a more precise fit between the purposes and the actions of the juvenile court by improving its fact-finding capacity (Burt 1971, p. 1293). The *Gault* decision does not proclaim, as such, that the state has no authority to pursue its beneficent purposes under any circumstances (see Schultz and Cohen, this volume).

In the later cases of *Yoder* and *Tinker* the Court appears to go somewhat further to limit the purposes that the state might pursue in displacing parental authority over children. The *Yoder* decision, in particular, raises doubt about authority for state intervention against contrary parental wishes even if that intervention might reliably foster a child's autonomy. In addressing the possibility that Amish parents might in the future be shown to "prevent . . . their minor children from attending high school despite their expressed desires to the contrary," the Court commented:

Recognition of the [State's] claim . . . would, of course, call into question traditional concepts of parental control over the religious upbringing and education of their minor children recognized in this Court's past decisions. It is clear that such an intrusion by a State into family decisions in the area of religious training would give rise to grave questions of religious freedom comparable to those raised here. . . . On this record we neither reach nor decide those issues (406 U.S. at pp. 231–32).

The Court's considerable deference to parental prerogatives appears to rest on two questionable premises. The first is that this dispute between the Amish and the state "is not one in which any harm to the physical or mental health of the child or to the public safety, peace, order, or welfare has been demonstrated or may be properly inferred" (406 U.S. at p. 230). But surely it is question-begging to assert that no harm at all to the "mental health of the child . . . may be properly inferred." Norms of mental health are necessarily culturally derived, none more so than the socially prized adult capacity of autonomous self-determination. Autonomy in a democratic society might be defined as the adults' capacity to choose what their parents might not have chosen for them or for themselves (Erikson 1963). Such a norm of mental health is at least inferentially at risk in this case.

The second questionable premise is the implicit conclusion that state action to support children's "expressed desires" to defy their parents would be "an intrusion by a State into family decision" while the absence of such action would not be an intrusion. But as long as state laws force children to remain in their parents' custody, and demand that all others who deal with them first gain parental consent (Foster and Freed 1972; Clark 1968), the state has equally intruded into family decisions. In other words, if the state can intervene on behalf of parents, it must also have authority to decide when public purposes would not be served by such intervention. It would follow that if state support of parental prerogatives disserves a value central to our democratic ethos—that is, an individual's capacity for self-determination—a court would be hard put to assert that some contrary constitutional principle forces deference to parents.

A Presumption Favoring Parental Prerogatives

These comments have quarreled with the *Yoder* opinion, not with its result. The *Yoder* result might be better justified, and rest more comfortably with other recent cases, on this principle: that when the state contravenes parental decisions in child rearing, with the claimed purpose of benefiting the child, the state must present a convincing case that its intervention in fact will serve its professed goal (see M. Wald, this volume).

So far the Supreme Court has eschewed adopting this standard. It was reluctant in the *Yoder* case to speak broadly of parental prerogatives. Instead it relied heavily on the "religious" aspect of the particular prerogatives claimed. *Tinker* and *Gault* ignored the parents' roles in resisting state intervention for their children; they spoke instead of the children's rights as if they could be asserted without considering their parents' intent. But the principle uniting these cases might best be understood to establish a constitutional presumption in favor of parental prerogatives over children. In the course of this discussion, the shortcomings of such a principle will become evident, but at least it may be a useful way station toward a general standard governing state substitute-parenting activities.

A presumption favoring parents corresponds to important realities: to the social reality that state child-rearing interventions are inherently difficult enterprises, and to the psychological reality that an intensely intimate bonding between parent and child lays the best developmental foundation for this society's most prized personality attributes (Goldstein, Freud, and Solnit 1973; Ellsworth and Levy 1969). Notwithstanding the language of the *Yoder* opinion, however, it makes no sense to endow this parental presumption with irrebuttable force in any particular aspect of child rearing. Rather, a court should view all state claims to contravene parental desires with the same skeptical eye—but it should be prepared to sanction all interventions that satisfy its generally applicable criteria.

Standards to Govern State Intervention

The proper criteria can readily be drawn from Supreme Court decisions protecting other "fundamental rights" from state intrusion. They are these: Has the need for the state intervention been convincingly identified, and is there a close correspondence between that need and the means proposed to satisfy it (Gunther 1972)? Application of such criteria would permit courts to gather data directly relevant to the purposes served by the presumption for parents. The presumption will be displaced only if the state can demonstrate that the psychological values achieved by close parent-child identity are in fact disserved in the particular dispute and that the historic inadequacies in state substitute-parenting techniques and resources have in fact been remedied for the particular case.

Of these two standards, the second will have special bite. The first criterion is more obviously value-laden and thus more easily satisfied by simple assertion that a child's optimal development is endangered by parental practices. But for the second criterion, what can the state say? Though the state may fervently and properly want to displace parental values, who has a magic wand to make parents disappear from their children's thoughts and lives? The psychological professions have amply documented that "efforts made to 'save' the child from his bad surroundings and to give him new standards are commonly of no avail, since it is his own parents whom, for good or ill, he values and with whom he is identified" (Bowlby 1965, p. 80). Frequently, state demands contrary to parental wishes only force children to choose between conflicting authorities when they have no satisfactory principle for choice. Unless the state can demonstrate that its proposed technique for intervention accounts for this psychological reality, there cannot be the clear correspondence between means and ends that would justify intervention.

The Court's action in *Yoder* illustrates both the child's dilemma and the Court's failure sensibly to comprehend it. This appears in the disagreement between the Court majority and Justice Douglas, who dissented on the ground that the religious freedom of the child alone—and not his parents—warranted judicial protection. Accordingly, Douglas argued, the record must affirmatively show that the child's own religious views were opposed to secondary education. Only one child had testified on this score, and Douglas concurred in exempting her from the state law because she "in fact testified that her own religious views are opposed to high-school education" (406 U.S. at p. 243).

The Court gave short shrift to this argument, asserting in effect that an identity of religious views between parent and child should be assumed unless the state can demonstrate that the child has "expressed desires to the contrary." But even this appears a grudging concession, as the Court observed that

there is nothing in the record or in the ordinary course of human experience to suggest that non-Amish parents generally consult with children up to ages 14–16 if they are placed in a church school of the parents' faith (406 U.S. at p. 232).

On the face of it, Justice Douglas appears a champion for the rights of children, for the view—as he puts it—drawn from *Gault* and *Tinker* that "children are 'persons' within the meaning of the Bill of Rights" (406 U.S. at p. 243). The Court's position might appear to ignore children and espouse their parents' "chattel rights" in them. But the question is more complex than this. In fact, there is little practical difference between these positions.

Both the Court and Douglas demand some express opposition from children before recognizing a conflict between parent and child. But how can we offer protection in this way to children caught between loyalties to and dependence on their parents and the desire to become adults autonomous of them? This is a classic psychological bind of adolescence (Erikson 1968). Undoubtedly the different upbringing of Amish children influences the timing and intensity of this bind for them as compared to adolescents in the more typical American culture. But for all children poised at adulthood, it is risky business to ask them whether they differ with their parents on matters crucial to both and to expect that the answer will give a reliable guide to action in the children's interest. Often the children's true feeling is deep ambivalence, and they are paralyzed into silence by that amibivalence or they mask it with a brash assertion that they agree or disagree with their parents. Justice Douglas' solution may indeed only harmfully intensify the psychological bind for these children by forcing them either publicly to disavow their parents or publicly to announce their acquiescence and consequent impotence in response to parental direction.

This is not to say that children of whatever age have no autonomous will. But the typical difficulty for children is clearly to identify (even to themselves) and crisply to announce their self-determination (Freud 1965b). Thus it would be wrong to demand a clear expression of the child's view (either for or against parents) as the first step in evaluating state claims to displace parents. The child's capacity to have an independent view is a proper goal, not the prerequisite, for state interventions.

From this perspective, the best resolution of the dispute represented by the *Yoder* case appears to have been the compromise proposal initially advanced by the Amish but rejected by the state. A secondary school primarily catering to Amish children and limited in curricular offerings would have given state school officials a forum in which children could be reached by outside influences which would not appear dramatically at odds with their parents' demands. As noted, this kind of compromise had been reached in other states with Amish parents.

It may be that if state school officials now proposed to compel Amish parents to send their children to such a school, the Court would retreat from its apparently blanket exemption for them.

Whatever the specific meaning of *Yoder* for future state dealings with Amish parents, that case and the *Tinker* decision have contributed to forcing state school officials generally to adopt different attitudes in responding to disputes with parents over children. Ten years ago parents locked in dispute with local schools were without recourse unless they could enroll their children in private school or move to a new jurisdiction. Today those parents bring suit. Not all such suits are, or deserve to be, successful. But court actions have forced substantial numbers of local schools to implement new discipline policies, to abandon hair length or school newspaper censorship regulations, to devise new testing procedures for placement in "slow learners" classes, and to adopt other significant changes in school policy. Schools are now on notice that they must be prepared to justify their substitute-parenting interventions to an external agency.

The Scope of the Standard

The substantive scope of the parental presumption rule is not clear. This obviously troubled the Court in the *Yoder* and *Tinker* cases. In *Yoder* the Court responded, as previously noted, by attempting to limit its ruling to traditional religions and to practices which were "obviously" not harmful to children, but neither limit will withstand close analysis. *Tinker,* on the other hand, attempted to limit its reach by restricting attention to grand issues and excluding school "regulation of the length of skirts or the type of clothing ... hair style or deportment" (393 U.S. at pp. 507-8). It has become apparent, however, that many students (and their parents) did not subscribe to the Court's hierarchy of importance, and substantial numbers of lower courts subsequently have used *Tinker* to strike down school regulations on precisely these matters (for example, *Hatter* v. *Los Angeles City High School District,* 452 F. 2d 673 [9th Circuit, 1971]).

But the absence of substantive clarity in this presumption for parents should not be troubling. In fact, doctrinal tidiness in these matters is neither possible nor desirable. State policy toward child rearing revolves around attempts to answer this question: Will children become what this society most wants (1) if parents are left to follow their own stars in child rearing, (2) if plural subcultural groups are free to shape norms of child rearing for parents, or (3) if the more inclusive state community is permitted to intrude and set limits on both parental and small-group impositions on children? The answer surely must be that there can be no conclusive answer favoring one contestant over the other.

Though it may seem paradoxical, that lack of answer is a central guide for court review of state child-rearing policy. If there can be no conclusive reply, courts should properly insist that the question remain adequately open. When, as in *Yoder* or *Tinker*, battle lines for resolution seem clearly drawn—when the state is patently attempting to override individual parental or subcultural group norms for child rearing and when the latter are patently resisting—it is important to assure that none of the combatants conclusively ousts the others.

This, after all, is the practical effect of the holdings in those cases. School officials in *Yoder* remain free to require elementary education for Amish children. Only state claims for compulsory higher education were rejected because the Court perceived that this would fundamentally "undermine . . . the Amish community and religious practice as it exists today" (406 U.S. at p. 218). In *Tinker*, school officials are still permitted to prescribe curriculum and thus dictate in important ways what their students think about. The Court only rejected school demands to dictate what students might say about the Vietnam War.

The constitutional presumption against state substitute-parenting might appear to be at odds with these results. It might be assumed that state claims would automatically be defeated no matter what. But this result would follow only if the presumption, with its accompanying presentational rhetoric, were accepted on its face. State efforts to override parental preferences will surely receive "strict scrutiny," in the grand tradition of constitutional exegesis. These efforts will often be invalidated. And the "strict scrutiny" formulation will remain substantively inscrutable (as the grand tradition demands) about when state claims will prevail. Ultimately, however, judicial precedent and experience will forge an appropriate accommodation of competing state and parental claims over children.

In these disputes, a number of elements must come together to bring judicial intervention. Adamant parents can enlist a trial court's sympathy (or, as will quite frequently be necessary, an appellate court's sympathy) only if they can invoke widely shared norms of child rearing and prove them by appeal to the judicial sense of community experience as enlarged by expert witnesses attesting to parental wisdom in the dispute. As judges are drawn more often into these disputes, they will undoubtedly sense what Justice Jackson observed in overturning the compulsory school flag salute for Jehovah's Witness children:

School boards are numerous and their territorial jurisdiction often small. But small and local authority may feel less sense of responsibility to the Constitution, and agencies of publicity may be less vigilant in calling it to account. . . . There are village tyrants as well as village Hampdens . . . (*West Virginia State Board of Education* v. *Barnette,* 319 U.S. 624, 637–38 [1943]).

As school litigation continues in frequency, school officials will learn what other habitual litigants know, that conviction of one's rectitude does not assure success in court. They should thus be led to temper rigid uniformity in school administration and to respond more flexibly to the demands of school clientele, if only to forestall the haphazard impact of litigation. Thus the process itself of holding available judicial review will tend toward achieving the basic goal of the constitutional norm—to enhance diversity and to combat any imposition of monolithic, authoritarian standards on children.

IMPLICATIONS OF THE STANDARD:
THE CASE OF "STATUS OFFENSES"
This discussion has implications for future impositions of constitutional norms on the juvenile court. Many have argued that state efforts through that court to aid "children in trouble" are at best quixotic and should be generally curtailed. One commentator has distilled this argument to "the basic injunction for public policy . . . : *leave kids alone wherever possible*" (Schur 1973). This dictate may be interpreted in two ways. One is that the state should refuse generally to impose any direct legal constraints on children, except when they violate laws equally applicable to adults. The other interpretation is that the state should continue to support parental authority over children but that it should abandon the substitute-parenting claims of the juvenile court. Those who argue for the abolition of the juvenile status offenses— state interventions, that is, exclusively applied to children— typically ignore the implications of state power supporting parents' authority over their children.

Status offenses appear to be the purest examples of juvenile
court claims to control children for their own welfare rather than
to protect the community from directly dangerous conduct. Even
if these offenses are abolished, however, it seems likely that much
of the conduct involved would be easily caught under adult
offense rubrics such as car theft, breaking and entering, disorderly conduct, drug possession, or the like. Abolitionist proposals would appear clearly to exclude only current truancy and
runaway laws from juvenile court coercive jurisdiction. But if
these status offenses are abolished, would some state agency
retain power to force the return of children to their parents?
Under current law, parents may file a complaint that their
children have fled and that complaint in effect authorizes police
authorities throughout the country to arrest those children and
forcibly return them home. If this state power is retained and the
state loses only the power to force (or perhaps even to offer)
alternative custodial placements for such juveniles, it may be
questioned whether children's interests are thus well served. It is
equally questionable whether any of this state coercive authority
over children in flight should be wholly abolished.

In flight from parents or from school, juveniles most directly
express adolescent efforts at self-definition in combat with constituted authority (Erikson 1968; Suddick 1973). Insofar as the
state intends to assist fleeing juveniles in resolving the developmental implications of their flight, the use of force seems to carry
great dangers. Whether coerced back into home, school, or other
arrangements, the coercion itself is likely to appear to the
juveniles (and to mean in fact) that their reasons for running have
been ignored and their autonomy overriden. But failure to exert
force can have equally disheartening meaning for juveniles. It
may mean that no one has taken up their dare to prove that they
are wanted. It may mean that no one will help them act on their
need to return to home or school while accommodating their
equally powerful need not to admit dependence (see Nir and
Cutler 1973). There can thus be quite important reasons to retain
state power to coerce in order to help some runaway children.

But the same dilemma presents itself here as in the earlier
discussion of other state parenting interventions. Though the case
can be made for beneficial application of state power, how
reliably beneficial can that power be in the hands of the state
agencies that traditionally exercise it? There is no assured answer

to this question. Yet in view of the developmental significance of runaway behavior, and the likelihood that withholding state intervention in many cases will lead to results no one (including the juvenile) wants, it seems worthwhile to try to develop more subtle mechanisms to control state power before jettisoning it altogether.

One possibility in particular appears worth exploring—that coercive invocation of state power for runaways be retained, but be made subject to strict time limits. Thus, for example, a juvenile court could command runaway children to remain in a state-sponsored foster home for two months but at the end of that time the option to remain there would belong wholly to the juveniles themselves. If they then decided to renew flight, the state might have authority to invoke another coercive placement—perhaps with the juvenile's parents or another foster family or in an institution. But there also would be time limits on these coercions. At some time, and after the failure of some number of forced placements to engage the juvenile's voluntary adherence, there should be no more state authority to exercise added coercions solely because of the juvenile's flight.

The ultimate time limit imposed would in one sense be arbitrary, since the juvenile's psychological needs for both freedom and coercion would remain unresolved, but it would prevent the juvenile from getting caught in a state-spun web where individual needs are both exacerbated and disregarded. The social reality is that state coercion of children too readily becomes an end in itself rather than a means for helping troubled children. If state power over runaways is to match its claimed purpose of assisting children toward greater capacity for self-determination, the state must be held rigorously to demonstrating that the goal is realized in individual cases.

The state must accordingly be forced, within a relatively limited time, to obtain the willing acquiesence of the child for continued state intervention. Unless the state must rely on persuasion, it will too readily rely on force. If state officials are permitted long-term indulgence of typical official fantasies that force cures all, they will have no adequate incentive to work toward enlisting the willing cooperation of the child, and the possibility of any beneficial purpose for the child will be jeopardized (Burt 1973). Further, if state officials knew that they were compelled quickly to find a place where runaway children were willing to remain, there would be incentive to relax the rigidly moralistic standards now followed by most juvenile court authorities in approving group or individual foster homes as alternative placements. Instead of imposing their definitions of the good life on hapless children, these state officials would be forced to collaborate with their charges to find an acceptable accommodation.

After runaway children had rejected every placement for which the state had time to coerce, this scheme would not leave them utterly without state protection. Such children, like all adults, would be protected against others' depravations by the criminal laws proscribing assaults, rapes, narcotics dealings, and the like. In many instances, these laws will not effectively protect roaming children from harm, but it is false to think that confining children for indefinite terms does effectively protect them. When the state locks children away—whether in secure state institutions or in their parents' homes from which they persistently flee and to which the police persistently return them—the harm is directly inflicted by state action. Accordingly, if state power over children is limited by some constitutional principle, the state cannot argue that the harm it imposes is no worse than what others might do to children.

This raises the further question: Does a constitutional principle compel some such limitation on state power over runaway children? This question is not readily answered by resort to the constitutional principle posited earlier in this discussion, that parents' disposition of children should presumptively prevail in disputes with the state. The parents of many runaway children willingly turn them over to state custody. For these children, should agreement between parents and the state justify unlimited exercise of power over children? For other runaway children, the state may want to force them again and again to return to their parents from whom they persistently flee. For these children, should the state be constitutionally permitted to adhere to the parental presumption no matter how persistently the child protests?

In other words, does the principle drawn from *Yoder* and the other cases discussed mean that parents have a constitutionally sanctioned role in their children's lives, or does it mean that the state has a constitutionally limited role in child rearing which typically, but not necessarily, is enforced by deference to parents? Traditional dictates against state authority to enforce ideological or moral conformity among its citizens—whether drawn from First Amendment roots or from more contemporary notions of "privacy rights"—support the latter interpretation. Many Supreme Court cases, though addressing child-rearing practices, speak directly to the limits on state power over all individuals, whether child or adult. The Court in most of its decisions has ignored the powerful psychological role played by the parents, and the disposition of the cases suggests that the Court has not deferred to parental views from respect for them but rather to limit the state power "to submerge the individual and develop ideal citizens" (*Meyer* v. *Nebraska,* 262 U.S. 390, 402 [1923]).

From this perspective, then, constitutional values are called into question whenever the state professes to act with children in the role traditionally taken by parents in this society. Rigorous standards for justifications should be imposed on state substitute-parenting actions, whatever the desires of the child's own parents may be. In applying those standards, the parents' acquiescence in state intervention may itself convincingly establish the need for it. But that acquiescence would not necessarily demonstrate the requisite close correspondence between the child's need and the means by which the state proposes to satisfy that need. Moreover, the state must be more limited in its claims to mold its citizens than parents in their claims. This is, simply put, because the Constitution directly limits the state, not parents.

Accordingly, in reviewing state runaway statutes, constitutional norms could properly be applied to require some firm limitation on the breadth of state power in order to ensure that the means of state intervention rigorously and reliably correspond to the purported purposes. Consideration of state runaway statutes sharply illuminates two aspects of the constitutional analysis underlying all of the preceding discussion—children are a subject population no matter who exercises authority over them, and all such authority (whether school teachers, juvenile court judges, or parents) is supported by state sanction, by legal artifact. Thus constitutional norms limiting state child-rearing activity, it would appear, must apply to all of its guises, including state support for parental authority over children.

This proposition echoes the constitutional law debates attempting to define "state action." Here, as in other contexts in this debate, it is possible to argue with formal logic that every interaction between parent and child is "state action" because state support for parental authority is so pervasive. By this logic, any imposition of parental discipline might require *Miranda* warnings (*Miranda* v. *Arizona*, 384 U.S. 436 [1966], mandating officials to inform suspects of various rights when questioned regarding possible criminal acts) and appointment of counsel for the accused child. This strained result obviously makes no sense, but to avoid this, it is not necessary wholly to ignore the reality that state support for parental authority pervades child-rearing policy in this society. Constitutional constraints on state support for parental authority could sensibly be applied only when battle lines are clearly drawn between parent and child (as when the child flees home) and overt state support is invoked by the parent. Where the state police power is thus made starkly visible, it is proper to apply constitutional norms generally applicable to such state power and to require that the state respect children's claims to developing autonomous individuality.

Conclusion

This discussion has addressed instances in which the state has assumed parenting roles—as teacher, judge, and custodian of children. Underlying these state activities is a basic historical reality. During the past century or more, extended kinship and close community ties in this country have visibly attenuated, leaving nuclear families and one-parent families increasingly isolated and vulnerable. As informal supports for troubled families diminished, the need arose for formal social institutions to fill the gap (Rothman 1971). But the very formality of the institutions that appeared brought impersonality, rigidity, and stigmatization, defeating their helping purposes.

In the past decade, beginning most openly with the assault on juvenile court procedure in *Gault*, court decisions have reflected (sometimes explicitly) the growing criticism directed at social welfare agencies. The cases discussed here, dealing with various aspects of the state's parenting activities, often appear to have been decided without cross-reference. But because such activities inevitably reflect uniform underlying social characteristics, it is not surprising that the decisions themselves cluster around the same themes, and that a unifying constitutional principle can be drawn from them. State substitute-parent authority is limited by both the presumption of parental prerogatives and the constitutional norms applicable to exercise of state power over any individual, child or adult.

Occasionally courts have fallen into a nostalgic rhetoric, romanticizing the family and implying that modern ills would be cured if we could return to (as Chief Justice Burger put it in *Yoder*) "the simple life of the early Christian era which continued in America during much of our early national life" (406 U.S. at p. 210). Wishful fantasies aside, the past cannot be undone and the need for formal state parenting interventions will not vanish. The harmful self-defeating aspects of these interventions will continue unless sensible remedies can be devised. One hopes that courts may be enlisted in an effort to limit the grandiosity of state claims over children and, at the same time, to assure reliable assistance from state agencies. The competence of courts to dictate state child-rearing policies may be questioned, but some external review is needed over the narrowly based state bureaucracies that now act as substitute parents in a broadening range of settings. This state activity affects fundamental libertarian values. Courts have traditionally spoken for these values in other contexts. Our children deserve as much.

BIBLIOGRAPHY

Bowlby, John. 1965. *Child Care and the Growth of Love.* 2d ed. Baltimore: Penguin Books.
Burt, Robert A. 1971. "Forcing Protection on Children and Their Parents: The Impact of *Wyman* v. *James.*" *Michigan Law Review* 69:1259–1310.
——. 1973. "The Therapeutic Use and Abuse of State Power over Adolescents." In *Current Issues in Adolescent Psychiatry,* ed. Joseph Schooler. New York: Brunner/Mazel. Pp. 243–51.
Clark, Homer. 1968. *The Law of Domestic Relations.* St. Paul: West.
Ellsworth, Phoebe C., and Levy, Robert J. 1969. "Legislative Reform of Child Custody Adjudication: An Effort to Rely on Social Science Data in Formulating Legal Policies." *Law and Society Review* 4:167–233.
Erikson, Erik. 1963. *Childhood and Society.* 2d ed. New York: W. W. Norton.

————. 1968. *Identity: Youth and Crisis.* New York: W. W. Norton.

Foster, Henry H., Jr., and Freed, Doris Jonas. 1972. "A Bill of Rights for Children." *Family Law Quarterly* 6:343-75.

Freud, Anna. 1964. *The Psychoanalytic Treatment of Children.* New York: Schocken Books.

————. 1965a. *Normality and Pathology in Childhood.* New York: International Universities Press.

————. 1965b. "On the Difficulties of Communicating with Children: The Lesser Children in Chambers." In *The Family and the Law,* eds. Joseph Goldstein and Jay Katz. New York: Free Press. Pp. 261-64.

Goldstein, Joseph; Freud, Anna; and Solnit, Albert J. 1973. *Beyond the Best Interests of the Child.* New York: Free Press.

Gunther, Gerald. 1972. "Foreword: In Search of Evolving Doctrine on a Changing Court: A Model for a Newer Equal Protection." *Harvard Law Review* 86:1-48.

Hostetler, John. 1968. *Amish Society.* Rev. ed. Baltimore: Johns Hopkins.

Nir, Yehuda, and Cutler, Rhoda. 1973. "The Therapeutic Utilization of the Juvenile Court." *American Journal of Psychiatry* 130:1112-17.

Rothman, David J. 1971. *The Discovery of the Asylum: Social Order and Disorder in the New Republic.* New York: Little, Brown.

Schur, Edwin M. 1973. *Radical Nonintervention: Rethinking the Delinquency Problem.* Englewood Cliffs, N.J.: Prentice-Hall.

Suddick, David E. 1973. "Runaways: A Review of the Literature." *Juvenile Justice* 24:47-54.

Watson, Andrew S. 1969. "The Children of Armageddon: Problems of Custody Following Divorce." *Syracuse Law Review* 21:55-86.

12 State Intervention on Behalf of "Neglected" Children: A Search for Realistic Standards*

Michael S. Wald

During the past ten years, many experts have advocated curtailing state intervention in cases involving criminal or quasi-criminal behavior by minors (President's Commission . . . 1967). At the same time, however, most experts have supported increased state intervention on behalf of "neglected" children (Foster and Freed 1972; Katz 1971; Young 1964). For example, efforts to overcome poverty resulted in concern for the "disadvantaged" child. The apparent inability of public schools to decrease performance differences between "advantaged" and "disadvantaged" children led experts from many disciplines to focus on family failures as the cause of disadvantaged children. In addition, publicity about the extent of physical abuse of children, spurred by descriptions of the "battered child syndrome" in 1962, led directly to new legislation establishing reporting schemes to improve the state's ability to find abusing parents.

It is the thesis of this chapter that a reappraisal of the neglect jurisdiction of juvenile courts is indeed necessary. In contrast to those who advocate extending the reach of neglect laws, I submit

*A previous version of this article appeared in the *Stanford Law Review* 27 (1975): 985–1040. © 1975 by The University of Chicago.

that a narrowing of neglect jurisdiction is needed. The sympathetic appeal of beaten, malnourished, or helpless children is a strong inducement for expanded intervention. Because legislators and judges presume the beneficence of such intervention, there is great temptation to intervene too often, and the usual restraints on the exercise of coercive state power are minimized or disregarded in the child neglect area. Since our society values the principles of family autonomy and privacy, we should carefully examine any decision to coercively limit parental autonomy in raising children. We should define the goals we seek by coercive intervention and the costs we are willing to absorb in the process. In addition, we should ask whether the resources exist, or can be developed, to make intervention into family affairs useful.

This chapter develops a statutory definition of neglect. I argue that a court should not be authorized to intervene coercively to protect children, either by ordering that children be removed from their homes or that their parents accept supervision and treatment as a condition of continued custody, unless one or more of the factors enumerated below are present. I address only the issue of statutory standards. Intervention need not occur every time a child is suffering one of the harms specified; on the contrary, coercive intervention may be inappropriate in some such cases. The proposed statute (see the appendix to this chapter) contains only a general authorization to intervene. The appropriateness of intervention in a given situation must be decided on a case by case basis, taking into account the programs and resources the court has available to help the family and the dynamics of the specific family.

BASIC PREMISES: PARENTAL AUTONOMY

Three basic policy issues must be analyzed in order to determine the appropriate scope of coercive state intervention. First, we must consider how child-rearing responsibility is to be allocated between parents and the state. Second, we must decide whether state intervention should be premised primarily on parental conduct or on evidence of damage, however defined, to a child. Finally, we must decide whether intervention is to be premised on general, vague descriptions of either parental conduct or harm to a child, or whether more narrow and specific bases for intervention can be developed. I contend that neglect laws should be premised on substantial deference to parental autonomy in child rearing, that neglect statutes should focus on the child, and that the harms to a child which warrant state intervention should be defined as specifically as possible.

A basic tenet of our laws holds that the family has great autonomy in child rearing. However, parents clearly do not have exclusive control over the lives of their children. Because children are presumed unable to protect their own interests fully, the state, under the doctrine of *parens patriae*, is seen as having a right and an obligation to protect children if their parents are performing "inadequately."

Advocates of increased intervention often imply that our laws should give less deference to parental autonomy. They contend that parents should be treated as trustees for their children. The state should monitor parental performance and intervene when the parents act in a manner which interferes with the child's optimal development (Gil 1970).

I believe that we should continue to give substantial deference to parental autonomy in deciding when coercive intervention is appropriate. Our political commitment to diversity of views, life styles, and freedom of religion is promoted by allowing families to raise children in a wide variety of living situations and with diverse child-rearing patterns. It is unlikely that such diversity would be encouraged in state-run child care or in a system that held parents merely to be trustees for children.

Moreover, a presumption in favor of family autonomy comports with our limited knowledge regarding child rearing and how to effect long-term change in a given child's development. Extensive state involvement in child rearing would require knowing not only the characteristics desired in children and adults, but also how parental behavior and home environment affect their development. No national consensus exists about what constitutes a healthy adult. Even less agreement exists on how to achieve a healthy child, however "healthy" may be defined. The few longitudinal studies that have been done all conclude that prediction of future behavior from observation of child-rearing practices is extremely difficult (Skolnick 1973; White 1973, vol. 1).

A system based on autonomy does not require agreement about the characteristics desired in children, the proper type of home environment, or the right way to raise children. Instead, it requires agreement about some basic harms from which we wish to protect all children. Intervention can be premised on the existence of these harms without trying to regulate all aspects of child rearing. Even then, as will be shown below, it is exceedingly difficult to delineate the basic harms which clearly justify intervention. The difficulty of deciding even the basic premises warns against a policy of intervention in less basic matters.

Third, there is substantial evidence that except in cases involving very seriously damaged children, we may be unable to improve a child's situation through coercive state intervention. In fact, intervention may harm the child. It is now well recognized that any intervention leading to removal of a child from the family entails substantial risks to the child (Mnookin 1973; Bowlby 1965). Even more limited types of intervention, such as requiring placement of children in day care or mandating supervision of the home, entail risks that should not be ignored (Goldstein, Freud, and Solnit 1973).

Moreover, it must be recognized that we lack both the knowledge and resources needed to make coercive intervention useful (Fischer 1973; Kadushin 1974). Most public welfare agencies have untrained or poorly trained staff. Turnover among caseworkers is very high (Campbell 1970; Levine 1973). Recordkeeping is so bad that case records do not even permit continuity of treatment among workers, let alone outside evaluation of effectiveness. The percentage of minority-group workers is very low, although in urban areas a significant proportion of the clients come from minority groups. Social work agencies are often thought to be applying middle-class standards to poor and minority parents and to be attempting to change their life styles to meet the social worker's expectations of proper parenting (Kay and Philips 1966).

Finally, our societal commitment to child welfare has not extended to providing each family with adequate income to assure that their children can receive basic nutrition, medical care, adequate housing, or any of the other advantages we would like parents to provide. Nor have governmental bodies been willing to make day care, homemakers, or other services available to all who would use them voluntarily. Yet every study shows a strong correlation between neglect and poverty. In a society committed to individual freedom and privacy, problems ought to be tackled by noncoercive means before attempting coercive methods (Bronfenbrenner 1974). For all these reasons, the standards proposed in this article will be premised on a presumption for parental autonomy.

Basic Premises: Specific, Child-focused Laws

Most state statutes define neglect in broad, vague language, which seems to invite virtually unlimited intervention. Typical of such laws is the California statute, which defines a neglected child as one:

(a) Who is in need of proper and effective parental care or control and has no parent or guardian, or has no parent or guardian willing to exercise or capable of exercising such care or control, or has no parent or guardian actually exercising such care or control.

(b) Who is destitute, or who is not provided with the necessities of life, or who is not provided with a home or suitable place of abode.

(c) Who is physically dangerous to the public because of a mental or physical deficiency, disorder or abnormality.

(d) Whose home is an unfit place for him by reason of neglect, cruelty, depravity, or physical abuse of either of his parents, or of his guardian or other person in whose custody or care he is (Calif. Welf. and Inst. Code §600).

The statutes all define neglect primarily in terms of parental conduct or home conditions. Rarely do they require any showing of actual harm to a child; they do not even specify the types of harm that are of concern.

The definitions of neglect offered by legal scholars are equally broad. For example, Sanford Katz writes that "child neglect connotes a parent's conduct, usually thought of in terms of passive behavior, that results in a failure to provide for the child's needs as defined by the preferred values of the community" (Katz 1971). According to Monrad Paulsen, "The meaning of the standard is given by community minimums in regard to family conduct" (Paulsen 1962).

The absence of precise standards for state intervention is said to be a necessity, even a virtue. Professor Katz says:

(Broad) neglect statutes recognize that 'neglectful' behavior can also vary, and thus cannot be easily or specifically defined....

The broad neglect statutes allow judges to examine each situation on its own facts (Katz 1971).

I contend that this position is incorrect. It is both possible and desirable to define more specifically both neglect and the types of damage that justify intervention.

Vague neglect laws increase the likelihood that decisions to intervene will be made in situations where the child will be harmed by intervention. Because the statutes do not reflect a considered analysis of what types of harm justify the risks of intervention, decision making is left to the ad hoc analysis of social workers and judges. There is evidence that their decisions to intervene often reflect personal values not supported by scientific evidence and result in removing children from environments in which they are doing adequately (Mnookin 1973). Only through carefully drawn statutes, delineating specific harms to the child, can we reduce the possibility that intervention will do more harm than good.

If judges and social workers need not justify their decision to intervene on the basis of specific harms, they are unlikely to make sound decisions about the appropriate disposition even where intervention is justified. Such decisions require weighing the harms to be prevented or alleviated against the harms likely to result from a specific intervention program. This cannot be done when the harms to be prevented are ill defined. It is also impossible for the decision maker, or others, later to evaluate the efficacy of the intervention, since the criteria of success or failure are unknown.

Finally, considering the seriousness of the decision to intervene from the parents' perspective, intervention should be permissible only where there is a clear-cut decision, openly and deliberately made by responsible political bodies, that the type of harm involved justifies intervention.

The problems caused by statutory vagueness are intensified because the statutes permit intervention solely on the basis of parental conduct without requiring evidence of specific harms to children. This encourages social workers to focus on the parents rather than on the child (Sherman et al. 1973). Yet all available evidence indicates that it is extremely difficult to correlate parental behavior or home conditions with specific harms to a child, especially if the predicted harm involves long-term, rather than immediate, effects (White 1973, vol. 1). Even in very "bad" homes, the impact of the environment will vary depending upon the age of a child, the nature of family interactions, developmental differences among children, and many other factors. Since significant harm can result from intervention, it is essential that laws be drafted so as to assure that these factors will be taken into consideration, thereby minimizing the danger of over-intervention. Even when the focus is on specific harm to the children, long-term prediction is still difficult. Therefore, focusing solely on parental behavior certainly increases the danger of intervention harmful to the child.

Recognizing the difficulty of prediction does not require ignoring that a substantial body of theory and data supports the hypothesis that a child's intellectual, physical, emotional, and social development is significantly affected by his home environment (Bronfenbrenner 1974; Freud 1965). Therefore, I believe that both state and federal governments should actively support, financially and legislatively, programs designed to help "disadvantaged families" who wish to have support. Programs providing comprehensive health care, day care services, preschool programs, and at-home training for mothers all show promise of helping both children and parents in disadvantaged homes. Participation in such programs should be completely voluntary since parental cooperation is probably essential for success (Bronfenbrenner 1974). Growing up in a so-called disadvantaged home is not a sufficient basis for coercive intervention.

Because neglect statutes usually imply that the concern is with parental misconduct, courts are often unwilling to intervene to protect a child who is suffering serious harm where there is no evidence of parental fault. If our concern is with helping children who are suffering harms, intervention should occur whenever the parents are unwilling to rectify the situation, regardless of who caused the harm.

By focusing on the child, it is possible to draft more specific statutes than if the focus is on the parents' behavior. Although there may be many types of neglectful behavior by parents, there are relatively few harms to children with which we should be concerned. By limiting intervention to cases in which these harms are present or are extremely likely to occur, the hazards of prediction are reduced, although not eliminated, and the law is made more efficacious. Specific laws do not prevent judges from examining each situation on its own facts to determine the appropriate disposition; rather they more clearly define for the judges the kinds of harm with which society is concerned.

In asserting that the grounds for state intervention should be drafted in terms of specific harms to a child, I am not arguing that parental behavior is irrelevant. In virtually every case we are concerned not only with the specific harm to the child, but also with the fact that a parent inflicted the harm or failed to provide the child with adequate protection from the harm or failed to provide adequate treatment for the harm. We intervene to protect the child from a specific harm, but the parental behavior is relevant because it helps indicate whether the harm is likely to recur. For example, we are more concerned when a child's leg is broken by a parent than by a fall from a bike, since we assume that inflicted injuries are more likely to recur.

Using parental behavior as an indicator of the likelihood of future harm, given the existence of a present harm, is far different from predicting a future harm based solely on parental behavior. Without present harm the chances of erroneous prediction increase greatly. It may be necessary in some cases, however, to act solely on the basis of parental conduct if there is sufficient reason to believe that the parental conduct will result in specific harm to the child in the near future.

DEVELOPING NEW STANDARDS: PRINCIPLES OF INTERVENTION

Ideally, parents ought to protect children from a large number of harms and make sure that they receive a variety of benefits. Obviously, parents should be required to feed and clothe their children. They also must comply with laws regarding compulsory education and child labor. Beyond these minima, parents should provide love, affection, and a home environment conducive to the development of mental and emotional stability. Ideally each home would provide each child the "best available opportunity to fulfill his potential in society as a civilized human being" (Goldstein 1968, p. 1076). Probably few families provide this ideal environment. Yet, in a system based on parental autonomy, the imperfections of parents should not justify intervention. Again, neglect statutes should be concerned with specific harms that a child is suffering or extremely likely to suffer, not with parental behavior as such.

In view of our limited knowledge and the limited alternatives to raising children in their natural families, I have adopted the following criteria for deciding when coercive intervention should be statutorily authorized, that is, how "neglect" should be statutorily defined: (a) the harm should be serious, and (b) it must be a type of harm for which, in general, the remedy of coercive intervention will do more good than harm.

These criteria reflect the judgment that certain categories of harm to children should not constitute a basis for intervention, even though in some individual cases intervention might be beneficial, because in the majority of cases intervention to prevent the harm will do more damage than good. The criteria are intended to insure that state views of child rearing will replace parental views only for harms of a magnitude that justify the risks and costs of intervention. Unless limited by statute, social workers and judges tend to intervene whenever a child is suffering some harm without adequately weighing the potential likelihood of the success of state intervention (Mnookin 1973; Tamilia 1973).

It must be recognized that courts are not the only agencies which apply neglect criteria. Statutory definitions of neglect provide the basis by which enforcement agencies, such as welfare departments, investigate homes. As in all areas of enforcement, investigations are likely to take place on the basis of information that proves unfounded or not serious enough to justify further intervention. Yet investigation in and of itself is undoubtedly traumatic for both the parents and children. The investigators may make the parents uncertain in dealing with their children. Interviewing children can frighten them. In some states, agencies ask courts to order psychiatric examinations of family members under investigation (Texas Family Code tit. 2, §34.05(c) [1973]). Agency contacts with neighbors may adversely affect the neighbors' attitudes toward the suspected parent and children.

The reach of agency intervention invariably extends beyond the scope of the statute (Boehm 1964). In fact, most child protective service agencies define their mission broadly to justify intervention in cases where court jurisdiction could not be sustained (American Humane Association 1967). Several commentators have documented the type of pressures agencies place on families to accept "voluntary" supervision, even though children are not suffering from a harm cognizable under the neglect statute (Handler 1973; Levine 1973). Agencies often pressure parents to "voluntarily" place their children in foster care; many such children are never returned (Campbell 1970). The potential harm from such agency action has been discussed above; the fact that most agencies cannot even deliver helpful services after such interventions makes me even more cautious in authorizing intervention.

Finally, limiting intervention to classes of harms which are most serious seeks to insure that the limited resources available for helping children will go to those in the most danger. Intervention should be concentrated on these cases since the risks of doing nothing are greatest.

For these reasons, the proposed statutory standards permit intervention only to prevent or alleviate certain serious harms to a child. It must be stressed again that state intervention should not occur every time it is alleged that a child is suffering from one of the harms enumerated by statute. Even when a child is suffering a harm which meets the statutory definition, the court must decide whether there is reason to believe that the services it can provide that child are likely to decrease the possibility of continued harm. However, my discussion here is confined to the question of which types of harms, in general, justify intervention and therefore should be included in a statutory definition of neglect. It does not extend to what standards and procedures courts can use in deciding the specific case (see Michael Wald 1976).

DEVELOPING NEW STANDARDS: HARMS TO BE INCLUDED IN A DEFINITION OF NEGLECT

Since most statutes define neglect in terms of parental behavior, the literature and cases understandably identify typical situations warranting intervention according to the parental conduct involved. Generally, neglect cases involve the following categories of parental behavior: physical abuse, inadequate supervision, emotional neglect, inadequate parenting, inadequate housekeeping, sexual abuse, failure to provide medical care, immoral or unconventional parental behavior, and parental conduct contributing to the delinquency of a minor.

The bases for intervention proposed in the following sections focus on the child. Parental behavior is relevant only insofar as it causes or is likely to cause a specific harm to the child. However, the discussion will be organized by current descriptive categories, in order to compare and contrast the proposed bases for intervention with present practices.

Physical Abuse

Probably the clearest case for intervention arises where a child has been physically abused. There is undoubtedly consensus that children should be protected from severe physical injuries. Killing, maiming, torturing, and severely beating other humans are not acceptable forms of behavior. There is no more reason to permit physical abuse which can result in death or permanent impairment, either physical or psychological, in a family than in society at large.

Intervention need not be premised on the likelihood of long-term harm. Physical abuse inflicts pain on children who are unable to protect themselves. Our society generally condemns inflicting unnecessary pain, and children should not be treated as exceptions to that rule.

In addition, there is substantial evidence of a correlation between parents becoming childbeaters and their being beaten as children. While we lack evidence indicating what percentage of abused children ultimately abuse their own children, studies have found that many child abusers suffered beatings when they were young (Gil 1970). Thus, intervention might be justified to break the pattern of this type of behavior.

Finally, physical injury is relatively easy to identify. To the degree that we want to be able to provide concrete standards for intervention to limit intervention based on subjective value judgments made by doctors, judges, or social workers, and to provide concrete issues subject to proof at trial, physical abuse offers a feasible basis of intervention.

There are, however, problems in intervening even for physical abuse. First, although there is a consensus that intervention is justified when a child has been treated in a manner likely to cause death or severe physical injury, it is difficult to define precisely other types of physical injuries that justify intervention. A recent nationwide study found that more than half the reported cases of physical abuse of children involved minor bruises or abrasions that did not require treatment (Gil 1970). Our society certainly accepts corporal punishment of children; the extent of the sanction varies among cultural groups. It is difficult to draw a line where such discipline stops and abuse begins.

In addition, diagnostic accuracy is limited despite recent advances. Doctors often cannot be sure that any particular injury was intentionally inflicted. Since intervention in abuse cases is premised on the likelihood that abusing parents may again injure their child, diagnostic accuracy is needed to insure intervention in appropriate cases.

These difficulties create a risk of some unwarranted interventions even in physical harm cases. As previously discussed, a family accused of child abuse is liable to pressure from state agencies. Family relations may be significantly disrupted by the trauma of court appearances, social workers' visits, compulsory psychiatric examinations for the parents or the child, and short- or long-term removal of children from the family while the case is being investigated. Children who were not actually abused may thus suffer significant harm as a result of intervention.

Except in cases where the beatings are so severe that death or maiming is likely to occur, it is difficult to predict the long-term negative consequences for the child. There is certainly evidence that parents who abuse their children have themselves been abused as children, but there are few data available on what percentage of abused children grow up to be abusers or in any other way maladjusted (Elmer and Gregg 1967).

There is no reason for children to suffer the short-term pain, trauma, and danger caused by severe beatings, but it is possible that in some cases coercive state intervention will not provide even a physically beaten child with a less detrimental environment, especially if the child can only be protected by removal from the family. Despite these reservations about when and how to intervene, state intervention should be authorized where there has been or is likely to be serious physical injury inflicted upon a child. The magnitude of the harm and the likelihood that intervention will lessen the danger to the child make it appropriate to include physical harm in a statutory definition of neglect.

In order to give courts and child welfare workers guidance to the types of injuries which justify intervention, I propose that serious physical injury be defined as "an injury, inflicted on a child by other than accidental means, which causes or creates a substantial risk of death, disfigurement, or impairment of bodily functioning." Such injuries indicate that the child has been willfully injured or, at a minimum, disciplined in an extremely abnormal manner. In either case, there is legitimate basis for concern that the child may receive further injuries unless afforded protection. On the other hand, the definition should prevent intervention simply because a neighbor, relative, social worker, or judge disapproves of a given parent's disciplinary measures. Although still open to interpretation, the proposed definition forces the intervener to focus on the specific consequences likely to result from parental action, not just on the parents' practice of physical punishment.

While restricting the types of physical injuries warranting state intervention, the proposed definition does allow intervention based on the "substantial risk" that the parental action may cause such an injury. This obviously requires making predictions. Regarding physical injuries, however, it is essential to take the risk. We now have conclusive evidence that some parents continually inflict injuries upon their children in a manner that creates a substantial likelihood of death, disfigurement, or impairment (Weston 1968). Children in these homes may be treated by doctors or hospitals on many occasions before court intervention is requested. Because in a given instance a child was not killed, disfigured, or substantially impaired, intervention should not be precluded if it can be shown that the injurious actions created a substantial likelihood of more serious injury. While courts should certainly be extra cautious in intervening when a child has not already suffered serious injury, they should not be required to wait until the child dies or suffers a more severe injury before intervening.

Moreover, in a system that focuses on the child, authority to intervene in physical abuse cases should not be limited to situations where the parent or guardian inflicts the injuries. Gil's study revealed that 11.5 percent of reported injuries were inflicted by siblings, relatives, boyfriends, or a person living with but not married to the child's mother (Gil 1970, p. 117). Intervention should be possible whenever the parent cannot protect the child from being injured by others.

Inadequate Protection of a Child's Physical Well-being

Under current practice, intervention often takes place when it is thought that the child's physical well-being is endangered, even though the child has not been intentionally injured. These cases involve a variety of situations. A parent may fail to adequately feed or clothe the child, home conditions may be so dirty that the child is physically endangered (by broken glass, uncovered fires, or serious diseases associated with filth), or a young child may be left unattended or inadequately supervised for long periods.

When a child actually suffers serious physical injury as a result of parental inattention or unsafe home conditions, statutory authorization for intervention is justified for the same reasons as in physical abuse cases. When no injury has occurred, however, the possibility of unwarranted intervention is increased. A court deciding whether to intervene must predict both the likelihood of the injury occurring and the likelihood that intervention will be beneficial. There is a great temptation to focus exclusively on the parental behavior and ignore the likelihood of injury. Intervention may be prompted by a social worker's repugnance to dirty homes or because a judge differs from the parents regarding the age at which a child may be left alone safely or at which an older child can care for a younger sibling.

Despite these possibilities, it would be unwise to allow intervention only after a child has been seriously injured as a result of inadequate conditions or supervision. For example, a court must be able to protect a five-year-old child left unattended for several days, even if the child has avoided injury. Therefore, intervention should be permissible when children have suffered physical injury causing disfigurement or impairment of bodily functioning or where there is a substantial risk that children will suffer imminent death, disfigurement, or impairment of bodily functions as a result of conditions created by their parents or the failure of their parents to provide adequate supervision.

The proposed standard is the same as the abuse standard when the child has actually suffered injury. However, when no injury has occurred, the proposed standard requires that the risk be substantial and imminent. These terms should limit the scope of acceptable prediction of harm. Of course, such terms are subject to interpretation. They may well be expanded to include situations where I would reject intervention, but the proposed language does place restraints on court actions and makes the court and welfare workers aware of legislative policy. It forces an agency bringing a neglect case to court to prove the likelihood of specific types of injuries occurring. Combined with adequate procedural changes, the proposed standard should substantially limit inappropriate intervention (Michael Wald 1976).

Emotional Neglect

Most recent criticisms of neglect laws have focused on the alleged failure of state statutes to include "emotional" neglect among the harms justifying intervention. Critics argue that focusing on physical health ignores current evidence on the serious emotional harms children also suffer (Katz 1971). Clearly children can be severely damaged psychologically as well as physically (Mac-Farlane, Clausen, and Yahraes 1971). Often the impairments are crippling and permanent. An increasing body of evidence shows that children who suffer early emotional disturbances often display later mental illness or antisocial behavior (Fontana 1973; Robertson 1962). As adults they may be incapable of caring for themselves or their own children (Goldstein, Freud, and Solnit 1973). If severely disturbed children are not receiving treatment, the reasons for intervening are little different from those justifying protecting children from physical injury.

Again, however, current efforts to expand neglect laws to include emotional harm generally focus on parental behavior rather than on the condition of the child. It is wrongly assumed that predictions of emotional harm can be based solely on parental conduct—usually defined extremely vaguely. Often mentioned is "inadequate" parental affection. For example, the Child Welfare League recommends that intervention take place to protect all children who are "denied normal experiences that produce feelings of being loved, wanted, secure and worthy . . . " (Child Welfare League of America 1973, p. 12). Even those commentators who recommend focusing on the child fail to offer specific guidelines to types of harm that warrant intervention. For example, Katz advocates intervention when a child's "mental health is damaged" (Katz 1971, p. 55). Moreover, some commentators advocate intervention based solely on the prediction of future harm. They argue that because the symptom in the child may not appear for many years, we should intervene early to prevent later harm (Max Wald 1961).

While emotional damage to a child should be a basis for intervention in some cases, it is essential that laws be drafted in a manner consistent with our limited knowledge about the nature and causes of psychological harm. Intervention should not be premised on vague concepts like "proper parental love" or "adequate affectionate parental association." Such language invites unwarranted or arbitrary intervention. It could be applied to parents who travel a great deal, leaving their children with housekeepers, who send their children to boarding school to get rid of them, or who are generally undemonstrative people. As a result, intervention might be so pervasive that parental autonomy would be effectively abandoned.

Our knowledge about the relationship between parental behavior and child development is too incomplete to permit intervention based solely on parental behavior, even specifically defined behavior. Sheldon White summarizes the findings of existing studies:

Neither theory nor research has specified the exact mechanisms by which a child's development and his family functioning are linked. While speculation abounds, there is little agreement about how these family functions produce variation in measure of health, learning, and affect. Nor do we know the relative importance of internal (individual and family) versus external (social and economic) factors (White 1973, vol. 2, p. 240).

Other commentators also assert that the impact of parental conduct on a given child will vary with the child's age and particular emotional makeup (Freud 1972; Gill 1960).

Therefore, it is essential that intervention for emotional neglect be premised solely on damage to the child. Without actual damage it is extremely difficult both to predict the likely future development of the child and to assess the impact of intervention. At a minimum, sound prediction would require extensive observations of the child and the family. At present we lack the resources to undertake such evaluations, and our knowledge of child development is still too limited to insure sound long-term predictions (Goldstein, Freud, and Solnit 1973; Sherman et al. 1973).

The efficacy of coercive intervention on behalf of emotionally damaged children also is certainly questionable. The problem is particularly acute when removal is utilized. To justify removal the decision maker must determine that there is emotional damage and that the emotional harms connected with removal will be less damaging than the emotional harm caused at home. As Mnookin (1973) has shown, this is an extremely difficult determination. The most efficient allocation of resources would be to use voluntary services for less serious situations and reserve coercive intervention for the most drastic cases.

With these problems in mind, I propose that, while coercive intervention should be permissible to aid a child evidencing emotional damage, the statutory standards must be very specific and narrow. I propose allowing intervention only if "the minor is suffering serious emotional damage, evidenced by severe anxiety, depression or withdrawal, or untoward aggressive behavior or hostility toward others, and the parents are unwilling to provide treatment for the child."

The proposed standard focuses on the child's behavior and is concerned with short-term, not long-term predictions. Since there is "no unanimity among mental health professionals regarding the definition of mental illness and serious emotional disturbances" (Joint Commission on Mental Health of Children 1969, p. 250), the suggested definition attempts to base intervention on the specific symptoms of serious emotional harm on which most mental health professionals seem to agree.

These are not the only symptoms that could have been included, and application of the standard obviously depends heavily on mental health professionals who may differ in their definitions. Despite these problems, reliance on specific terminology is necessary to limit the scope of intervention, to make clear to all decision makers the types of harm that justify official action, and to place some constraints on expert testimony so that it will not be based solely on individual views regarding proper child development. If conscientiously applied, the standard will require judges to consult mental health professionals before deciding whether intervention is justified. This should encourage more adequate evaluations of the presence and causes of emotional harm and the design of better treatment plans.

The proposed standard does not require that the emotional damage be caused by parental conduct. If a child evidences serious damage and the parent fails to provide help, intervention is justified whatever the cause of harm. Fault concepts, stemming from the parent orientation of existing law, are discarded, as they add an often unprovable (as well as misconceived) element to fact finding that thwarts necessary intervention.

Concededly, by restricting coercive intervention to only the most serious cases, some children who might benefit from coercive state intervention will not get needed help. The proposed standard assumes that overintervention and overremoval are more significant problems than underintervention, and that restricting coercive involvement will benefit more children than it will harm.

Inadequate Parenting

While we lack statistical breakdowns of the reasons for intervention in neglect cases, probably the largest category of cases involves persons characterized as "inadequate parents." All commentators agree that the great majority of neglect cases involve very poor families who are usually receiving welfare. In addition to the problems directly caused by poverty—poor housing, inadequate medical care, poor nutritional practices—many of the parents can be described as extremely marginal people, that is, they are continually at the borderline of being able to sustain themselves—economically, emotionally, and mentally (Cohen, Mulford, and Philbrick 1967).

Their plight is reflected in their homes, which are often dirty and run-down. Feeding arrangements are haphazard. One or both parents may have a drinking or drug problem, suffer from mental illness, or be retarded, which may affect the quality of their child care. If there are two parents, constant bickering and fighting may occur, or the husband may periodically disappear. Often the children live in uncertainty and chaos.

Such parents may provide little emotional support for their children. While their children may not be physically abused, left unattended, dangerously malnourished, or overtly rejected, they may receive little love, attention, stimulation, or emotional involvement. The children do not usually evidence emotional damage as serious as that previously discussed, but they may be listless and do poorly in school and in social relations (Polansky, Borgman, and DeSaix 1972; White 1973, vol. 1).

It is certainly tempting to intervene to help such children. Intervention might be justified to protect the children by providing them with an environment in which they can better reach their potential and also to protect the state, since it is claimed that such children will probably end up as delinquents, criminals, or welfare recipients. Without intervention, we may be perpetuating a "culture of poverty" (Chilman 1966; Cohen, Mulford, and Philbrick 1967).

Despite the appeal of these arguments, parental "inadequacy" in and of itself should not be a basis for intervention, other than the offer of services available on a truly voluntary basis. The term "inadequate home" or "inadequate parents" is even harder to define than emotional neglect. There is certainly no consensus about what types of inadequate bahavior would justify intervention. Given the vagueness of the standard, almost unlimited intervention would be possible. Neither can we predict the consequences for a child of growing up in a home lacking affection or stimulation, or with a parent who suffers from alcoholism, drug addiction, mental illness, or retardation:

Given the tenuous evidence showing a causal relationship between home environment and social class on the one hand and retarded child development on the other, it would seem ill-advised for public policy to be based on either home environment or social class (White 1973, vol. 1, p. 74).

In fact, by focusing solely on parental behavior, child care workers often ignore the many strengths a given child may be deriving from his environment. As I have stressed, the complexity of the process by which a child relates to any environment defies any attempt to draft laws solely on the basis of environmental influences.

There is also reason to be pessimistic about the utility of coercive intervention. The services necessary to help these families are generally unavailable. More day care centers, homemakers, health facilities, and job training programs would all be needed to make intervention anything more than periodic visits by a social worker. Such visits themselves are costly, have not been shown to be effective, and may be resented by the parent who will blame the child for the outside meddling.

Even when inadequate parents seek help, agencies often lack the resources or ability to alleviate undesirable home conditions (New York State Assembly Select Committee on Child Abuse 1972). The chances of success are even lower when the family resists intervention (Polansky, DeSaix, and Sharlin 1972). Few communities have sufficient personnel and programs to permit meaningful intervention, even in cases involving physical abuse or severe emotional damage. It is highly questionable whether limited resources ought to be expended on families with less severe problems, unless they request services or accept them voluntarily.

In an ideal world, children would not be brought up in inadequate homes. However, our less than ideal society seems unable or unwilling to provide better alternatives for these children. The best we can do is to expand the social welfare services now offered families and make them voluntary. Adopting income maintenance and comprehensive health care programs for both adults and children and increasing the number of day care centers would also alleviate some problems.

It is also important to recognize that intervention may take place if, as a result of inadequate parenting, a child comes under one of the categories that would justify intervention. For example, a dirty, run-down house or haphazard feeding arrangements might create an imminent and substantial threat of serious injury or disease for a child. While I would not encourage judges to expand "physical danger" as a means of avoiding the limitations imposed by the proposed guidelines, it seems to me highly unlikely that a judge would not authorize intervention if a child appeared seriously endangered. Statutes can place general constraints on judges, but in my experience juvenile court judges often find ways to do what they want to do, regardless of the statute.

Sexual Abuse

Perhaps the most universally condemned behavior of a parent or other family member toward a child involves sexual conduct (Weinberg 1955, chap. 3). Thus, it may seem apparent that "sexual abuse" ought to justify intervention. While few state statutes specifically mention sexual abuse in neglect statutes, courts do regularly intervene on this basis.

In the proposed guidelines, the case for state action to protect children from sexual contact with their parents is not so clear. There is no generally accepted definition of sexual abuse. It clearly includes intercourse, accomplished with or without force or threat. When the activity is less specific than intercourse, definition becomes harder. As a factual matter, it may be difficult to distinguish between appropriate displays of affection or fondling and other possibly disturbing behavior.

More importantly, despite an abundance of theoretical material about the harm of sexual activity within the family, there are very few studies demonstrating the negative impact of sexual abuse (see Michael Wald 1975, p. 1025, n. 209). The damage, if there is any, is usually emotional and the symptoms may not be manifest. Often, the offending contact was going on long before it was discovered and the child had demonstrated no overt physical or emotional problems as a result of the condemned behavior. On the basis of available evidence, intervention because of emotional damage, as defined herein, would not seem possible in all cases.

In addition, any intervention that requires children to tell their story to the police, welfare workers, and court, may cause more trauma than the condemned parental behavior (Bender and Blau 1937). There is little evidence about the efficacy of treatment programs following intervention that might justify this added trauma.

While these factors militate against including sexual abuse among the harms justifying intervention unless there is evidence of emotional damage, there are several considerations unique to sexual abuse cases that require the application of different standards. Sexual abuse is usually only one of several negative factors in families where it occurs. Several studies report that the father often has physically beaten the children or created an atmosphere of terror in the house (Reimer 1940; Tormes 1968; Weinberg 1955). Even though the home situation might not justify intervention if there were no sexual abuse, the added problems caused by the charges of sexual abuse might justify singling out these families for special attention. It is likely that, while the behavior may have been condoned by both parents and acquiesced in by the child before it became public, the fact that the sexual conduct has been reported will drastically alter the family situation. The child is then likely to feel guilt or shame. It may be essential to intervene in order to assess the impact of the discovery on the child and to insure that the conduct is discontinued.

Finally, sexual abuse cases involve a factor not generally

present in neglect situations: the likelihood of a criminal prosecution against the parent. While most criminal statutes forbidding child neglect cover conduct other than sexual abuse, the little available evidence indicates that such charges are most frequently brought in sexual abuse cases. Criminal proceedings can be extremely harmful to the child. Filing charges means that the child will have to undergo the trauma of interviews and testifying. In many cases additional pressure is created by the parents who encourage the child not to cooperate with the prosecuting authorities. Criminal prosecution often results in the father's imprisonment. Several recent reports contend that splitting up the family and imprisoning the father may add to the child's problems. Treatment should involve the entire family (Eist and Mandel 1968).

While neglect charges may necessitate questioning the child both in and out of court, the chances are greater that the negative effects can be avoided or minimized in a neglect hearing rather than in a criminal proceeding. Interviews can be conducted by social workers, accustomed to dealing with children, rather than by prosecutors. Without the threat of criminal sanctions, the parent may choose not to contest the charges. If a hearing is necessary, the lower standard of proof in a neglect proceeding may make it unnecessary for the child to testify. In any case, the hearing is generally private rather than before a jury and testimony can be taken in chambers. Finally, the court in a neglect proceeding is concerned with the well-being of the child and open to a greater range of dispositions than the criminal court. These proceedings likely will be less punitive and more treatment-oriented than criminal proceedings.

Therefore, criminal penalties for sexual abuse by parents or other family members really should be eliminated. The availability of neglect proceedings, through which the child can be protected, negates, from the child's perspective, the need for criminal proceedings. Realistically, however, given the strong moral condemnation evoked by such behavior, it is highly unlikely that any legislature would repeal these laws unless assured that all cases can be subject to the scrutiny of the juvenile court. For this reason, as well as those previously noted, coercive intervention should be permissible when a parent or other family member has sexually abused a child in the family, or when a parent cannot protect the child from sexual abuse by others.

Failure to Provide Medical Care

Many statutes now authorize court intervention when a parent fails to provide a child with adequate medical care. Typically, these statutes provide little guidance to when intervention is justified. Despite the broad mandate, courts often have been reluctant to intervene under this power (Baker 1969).

Most frequently, medical care cases involve parents who, because of religious objections, refuse to consent to an operation or blood transfusion recommended by a doctor, school official, or social worker. Occasionally, the parents refuse consent because of the risks of the proposed treatment. If there is a serious risk of death to the child unless the treatment takes place, courts virtually always intervene. When the proposed treatment is necessary to alleviate some lesser impairment, such as a serious deformity or disabling disease, however, courts have adopted divergent positions. Some courts refuse to intervene unless the condition is drastic and likely to be irremediable. Other judges have been willing to intervene "if in the court's judgment the health, safety and welfare of the child require it" (*In re D.*, 335 N.Y.S. 2d 638, 648 [Richmond Co. Fam. Ct. 1972]).

I assume, for purposes of discussion, that there are no constitutional impediments to court intervention when a child may suffer substantial harm. The analysis is solely concerned with when coercive intervention is justified. Leaving out the constitutional issues, which arise whenever parents state religious objections to medical procedures, makes it easier to determine whether there are peculiar elements in medical neglect cases that justify either more limited or more expansive intervention than in other types of neglect cases.

Both courts and commentators have specified a number of reasons for restricting intervention in medical neglect cases (Council of Judges, National Council on Crime and Delinquency 1968). However, their reasons are relevant in deciding whether to intervene in a specific case, not in determining the appropriate statutory standards for authorizing intervention.

First, it is argued that operations often involve substantial risk for the child. Courts obviously should be concerned if the proposed medical treatment entails the risk of death or permanent impairment. They should be especially reluctant to impose such risks when the chances of success are not very high, but this same concern should be central in any intervention decision. All forms of intervention involve risks to the child. In fact, it is often possible to derive a much more accurate picture of the potential costs and benefits of surgical intervention than to make an analogous calculation in other cases, where the means of intervention are less precise.

Courts are also reluctant to intervene if the child does not want the treatment. Such a policy is certainly sensible, since if a child shares the parental objections to medical treatment, it lessens the operation's chance of success and creates a risk of emotional damage. Again, however, this factor is relevant to determining the appropriate course in a given case, but not to deciding the legislative standard.

It is particularly appropriate to limit intervention statutorily in medical neglect cases to instances where the proposed action is needed to prevent the child's suffering serious physical injury or emotional damage. By their very nature, medical neglect cases raise special problems. Whenever intervention entails authorizing an operation, parental support will be necessary for the child before, during, and after the operation. If the medical problem involves continuing care, parental cooperation—emotional as well as physical—may be essential. Because parental cooperation is so vital to the child's well-being, parental wishes should be followed unless the potential consequences to the child are extremely dangerous.

Moreover, it must be recognized that in medical neglect cases the party requesting intervention does not represent "the best interests of the child" as objectively defined but merely another view on the issue (Keith-Lucas 1973). The parents also believe that they are acting in the child's best interest. It is reasonable to assume that parents are particularly sensitive to their child's needs and development. Not only are the parents in a unique position to gauge the likely impact of the proposed action on the child, but the child will also look to the parents in forming her or his own views. Thus, the child may be extremely fearful of any treatment the parents reject. In contrast, where intervention is premised on physical abuse, sexual abuse, or parental behavior causing emotional damage, rarely can the parents' actions be accepted as an alternative means of promoting the child's best interest. Thus, it is even more reasonable to require serious harm in medical neglect cases than in these other types of cases. I therefore propose that coercive intervention should be authorized only when a child is suffering serious physical injury or emotional damage, as previously defined, which can be alleviated by medical treatment.

I intend this definition to allow intervention in "failure to thrive" cases. Children who evidence severe malnutrition, extremely low physical growth rates, delayed bone maturation, and significant retardation of motor development need medical care which their parents are usually unwilling to give. There is pervasive evidence that coercive intervention will significantly improve the child's health. Without intervention many children suffer brain damage, emotional disorder, and even death.

"Aberrant" Child-rearing Practice, "Immoral" Homes, or "Undesirable" Life Styles

Historically, neglect laws were concerned primarily with the moral conduct of the parents (Thomas 1972). Even today, more states have statutes regulating moral neglect than physical neglect (Sullivan 1968). A review of appellate cases indicates that courts still remove children because they disapprove of the parents' life style or child-rearing practices. Courts have removed children because the parents were not legally married; because the mother frequented taverns or had men visitors overnight; because the parents adhered to "extreme" religious practices, or lived in a communal setting; or because the parent was a homosexual, or the mother of an illegitimate child. In none of these cases was there evidence of harm to the children (see Michael Wald 1975, p. 1033, n. 254-58). While it is unlikely that the reported cases constitute a significant percentage of the total cases handled by welfare agencies and juvenile courts, it is clear that once a "moral neglect" case is brought to a court's attention, judges are apparently quite ready to intervene and remove children, even from quite stable home environments.

Moral neglect cases epitomize the unrealistic orientation of current neglect statutes. They focus on parental behavior, rather than on the problems of the child. Intervention occurs even when there is no evidence that the indicted behavior has affected the child in any way. The statutes are drafted in vague terms, so that intervention is likely to be haphazard and subject to the intervener's personal value judgments. Since the basic purpose of the proceeding is to condemn and punish the parent, the children are usually removed from the home despite the harms caused by such action. A policy that attempts to increase socialization at the cost of increasing emotional damage should be unacceptable. Moreover, if the children do identify with the parents, it is unlikely that their views can be changed by removal. As John Bowlby has written, "Efforts made to 'save' the child from his bad surroundings and to give him new standards are commonly of no avail, since it is his own parents who, for good or ill, he values and with whom he is identified" (Bowlby 1965, p. 80).

It is unlikely that child neglect laws can be used successfully to enforce social norms that society in general cannot enforce. More importantly, it is unconscionable to use children as pawns to achieve these ends. For all of these reasons, the morality of the parents and the type of upbringing they provide should not constitute a basis for state intervention.

Contributing to Delinquent Behavior

While a parent's immoral conduct as such should be irrelevant, intervention should be authorized where the minor is committing delinquent acts as a result of parental pressure, guidance, or approval. The harm in this instance is already defined by the state. Intervention is necessary to prevent the minor from continuing the undesirable behavior. However, intervention should be limited to cases where the parent actually encourages the delinquency.

At present a social worker or probation officer may file a neglect allegation, feeling that a child's behavior is related to poor home conditions, even though the parent neither encouraged nor approved the child's actions. In such situations the neglect allegation is essentially used as a lesser charge, a substitute for delinquency allegations, in order to mitigate the harshness of a delinquency adjudication. Such practices should not be continued. Unless the parents directly encouraged or participated in the delinquent act, it is virtually impossible to show that a minor committed a given offense because of parental neglect. Issues of responsibility, causation, and the role of the family could arise in all delinquency cases. Neglect charges should be permissible only when the minor's delinquent acts are directly caused by the parent.

Neglect charges are also sometimes used in lieu of "predelinquency" charges—for example, truancy, incorrigibility, or curfew violations. Such conduct does often involve a family problem, but the proposed standard is not meant to be applicable to such situations unless the parent directly encourages or causes the proscribed behavior. Many commentators question the wisdom of any coercive intervention to prevent quasi-criminal behavior, unless the child is very young. There is no room here to try to resolve the difficult issues regarding appropriate state policy toward children who engage in "predelinquent" conduct, but certainly merely changing the name of the proceeding will not eliminate the problems raised by state intervention in such cases.

CONCLUSION

The preceding sections delineate guidelines for state intervention to protect endangered children whose parents are unwilling to protect them. The guidelines are premised on parental autonomy, partly because we lack sufficient knowledge and agreement about child development and proper parenting to justify state effort either to undertake the functions now assumed by parents or to assume a more extensive role in monitoring parental decision making.

The standards advocated are relatively specific and designed to minimize state intervention. Basically, intervention is permitted only in cases where a child evidences serious physical or emotional damage. The guidelines are not designed to insure that every child receives adequate housing, medical care, education, or supportive home environment. Many children need more than they now have, but their needs should not be met through neglect proceedings, which even in the best circumstances will be perceived as punitive, rather than helpful, by parents. Instead, the state should establish general programs to help all families provide adequately for their children and intervene coercively only if the statutory grounds proposed herein are met.

If the law required all parents to provide a home environment that provided maximum opportunity for their children to realize their inherent potentials, intervention might be necessary in most American homes. Such a system is possible. According to one observer, in the Soviet Union when "mothers take their babies to the clinics, they are given quizzes to see if they know the right answers, if they are doing the 'right thing.' Workers are frequently sent into the homes to observe the parents' relationship with each other—and with their children" (Luckey 1964, p. 271). Given the plight of many children, it is tempting to consider policies along these lines. However, the history of failure of previous state efforts to improve children's lives through substitute-parenting demands rejection of this notion.

It is to be hoped that adopting a policy of minimal coercive intervention may encourage the creation of more extensive services available on a voluntary basis to all families. This would improve the well-being of many more children than now are aided through the almost haphazard application of neglect laws.

The proposed standards will leave room for discretion. Certainly a neglect statute cannot specify every circumstance which warrants intervention. However, the standards attempt to provide more specific guidelines than presently exist. I believe that the greater specificity will eliminate intervention in most cases in which it is unwarranted.

To be sure, narrowing the scope of court jurisdiction may result in excluding from protection some children who would benefit from intervention. Unfortunately, it is impossible to draft a statute or devise a system whereby intervention will occur only when necessary and beneficial and always when necessary. I believe more harm than good will be done overall if we do not limit intervention to the categories I suggest. Perhaps, as we acquire more knowledge about child development and about the capacity of our institutions to help families and children, and when society is willing to expend more resources to provide services to children, different standards will be appropriate.

The approach suggested may be seen by some readers as more solicitous of parents' rights than of children's rights. As such, it may be interpreted as a defense of the old system against the mounting call for emphasis on children's rights and greater state protection for children. To me, such charges are unwarranted. Existing policies have too often destroyed families rather than helped them become viable units. The result has not only harmed the parents, it has failed to benefit the children. A new approach is needed if we are really to protect children's rights.

APPENDIX: PROPOSED STATUTORY GROUNDS FOR INTERVENTION
1. General Principles

1.1 Laws structuring a system of coercive state intervention on behalf of endangered children should be based on a strong presumption for parental autonomy in child rearing. State intervention either through active state involvement in child care or through extensive monitoring of each child's development should be available only as an opportunity provided on request of, or without objection by, the parent, except when a child is suffering harm, as defined in part 2, section 2.1.

1.2 Coercive state intervention should be premised upon specific harms to a child, not on the basis of parental conduct.

1.3 Coercive state intervention should be authorized only for those categories of harm where

(a) A child is suffering or there is substantial likelihood that he or she will imminently suffer a serious injury; and

(b) Coercive intervention to alleviate the general category of harm will, in most instances, be able to prevent the harm without creating in the process new harms for the child greater than the harm leading to intervention.

1.4 The grounds for coercive intervention should be defined as specifically as possible. Vague or general laws are both undesirable and unnecessary for protecting children.

1.5 Fault concepts should not be relevant to determining the need for intervention.

1.6 All standards for intervention should take into account cultural differences in child rearing and all decision makers should examine the child's needs in light of his or her cultural background and values.

2. Harms for Which Intervention Is Permitted

2.1 In cases where it is alleged that a child is endangered, courts should be authorized to assume court jurisdiction in order to condition continued parental custody upon the parents' accepting supervision or to remove a child from his/her home, only if the court finds that the child comes within one or more of the provisions in subsections 2.1 (a)–(f).

(a) A child has suffered a physical injury, inflicted upon him/her nonaccidentally, causing disfigurement, impairment of body functioning, or severe bodily harm, or there is a substantial likelihood that the child will imminently suffer such an injury.

(b) A child has suffered physical injury causing disfigurement, impairment of body functioning, or severe bodily harm as a result of conditions uncorrected by his/her parents or by the failure of his/her parents to adequately supervise or protect him/her; or when there is a substantial risk that the child will imminently suffer such harm as a result of conditions uncorrected by his/her parents or by the failure of his/her parents to adequately supervise or protect him/her.

(c) A child is suffering serious emotional damage, evidenced by severe anxiety, depression or withdrawal, or untoward aggressive behavior toward others, and his/her parents are unwilling to provide, when financially able to do so, or permit necessary treatment for him/her.

(d) A child has been sexually abused by a member of his/her household.

(e) A child is in need of medical treatment to cure, alleviate, or prevent him/her from suffering serious physical harm which may cause death, disfigurement, or substantial impairment of bodily functioning, and his/her parents are unwilling to provide, when financially able to do so, or consent to the medical treatment.

(f) A child is committing delinquent acts as a result of parental encouragement, guidance, or approval.

2.2 Intervention under Definition

The fact that a child is endangered in a manner specified by statute is a necessary but not sufficient reason for a court to declare the minor neglected and make the minor a ward of the court. In every case a court should also find that the child will be placed in a less detrimental position as a result of the proposed intervention.

BIBLIOGRAPHY

American Humane Association, Children's Division. 1967. *Child Protective Services.* Denver.

Baker, James A. 1969. "Court-Ordered Non-emergency Medical Care for Infants." *Cleveland-Marshall Law Review* 18:296–307.

Bender, Lauretta, and Blau, Abram. 1937. "The Reaction of Children to Sexual Relations with Adults." *American Journal of Orthopsychiatry* 7:500–18.

Boehm, Bernice. 1964. "The Community and the Social Agency Define Neglect." *Child Welfare* 43:453–64.

Bowlby, John. 1965. *Child Care and the Growth of Love.* 2d ed. Baltimore: Penguin Books.

Bronfenbrenner, Urie. 1974. *Is Early Intervention Effective? A Report on Longitudinal Evaluations of Preschool Programs,* vol. 2. Department of Health, Education, and Welfare. Washington, D.C.: U.S. Government Printing Office.

Campbell, Catherine E. 1970. "The Neglected Child: His and His Family's Treatment under Massachusetts Law and Practice and Their Rights under the Due Process Clause." *Suffolk University Law Review* 4:631-88.

Child Welfare League of America. 1973. *Standards for Child Protective Services*. Rev. ed. New York: Committee on Standards for Protective Services.

Chilman, Catherine S. 1966. *Growing Up Poor: An Overview and Analysis of Child-Rearing and Family Life Patterns Associated with Poverty*. Department of Health, Education, and Welfare, Welfare Administration, Division of Research. Washington, D.C.: U.S. Government Printing Office.

Cohen, Morton I.; Mulford, Robert; and Philbrick, Elizabeth. 1967. *Neglecting Parents: A Study of Psychosocial Characteristics*. Denver: American Humane Association, Children's Division.

✓ Council of Judges, National Council on Crime and Delinquency. 1968. "Guides to the Judge in Medical Orders Respecting Children." *Crime and Delinquency* 14:107-20.

Eist, Harold I., and Mandel, Adeline U. 1968. "Family Treatment of Ongoing Incest Behavior." *Family Process* 7:216-32.

Elmer, Elizabeth, and Gregg, Grace S. 1967. "Developmental Characteristics of Abused Children." *Pediatrics* 40:596-602.

Fischer, Joel. 1973. "Is Casework Effective? A Review." *Social Work* 18:5-20.

Fontana, Vinçent J. 1973. *Somewhere a Child Is Crying: Maltreatment—Causes and Prevention*. New York: Macmillan.

Foster, Henry H., Jr., and Freed, Doris Jonas. 1972. "A Bill of Rights for Children." *Family Law Quarterly* 6:343-75.

Freud, Anna. 1965. *Normality and Pathology in Childhood: Assessments of Development*. New York: International Universities Press.

————. 1972. "The Child As a Person in His Own Right." *Psychoanalytic Study of the Child* 27:621-25.

Gil, David G. 1970. *Violence against Children: Physical Child Abuse in the United States*. Cambridge: Harvard University Press.

Gill, Thomas D. 1960. "The Legal Nature of Neglect." *National Probation and Parole Association Journal* 6:1-16.

Goldstein, Joseph. 1968. "Psychoanalysis and Jurisprudence." *Yale Law Journal* 77:1053-77.

✓ Goldstein, Joseph; Freud, Anna; and Solnit, Albert J. 1973. *Beyond the Best Interests of the Child*. New York: Free Press.

Handler, Joel F. 1973. *The Coercive Social Worker: British Lessons for American Social Services*. Institute for Research on Poverty Monograph Series. Chicago: Rand McNally.

Joint Commission on Mental Health of Children. 1970. *Crisis in*

Mental Health: Challenge for the 1970's: Report. New York: Harper and Row.

Kadushin, Alfred. 1974. *Child Welfare Services.* 2d ed. New York: Macmillan.

Katz, Sanford N. 1971. *When Parents Fail: The Law's Response to Family Breakdown.* Boston: Beacon Press.

Kay, Herma, and Philips, Irving. 1966. "Poverty and the Law of Child Custody." *California Law Review* 54:717-40.

Keith-Lucas, Alan. 1973. "'Speaking for the Child': A Role Analysis and Some Cautions." In *The Rights of Children: Emergent Concepts in Law and Society,* ed. Albert E. Wilkerson. Philadelphia: Temple University Press. Pp. 218-31.

Levine, Richard E. 1973. "Caveat Parens: A Demystification of the Child Protection System." *University of Pittsburgh Law Review* 35:1-52.

Luckey, Eleanore Braun. 1964. "Family Goals in a Democratic Society." *Journal of Marriage and the Family* 26:271-78.

MacFarlane, Jean W.; Clausen, John A.; and Yahraes, Herbert C. 1971. "Childhood Influences upon Intelligence, Personality, and Mental Health." In *The Mental Health of the Child: Program Reports of the National Institute of Mental Health,* by Antoinette Gattozzi, Gay Luce, Maya Pines, Clarissa Wittenberg, and Herbert Yahraes; ed. Julius Segal. Rockville, Md.: National Institute of Mental Health Program Analysis and Evaluation Branch Office of Program Planning and Evaluation. Pp. 131-54.

Mnookin, Robert H. 1973. "Foster Care—In Whose Best Interest?" *Harvard Educational Review* 43:599-638.

New York State Assembly Select Committee on Child Abuse. 1972. *Report of the Select Committee on Child Abuse.*

Paulsen, Monrad G. 1962. "The Delinquency, Neglect, and Dependency Jurisdiction of the Juvenile Court." In *Justice for the Child,* ed. Margaret K. Rosenheim. New York: Free Press of Glencoe. Pp. 44-81.

Polansky, Norman Alburt; Borgman, Robert D.; and DeSaix, Christine. 1972. *Roots of Futility.* San Francisco: Jossey-Bass.

Polansky, Norman Alburt; DeSaix, Christine; and Sharlin, Shlomo A. 1972. *Child Neglect: Understanding and Reaching the Parents.* New York: Child Welfare League of America.

President's Commission on Law Enforcement and Administration of Justice. 1967. *The Challenge of Crime in a Free Society.* Washington, D.C.: U.S. Government Printing Office.

Reimer, Svend. 1940. "A Research Note on Incest." *American Journal of Sociology* 45:566-75.

Robertson, Joyce. 1962. "Mothering as an Influence on Early

Development: A Study of Well-Baby Clinics." *Psychoanalytic Study of the Child* 17:245-64.

Sherman, Edmund A.; Phillips, Michael H.; Haring, Barbara L.; and Shyne, Ann W. 1973. *Service to Children in Their Own Homes: Its Nature and Outcome.* [New York]: Child Welfare League of America Research Center.

Skolnick, Arlene S. 1973. *The Intimate Environment: Exploring Marriage and the Family.* Boston: Little, Brown.

Steele, Brandt F., and Pollock, Carl B. 1968. "A Psychiatric Study of Parents Who Abuse Infants and Small Children." In *The Battered Child,* eds. Ray E. Helfer and C. Henry Kempe. Chicago: University of Chicago Press. Pp. 103-47.

Sullivan, Michael F. 1968. "Child Neglect: The Environmental Aspects." *Ohio State Law Journal* 29:85-115.

Tamilia, Patrick R. 1973. "Neglect Proceedings and the Conflict between Law and Society." *Duquesne Law Review* 9:579-89.

Thomas, Mason P. 1972. "Child Abuse and Neglect. Part 1: Historical Overview, Legal Matrix, and Social Perspectives." *North Carolina Law Review* 50:293-349.

Tormes, Yvonne M. 1968. *Child Victims of Incest.* Denver: American Humane Association, Children's Division.

Wald, Max. 1961. *Protective Services and Emotional Neglect.* Denver: American Humane Association, Children's Division.

Wald, Michael S. 1975. "State Intervention on Behalf of 'Neglected' Children: A Search for Realistic Standards." *Stanford Law Review* 27:985-1040.

———. 1976. "State Intervention on Behalf of 'Neglected' Children: Standards for Removal of Children from their Homes, Monitoring the Status of Children in Foster Care, and Termination of Parental Rights." *Stanford Law Review* 28:623-706.

Weinberg, Samuel Kirson. 1955. *Incest Behavior.* New York: Citadel Press.

Weston, James Tuthill. 1968. "Pathology of Child Abuse." In *The Battered Child,* eds. Ray E. Helfer and C. Henry Kempe. Chicago: University of Chicago Press. Pp. 77-100.

White, Sheldon. 1973. *Federal Programs for Young Children: Review and Recommendations.* 4 vols. Washington, D.C.: U.S. Government Printing Office.

Young, Leontine Ruth. 1964. *Wednesday's Children: A Study of Child Neglect and Abuse.* New York: McGraw-Hill.

IV

**JUSTICE FOR THE CHILD:
OTHER TIMES, OTHER PLACES**

13   Juvenile Justice and the National Crime Commissions

Michael H. Tonry

Large criminals from small delinquents grow.

So said the National Commission on Law Observance and Enforcement in 1931, the President's Commission on Law Enforcement and Administration of Justice in 1967, and the National Advisory Commission on Criminal Justice Standards and Goals in 1973.

The three principal American national crime commissions are said to share more than that modest maxim. Critics of American criminal justice have asserted repeatedly that the three commissions recorded near-identical failings of the system and offered near-identical reform agendas. The critics are basically correct, but the national crime commission reports are important nonetheless. The commission reports—in their views of the nature and causes of delinquency, the problems and possibilities of juvenile justice, and directions for the future—have important implications for present proposals for change.

The advent of the juvenile court was heralded with elaborate rhetoric about child saving. Implicit in the rhetoric were assumptions about the propriety of state intervention in children's lives and the likely success of that intervention, both of which assumptions have continued controversial to the present.

In an effort to make theoretical sense of America's three-quarter-century juvenile court experiment, Edwin Schur in *Radical Nonintervention: Rethinking the Delinquency Problem* (1973) chronicles the evolution of American delinquency theory. He offers a useful typology of theories and strategies, which will be employed here as a measure for the reports of three crime commissions.

Schur suggests three "patterned reactions to delinquency": individual treatment, liberal reform, and radical nonintervention. Schur also notes, but does not develop, a fourth patterned reaction to delinquency: the get-tough antipermissive approach to crime so popular in political campaigns. This fourth reaction is seldom developed theoretically outside of jurisprudential debates on law and morality (see Ewing 1970; Devlin 1965).

Individual treatment explains delinquency in terms of differences among individuals and proposes to reform defective and inadequate people. Delinquency results from internal failing which must be cured. Individual treatment allows for both utilitarian and positivist explanations of crime. With that inherent ambiguity, it was the prevalent delinquency ideology of the separate-treatment-for-juveniles movement and it survives in the assumptions of the present juvenile justice system.

Liberal reform is positivist and portrays delinquency largely as a lower-class phenomenon, determined by social environment. Individuals don't fail. Social organization does. Delinquency can be dealt with only through environment, whether by facilitating individual adaptation, by removing the troubled child, or by changing the environment. Symbolized by the street worker and community programs, liberal reform ideologies have been influential during most of this century, from Shaw and McKay to Cloward and Ohlin. Schur describes individual treatment and liberal reform as inevitably overlapping and suggests that "most delinquency research and policy has reflected their combined influence," which should be no surprise. Most lay theories of crime allow both for criminals who are weak, self-indulgent, and undisciplined and for others who are victims of a "bad home life" or the "wrong side of the tracks."

Radical nonintervention describes delinquents as sufferers of contingencies and not as people with special personal problems or as victims of socio-economic constraints. Nonconforming behavior by the young is ubiquitous; those who experience the fortuities of apprehension and processing become "delinquents." Building on labeling theory and self-report and other studies that suggest that characterization as delinquent is the most reliable predictor of delinquency, radical noninterventionists argue that nonconforming behavior is more widespread, geographically and socially, than is generally recognized and that most children will outgrow it if left alone. A second radical nonintervention focus is compulsion. Whether its purpose is treatment or correction, they are against it, although some allow a frankly punitive use. They oppose compulsion for moral and practical reasons. Moral, because of the sanctity of human autonomy and the class bias of the operation of the criminal justice system. Practical, because there is no compelling evidence that coerced rehabilitation works. Indeed, present evidence suggests that the more intensive and constraining the intrusion into children's lives, the greater the likelihood that a delinquent incident will lead to a criminal career.

The perspectives of the three major United States crime commissions approximate Schur's three patterns of reaction. The first commission was the National Commission on Law Observance and Enforcement, known as the Wickersham commission. Its report on juvenile justice, *The Child Offender in the Federal System of Justice* (National Commission . . . 1931) is an optimistic document. It parrots the effusive praise for the juvenile court's beneficence contained in the early judicial decisions upholding the court's constitutionality. The report enthusiastically endorses a delinquency strategy which, while immature and incomplete, would be successful if money and will held out. The failures which *The Child Offender* describes are failures of execution, not of concept. The basic analysis portrays delinquency as failures of children, soluble by compassionate individualized rehabilitation.

In 1965 Lyndon B. Johnson appointed the President's Commission on Law Enforcement and Administration of Justice, popularly called the President's Crime Commission. Its report, *The Challenge of Crime in a Free Society* (President's Commission . . . 1967a), offers a liberal reform perspective with radical nonintervention slanting. Delinquency is described as a product of economic disadvantage, family instability, and myriad other social factors. Until those social conditions are ameliorated, no delinquency strategy can work. The only realistic goals of reform are to make the instruments of justice fairer and the exercise of their authority more principled. Children should be spared the excesses of child-saving institutions and attempt should be made to compensate for criminogenic environments by establishing all-purpose youth support agencies, called youth service bureaus, in the neighborhoods.

Most recently, the Nixon administration appointed a National Advisory Commission on Criminal Justice Standards and Goals, known as the Standards and Goals commission. Its report, *A National Strategy to Reduce Crime* (National Advisory Commission . . . 1973*a*), questions the juvenile justice system's effectiveness and proposes an agenda of nonintervention. It accepts the view that any intervention is likely to be more harmful than no intervention and offers numerous proposals for saving children from the child savers.

THE WICKERSHAM COMMISSION AND THE WHITE HOUSE CONFERENCE ON CHILD HEALTH AND PROTECTION

The Wickersham commission was a product of Prohibition. Herbert Hoover, during the 1928 presidential campaign, promised if elected to investigate enforcement of the national prohibition laws. In early 1929, with rhetoric foreshadowing the sixties, he declared:

Every student of our law enforcement knows well that it is in need of vigorous re-organization; that its procedure unduly favors the criminal; that our judiciary needs to be strengthened; . . . that justice must be swift and sure. In our desire to be merciful the pendulum has swung in favor of the prisoner and away from the protection of society (as quoted in Wickersham 1929, p. 377).

On 28 May 1929, he appointed the National Commission on Law Observance and Enforcement, chaired by George W. Wickersham, former Republican attorney general and president of the American Law Institute. The other ten members included Harvard Law School Dean Roscoe Pound, Radcliffe College President Ada Louise Comstock, three sitting federal judges, and four distinguished private attorneys. Their mission, President Hoover told Congress in his annual message of 3 December 1929, was to conduct

an exhaustive study of the entire problem of the enforcement of
our laws and the improvement of our judicial system, including
the special problems and abuses growing out of the prohibition
laws. The Commission has been invited to make the widest inquiry into the shortcomings of the administration of justice and
the causes and remedies for them (as quoted in Wickersham
1930, p. 654).

The commission formed fourteen subcommittees and hired leading academics and writers to head research programs. Included
were Clifford Shaw and Benjamin McKay on causes of delinquency, Hastings Hart on penal institutions, William O. Douglas
and Thurman Arnold on the federal courts, and Edith Abbott on
crime and the foreign-born. With two years, half a million dollars,
expert research teams, and an enthusiastic membership, the
commission produced fourteen reports in fifteen volumes.

The Wickersham commission's juvenile justice report was
undertaken as a collaborative effort with the 1930 White House
Conference on Child Health and Protection. The product was to
be published in two parts: part 1 on the child offender in the state
systems of justice by the White House Conference and part 2 on
the child offender in the federal system of justice by the Wickersham commission. Miriam Van Waters, a contemporary juvenile
justice authority, was to be the research director of the combined
study. The Wickersham commission and Dr. Van Waters refer to
the joint sponsorship and the intended complementary publications. The relevant White House Conference report does not.

George Wickersham submitted Report no. 6, *The Child
Offender in the Federal System of Justice,* to President Hoover on
28 May 1931. *The Child Offender* is representative of Wickersham commission reports although, because of the apparently
abortive collaboration, it is not as comprehensive as most. The
juvenile justice staff, social-work dominated, was experienced and
well qualified. Dr. Van Waters was research director. Extensive
research, largely empirical, was undertaken concerning the operation of the federal criminal justice system as it affected children.
The federal reformatories and similar state juvenile institutions
were investigated. The report contains numerous detailed and
occasionally quite sophisticated statistical tables.

Appearing about thirty years after the first juvenile courts
began operation, at a time when forty-six states had established
juvenile courts, *The Child Offender* (National Commission . . .

1931) offers the following statement of the juvenile court concept:

The creation and development of the juvenile court in the American States has been made possible by a line plainly drawn between child and adult in the State law. The child offender is generally dealt with on a non-criminal basis and has been protected from prosecution and conviction for crime. The State has come to regard him as its ward. It has undertaken to safeguard, train and educate rather than punish him. It has substituted social for penal methods, the concept of juvenile delinquency for that of crime (p. 2).

The report's approach to the juvenile justice system is to ask whether individualized treatment in a humane and compassionate setting has been achieved. The concluding paragraph of a survey of juvenile correctional institutions begins: "Individualization of treatment has not been accomplished" (p. 106).

The Child Offender never abandons its enthusiasm for the child-saving experiment. While the report acknowledges that in the best juvenile correctional institutions "no sense of beauty, personal loyalty, or confidence in human relationships is given support or outlet" and that "individualization of treatment has not been accomplished.... The need of the spirit for creative outlets, personal guidance and satisfying human relationships are [*sic*] unfulfilled" (p. 106), it expresses no doubt about the soundness of the juvenile court system's basic concepts. On the basis that the states' juvenile court reforms were conceptually sound and the number of federal juvenile offenders too small to warrant a parallel system, the principal reform recommendations for the federal system were that the juvenile court concept of the child-as-ward be adopted and that all juveniles arrested for federal offenses be referred to state juvenile courts for handling.

The intended companion report, *The Delinquent Child* (White House Conference ... 1932), affirms its individual treatment orientation explicitly in two "basic principles":

(1) reaffirmation of the idea that delinquency is a symptom, in that it is a rather naturally expected expression of some earlier, deeper or more pervasive maladjustment; (2) recognition that it is the delinquent rather than the delinquencies which requires and merits study (p. 24).

The Delinquent Child was produced by the Committee on the Socially Handicapped and Delinquency of the 1930 White House Conference. Chaired by Judge Francis P. Cabot of the Boston

Juvenile Court, the report shows the intellectual domination of
William Healy, a prolific exponent of his own psycho-social
theories of multiple-factor explanations of delinquency. The
committee's research director was Katherine F. Lenroot, assistant
chief of the United States Children's Bureau, who had been
Dr. Van Waters' deputy on the Wickersham commission. Subcommittees prepared chapters on the child himself and his
relationships with his family, education, employment, religion,
community, and the state. The committee and its staff were
mostly social workers and juvenile justice system professionals.

The Delinquent Child approves and elaborates on the Wickersham commission's endorsement of the juvenile court concept
and echoes most of its criticisms and reform prescriptions. The
report describes the system's concrete failures:

unnecessary arrests; detention in police stations and jails; juvenile
courts, presided over by poorly paid judges not especially prepared or selected for children's work, and without the services of
an adequate number of qualified probation officers; absence of
psychiatric services; inadequate facilities for foster home or institutional care; absence of an effective parole system (p. 21).

Shortcomings notwithstanding, the report expresses no doubt
that the juvenile court system is the answer to delinquency. Its
recommendations are the familiar litany of more, better paid, and
better qualified personnel, development of more rehabilitative
programs, and the use of institutionalization as a last resort. The
report adopts as its own the Juvenile Court Standards jointly
developed by the United States Children's Bureau and the
National Probation Association.

The Child Offender and The Delinquent Child span the field of
official intervention, federal and state, in the lives of troublesome
children. Both describe squalid and brutal institutions, over-
worked and underpaid personnel, and inadequate resources.
Both argue that delinquency results from soluble individual
problems of children. Both accept the juvenile court individual
treatment model as sound but, because of inadequate resources
and personnel, untested.

Neither report appears to have had significant impact. The
Delinquent Child, like most conference reports, was little reviewed and apparently had little influence. The Child Offender
was drowned in alcohol.

Partisan crime problems produce bad national commission

reports. With striking similarity to the insipid marihuana report of the National Commission on Marihuana and Drug Abuse (1972), the Wickersham reports on Prohibition are unprincipled, self-contradictory, and divisive. Although the commission dealt with every aspect of criminal justice, the fourteen reports were reviewed in only three American legal periodicals, none of which considered all of them. Columbia Law Professor John Hanna (1931) observed in the *Harvard Law Review*:

It is a matter of common knowledge, however, that the initial reaction of the public to the report was unfavorable, and that the Commission has received a surprising amount of abusive criticism much of which has been ribald and unembarrassed by any familiarity with the report (p. 1005).

Wickersham (1931) himself later acknowledged that the controversy surrounding the Prohibition reports overshadowed the commission's other efforts.

THE PRESIDENT'S CRIME COMMISSION

Thirty-six years after Hoover's preelection pledge to investigate Prohibition, Senator Barry Goldwater laid the foundation for the second national crime commission in another presidential campaign by his attempt to raise "crime in the streets" as an anti-administration issue. There are many accounts of the background to President Johnson's decision to appoint a crime commission; most focus on Goldwater's failure to make "crime in the streets" a potent issue in the 1964 campaign and Johnson's successful effort to avoid it. In the longer run, the issue, renamed law and order, did become politically important and Johnson apparently felt obliged at least to appear to take the issue seriously. Whatever his motivation, President Johnson by executive order on 23 July 1965, created the President's Commission on Law Enforcement and Administration of Justice. The nineteen-member commission bore a striking resemblance to its Wickersham predecessor in both membership and approach. None of its members were elected politicians. Its chairman was Nicholas deB. Katzenbach, then United States Attorney General. Other members included the president of Yale University, two sitting federal judges, a state supreme court judge, and several distinguished private attorneys. The Wickersham and White House Conference juvenile justice staffs were composed mostly of social workers. The

President's Crime Commission's staff were largely lawyers. The research program of the President's Crime Commission was highly centralized. Extensive surveys and statistical studies were commissioned. Numerous consultants prepared papers and drafts of the reports. One count numbered the commission's hired hands at 65 staff members, 175 consultants, and hundreds of advisors. The President's Crime Commission produced a general report, *The Challenge of Crime in a Free Society* (President's Commission . . . 1967*a*), and nine task force reports including one entitled *Juvenile Delinquency and Youth Crime* (President's Commission . . . 1967*b*).

The juvenile justice system was under heavy attack when the President's Crime Commission began its work. Most critics focused on the system's denial of procedural protections to juveniles without a corresponding increase in its humanity and effectiveness. Justice Abe Fortas, in *Kent v. United States* (383 U.S. 541 [1966]), the first of the Supreme Court's important juvenile court decisions, wrote:

While there can be no doubt of the original laudable purpose of juvenile courts, studies and critiques in recent years raise serious questions as to whether actual performance measures well enough against theoretical purpose to make tolerable the immunity of the process from the reach of constitutional guarantees applicable to adults. There is much evidence that some juvenile courts, including that of the District of Columbia, lack personnel, facilities and techniques to perform adequately as representatives of the state in a parens patriae capacity, at least with children charged with law violations. There is evidence, in fact, that there may be grounds for concern that the child receives the worst of both worlds: That he gets neither the protections accorded to adults nor the solicitous care and regenerative treatment postulated for children (p. 556).

The President's Crime Commission shared Justice Fortas' concern.

The Challenge of Crime in a Free Society declares delinquency to be the product of adverse social conditions. More than two-thirds of the *Challenge*'s chapter on juvenile delinquency and youth crime describes the social setting of delinquency; the remainder discusses the state's reactions. The solution to delinquency lies not in reformation of juvenile justice institutions, but in social reform:

The Commission finds, first, that America must translate its well-founded alarm about crime into social action that will prevent crime. It has no doubt whatever that the most significant action that can be taken against crime is action designed to eliminate slums and ghettoes, to improve education, to provide jobs, to make sure that every American is given the opportunities and the freedoms that will enable him to assume his responsibilities. We will not have dealt effectively with crime until we have alleviated the conditions that stimulate it. To speak of controlling crime only in terms of the police, the courts and the correctional apparatus, is to refuse to face the fact that widespread crime implies a widespread failure by society as a whole (p. 15).

The entire juvenile justice system is a disaster. The juvenile court "has not succeeded significantly in rehabilitating delinquent youth, in reducing or even stemming the tide of delinquency, or in bringing justice and compassion to the child offender." Juvenile probation means "minimum supervision at best ... caseloads are typically so high that counselling and supervision take the form of occasional phone calls and perfunctory visits." Custodial institutions often mean "storage—isolation from the outside world—in an overcrowded, under-staffed security institution with little education, little vocational training, little counselling or job placement, or other guidance or release" (p. 80).

The explanations for the system's failures are various: delinquency is only a symptom of profound social failures and cannot be redressed by any reactive institutions; material and manpower resources are inadequate; the juvenile justice system, like all social welfare programs, suffers from low priority; juvenile justice is not in a position to demand a substantial wedge of the state's fiscal pie. Nonetheless, *The Challenge* does not recommend that America "jettison the experiment and remand the disposition of children charged with crime to the criminal courts of the country." The reason: the problems of the criminal courts are even graver than those of the juvenile courts and the "ideal of separate treatment of children is still worth pursuing" (p. 81).

The reforms proposed by the President's Crime Commission are a juvenile court with added procedural protections and a reduced jurisdiction (basically limited to conduct that would be criminal if committed by an adult) and establishment of youth service bureaus—neighborhood facilities designed to provide individually tailored support services in a largely noncompulsory setting. The juvenile justice reform proposals of *The Challenge* have been summarized as diversion, due process, and deinstitutionalization (Empey 1973). The alliterative catchwords embody a view that any official processing of children in the juvenile justice system is likely to damage them and that the state should minimize harm by interfering in their lives as infrequently and unobtrusively as community safety (narrowly defined) will allow. While "less harm" is more a concept of radical nonintervention than liberal reform, the focus on the social causes of delinquency, the view that delinquency is largely a problem of the lower classes, and the recommendation for development of youth service bureaus places *The Challenge* well into the liberal reform camp. Despite many concrete recommendations, *The Challenge* contains a fatalistic prognosis that the best we can do is stumble along as before but hopefully—by diversion, due process, and deinstitutionalization—cause less harm to fewer children.

THE STANDARDS AND GOALS COMMISSION
The third major national crime commission, the National Advisory Commission on Criminal Justice Standards and Goals, derived not from election polemics but from the Nixon administration's preoccupation with law and order and from the spate of prison uprisings of the early seventies. Appointed by Jerris Leonard, then administrator of the Law Enforcement Assistance Administration, the twenty-two-person commission substantially completed its work in little more than a year, presenting a preliminary version of its report to a National Conference on Criminal Justice in early January 1973. The final version of the six-volume report—including a summary volume and five specialized reports on police, courts, corrections, community crime prevention, and the criminal justice system—trickled out during the summer and fall of 1973.

The Standards and Goals commission differed from its predecessors in important respects. For the first time a national crime commission contained elected politicians: five, nearly a quarter of its membership; Republican Governor Russell Peterson of Delaware was chairman. Unlike the blue-ribbon generalists who manned its predecessors, this commission had a distinctly professional hue and was composed largely of criminal justice professionals. Each commission has had an academic member: the Wickersham commission included Harvard Law School's dean; the President's Crime Commission included Yale's president; the Standards and Goals commission's academic member was chairman of the humanities department of Spencerian Business College in Milwaukee.

The Standards and Goals commission does not define its mission encyclopedically or support extensive fact-gathering research. Its avowed goal is to build upon existing information and articulate clear standards for reforming the methods and institutions of American criminal justice. Its aim is to "formulate for the first time national criminal justice standards and goals for crime reduction and prevention at the State and local levels" (National Advisory Commission . . . 1973a, p. v). In part, no doubt, the Standards and Goals agenda is an answer to "Why another commission?"

Goals for criminal justice reform are set: by 1983, reduce homicide, forcible rape, and aggravated assault rates by 25 percent, robbery and burglary by 50 percent. While the report acknowledges that "the selection of these crimes and percentages of reduction will arouse the doubts of skeptics," it confidently opines, "The goals can be attained" (p. 8). Asserting that adult criminals are made, not born, its principal reform strategy is an assault on delinquency. To achieve its goals, the commission offers concrete standards for reform, blueprints to be adopted by state criminal justice systems. In the main, the Standards and Goals commission adopts the recommendations of the President's Crime Commission, occasionally going further. It could live with an agenda of diversion, due process, and deinstitutionalization.

Some of the commission's recommendations—notwithstanding the establishmentarian backgrounds of the commissioners—are relatively radical. While few of the commissioners would be likely to describe themselves as radical critics of American society generally, or of the criminal justice system particularly, a strong case can be made that Schur's radical nonintervention category summarizes the ideology of the Standards and Goals report. The commission notes that

a number of studies . . . suggest that many children mature out of delinquent behavior. If this is true, the question is whether it is better to leave these persons alone or put them into the formal juvenile justice system. . . . There is a substantial body of opinion which favors "leaving alone" all except those who have had three or four contacts with the police (p. 109).

Every significant standard involving juveniles urges leaving them
alone and saving them from the juvenile court and its backup
institutions. Like the President's Crime Commission's report, this
report proposes that police, juvenile court intake workers, and
juvenile court judges divert all possible children from official
processing and urges development and extensive use of youth
service bureaus, though with some of their compulsory features
removed.

The Standards and Goals commission's most important juvenile justice recommendation is the effective renunciation of the
juvenile court concept. Paying rhetorical respect to the juvenile
court, the report asserts, "The objective of reform should not be
to render the court processing of juveniles indistinguishable from
the processing of adult criminal defendants" (National Advisory
Commission ... 1973b, p. 291). But, with two exceptions—
juveniles should not be tried before adult criminal courts, and
dispositional alternatives at postconviction sentencing hearings
should be wider for juveniles—the effect of the report's juvenile
court recommendations would be precisely that.

The juvenile court's jurisdiction would be incorporated into
new "family courts" which would be responsible for most legal
matters involving family organization and children:

This jurisdiction should include delinquency, neglect, support,
adoption, child custody, paternity actions, divorce and annulment
and assault offenses in which both victim and alleged offender are
members of the same family (National Advisory Commission ...
1973a, p. 109).

The family court would inherit allegations of "conduct criminal
if committed by adults" and neglect cases, but not dependency
cases, which should be the responsibility of social service agencies. The report takes no position on MINS-PINS-CHINS jurisdiction but urges that "conduct illegal only for children" should
never result in either a finding of delinquency or placement in
institutions for delinquent children.

The report further recommends that children accused of acts
criminal by adult standards, who are not diverted from the
system, should be entitled to nearly all the procedural protections
of the adult criminal court, including a right to a fully adversary
counsel answerable only to the child regardless of the child's
"best interests" or the wants of parent or guardian. (The most

notable exception is a right to trial by jury, a right which the Supreme Court has decreed does not belong to children. See *McKeiver* v. *Pennsylvania,* 403 U.S. 528 [1970].) Proceedings should be divided into separate adjudicatory and dispositional hearings; only at the latter should procedures differ from adult cases and then only to the extent that a wider range of dispositional alternatives should be available. In all other respects the dispositional hearings should resemble adult sentencing hearings (which the commission would also remodel by infusion of numerous procedural protections).

The recommendations for sanctions again reflect a view that less harm will be caused to juveniles if formal processing is kept to a minimum. Like the President's Crime Commission's report, the Standards and Goals report urges (1) development of community-based institutions and (2) institutionalization only as a last resort. Finally it urges that other states follow the lead of Massachusetts and abolish all large juvenile institutions.

THE REPORTS REAPPRAISED

Every commonsense assumption about the three commissions would suggest a disagreement on policy recommendations for juvenile justice reform. The Wickersham and President's Crime commissions were blue-ribbon affairs and included few politicians or practitioners; the Standards and Goals commission was composed largely of politicians and professional administrators. The Wickersham and the Standards and Goals commissions were appointed by, or under, conservative Republican presidents, the President's Crime Commission by the domestically liberal Democrat, Lyndon Johnson. Social workers dominated Wickersham's research staff; the President's Crime Commission staff was the creature of lawyers; the Standards and Goals commission staff was—probably because the commission did not sponsor substantial original research—basically administrative.

The Wickersham report is sanguine about the child-saving institutions' potential. It perceives delinquents as different and damaged. The 1967 report is fatalistic in both its rhetoric and its views. It describes children as victimized by their environments; future generations of children will suffer similar fates until dramatic social reforms materially alter that environment. The Standards and Goals report is rhetorically optimistic, but offers

an agenda that would abandon the child-saving experiment. It
views problem children as the joint product of social conditions
and the juvenile justice system: "The highest priority must be
given . . . to minimizing the involvement of young offenders in
the juvenile and criminal justice system." Why? Because "the further an offender penetrates into the criminal justice process, the
more difficult it becomes to divert him from a criminal career"
(National Advisory Commission . . . 1973a, p. 23).

The reports do, however, have important similarities. Each was
appointed in response to a crime crisis. The precise criticisms of
the three reports—impersonal institutions; arbitrary decisions;
brutality; insufficient resources; and inadequately trained personnel—are interchangeable. And their solutions to these problems are strikingly similar—more money; better trained personnel; centralization and rationalization of systems. Despite
reasons to expect fundamentally different reform recommendations, the three commissions recommended the same basic
package. Why?

The lesson of the crime commission chronicle may be that
Schur's noninterventionists are right: the juvenile court child-
saving system does not and cannot work. Credible explanations
include the low level of financial support obtainable by any social
welfare program, the nature of bureaucratic institutions, and our
limited knowledge of the technology of rehabilitation.

The commissions' consistent accounts of the system's failure
accord with contemporary views of the failings of criminal justice
generally. Sufficient financial support is never available. When it
is available the inevitably staff-centered institutions compromise
the pursuit of rehabilitative goals. When the pursuit is not so
compromised, there is no convincing evidence that rehabilitative
programs work. Finally, labeling a child a "problem child," the
socially discriminatory treatment of juvenile justice system alumni
in the outside world, and contamination of the child by other
problem children—these constant features of the system appear
to do more harm than any imaginable system could do good.

Had the commissions posed different questions, they might
have been able to offer more promising answers. Their accounts
of an ineffective system raise serious questions about the key
underlying concepts of "adolescence," "delinquency," and
"crime." None of the commissions explicitly dealt with those

definitions, although the later two approached them implicitly. The modern commissions should have reconsidered the first principles of juvenile justice: that children are qualitatively different from adults and therefore should be treated differently. Those principles cause many of the systemic excesses. They permit the exchange of procedural protections for ostensibly benevolent paternalism and further development of delinquency definitions which expose children to state interference not experienced by adults.

Neither the President's Crime Commission nor the Standards and Goals commission discusses disavowal of jurisprudential significance for adolescence, but both contain recommendations, the due process recommendations, which point in that direction. The President's Crime Commission recommended retention of the juvenile court with greater elements of due process; the Standards and Goals commission recommended abandonment of the juvenile court and the creation of a family court which would hear most legal matters relating to marriage and the family, also with greater due process. Both commissions recommend something like a juvenile criminal court, differing from the adult court principally in the ages of its clients and its separateness. Had the two commissions explicitly addressed the question of abandoning legal recognition of adolescence, their results would have been more controversial, but their recommendations might have been more striking and persuasive.

Accepting that children will continue to be treated differently from adults, the other definitions which the commissions should have faced explicitly (although again the later two did so implicitly) were "crime" and "delinquency." The three commissions agree that the answer to crime lies in our treatment of juveniles in trouble.

The present definitions of "crime" and "delinquency" differ in that the latter contains the content of the former plus behavior which legal recognition of adolescence makes subject to the juvenile court: being dependent, being in need of supervision, being a truant from school, or a curfew violator, or having "bad companions," or myriad other acts and statuses that are unlawful only for children.

It is a truism that crime could be decreased by repealing criminal laws; the argument is usually offered in connection with victimless crime. The commissions could have dealt with many delinquent acts by recommending that the definition of crime be narrowed and major parts of the criminal law be repealed. Narrowing the content of "crime" would necessarily narrow the scope of "delinquency." Because delinquency is broader, however, there is more room for narrowing.

The later two commissions partially deal with the definition of delinquency when they suggest that the jurisdiction of courts over juveniles be reduced to conduct that would be criminal if committed by an adult and when they recommend that no child should be declared delinquent who has not committed such acts. To the extent that the courts are divested of delinquency jurisdiction now exercised over children who are in fact "dependent," "in need of supervision," or engaging in acts permitted to adults, the definition of delinquency will have been narrowed.

The similarities of the commissions' descriptions and many of their recommendations result from commitment to a set of institutions which appear to be constitutionally incapable of achieving their goals. Such differences as appear among the commissions stem from a willingness of the later two commissions to consider, however gingerly, the implications of "adolescence" and "delinquency." If these terms are used to frame the agenda of a yet-to-be-proposed fourth national crime commission, the diagnosis and prescription should look different and better.

BIBLIOGRAPHY

Devlin, Patrick. 1965. *The Enforcement of Morals.* London and New York: Oxford University Press.
Empey, Lamar T. 1973. "Diversion, Due Process and De-institutionalization." In *Prisoners in America,* ed. Lloyd E. Ohlin. Englewood Cliffs, N.J.: Prentice-Hall. Pp. 13–48.
Ewing, Alfred C. 1970. *The Morality of Punishment, with Some Suggestions for a General Theory of Ethics.* Patterson-Smith Reprint Series in Criminology, Law Enforcement and Social Problems. Montclair, N.J.: Patterson-Smith.
Hanna, John. 1931. Book Review. *Harvard Law Review* 44: 1001–5.
National Advisory Commission on Criminal Justice Standards and Goals. 1973a. *A National Strategy to Reduce Crime.* Washington, D.C.: U.S. Government Printing Office.

National Advisory Commission on Criminal Justice Standards and Goals. 1973*b*. *Report on Courts.* Washington, D.C.: U.S. Government Printing Office.

National Commission on Law Observance and Enforcement. 1931. *The Child Offender in the Federal System of Justice.* Washington, D.C.: U.S. Government Printing Office.

National Commission on Marihuana and Drug Abuse. 1972. *Marihuana: A Signal of Misunderstanding.* Washington, D.C.: U.S. Government Printing Office.

President's Commission on Law Enforcement and Administration of Justice. 1967*a*. *The Challenge of Crime in a Free Society.* Washington, D.C.: U.S. Government Printing Office.

———. 1967*b*. *Task Force Report: Juvenile Delinquency and Youth Crime.* Washington, D.C.: U.S. Government Printing Office.

Schur, Edwin M. 1973. *Radical Nonintervention: Rethinking the Delinquency Problem.* Englewood Cliffs, N.J.: Prentice-Hall.

White House Conference on Child Health and Protection. 1932. *The Delinquent Child.* Report of the Committee on Socially Handicapped-Delinquency. New York and London: Century Co.

Wickersham, George W. 1929. Presidential Address to the American Law Institute. *American Bar Association Journal* 15:338, 376–77.

———. 1930. Presidential Address to the American Law Institute. *American Bar Association Journal* 16:654–61.

———. 1931. Presidential Address to the American Law Institute. *American Bar Association Journal* 17:359–63.

14 Juvenile Justice in Great Britain: Cautions, Hearings, and Courts

Michael J. Power

Over the last decade there has been a continual review of the methods used to regulate the social behavior of older children in Great Britain. (See generally, Conservative Political Centre 1966; Labour Party 1964; Gt. B. Parl. Papers ... 1945-46, 1959-60, 1964-65, 1967-68; Gt. B. Pub. Gen. Acts ... 1963, 1969.) A Committee of Enquiry, two detailed sets of recommendations from the political parties, two government White Papers, and two major Acts of Parliament, are evidence of the concern shown to find new ways of assisting delinquent children by a fair and just procedure. This search has been international and accounts elsewhere in this book describe other attempts to formulate a sane and liberal policy that protects the community by regulating behavior without further harming the delinquent child. In fact, this recent concern is only one aspect of the long-term emancipation of children from the virtual slavery of child labor—rural and urban (see Roberts 1971; Seebohm-Rowntree 1913).

The Historical Background—The Long View

At the beginning of the nineteenth century, as the industrial revolution in England gathered momentum, children in towns and country worked as hard as adults, and for as long each day. They frequently had less to eat because their contribution to the family income was small, and, of course, holidays were unknown. In law, children had no separate protected status, received no education and consequently, like their parents, were for the most part illiterate. A child's conviction for stealing might lead to hanging or transportation. The children of the well-to-do were protected, yet frequently they were educated in boarding establishments of spartan simplicity, rigid rules, and sadistic punishment.

By the first decade of this century half the population of England's industrial cities were unskilled manual laborers and their families. With an average annual income of £75, it was not surprising that as recently as 1912 the Poor Law workhouses held 280,000 paupers out of a total population in England and Wales of 30 million. For those who managed to stay outside, average weekly expenditure on food for a family with three dependent children amounted to 70p (then equivalent to $2). This might be half the average income for the family. Men averaged £1.25 a week, while half the working women in the country earned less than 50p for a 54-hour week. As outworkers, women might put in 14 hours a day making artificial flowers to earn 3p a gross; 25p for 18 hours' work putting hooks on cards. In such poverty it was the dependents, children and old people, who suffered most. With no pensions of any sort, the old had to seek parish relief as paupers. At the turn of the last century, one-quarter of all aged 65 and over were regarded as paupers, with half of them dying in the workhouse. Children fared no better—and with five or six children per family on the average, at least one was likely to die as an infant during the first year of life. Well into this century, infectious diseases and malnutrition continued to take their toll. But for those who survived, the future was brighter, because the one great reform that had been gradually gaining momentum for thirty years—universal education—took children out of the factories. Many went into classes of 100 or more, in charge of untrained teachers who, by 1908, might earn only £110 per year. Yet even in these circumstances it was possible to start tackling illiteracy and malnutrition.

By 1906 the Education (Provision of Meals) Act was passed. Yet stunted growth was to be widespread for another twenty years. At the beginning of the First World War in 1914-15 large numbers of unskilled working-class men volunteered. The doctors who examined them were appalled at their poor health and rejected thousands as unfit.

Child protection had focused upon factory legislation and compulsory education. Penal reform was limited to industrial and reformatory schools, for the child vagrant and the young incorrigible criminal. Not until 1933 did a law concern itself exclusively with welfare provisions for children, by setting the minimum age of criminal responsibility at eight years and establishing a network of juvenile courts (Gt. B. Pub. Gen. Acts . . . 1932). It also licensed certain mainly rural, privately managed "approved" boarding schools to receive delinquent children.

The Shorter View

The Second World War profoundly affected the civilian population. Mass evacuation from cities to rural areas revealed once more the extent of malnutrition and the neglect of the city child. A review of the plight of children not living with their families showed the backward, handicapped, emotionally sick, and delinquent all housed together in large and impersonal institutions that in the middle of the twentieth century provided a nineteenth-century childhood (Gt. B. Parl. Papers . . . 1945-46). The shock created by this report of the Care of Children Committee of Parliament formed the ground swell of another reforming movement, focused this time not upon getting the children out of the factories and into schools, but upon their social and, in a less certain way, emotional care.

A special child care agency was formed to be responsible at central and local level for all aspects of children's welfare. To begin with it was concerned with children without families. A powerful influence in the care of such children came from studies of parent-child separation indicating that, if at all possible, the bond between parents and children should remain intact. Consequently child care agencies became more concerned to reach children in difficulty still living with their parents to avoid the breakup of the family.

In 1963 a new law affecting England and Wales gave impetus to attempts to reduce the numbers needing residential care. So far the effect of these preventive measures has been limited, partly because resources have never permitted early help on any major scale to families not yet in serious trouble. From the beginning, social workers were extensively involved in trying to help families who were deprived economically, socially, and psychologically. Frequently ill, parents on low income in overcrowded conditions struggled to raise their children, who, in turn, seemed to experience the same deprivation as their parents. Because it was believed that such children, as they grew older, were especially vulnerable to delinquent behavior, the view developed that their burdens should not be added to by making them accountable to a court of law and that their best interests, and therefore in the long term those of society, would be served by the provision of a reorganized and improved family service that would permit social workers and parents alike to get to the underlying reasons for delinquency.

This belief that juvenile delinquency is primarily a manifestation of family stress found expression in government proposals, made in 1965, that the juvenile courts should be replaced by family panels, to consist of laymen with administrative responsibility to receive specialist advice and make recommendations for the treatment of delinquent children. The age of criminal responsibility was to be raised to sixteen so that those of compulsory school age would no longer be legally accountable (Gt. B. Parl. Papers . . . 1964–65).

These proposals for an administrative alternative to the courts met much opposition. Magistrates and probation officers claimed that the courts safeguarded children's rights by testing in law the allegations made and in particular ensuring that loss of liberty in the form of removal from home could not be an administrative decision. Many expressed the view that certainly by fourteen years children should accept some legal responsibility, in certain circumstances, for their behavior. Reservations also came from those who believed that not all delinquency was family-based and measures were required beyond family casework, for example, school- or neighborhood-based action.

The debate that followed in Parliament and elsewhere led to much "nineteenth-century" argument around whether delinquent children were "deprived" or "depraved." These proposals were made at a time of rising crime rates, including juveniles, so that some maintained that it was inappropriate to relax controls when the rules were being broken with ever-increasing frequency. Despite the controversy, no attempt was made to evaluate the effectiveness of the existing juvenile court system, or of the new proposals; but in the face of continued criticism, further government proposals were made in 1968 for the retention of the juvenile courts in modified form, but to deal with fewer children (Gt. B. Parl. Papers ... 1967–68). They recommended raising the age of criminal responsibility to twelve years and bringing children under fourteen to court only if their family circumstances were such that they needed social work help that could only be provided by a court order. Over thirteen years of age, and under seventeen, children could be brought to court either under civil proceedings similar to those used for under-fourteens or under criminal proceedings. In 1969 a new Children and Young Persons Act for England and Wales gave effect to these proposals by aiming to reduce substantially the numbers dealt with in court, by changing the age of criminal responsibility from ten to twelve and by altering the legal basis on which children may be brought. At the same time public authorities were made responsible for the residential care of delinquent children by taking over the "approved" school system, thus removing it from the field of private provision.

Since the Act came into force in 1971, the controversy has continued ("Disagreement ... " 1975; "Women Seek ... " 1975; Symon 1975). Briefly, this seems to be due to four factors: (1) there has been no reduction in the number of juveniles before the courts; in fact, the pressure has increased; (2) the residential homes for delinquent children have been reorganized and in particular their staffs have now the right to select children for admission when previously they had no such choice; this means, at least temporarily, fewer places available; (3) the part of the Act that transferred from the courts to the local authority the responsibility for deciding that residential care was needed, caused difficulty in administering the care order; (4) the reorganization of the social services saw a dispersal and dilution of child care skills.

The pressure on the courts comes partly from the 15 percent increase in official juvenile delinquency in 1974–75, one of those upswings that reflect conditions in urban society and for which the cause is still unknown. At a time of increasing numbers in court, the shortage of residential places in "community homes"

meant that children under care orders were still living at home
with their families awaiting admission. If they were again delinquent and brought back to the same juvenile court, the magistrates were powerless to take sterner measures. Only by making
custodial orders that should more properly be reserved for older
adolescents and young adults (the seventeen to twenty age group)
can the court protect society further from serious property
offenses. In fact, detention center orders and borstal training
committals have increased for fifteen- to sixteen-year-old juveniles during 1974.

Another result of the pressure on the courts and social services
has been a change in social worker attitudes toward children
committed under the 1969 Act. At the beginning, when the court
made a care order because magistrates felt the child should be
given residential help, many social workers considered it inappropriate for deprived children to be removed from their
families or punished in any way. Against a background of
continuing delinquency, it is noticeable that attitudes have hard-
ened among some social workers who now recommend detention
center or borstal "too early" because they know that places in
community homes are impossible to find. In this situation
magistrates can sometimes find themselves unwilling always to
adopt the social worker's advice for a custodial order, thus
reversing the earlier positions. Such fluctuations in approach
illustrate the difficulty of implementing an intended reform
without adequate resources.

In this respect it is interesting that there has been no real public
dissatisfaction with the Scottish system except that voiced by
some senior police officers.

The dissatisfaction with the working of the 1969 Act in
England and Wales has led to an internal governmental review,
with particular attention being given to the possibility of restoring
the power to the judiciary to enforce a residential order. This, of
course, would be difficult as the law now stands because central
government no longer controls the admissions to community
homes and the current economic stringency limits capital expenditure that eventually would provide the local authority with
more places. More likely, in the short term, is some limitation on
the right of community homes to refuse to admit children when
they have vacancies.

In Scotland a similar trend was evident, but the path to reform has so far been easier. In 1964 the Kilbranden committee recommended that courts for most children should be abolished and replaced by an educational approach (Gt. B. Parl. Papers . . . 1963–64). Unlike England and Wales, Parliament passed legislation for Scotland that acted upon the committee's recommendations and, since 1971, most children in trouble with the police have been dealt with by a civil administrative system, known as "children's hearings," with only disputed matters going first to the courts for determination. The success of all these many proposals depended in part upon additional resources, particularly more social workers and specialized residential care for disturbed children. Training facilities for social workers have been greatly expanded, but the reorganization of the social services in 1970, to produce a unified single authority responsible in each locality for all forms of social care, has of necessity meant that other forms of social distress—particularly affecting the elderly and the mentally ill—are for the first time receiving consistent attention. Previously these services were the least developed in many parts of the country, while generally children's services were the most advanced. Despite annual increases in social service budgets of about 10 percent until 1975, there are still chronic shortages.

A parallel but less publicized development relates to police practice. In some parts of the country for many years it has been an established procedure for the police officially to caution younger offenders coming to their notice for the first time. In London, in 1969, teams of experienced police men and women were given responsibility for police work with children. All cases are referred to the team unless the alleged offense is disputed, when it must go to court. After a family investigation the team (called the "Juvenile Bureau") decide which course of action is most suitable: a formal reprimand by a senior policeman or a court appearance. Over the last three years court appearances by juveniles, particularly the younger ones, have decreased while cautioning has increased (Gt. B. Parl. Papers . . . 1972–73). Underlying these changes in police practice is a view, held by some policemen, that taking children to court is a time-consuming and unrewarding business best avoided. One result of the cautioning schemes has been closer ties between police, social services, and schools. While this varies considerably with locality, generally there is greater understanding among teachers, social workers, and policemen of the other's job and attitude to children in difficulty.

In one sense, the last decade has been a major exercise in "diversion." The disagreements and indecisions have been about the relative merits of different proposals. At times the advocacy of a particular administrative or judicial model has assumed the character of an ideological debate, unhindered by evidence. In the absence of a complete understanding of delinquent behavior there is no agreement on who is really the guilty party: the child, the parents, or society. Although a good deal is known about predisposing factors, much remains to be understood. Some observers see urban life as increasingly stressful and seriously deficient in the essential psychological and social experiences, traditionally provided by the family, that are thought to be necessary for normal development (Bronfenbrenner 1974). Certainly the rules that govern urban life are increasingly complex.

The search for more successful and fairer ways of dealing with delinquent children continues and would be greatly helped by some knowledge of what works, with whom, and in what particular circumstances. In Great Britain at the present time there are three parallel but different ways of dealing with delinquent children: the police use of cautioning—an executive decision; the Scottish children's hearings—an administrative tribunal with legal backing; and the English juvenile court—a judicial institution with welfare responsibilities. Data have been collected on the operation of these three systems of juvenile justice and the rest of this chapter presents some first results as a factual basis for further discussion.

THREE WAYS OF DEALING WITH JUVENILES
Despite the 1969 Act, the age of criminal responsibility continues to be ten. A juvenile becomes an adult under the criminal law on his or her seventeenth birthday. There are approximately 5.5 million children in this age group; all but half a million are of school age, and at the present time there are 3 percent more boys than girls. By their seventeenth birthday one in eight of all boys in England and Wales will have either been officially cautioned by the police or appeared in court (Douglas,

Ross, and Simpson 1968). The corresponding proportion for girls is about one in thirty. As elsewhere, the cities see more of this problem; for example, inner London, with a total population of 3.5 million, has one boy in five officially delinquent; and within that inner London area there are boroughs where one-quarter of all boys are officially known by the police and the courts. Boys are almost always dealt with for an offense under the criminal law—generally, about 80 percent of them are concerned with theft or burglary. The older boys in the age range are increasingly likely to be concerned with minor assualt, disorderly behavior that threatens a breach of the peace, or joy-riding on motorcycles or in cars. Among juveniles, violence is still rare—only 2 percent of all delinquents are charged with anything more serious than schoolboy bullying.

There are a group of civil cases, known as care proceedings, that mainly deal with cases of neglect of infants or young children. Infrequently boys of school age may be in need of the protection afforded by the court because of severe beatings by parents or because they have been the victims of sexual assault or interference. By contrast, these care cases are much commoner with girls—invariably the result of difficulties between adolescents and parents that have resulted in a daughter running away from home. When girls are in court charged with an offense, it is more likely to be as the result of shoplifting or cheating the public transport system. There is no equivalent to the laws of many states of America concerned, for example, with curfew breaking or other misdemeanors. Occasionally, demonstrations or sporting events lead juveniles to vandalism and fighting, but the social regulation of adolescent group behavior is not a major concern of the juvenile courts unless a specific offense has been committed.

Cautioning

In 1969 the Metropolitan Police for London, responsible for an area that includes one-fifth of the population of England and Wales, started a major exercise in "diversion." While it has always been recognized that individual policemen exercised discretion and dealt with much minor delinquency informally, the Metropolitan Police, unlike other English police authorities, held the view that, if a crime was committed involving a juvenile, the matter should come to court. This sometimes led to young first

offenders appearing on trivial matters and, as it was known that
about half the boys who made a first court appearance did not
reappear (at least as juveniles), it seemed unnecessarily cumbersome always to invoke court proceedings with its possible stigma
and certainly time-consuming hearings. While in theory it seemed
eminently sensible to deal with single or occasional offenders by a
police caution, the difficulty was to identify reliably the half of all
boys known for a first time and unlikely to reappear. The Juvenile
Bureau screens all cases referred to them by their colleagues by
seeing the boys and visiting their families; inquiries are also made
about school progress and previous referral to the social services.
On the basis of these inquiries, a decision is made that in part
reflects a view of the likelihood of reappearance; if it is thought
unlikely, then cautioning is indicated. There are certain technical
limitations to this; for example, if a child denies the offense, the
case must be heard in court.

In order to evaluate this new scheme it was agreed to study all
boys living in one borough coming to the notice of the Juvenile
Bureau for a first time during its first year. A sample of 195 local
boys, aged eleven to fourteen, was investigated. There were, in
addition, eighteen boys for whom no action was taken mainly
because of insufficient evidence.

Table 1 shows that just over two-thirds of the sample were
cautioned. Forty-eight of the sixty boys who appeared in court did
so for the kinds of technical reasons already mentioned. In six of
the remaining twelve cases court proceedings were decided upon
for welfare reasons—that is, it was considered that the family
would only accept social work help ordered by a court.

TABLE 1
*Boys Aged 11-14 First Notified to the
Juvenile Bureau 1969-70: Police Decision*

Police Decision	No.	%
Court	60	31
Caution	135	69
Total	195	100

The offenses in which these 195 boys were concerned have been
grouped in table 2 under three headings: (1) those against

property which include theft, handling, burglary, malicious
damage; (2) those against the person which include threatening or
insulting behavior likely to cause a breach of the peace, obstruc-
tion of the police, assault, possession of an offensive weapon or
firearm, and robbery; and (3) those concerned with "taking and
driving away" (TDA in the table) motor vehicles, mainly a form of
joy-riding. Table 2 shows that most offenses concerned property,
and there is no suggestion that the type of offense influences the
police in their decision.

TABLE 2
*Boys Aged 11-14 First Notified to the Juvenile Bureau 1969-70: Police
Decision and Offense Group*

Police Decision	Property		Offense Group Person		TDA*		Total	
	No.	%	No.	%	No.	%	No.	%
Court	47	78	7	12	6	10	60	100
Caution	107	79	15	11	13	10	135	100
Total	154	79	22	11	19	10	195	100

* Taking and driving away.

As a visit to the home and an assessment of the family
circumstances form the central part of the Juvenile Bureau's
investigations, it could be expected that the results of these visits

TABLE 3
*Boys Aged 11-14 First Notified to the Juvenile Bureau 1969-70: Police
Decision and Family*

Police Decision	Intact*		Family Broken†		Not Stated		Total	
	No.	%	No.	%	No.	%	No.	%
Court	42	70	15	25	3	5	60	100
Caution	110	81	24	18	1	1	135	100
Total	152	78	39	20	4	2	195	100

* Both natural parents at home.
† One natural parent at home.

influence them. Table 3 classifies the boys by their family background: "intact" means both natural parents at home; "broken" means one or both parents permanently absent through marriage breakdown or death. Overall, 20 percent of the boys in table 3 came from broken homes, with rather more in the smaller number sent to court than was the case with those who were cautioned. The suggestion here is that the police cautioned virtually all those boys where there was a choice to be made, whether or not they came from broken homes.

TABLE 4
Boys Aged 11–14 First Notified to the Juvenile Bureau 1969–70: Police Decision and Renotification

Police Decision	Renotification within Two Years					
	None		One or More		Total	
	No.	%	No.	%	No.	%
Court	25	42	35	58	60	100
Caution	77	57	58	43	135	100
Total	102	52	93	48	195	100

Table 4 shows the results when, two years after first notification, each boy's record was checked to see if during this period he had been renotified. As expected, overall 48 percent of the total were renotified, and it follows that the cautions, representing over two-thirds of the total, showed a similar proportion. However, the third going to court were more likely to be renotified (58 percent against 43 percent of those cautioned).

In table 5, 28 of the 47 boys before the courts were renotified, showing the expected trend, with those from broken homes at greater risk of reappearance (Douglas, Ross, and Simpson 1968). This is in contrast to the reappearance experience of boys who were cautioned, where 57 of the 134 boys were renotified, but those from broken homes proportionately did not reappear more than those from intact families. As the numbers in the series are small, it is unlikely that a statistically significant result could be expected and the difference in reappearance was not, in fact, significant.

TABLE 5
Boys* Aged 11-14 First Notified to the Juvenile Bureau 1969-70: Family Circumstances and Renotification (N = 181)

| Police Decision | Intact | | | Broken | | | |
	Original Sample	Renotified	%	Original Sample	Renotified	%	Total Renotified
Court (47)	33	19	58	14	9	64	28
Caution (134)	110	47	43	24	10	42	57

*Of the total number of boys in the study (195), 14 were excluded: 10 court cases were dismissed and in 4 others (3 court and 1 caution) family background was not known.

Because this study of police practice is part of a long-term study of juvenile delinquency in one community, comparative data were available on the way the local courts dealt with all boys before cautioning started. The most lenient decision open to the court and used extensively with first offenders was to discharge the boys upon condition that they did not get into further trouble over a specified period of time—usually one year. During the twelve months before the cautioning scheme, 157 such discharges were given to boys of the same age group from the same locality before the courts for the same kinds of reasons. As part of the delinquency study, detailed family circumstances were obtained for all boys cautioned or in court by investigators independent of the police and the courts. In this way, both groups could be placed into "low" and "high" risk categories according to their family circumstances. As the "cautioned" boys were revisited for social work assessment after the police interview, using the same procedure developed for earlier studies (Power, Benn, and Morris 1972; Power et al. 1974), a more detailed classification than just "broken homes" was possible. Table 6 shows the percentage renotified for the discharged and the cautioned groups.

Those boys in court and conditionally discharged showed the expected trend, with a higher percentage renotified where there were difficult family circumstances (as defined); yet for those cautioned the percentage reappearing is the same, irrespective of differences in the family circumstances.

TABLE 6
Boys Aged 11–14 First Before the Courts 1968; First Cautioned 1969–70: Family Circumstances and Renotification (N = 253)

| Decision | Family Circumstances | | | | | | |
| | Low Risk* | | | High Risk† | | | |
	Original Sample	Renotified	%	Original Sample	Renotified	%	Total Renotified
Conditional discharge (157)	118	47	40	39	22	56	69
Caution (96)‡	68	32	47	28	13	46	45

*Intact without severe problems.
†Intact with severe problems or separation of parents.
‡Of the 135 boys originally cautioned, 39 are excluded here: 5 families refused home visits and 34 "controls" were not visited.

Two provisional observations may be made from these data. School boys of the same age, from the same locality, concerned with similar offenses, do not get into more trouble if cautioned by the police instead of appearing before a juvenile court. It should be remembered that all the boys cautioned admitted what was alleged and that the court would still be necessary for those who denied the offense. However, by far the most interesting suggestion to arise from these data is the possibility that cautioning rather than court is the best course to take with boys from difficult family circumstances. Those most vulnerable because of their fragile environment do better if kept out of the courts. This is the opposite assumption to that made by the police and by the architects of the 1969 Act. They wanted to reduce the chances of court appearance for boys in ordinary family circumstances and reserve the court as the agency responsible for mobilizing maximum aid for those in stressful family conditions. In turning this upside down, it may be that the children's and society's best interest are served by not further traumatizing those already in a state of shock. Further studies on larger populations of boys are needed to examine this hypothesis.

The Children's Hearings in Scotland

Whatever the longer-term benefits may be, one undoubted result of radical change in juvenile justice is a break with traditional ritual. Much that goes on in the relative informality of an English juvenile court has its origins in legal history. The ritual emphasizes the independence of the judiciary while the complex rules relating to evidence and highly stylized procedure aim to close the gap between what is said to have happened and what actually happened by admitting only relevant evidence under controlled conditions.

One difficulty is that the ritual in the juvenile court may not make much sense to some children or, for that matter, to their parents. Consequently their ability to contribute is limited by bewilderment; yet without their involvement the court has less chance of successfully modifying a child's behavior. Alienation from an institution frees the individual of obligation to accept the rules that govern conduct.

The Children's Hearings that started in Scotland in April 1971 are a break with tradition. Screening decisions are made by a full-time official, known as the reporter, to whom the police and others refer all cases of juvenile delinquency. The reporter makes the initial assessment, deciding whether a child need go to a hearing. If the allegation is denied by the child, the case must go to court and then, if proved, be referred back to the reporter. This happens in approximately 6 percent of all cases. The initial screening undertaken by the reporter aims to identify the children with previous good history and settled family circumstances thought unlikely to get into further trouble. If social work is needed, an informal referral may be made and the child's willingness, together with that of his parents, to seek and accept help is a major consideration. If the reporter decides that a child should appear at a hearing, family and school reports are obtained beforehand.

An advantage of any new system of juvenile justice is that a fresh approach may be made to the question of how many people and how much money is needed. This new start has meant that proportionately nine times the number of personnel are available to Scotland's largest city—Glasgow—compared to inner London, although both have about the same level of juvenile crime. This meant that the hearings, timed for evenings as well as during the day, may last on the average five times longer than a comparable case before an English juvenile court.

The hearing is conducted by the senior member of the panel. Present are the three panel members, the reporter, and a social worker who has visited the family, as well as parents and child. All concerned sit around a table. After confirming formally that the child admits the offense, all panel members then conduct a wide-ranging discussion with the family into the nature of the delinquent act and its possible cause. As the hearing is not a court of law, there are no further procedural rules or limitations on evidence. However, there are legal powers when it comes to disposing the case. The panel may decide to make no order at all; or it can decide that supervision should be provided by the social work department for the children, either with them continuing to live at home with their families or living away from home in a children's home. The panel must follow up all cases, irrespective of the decision, every six months.

It will be of considerable interest to compare the outcome of children dealt with in Scotland by the panels with those dealt with in England and Wales through the juvenile courts. It is as yet too soon to make such comparisons, but it is possible to look at the decisions reached by the reporter and the panel (see figure). So far, almost all referrals to the reporter come from the police, although it was visualized that others concerned with child care— teachers and social workers—might also wish to have the expert advice of the reporter.

During 1973 the reporter decided that 37 percent of all children did not need further help of any kind, while a further 12 percent could be dealt with either formally by a warning from the police or by direct referral to the social work department. In this way the reporter disposed of half of the cases, a fact that emphasizes the importance of his task. This major screening exercise achieves a systematic diversion of cases. The 21 percent of all children for whom "no order" is made include a number where short-term action was taken, for example, an informal piece of community service in a case of vandalism before the final decision.

Overall, decisions taken in the second full year of the new

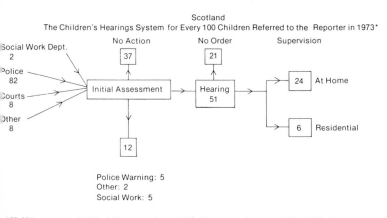

Scotland
The Children's Hearings System for Every 100 Children Referred to the Reporter in 1973*

Police Warning: 5
Other: 2
Social Work: 5

*29,384 reports on 20,939 children; see Social Work Statistics, Scotland 1973 HMSO 1975, tables 2-5 to 2-68.

system, by a new group of selected, specially trained lay panel
members and the professional reporter, are broadly similar to the
kinds of outcome to be found in the English juvenile courts. In
Scotland, in 1973 one way or another, 70 percent of cases resulted
in no action, no order, or a police warning; social work intervention was invoked in 30 percent of the cases. Perhaps it is not
surprising that, faced with the same range of behavioral problems, overall the decisions are similar for both hearings and
juvenile courts. Although the number of choices open to the panel
is restricted, as the reporter has screened out half of all cases,
there may be understandably a disposition to think that, if a case
gets to a hearing, something should be done; but apart from the
imaginative use of short-term adjournments before a formal "no
order," the panel must rely on the social work department for
supervision at home or in residential care. By comparison,
juvenile courts in England and Wales have eight possible
decisions.

Communication in the Juvenile Court

The fact of appearing at a juvenile court and receiving the
decision are believed by many to play a part in influencing
children against further delinquency. Such considerations are

uppermost in the minds of magistrates and social workers when a child is in court the first time. The decision reached partly reflects a view of the child's chances of reappearance. Those thought unlikely to reappear are mostly fined or conditionally discharged. If there are family or other difficulties, social work may be needed so that the decision is more likely to enable this through a supervision or—more rarely at first appearance—a care order. The latter places the child under the legal guardianship of the social services, who may arrange placement in a children's home if they think this is called for.

This overall view of "low risk" and "high risk" should be related to outcome as measured by the proportion reappearing. Table 7 shows this for two samples of London children, followed up for five years. The samples in table 7 are (a) for boys and girls appearing in 1957 before the courts for all types of offense, and (b) more reliably, for boys only, aged 11–14, in one London borough, all concerned with stealing.

TABLE 7
Juveniles First Before the Courts (Cases Proved): Court Decision and Percent Reappearing within Five Years

Court Decision at First Appearance	(a) N =901 Greater London Aged 10–16 (1957) All Reasons	(b) N =451 Tower Hamlets Boys Aged 11–14 (1958–60) "Stealing"*
	Percent Reappearing Five Years Later	
Fine	34	45
Conditional discharge	43	51
Probation order	58	69
ASO/FPO†	70	83
Other	‡	77§
All	48	57

* "Stealing" then was breaking and entering, larceny, enclosed premises, receiving.
† Approved School Order/Fit Person Order.
‡ Only four cases.
§ Thirty-one cases.

More recent data are shown in table 8, again for a sample of boys aged 11–14 in one London borough, first before the courts in 1968 and followed up for two years.

TABLE 8
246 Tower Hamlets Boys Aged 11–14 First Before the Courts 1968: "Sentence" and Reappearance

Court Decision at First Appearance	No. of Boys	Percent of These Reappearing within Two Years	
		At Least Once	At Least Twice
Discharge*	173	43	23
Fine	26	42	23
Probation or supervision order	39	69	36
Fit Person Order	8	50	38
All	246	48	25

*Absolute or conditional discharge; no order.

The obvious lack of success in sorting out boys at "low risk" of reappearance is shown in these tables. Furthermore, the 1968 series (table 8) shows that those given a conditional discharge and therefore initially considered at "low risk" were likely to reappear more than once. Over the decade covered by these three samples, juvenile crime rates nationally, for greater London and for the one inner London borough, have all doubled; yet the reappearance picture is remarkably consistent, with about half of all first offenders officially coming to notice again and, in turn, half of all second offenders appearing a third time.

The regularity of the proportions reappearing is one of the most puzzling features of recidivism. What could be the explanation for this, and for the court's inability to focus successfully on those really at risk? As mentioned earlier, even the informal juvenile court is a highly structured social system where magistrates, social workers, the police, and other officials have clearly defined roles. All are familiar with the complex proceedings and the ritual, and with experience, perform competently. By contrast, parents and children—in one sense the principal actors in the court—have no previous experience and many go legally unrepresented and quite unprepared. When questioned outside the courtroom at the close of the case, families vary considerably in their understanding of the proceedings. A few had understood nothing, not even the result; most families had understood part, including the result—but felt they had been unable to contribute and were bewildered by the proceedings. A further group had a good understanding of all that had happened. Nearly all reported that they were at a disadvantage.

One reason frequently given for preferring a court system of justice for children is that their rights are safeguarded, but these "consumer" reports cast doubts on the usefulness of safeguarding the rights of children and parents many of whom do not consider they had a fair opportunity of putting their case. That they had not been able to do so does not necessarily reflect upon the people working in the courts; they may in all sincerity believe they had given the family every opportunity. It may have more to do with the complicated legal procedure, differences in social background and language between defendants and magistrates, and the inhibiting effect of the anxiety felt by the children and parents because they are worried about the decision the court will impose. All this may well have an alienating effect so that both children and parents are inclined to interpret the experience as one for which they had no part or responsibility.

In order to test this, an experiment was designed in two stages. The first involved the special preparation by interviewers experienced in court work of a randomly allocated one-half of all children making a first court appearance together with their parents. All children, whether specially prepared or not, were interviewed immediately outside the courtroom and asked to give an account of the hearing. These accounts were then sent "blind" to ten independent assessors. They were asked to identify the accounts given by families who had some preparation. Although no one of them identified correctly all families interviewed before the hearing, most could pick out most of the families and a statistical test applied to these results showed that such a selection as correct as that made could only happen by chance once in a hundred times.

As this suggested that preparation did increase the family's understanding of the proceedings, the experiment was repeated, again using random allocation and again with one of the two groups specially briefed beforehand. The experiment was conducted in three inner London juvenile courts between October 1969, and January 1970. After a number of exclusions for technical reasons, the sample was still reasonably representative of all first offenders in age, sex, and offense. Over the three months, 88 children were allocated to one of the two groups and table 9 compares them for age, reason for court appearance, and result.

TABLE 9
88 Children in Court: "Briefed" and "Not Briefed"

Age	11	12	13	14	15	16	Total
Briefed	3	10	1	8	8	16	46
Not briefed	3	4	5	14	7	9	42
Total	6	14	6	22	15	25	88

Reason*	Property	Person	Traffic	TDA	Welfare	Other	Total
Briefed	15	5	9	9	4	4	46
Not briefed	16	2	6	5	8	5	42

Result*	Fine	CD	PO/SO	ASO/FPO	Other	Total
Briefed	20	16	8	1	1	46
Not briefed	9	18	10	2	3	42

*CD, conditional discharge; PO/SO, probation order/supervision order; ASO/FPO, Approved School Order/Fit Person Order; TDA, taking and driving away.

Allowing for the small numbers, the two groups have broadly similar characteristics in these respects, although there is a slight excess of sixteen-year-olds, and consequently of traffic offenses and fines, in the "briefed" group. As well as the interview immediately after the hearing, a transcript was obtained of the hearing to compare with the account given by the family. A home visit was made six months later to establish how much the child and parents recalled of the hearing and to estimate the continuous impact, if any, of the experience for the family. Finally, at eighteen months from the court appearance, a documentary check was made to establish whether the child had been in court again. The refusal rate was low (10 percent) for such a study and all concerned cooperated generously. Follow-up interviews and home visits yielded much that was of interest; for example, although six groups of magistrates were concerned with the cases in the series, the transcriptions of the court hearing showed how similar the approach adopted was. Once again, as "consumers" of justice, the families varied in their reaction to the court hearing, some considering it fair, others indignantly asserting they had no chance to state their case. Generally, those specially briefed beforehand welcomed the preparation.

When the records were checked eighteen months later, 30 of the 88 boys and girls (34 percent) had reappeared. Table 10 shows the proportion for those briefed and for those not briefed.

TABLE 10
Follow-up at Eighteen Months: Proportion of Children Reappearing

	No. of Court Reappearances*		
	None	One or More	% Reappearing
46 Briefed	33	13	28
42 Not briefed	25	17	40
Total	58	30	34

*Cases proved.

Although there is a distinct trend, on the numbers in this sample, it was not a statistically significant difference. Identification of the more comparable age groups of 11–14-year-olds gave the same result. Nine out of the 22 of those briefed (41 percent) gave the same trend when compared with 15 out of 26 of those not briefed (54 percent).

Once again it was possible to look at reappearance for these younger boys by decision made at their first appearance. Table 11 once again suggests that the proportion reappearing is approximately the same for each type of decision.

TABLE 11
48 Children Aged 11-14: Decision at First Appearance and Follow-up at Eighteen Months

Court Decision at First Appearance	No. of Children	No. Reappearing
Fine	3	1
Conditional discharge	23	9
Probation or supervision order	16	10
Approved School Order	1	0
Other	5	3
Total	48	23

It was possible to look at reappearance in relation to the length of the hearing, as measured by the total number of contributions from all concerned. Transcripts were available in 68 of the 88 cases. Thirty-two of the cases were designated as short, with between 10-53 contributions; the other 36 were long, with between 54-226 contributions. Thirty-two percent of the 68 children reappeared, compared with the 34 percent for the complete sample. Table 12 gives the percentage reappearing by length of hearing.

TABLE 12
68 Children Aged 11-16: Length of Hearing and Reappearance

Length	No. of Children	Reappearance No.	Reappearance %
Short	32	8	25
Long	36	14	39
Total	68	22	32

There is a tendency for longer cases to have a higher risk of reappearance, but this may reflect the gravity or complexity of the particular cases, together with the number of children involved. Perhaps a better approach to estimating the impact made upon short or long exposure in court is given by identifying only the direct exchanges between the chairman of the magistrates panel and the family. Counting only those contributions—the essential "core" of the hearing—the cases were divided once again into short and long (table 13).

TABLE 13
68 Children Aged 11-16: Magistrate/Family Discussion and Reappearance

| Length | No. of Children | Reappearance | |
		No.	%
Short	34	11	32
Long	34	11	32
Total	68	22	32

Clearly the length of discussion has no bearing on the risk of reappearance. This, of course, only relates to how much was said from both sides, not what was said, or the manner in which it was delivered.

Finally, it was possible to make a start to answer the question of whether the impact upon the child of a court appearance had any lasting effect, apart from that measured by subsequent reappearance. Fifty-six children were visited at home six months later. A further twenty replied saying that they did not wish to be visited, regarding the whole affair as over and unwilling to discuss it again. It is of interest that the reappearance rate for this group was only 22 percent, compared with 41 percent for those who were willing to receive a visit. It may be that those for whom the court experience really acted as a deterrent could not face another reminder, although, once again, with the numbers at this stage in the study it could be no more than a suggestion for further inquiry.

At the home visit a four-point attitudinal scale was used to identify (1) those who were indifferent to the appearance at the time of the hearing and who six months later had forgotten the details; (2) those who were indifferent at the hearing, but still thought about it six months later; (3) those who were worried at the time of the hearing but had forgotten about it later; and (4) those who were worried at the time of the hearing and were still thinking about it six months later. An independent assessor placed twenty-six of the fifty-six children into the last category, that is those who reported being worried at the hearing and were still worried later. On follow-up one year after the home visit, twelve of those twenty-six children (46 percent) had reappeared. At the other end of the scale a further nine children had been assessed as indifferent at the hearing and having forgotten about it later; five of these had reappeared at the end of the follow-up period.

This study, essentially exploratory, set out to identify the part played by the court in reducing the risk of reappearance. There is a suggestion that special preparation did make a contribution, but if so it was marginal and with these numbers not statistically reliable. The type of decision made by the magistrates, the length of the actual proceedings, the impact of the experience assessed six months later and then followed for another twelve months—all showed no relationship to subsequent likelihood of reappearance in court. It may be that other characteristics of the court not investigated here play an important part. There is, for example, the suggestion of the evidence of those refusing a home visit six months later (excluding children who had already by then reappeared) showing a lower risk of reappearance because the experience was still painful to some of them. It was, of course, encouraging that the experiment was possible at all. Traditionally, the courts have not been the easiest place to undertake work of this kind. The cooperation offered reflected the genuine concern of magistrates, social workers, and others, as well as the willing cooperation of families, to enter into experiments that might provide clues to increased effectiveness when dealing with the persistent juvenile offender.

CONCLUSION
These three examples of work in progress are concerned with evaluating services and they reflect an increasing willingness to acknowledge that the regulation of social behavior among children and adolescents should be handled sensitively and appropriately. This is difficult to achieve. All this century, greatly improved economic and social conditions have made children healthier, better educated, and more independent. To say this does not go against the recognition that in our society there are still highly vulnerable groups who have not shared in this general progress. There is a long literature to suggest that official juvenile

delinquency is disproportionately to be found among the under-privileged. But such deprived children only account for a minority of all those before the courts. Recent studies in the United States and in England show many delinquents come from intact and well-functioning lower- and middle-class families. The "delinquent" and the "deprived" are not the same population of children, although there is some overlap.

Parallel to children's improved health and circumstances has been the gradual growth of the idea that childhood should have a separate and protected status. It started because children were being economically exploited, but now it is linked to the idea that urban life in particular is complex, demanding, and stressful. The very independence children have achieved carries risks; and the belief is that if children fail to negotiate successfully all the hazards of city life, with its complex rules, pressure from the media, and sharper pace, allowances should be made. In such settings it is difficult to develop a system of juvenile justice that is fair to all. Children have a right to be heard, and that means that administrative decisions profoundly affecting their lives should not be made in their absence; but the right to be heard is not met simply by insuring that they are present when the decisions are made. Conditions have to be provided that will permit children and their parents to have their views heard. This is a problem for busy courts. Finally, despite their protected status, over a certain age children are reckoned to be accountable to some extent for their behavior. Frequently there are victims, and children should be helped to find constructive ways of expressing their regret and making appropriate reparations.

BIBLIOGRAPHY

Bronfenbrenner, Urie. 1974. "Children, Families and Social Policy: An American Perspective." In *The Family in Society: Dimensions of Parenthood.* London: Department of Health and Social Security, HMSO.
Conservative Political Centre. 1966. *Crime Knows No Boundaries: A Policy Study by a Group under the Chairmanship of the Rt. Hon. Peter Thorneycroft, M. P. London.*
"Disagreement on Act." 2 February 1975. *The Times* (London).
Douglas, James W. B.; Ross, Jean Mary; and Simpson, Howard Russell. 1968. *All Our Future: Longitudinal Study of Secondary Education.* London: Peter Davies.

Great Britain Parliament. Papers by Command. *Report of the Care of Children Committee.* Cmnd. 6922. (Session 1945–46.)
————. *Report of the Committee on Children and Young Persons.* Cmnd. 1191. (1960.) (Session 1959–60.)
————. *Children and Young Persons (Scotland).* Cmnd. 2306. (1964.) (Session 1963–64.)
————. *The Child, the Family, and the Young Offender.* Cmnd. 2742. (Session 1964–65.)
————. *Children in Trouble.* Cmnd. 3601. (1968.) (Session 1967–68.)
————. *Criminal Statistics, England and Wales, 1972.* Cmnd. 5402. (Session 1972–73.)
Great Britain. Public General Acts and Church Assembly Measures of 1932. *Children's and Young Persons' Act of 1932.* Chap. 12.
Great Britain. Public General Acts and Church Assembly Measures of 1963. *Children's and Young Persons' Act of 1963.* Chap. 37.
Great Britain. Public General Acts and Church Assembly Measures of 1969. *Children's and Young Persons' Act of 1969.* Chap. 54.
Labour Party. 1964. *Crime: A Challenge to Us All.* London.
Power, Michael J.; Benn, R. T.; and Morris, J. N. 1972. "Neighbourhood, School and Juveniles before the Courts." *British Journal of Criminology* 12:111–32.
Power, Michael J.; Ash, Patricia; Shoenberg, Elizabeth; and Sirey, E. Catherine. 1974. "Delinquency and the Family." *British Journal of Social Work* 4:13–38.
Roberts, Robert. 1971. *The Classic Slum: Salford Life in the First Quarter of the Century.* Manchester: Manchester University Press.
Seebohm-Rowntree, B. 1913. *How the Labourer Lives: A Study of the Rural Labour Problem.* London: Thomas Nelson and Sons.
Symon, Penelope. 15, 17–19 March 1975. "The Young Offenders." 4 pts. *The Times* (London).
"Women Seek Changes in 1969 Children Act." 23 January 1975. *The Times* (London).

15

The Scandinavian System of Juvenile Justice: A Comparative Approach

Tove Stang Dahl

Is the Scandinavian system of juvenile justice substantially different from the American one? Both were established around the turn of the century; their prehistories and early years show many parallel developments; even current problems are much alike. Similarity, however, is usually not the theme when the two systems are discussed. When juvenile justice problems arise, frequent reference is made to the attributes of other systems. The Scandinavian welfare model is often invoked in the American juvenile court debates, while the American juvenile court is invoked when due process arguments are raised in Norway.

The traditional focus on differences derives in part from scarcity of information. Little has been written about Scandinavian child welfare, and even less in English (see Nyquist 1960). Information is normally obtained through personal contact at conferences and during travels, from official representatives of the foreign system and professional colleagues. The officials will often provide a strictly formal picture of the situation, underlining the differences between their and other systems. Professional colleagues will tend to respond to the expectations and interests of questioners. When they are critics of their own systems, eager to detect differences, differences will be described.

Whatever the reason, the American and Scandinavian systems of juvenile justice are generally believed to be very different. In fact I do not think they are. While distinctions between the American juvenile court and the Scandinavian child welfare board are useful analytically as models, they are operationally misleading. As operating systems, Scandinavian and American efforts to deal with problem children are, I believe, more alike than different.

After surveying the Scandinavian system of juvenile justice, this chapter will briefly compare the American and the Scandinavian system. My purpose is partly to provide additional information about the Norwegian child welfare boards, and partly to argue that differences in formal solutions may easily be overestimated, both with regard to intersystem comparisons and to intrasystem evaluations of the numerous "pioneering" reforms in juvenile justice. I will conclude with a short discussion of the basic, but awkward, issue of the efficacy of law as a means of social change within the field of juvenile justice.

THE SCANDINAVIAN SYSTEM
The Invention of the Child Welfare Board

The prototype of the Scandinavian system of welfare boards for dealing with children in trouble was established by the Norwegian Neglected Children's Treatment Act of 1896. Although aiming mainly at crime prevention, the law appeared as an educational statute administered within the school system. Young offenders were not to be punished, but educated. The state undertook a prophylactic responsibility to prevent crime by identifying pre-delinquent children, and established a totally new legal body to identify those children.

Norway was the first country to create a modern system of child welfare, three years before the first Juvenile Court Act was passed in Illinois, and twelve years before the passing of the Children's Act in Britain. The Norwegian solution spread to Sweden in 1902 and Denmark in 1905, and to Finland in 1936 and Iceland in 1947.

The double character of the Norwegian law as a criminal law in purpose and a school law in words caused considerable controversy during the law-making process, especially about the provisions on administration and legal procedure (Dahl 1974). Responsibility for administering the new system was given to the Department of Education, not the Department of Justice; local

responsibility was entrusted neither to local boards of education—as preferred by many teachers—nor to the ordinary courts
or any special criminal court as the lawmakers considered but
finally rejected. Instead, each municipality or commune (the local
unit of administration in Norway) was to elect its own board of
guardians, from 1953 to be called child welfare boards. The board
of guardians was composed of laymen, professionals, and representatives from the state authorities. Of the four laymen, one or
two were to be women. (This was the first time women in Norway
were allowed to participate in an official body; the exception was
of course made because of their supposed special competence to
decide about children—even if they had not yet obtained the right
to vote.) The professions and the state authority were represented by the local judge, the vicar, and the district doctor.

Originally the judge was to be chairman of the board, for the
double reason of state control and due process; in Parliament,
however, the left objected. For political reasons the liberals
generally opposed the influence of lawyers whom they regarded as
representatives of Norway's conservative ruling class. Educationists, who tended to be liberals, invoked the formal purpose of the
law, the replacement of punishment by education, and argued that
a judge in the chair would give the boards the appearance of courts,
with stigma inevitably following. The political compromise was to
include the judge, but as a member only, with the vicar, the doctor,
and the four lay members in the new corporation which, in the
opinion of the lawmaker,

combined the intimate, personal insight with objective knowledge; local community with the wider society; lay elements with
state authority—all of which is represented by persons whose
vocations place them particularly close to the broader and lower
classes of the population (*Storthingsforhandlinger* 1893; translated by the author).

The boards had extensive authority. Their clients were lawbreakers under the age of criminal responsibility which was con-
currently raised from ten to fourteen years. Offenders between
fourteen and sixteen years could also be assigned to the board if
either the prosecution authorities or the court referred the case to
the board as an alternative (and sometimes in addition) to punishment. Finally, the board could intervene with "predelinquents,"
neglected or morally depraved children up to the age of sixteen

seemingly about to become delinquent. The clients, subject to control until age eighteen, were subject to a fairly wide range of "educational" measures, from admonitions and warnings to the children and their parents, to placing the children in children's homes, foster homes, or special schools—the latter corresponding to the Anglo-American reformatories. The board's proceedings followed certain rules laid down in the law of criminal procedure, but were on the whole much more informal than courts. Some of the decisions could be appealed to the Department of Education.

Basically, the system established in 1896 is still in operation, although altered in ideology and material resources. New legislation regulating juvenile justice—the Child Welfare Act—was enacted in 1953. This was no educational law, but a welfare law rationalized as social policy, and the administration was given to the Department of Social Affairs. Child welfare boards, integrated in the general municipal organization of social administration, have replaced the old boards. The latter were increasingly regarded both by clients and the public opinion as akin to criminal courts. The child welfare boards were consequently stripped of the old features of criminal procedure and moralism, and the proceedings were made less formal than before. The boards no longer had a judicial member, although a judge has to be called in to assist in cases of coercive separation of children from parents and in other similar measures. The vicar and the doctor are also gone, the former to lower the element of moralism on the board, the latter for purely practical reasons. The present board consists of five laymen, men and women, at least one of them a member of the local social board (the official body enforcing the general Social Care Act of 1964). To be a member of the child welfare board requires no special competence save a general interest in and if possible a special insight into children and young people. None of the members should be more than sixty-six years old.

The use of locally elected boards accords with Scandinavian traditions of local self-government and lay participation in administration and justice. The work of the child welfare boards, however, has been increasingly supplied by a growing milieu of professionals, above all through the growth in local social administration and the employment of social workers in most of the four hundred or so communes. Normally, a trained social worker is supposed to work out the agenda of the board's meetings; on the regional level a special child welfare officer advises and coordinates the board's work. Finally, the board has a right and sometimes an obligation to consult a medical doctor or other specialist before making decisions in important matters.

The field of operation is defined more widely by the 1953 law than before. Crime and delinquency form but one set of the symptoms worth alarm. In principle, child welfare encompasses any child in trouble or in need of help, whether for sickness, physical handicaps, maladjustments, unhealthy living conditions, or neglectful parents. The clients are now persons up to the age of eighteen, who can be kept under care until their twenty-first birthday. The age of criminal responsibility is still fourteen (fifteen in the other Scandinavian countries) and offenders under this age are dealt with by the child welfare board exclusively. As under the 1896 law, juvenile offenders above the age of criminal responsibility but below the age of eighteen face a double-track system: they can be subject to regular prosecution in the courts, or they can be given over to the child welfare board by the prosecution authorities or by the court itself.

The years between 1896 and 1953 saw a rapid decline in the belief in institutions. The 1953 law, therefore, prescribed the use of preventive measures before children were removed from home, preventive measures meaning any aid given to the children within their own environment: economic or material support, facilities for school attendance, and so on. When preventive measures are futile, children can be placed in a foster home, a children's home, a special school, or in suitable treatment elsewhere. Apart from the institutions for physically handicapped and mentally retarded children, which were incorporated into the child welfare system in 1953, the institutions in question are much the same as those under the old law, though they have of course been renamed. New children's institutions created under the Mental Health Act of 1961 have been established since the Second World War.

The Reasons for Child Welfare

In its broadest context child welfare is linked to the development of industrial capitalism as an international mode of production. Urban crowds and working class poverty created social problems of a specific and intolerable kind. Everywhere charitable measures of "child saving" were sought to take care of the poor, vagrant, and criminal children. In contrast, governmental institutions emerging at the end of the nineteenth century were based in part on new insight provided by the progress in social sciences. Positivism in social science may be interpreted quite simply as a new method of handling growing social problems: it led to a renewal of interest in institutions and methods of socialization, above all in education, but also to the creation of a new penology following the growth of the science of criminology from the 1870s onward.

The Norwegian context of child welfare demonstrates these points quite clearly. Norway was in many respects a surprising country to have originated one of the basic Western models for legal handling of problem children. Norway, in 1896, was a small country with a population of some 2 million and only modest industrial development, although Kristiania (later Oslo), the capital, nearly doubled its population between 1880 and 1900. As in other countries experiencing capitalist growth, poor workers concentrated in the cities (many of them poised for emigration to the United States), aggravating unemployment, bad health, and adult and child vagrancy.

But the problems of urban or industrial growth do not appear to have been worse in Norway than in other European countries or in the United States. Rather the opposite seems to have been true. Neither is there any evidence that the problems of "the dangerous classes" were regarded as more serious in Norway than elsewhere. The reason for child welfare in this country must be sought in the new scientific penology and in the modern ideology of social defense, which was introduced through a sweeping reform of the whole Norwegian criminal justice system in the 1890s. If ever the notion of a "legal revolution" may be justified, it was in Norway between 1887 and 1902. The outcome was a new law of criminal procedure, a new criminal law, a prison law, a public vagrancy law, and a child welfare law, offering a widely differentiated system of punitive and preventive measures. In addition to fines and imprisonment came waiver of prosecution, suspended sentence, indeterminate sentence, and release on parole. Children were "educated," the mentally disturbed and psychopaths "treated" (some in addition to punishment), vagabonds and alcoholics sent to forced labor. The "rehabilitative ideal" (Allen 1964) made its way into Norwegian criminal justice, helped by the new science of criminology.

In Norway, therefore, the reasons for child welfare were ideologically rather than socially grounded. Problems of crime and urban growth existed, of course, and they were frequently referred to by the lawmakers. Their arguments, however, reflected the specific professional interests of lawyers and prison administrators and scarcely provided sufficient reasons for opening up a totally new responsibility of the state. There is reason to assume (Dahl 1974) that the 1896 law would never have been passed by Parliament had it not been fostered by another set of professional interests, those of teachers and educationists. The great issue in Norwegian education in the 1870s and 1880s was the development of a democratic school system. The new comprehensive school was intended to become a school for all social groups, even the highest, but this would require raising its social respectability. To be comprehensive and yet respectable, these schools needed some means to segregate the "moral infectious matters" offending the upper classes. Such an outlet was precisely what the educationists saw in the projected child welfare system, and their professional interest gave decisive support to the law in Parliament in 1896.

A common trait of all the different interest groups taking part in the creation of Norwegian child welfare—criminologists, penal reformers, correctionalists, educationists, and teachers—is their orientation toward their own professional interests, that is, toward purposes and clients other than those of the child welfare itself. With the passage of the law it was possible for criminologists to produce science, correctionalists to raise the status of their work, penal reformers to strengthen social defense, educationists to make the comprehensive school safe for democracy, and teachers to secure a means of segregating troublesome children. Of all the groups, the educationists seem to have been the most orientated toward their own purposes, whereas the entrepreneurs of social defense rested on a fundamental notion of a common interest shared by the society and the neglected child.

By contrast, the reforms introduced by the law of 1953 were initiated neither by professional interests nor by changes in ideology, nor even by any direct increase in the problems of juvenile delinquency. The original initiative was largely bureaucratic, motivated by a wish to simplify and centralize the administrative and legal network which had developed since the turn of the century. During the law-making process, however, the direction of professionalism within health and social service in the late forties and early fifties did leave its stamp on the law. Thus, child welfare was transformed from school policy to social policy, with a substantial swing in ideology toward the concepts of treatment and welfare.

Today, child welfare is an aspect of the welfare state. It is not clear what this means, since the ideology of the welfare state is quite vague and little has been said either by politicians or social scientists to clarify it. Above all it has served as a political banner signifying that postwar social democratic Scandinavia has reached a level of progressive development where each individual enjoys the freedom from need and deprivation and the right to live a decent life. The more theoretical efforts to clarify the concept have tended to support this positive value by describing the welfare state as a society where the market economy is under control to make human care a definite and well-protected purpose of the social machinery. The relationship between citizen and the state is supposed to be in balance, in the sense that the citizens' duties to support the common aims are as universally recognized as the society's duty to shelter them from the crises and pains they cannot cope with alone.

More concretely, the welfare state is supposed to consist of an interplay of three distinguishable elements. First, there is the end itself: a dual ideology of well-being (meaning the right to live a decent and insured life) and of equality (meaning equal distribution, both socially and economically, of these rights). Then there are the two means: on the one hand, a strongly developed public sector of the economy, with state control over private enterprises; on the other hand, a highly developed system of social security and a social policy that increasingly distributes surplus wealth from the richer to the poorer part of the population.

Child welfare clearly belongs to the latter element. Social policy itself, however, may be divided functionally into a "strong" and a "weak" part, the first dealing with rights, the second with needs. Child welfare is based on needs. In the needs-related social policy sector, support is not given automatically in response to a certain state or situation on the part of the client, such as in the general social security. The family allowance, for example, is not administered by child welfare boards, nor is state support for youths during their education. Child welfare belongs to the "weak" part of social policy, the locally administered social service directed at people in temporary need of help. This service is not aimed at "normal" crises of the population but at particularly vulnerable groups, such as alcoholics, children, and other persons "unable to live on their own incomes or to take care of themselves," to quote the Social Care Act of 1964. Aid is not offered according to automatic standards but is granted after a consideration of the client's total situation. The consideration may quite naturally take the form of a collection of proofs for and against the client. His need for help and his decision to ask for it may not even rest with himself but with others in whose interest the board is asked to intervene. Since the client may not know what is good for him, child welfare boards, like the boards aiding alcoholics, have the right to use coercive measures.

At the same time the rather limited resources at the board's disposal normally do not permit more than modest economic help. The local or communal social services represent a transformation of the former poor laws and various local institutions for social control. (Indeed, the emergence of child welfare in Norway may be seen as a synthesis of criminal law and poor law institutions taking the shape of an educational measure. A detailed account of this has not yet been written.) Poverty in the welfare state is in a certain sense reproduced via the self-governing communes inasmuch as such small and poor communities usually cannot afford the expensive social policy that the official standards of the welfare state require.

Once, however, the client qualifies for objective measures of aid—for instance, by achieving a certain percentage of physical disability or a specific maximum age—the welfare state comes into operation even in the remote parts of the country. In child welfare this applies to sick clients, whether the symptoms are physical or mental or just related to the client's pattern of behavior. In these cases the local boards have a wide range of regional and governmental institutions at their disposal, offering treatment differentiated according to the various diseases and not according to their social causes.

The concept of sickness has widened considerably during the history of social welfare in Norway and by now encompasses many social phenomena formerly understood as forms of behavior. The scientification of criminal policy was well under way in the 1890s, and by the law of 1953 the child welfare boards were instructed to cooperate closely with teams of doctors, psychiatrists, psychologists, and social workers. Criminal politics of the 1950s were on the whole thoroughly influenced by the advance of the positivistic concept of sickness. Old slogans about the need to combat crime were replaced by new ones advocating the struggle against punishment. In 1952 the Scandinavian Congress of Penologists gathered to discuss "medical, psychological and pedagogical treatment of criminals." Scandinavia in general, and Sweden in particular, came to be known for an experimentally open-minded realization of the rehabilitative ideal in criminal justice. Concerns were raised about protecting clients from administrative arbitrariness, but only with limited effect. At that time they appeared as expressions of conservative skepticism about removing the moral element in criminal justice (see Andenaes 1965; Christie 1971).

The shift of ideologies following the development of social policies is a very complicated theme; little research has been done and there is no general understanding of the nature of social politics. For this reason, the present outline of the development of child welfare ideology is far from systematic. A certain pattern does emerge, however, as one observes the client's route from prison to school and from school to hospital. The pattern of decreasing moralism and increasing scientism is indicated by the sequence of devices from punishment to education and to treatment. Such a development is well in accordance with what might be called the official ideology of juvenile justice. In the following section I shall try to modify this impression of a linear, evolutionary development of child welfare. The American juvenile courts will, I hope, provide the necessary contrast for a clear picture.

Juvenile Justice in Scandinavia and in the United States: A Comparison

The Board and the Court: A Model Approach

Formally regarded, the Scandinavian child welfare boards and the American juvenile courts represent two different models of decision making, the administrative model and the judicial model. I will show the differences between the two models by sketching them as ideal types of decision making (see generally Aubert 1958; Eckhoff 1966; Eckhoff and Jacobsen 1960). Any such type is of course highly abstract and does not correspond to living realities. I use the ideal types here only to mark the two extremes of a practical continuum where both the boards and the courts lie well in the middle, but not, as I hope to show, on the same plane.

The judicial model is based upon the conflict as impetus for a decision, with the court as the typical organization for solving the problem. The structure of both the criminal and the civil court, as well as the rules of procedure, originate from this fact. The model therefore can be outlined as a triangular structure of decision making, with two parts in conflict and the impartial third party, the conflict solver. Hence the necessity to have principles of accusatory process separating the prosecution from the decision as prescribed in the rules of criminal procedure. The aim of the rules is to make the solution as correct and as just as possible. The model implies the use of coercive enforcement.

Judicial decision making requires a specific act, or an omission, of the past. The facts of the past are classified according to legal categories and included under other legal categories which indicate the result. A correct solution is secured by the rules regulating the presentation of the facts. The two parties have a number of specific rights, whereas the judges are bound by rules limiting the number of factors they may regard as relevant. A just solution is secured by the two principles of equality of the parties before the court and of proportionality between the act and the legal reaction to it. The network of rules is intricately structured and requires a special professional competence on the part of the decision maker. The two parties also normally rely on legal expertise to control the process and the solution. Other means of control are processes such as public proceedings, participation by laymen, and the right to appeal.

The administrative model differs fundamentally from the court model in respect to the purposes of the decision. Where the court's function is to clarify past facts and organize them under fixed rules, administrative decision making aims to fulfill certain future ends by means presently available. The typical judicial handling of a social problem is to respond to an act already done, whereas the typical administrative handling is to prevent such acts in the future. The aim indicates the choice of means. To be rational, administrative decision making involves such processes as outline of future effects attached to various means, calculation of the probability of each effect, and the final choice of means. Social utility is a central value in the administrative model, whereas justice and truth rate highest with the court (Eckhoff 1963).

This points to another important difference. In administrative decision making, causality and hence prediction play a major role. The causal relationship may be tested empirically, and scientific methods applied to the calculation of the various probabilities. Administrative authority, then, has an advanced expertise at its disposal, whereas court decisions rest on dogmatic and, empirically speaking, nonscientific know-how.

The administrative model is not based on conflict, either in structure or procedure. There is no need for a triangular model and the relationship of the administrative body and the client is generally bilateral. This does not mean that conflicts do not exist. Administrative decisions, when involving a conflict between a public administrator and a client, may be even more coercive than a court decision. The pov.er to decide and the control over material goods in the hand of the administrator may be overwhelming. But conflict solving is not the formal purpose of the decision making. So the bilaterality does not indicate a balance between the two parts. When resources are scarce as they often are within the "weak" sphere of social politics, the distributive power rests one-sidedly with the official body. Even if clients should want to reject the offer, they may be forced to accept. Compulsion is, however, not the usual way of fulfilling the decision. The administrator is not limited by rules to the same extent as the judge. Conflicts, then, may be veiled and the use of force less visible than in the court.

The two contrasting models appear to indicate extremely important differences between a system of juvenile justice organized by a court versus a child welfare system centered in an administrative board. In general, however, modern criminal justice shows signs of a definite rapproachement with the administrative model, and juvenile justice even more so.

Logically speaking, a decision may be unjust but socially useful, or just but socially useless. Eckhoff has argued that in situations where both justice and utility are relevant dimensions, there seems to be a psychological tendency that the same (positive or negative) position is more likely to be taken than the opposite. As Eckhoff puts it,

conceptions of "justice" and "social utility" are well suited to be molded into harmony with each other because of their vagueness and because of the uncertainty connected with some of their premises (e.g., the predictions of consequences in utility considerations) (Eckhoff 1963, p. 83).

Such a molding goes on not only in the mind of the individual decision maker. It is an important element in any process of political legitimation. The molding which took place in the late nineteenth-century scientification of criminal justice was at the same time both legal and political. Crime was to be met by punishment as well as prevention, which meant that both justice and social utility had to be considered. The new penal philosophy stated two postulates about the limits of punishment, later expressed by the French neoclassical school of criminal law: *ni plus qu'il n'est juste, ni plus qu'il n'est utile* (Andenaes 1965). The consequence was an extensive use of individually directed measures beyond the former process of criminal justice: education, treatment, aid, and detention, applied partly instead of and partly in addition to punishment.

In criminal justice, then, the pure court model has been mixed with numerous administrative elements. The two concepts of justice and social utility—proportionality between crime and punishment and efficiency in the process of rehabilitation—are harmonized by various means: by the notion of a common interest shared by the offender and the society, by the doctrines of limited punishment, by the splitting up of criminal procedure in two parts (clearing the question of guilt by the triangular procedure and measuring the penality through administrative decision), and finally by establishing separate administrative systems.

As I have said, the two models of decision making seem to be useful as marking the extreme ends of a continuum rather than serving as two alternatives. If this is so, the two systems of juvenile justice in Scandinavia and the United States may be located at certain positions on a continuous line between the models of court and administration. In the following section of the chapter I will try to locate the models tentatively, to see what possible insights we may gain as to the differences and similarities between the two systems.

The Administrative-Legal Continuum: A Practical Approach

The Norwegian child welfare boards are administrative bodies. According to the law, they carry a wide responsibility to care for the general conditions of children and youth in the community. Time has shown, however, that little is done in this general field by the child welfare boards. Their main occupation has been decision making in individual cases (Benneche 1967; Tiller 1973).

The purpose of the 1953 law was neither punishment nor conflict-resolution but aid to the client by means which point solely to the future. (My theme here being the conflicts between client and society, I take the client to be both the child and the parents, deliberately underplaying the sometimes conflicting interests between child and parents.) For this reason the criteria for intervention, in themselves vaguely formulated, are open for evaluation. Measures are justified not by children's actions in the past but by their situation broadly considered, where delinquency may be a mere symptom of more general difficulties. The measures, therefore, are not supposed to be proportionate to any particular situation in the past.

The board's procedure is inquisitorial; it is responsible both for the clarification of social facts and for decisions. In serious cases, when compulsion is necessary, the procedure comes closer to the triangular model inasmuch as a judge takes the chair. A triangular element may also appear when the communal social worker presents the case and the board is left only with the decision. This procedure, however, is established to provide the board with additional expertise, not to safeguard its impartiality. Children or their parents have the right to be heard and they are free to engage an attorney; this right derives from the general Administrative Procedure Act of 1967 but in fact seldom happens. The board is obliged to deliver a written report of its decision which also gives the reasons for the result. The clients have the right to complain, ordinarily to a higher administrative level, but in some cases also to a civil court. Apart from this, the work of the board is regulated by a minimum of written rules and the proceedings are not open to the public.

The informality is rationalized by the benevolent purposes of service. Some formal rules do of course exist to secure fair decisions in the distribution of the limited resources at the board's disposal. Time has shown, however, that these resources are scarce and that the primary aim of applying preventive measures in the child's own environment has been illusory. This means that the benevolent purpose is frequently implemented by removing children from family and peers. In such cases legal procedure may be of great importance to the client. A study of the law in action, however, suggests that even the few safeguards laid down in law do not work (Benneche 1967). The gap between the law in books and the law in action is partly due to the lack of legal knowledge among board members and partly to social workers' neglect of the value of due process. Even some judges seem to forget their legal training when joining the benevolent atmosphere—and the administrative structure—of the board.

A rough estimate indicates that the judge participates in about 10 percent of those cases involving removal from homes. The study mentioned argues that although the frequency is low the possible intervention of legal authorities and the mere threat of using force may neutralize actual conflicts. Parents may accept decisions without protest, whereas the board may prefer the more simple way of dealing with a case even if the law requires a more complicated procedure.

In this sense the decisions of the Norwegian child welfare board obviously may be regarded as products of a mixture of administrative and legal authority, carrying with them the inherent conflict of service objectives with the necessity for coercion (see Aubert 1958; see also Christie 1965 and Blegvad 1968). The many hundred individual boards have responded differently to this potential conflict. Colored also by local peculiarities, they have developed into certain distinguishable types of boards, some of which aim foremost at control, others at service.

Formally, the American juvenile courts are courts, incorporated in the general court system and in essential respects similar to the courts. Consequently, they differ from the Scandinavian boards in several ways. The decision maker is a judge and the rules of procedure are more elaborate. The rules for intervention are more limited, and so are the actual problems brought in and the measures and services at disposal. Yet the administrative elements are so prominent that Tappan has written of an "administrative hegemony" (Tappan 1962, p. 145). On the whole, judging from the extensive literature about juvenile courts and especially that from the 1960s, the dichotomy between judicial and administrative justice seems to be a fairly common subject of discussion in the United States. The reasons are apparent. Prison reform and scientific criminology were among the driving forces in creating the new courts at the end of the nineteenth century (Platt 1969; Platt 1974). Children were no longer to be punished and so the procedure differs from the adversary process of the triangular model of criminal courts. The jurisdiction engulfs vague categories of delinquency, neglect, and dependency (Tappan 1962, pp. 145–49). The alleged origin in chancery and the doctrine of *parens patriae* have justified this departure from the safeguards of criminal court. Even delinquency cases differ a great deal from criminal cases in procedure, particularly concerning grand jury indictment, preliminary hearing, jury trial, "sentencing," and amount of formality in general (see Hazard, this volume).

The juvenile court has on the whole been guided by its generally benevolent and administrative purpose. Thus Platt's description of the classical case:

A child was not accused of a crime but offered assistance and guidance; intervention in the lives of "delinquents" was not supposed to carry the stigma of criminal guilt. Judicial records were not generally available to the press or the public, and juvenile hearings were typically conducted in private. Court procedures were informal and inquisitorial, not requiring the presence of a defense attorney. Specific criminal safeguards of due process were not applicable because juvenile proceedings were defined by statute as in civil character. . . . The role model for juvenile court judges was doctor-counselor rather than lawyer. "Judicial therapists" were expected to establish a one-to-one relationship with delinquents. . . . Juvenile courtrooms were often arranged like a clinic and the vocabulary of its participants was largely composed of medical metaphors (Platt 1974, pp. 377–78).

Paternalism and belief in the rehabilitative ideal has blurred the possible conflict between client and society, even in the judicial model system (Allen 1964, pp. 43–61). The decline of the rehabilitative ideal parallels the Scandinavian development and may be attributed to a growing concern with the gap between ideals and realities, a gap due to former overestimation of the potential of science, to the basic needs for social and political control, and to the lack of resources. Clearly, the American system has its place on the same continuum between court and administration as the Scandinavian one. From the outset the American position was closer to the court model than was the Norwegian child welfare board, but its location produced much the same problems as affected the latter and there have existed the same degree of differences from tribunal to tribunal (Lemert 1970).

Each system's exact position has of course changed through time but not, as is sometimes thought, in one direction only. The Norwegian laws of 1896 and 1953 mark a considerable push in the same direction, away from the court model and toward the administrative ideal of welfare. During the 1960s, however, legal influences moved the system back again a bit, partly for control purposes and partly to enhance due process. In 1965 the growing concern about juvenile delinquency—which virtually exploded in official statistics during the late 1950s—was followed by increasing skepticism about the soft line of the child welfare boards and concern about their general inadequacy in dealing with young criminals. In the name of law and order the police were allowed the right to take cases back from a passive board. Perhaps more boards felt a pressure to satisfy the controlling functions and the prosecution authorities let more youths be prosecuted according to the general Criminal Procedure Act. On the other hand, there was a change in 1969 caused by a growing concern for the fate of civil rights both in child welfare in particular and in social welfare in general. Grave defects in procedure were revealed during the 1960s and the remedy advanced was to make some of the board's decisions appealable to regular courts. In the 1970s we seem to be witnessing a slide back toward administration but for quite different reasons than before: growing distrust of coercion in the process of treatment is spreading from the medical health service to social politics as a whole. Several official commissions in recent years have hesitated to advocate the use of compulsory measures. There is a growing tendency to prefer pure models to blurred mixtures and to regard treatment and aid as quite incompatible with compulsion.

The American development is of course not all that different. The failure of the juvenile court to fulfill its rehabilitative promise caused a renewed concern for due process in the 1960s. Numerous articles of lawyers and sociologists, legal changes in New York, California, and Illinois, the President's Crime Commission report, and the Supreme Court decision in *In re Gault* (378 U.S. 1

[1967])—all contributed to the retreat of juvenile courts in the direction of the "pure" court model. At the same time there is apparently a consensus about diverting "soft" cases to nonjudicial institutions and narrowing the jurisdiction of the new and increasingly legalistic juvenile court (see, for example, President's Commission . . . 1967, pp. 78–89; Lemert 1970). The solution proposed by the President's Crime Commission is to hand these youths over to administrative agencies—Youth Service Bureaus— thus removing them from a court for a second time (President's Commission . . . 1967, p. 83). Indeed, the purification of one model seems to demand the development of institutions on the other side of the continuum.

The Crime Commission's Youth Service Bureaus are welfare institutions similar to the Scandinavian boards, based on community service and neighborhood control instead of sentences and confinement. They are proposed in order to act as "central coordinators of all community services" for young people—the initial purpose of the Norwegian Child Welfare Act of 1953. A Scandinavian reader will easily recognize the need to avoid "the stigma of being processed by an official agency regarded by the public as an arm of crime control." The broad range of services is also very similar (although one is not mentioned by the Crime Commission: direct economic support). Even the ambivalence toward coercion is the same: on the one hand, the YSB's services shall be essentially voluntary, on the other hand, "it may be necessary to vest the Youth Service Bureau with authority to refer to the court" (President's Commission . . . 1967, p. 83). By moving juvenile courts in a legalistic direction and leaving the heaviest cases there, while at the same time establishing new administrative agencies with welfare purpose, a dual system not very different from the Scandinavian "double-track" system for youths is now obviously being advocated in the United States.

The similarities between problems and solutions in the two countries are in fact quite striking. No wonder then that as Americans study Scandinavia, so too critics of the American system are studied with great interest in Scandinavia, let it be Platt's critique of the system in general or of the President's Crime Commission's proposals in particular (Platt 1974), Hazard's pessimistic concession of the symbolic rather than material significance of legal devices for the control of deviance (this volume), or Lemert's more optimistic views about the consequences of "revolution within juvenile court" (1970).

CONCLUSION

There is no such thing as a "Scandinavian model" of juvenile justice and no fixed Scandinavian solution which can be copied with substantial results in other countries. There are only arguments for and against moving from one point of possibility to another on the vast continuum between ideal types of solutions. Legal changes have from time to time pushed the Scandinavian as well as the American system back and forth along this continuum, just as the positions of individual welfare boards and juvenile courts inside each system have varied and still vary considerably within the same frames.

In the sphere of formal solutions, one might conclude that it is impossible to administer welfare functions by means of due process. On the other hand, a purely administrative model of social service is not so easily achieved either. Such a model does not exist in Scandinavian juvenile justice or in the American system because of the compulsory element in the present notion of social policy. The Scandinavian debate about compulsion in welfare administration will probably never end, but it will almost certainly result in further steps toward a welfare model based on voluntarism, confronting the question of the client's participation and right to self-determination. At the same time, the purification of this model will develop solutions at the other side of the continuum and formal compulsion will be transferred where it rightly belongs, to the court.

It is often thought that change can bring about a novel solution in child welfare. In Norway, legal changes have been substantial, ideological changes perhaps even fundamental. But legal actions have in fact changed very few of the social realities of child welfare. The selection of clients follows the same old class criteria under the 1953 law as before, and traditional poor relief has not been replaced by any large-scale redistribution of wealth with the wider aims of promoting economic equality, social mobility, and a further distribution of political power. Changes have of course occurred, most of them in accordance with the general rise in social standards; life in the institutions is just like life outside, less ugly than before. But no basic functional changes have taken place. The material problems are the same. There are deviant children and young people, some of whom will be controlled and others aided. The fundamental questions are what sort of behavior constitutes deviancy, what sort of youngsters are punished, and in whose interest does it all happen. The answers are very much alike for the 1890s and the 1970s. Child welfare as a mirror to society shows much the same picture.

Many features of the American development point in the same direction, as does also the comparison between the Scandinavian and the American systems. Child welfare and juvenile justice alike seem to reflect some serious social problems in the West rather than to solve them.

The common belief in the importance of legal reforms may, I think, be seriously questioned with regard to juvenile justice. Certain improvements, important for the clients, may of course be engineered by legal means. But not the social problem itself, which seems to be inherent in the social structure of capitalism. The social marginality as well as the political powerlessness of the child welfare system makes the law itself rather unimportant. Change in our society obviously cannot start with changes in child welfare.

BIBLIOGRAPHY

Allen, Francis A. 1964. *The Borderline of Criminal Justice.* Chicago: University of Chicago Press.
Andenaes, Johannes. 1965. *The General Part of the Criminal Law of Norway.* New York: Publications of the Comparative Criminal Law Project of New York University.
Aubert, Vilhelm. 1958. "Legal Justice and Mental Health." *Psychiatry* 21:101–13.
Benneche, Gerd. 1967. *Rettssikkerheten i barnevernet* (Legal Safeguards in Child Welfare). Oslo: Universitetsforlaget.
Blegvad, Britt-Mari Persson. 1968. "A Case Study of Inter-organizational Conflict." *Scandinavian Studies in Criminology* 2:19–40.
Christie, Nils. 1965. "Temperance Boards and Inter-institutional Dilemmas: A Case Study of a Welfare Law." *Social Problems* 12:415–28.
———. 1971. "Scandinavian Criminology Facing the 1970s." *Scandinavian Studies in Criminology* 3:121–49.
Dahl, Tove S. 1974. "The Emergence of the Norwegian Child Wel-

fare Law." *Scandinavian Studies in Criminology* 5:83-98.

Eckhoff, Torstein. 1963. "Justice and Social Utility." In *Legal Essays: A Tribute to Frede Castberg*. Oslo: Universitetsforlaget. Pp. 74-93.

———. 1966. "The Mediator, the Judge and the Administrator in Conflict-Resolution." *Acta Sociologica* 10:148-72.

Eckhoff, Torstein, and Jacobsen, Knut D. 1960. *Rationality and Responsibility in Administrative and Judicial Decision-Making: Interdisciplinary Studies from the Scandinavian Summer University*, vol. 5. Copenhagen: Munksgaard.

Lemert, Edwin M. 1970. *Social Action and Legal Change: Revolution with the Juvenile Court*. Chicago: Aldine.

Nyquist, Ola. 1960. *Juvenile Justice: A Comparative Study with Special Reference to the Swedish Child Welfare Board and the California Juvenile Courts System*. London: Macmillan.

Platt, Anthony M. 1969. *The Child Savers: The Invention of Delinquency*. Chicago: University of Chicago Press.

———. 1970. "Saving and Controlling Delinquent Youth: A Critique." *Issues in Criminology* 5:1-24.

———. 1974. "The Triumph of Benevolence: The Origins of the Juvenile Justice System in the United States." In *Criminal Justice in America: A Critical Understanding*, ed. Richard Quinney. Boston: Little, Brown. Pp. 356-89.

President's Commission on Law Enforcement and Administration of Justice. 1967. *The Challenge of Crime in a Free Society*. Washington, D.C.: U.S. Government Printing Office.

Tappan, Paul W. 1962. "Juridical and Administrative Approaches to Children with Problems." In *Justice for the Child: The Juvenile Court in Transition*, ed. Margaret K. Rosenheim. New York: Free Press. Pp. 144-71.

Tiller, Per Olav. 1973. *Den offentlige barneomsorg: Endringer i praksis gjennom ti aar og geografiske variasjoner i barnevernets virksomhet* (Official Child Welfare: Changing Practices during Ten Years and Geographical Variations in Child Welfare Work). Oslo: INAS Rapport.

CONTRIBUTORS

EGON BITTNER Coplan Professor in the Social Sciences, Brandeis University; author, *The Function of Police in Modern Society*

ROBERT A. BURT Professor of Law, Yale University; Reporter, Juvenile Justice Standards Project

FRED COHEN Professor of Law and Criminal Justice, State University of New York at Albany; Reporter, Juvenile Justice Standards Project

TOVE STANG DAHL Associate Professor, Institute of Criminology and Criminal Law, University of Oslo

GEOFFREY C. HAZARD, JR. Professor of Law, Yale University

ROBERT MAYNARD HUTCHINS Life Fellow, Center for the Study of Democratic Institutions; previously Chancellor, University of Chicago

CHARLES E. LISTER Member of the firm, Covington and Burling, Washington, D.C.

JEROME MILLER Director, Office of Children and Youth, State of Pennsylvania; previously Commissioner of Youth Services, Commonwealth of Massachusetts

PAUL NEJELSKI Assistant Executive Secretary, Judicial Department of Connecticut; previously Director, Institute of Judicial Administration

LLOYD E. OHLIN Roscoe Pound Professor of Criminology, Harvard Law School; author, *Delinquency and Opportunity: A Theory of Delinquent Gangs* (with Richard Cloward)

MICHAEL J. POWER Research Fellow, Department of Social Administration and Social Work, University of Bristol; previously research scientist, Social Medicine Unit of Medical Research Council

MARGARET K. ROSENHEIM Helen Ross Professor, School of Social Service Administration, University of Chicago; editor, *Justice for the Child: The Juvenile Court in Transition*

J. LAWRENCE SCHULTZ (Deceased) Formerly Director and Reporter, Juvenile Justice Standards Project

CHARLES H. SHIREMAN Professor, School of Social Service Administration, University of Chicago; editor, *Social Work Practice and Social Justice* (with Bernard Ross)

MICHAEL H. TONRY Attorney, Dechert, Price and Rhoades; previously Lecturer in Law and Criminology, University of Birmingham, England

MICHAEL S. WALD Professor of Law, Stanford University; Reporter, Juvenile Justice Standards Project

PATRICIA WALD Attorney, Mental Health Law Project, Washington, D.C.; Trustee, Ford Foundation

MARGUERITE Q. WARREN Professor of Criminal Justice, State University of New York at Albany; previously principal investigator, Community Treatment Project, California Youth Authority

Index

GLASSBORO STATE COLLEGE